Kurt Busiek's

ASTRO

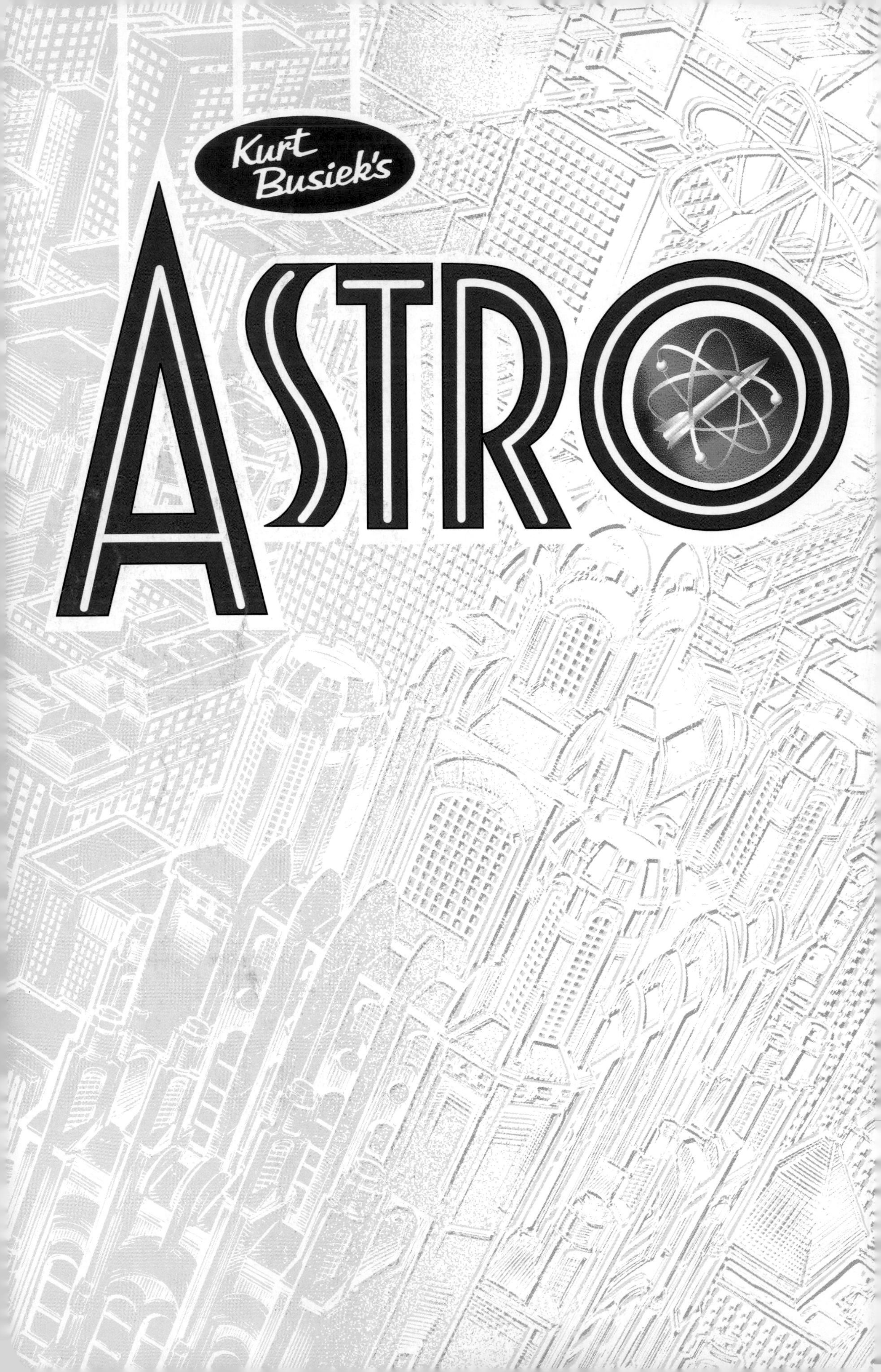

CITY

LIFE IN THE BIG CITY

KURT BUSIEK
WRITER

BRENT E. ANDERSON
ARTIST

RICHARD STARKINGS
AND **COMICRAFT'S**
JOHN GAUSHELL
LETTERING & DESIGN

STEVE BUCCELLATO
AND **ELECTRIC CRAYON**
COLOR ART

ALEX ROSS
COVERS

BUSIEK, ANDERSON & ROSS
ARCHITECTS & CITY PLANNERS

JUKE BOX PRODUCTIONS

"COMICRAFT"
Purveyors of Unique Design & Fine Lettering

HOMAGE COMICS ®

ANN HUNTINGTON BUSIEK
MANAGING EDITOR,
JUKE BOX

CHAPTER DIVIDER
FIGURES BY
CURT SWAN &
MURPHY ANDERSON,
GEORGE TUSKA
& JOE SINNOTT,
JIM MOONEY
JOHN ROMITA, SR.

CITYSCAPE BY
ART NICHOLS

JENETTE KAHN
PRESIDENT & EDITOR-IN-CHIEF

PAUL LEVITZ
EXECUTIVE VICE PRESIDENT & PUBLISHER

JIM LEE
EDITORIAL DIRECTOR - WILDSTORM

JOHN NEE
VP & GENERAL MANAGER - WILDSTORM

SCOTT DUNBIER
GROUP EDITOR

RICHARD BRUNING
VP - CREATIVE DIRECTOR

PATRICK CALDON
VP - FINANCE & OPERATIONS

DOROTHY CROUCH
VP - LICENSED PUBLISHING

TERRI CUNNINGHAM
VP - MANAGING EDITOR

JOEL EHRLICH
SENIOR VP - ADVERTISING & PROMOTIONS

ALISON GILL
EXECUTIVE DIRECTOR - MANUFACTURING

LILLIAN LASERSON
VP & GENERAL COUNSEL

BOB WAYNE
VP - DIRECT SALES

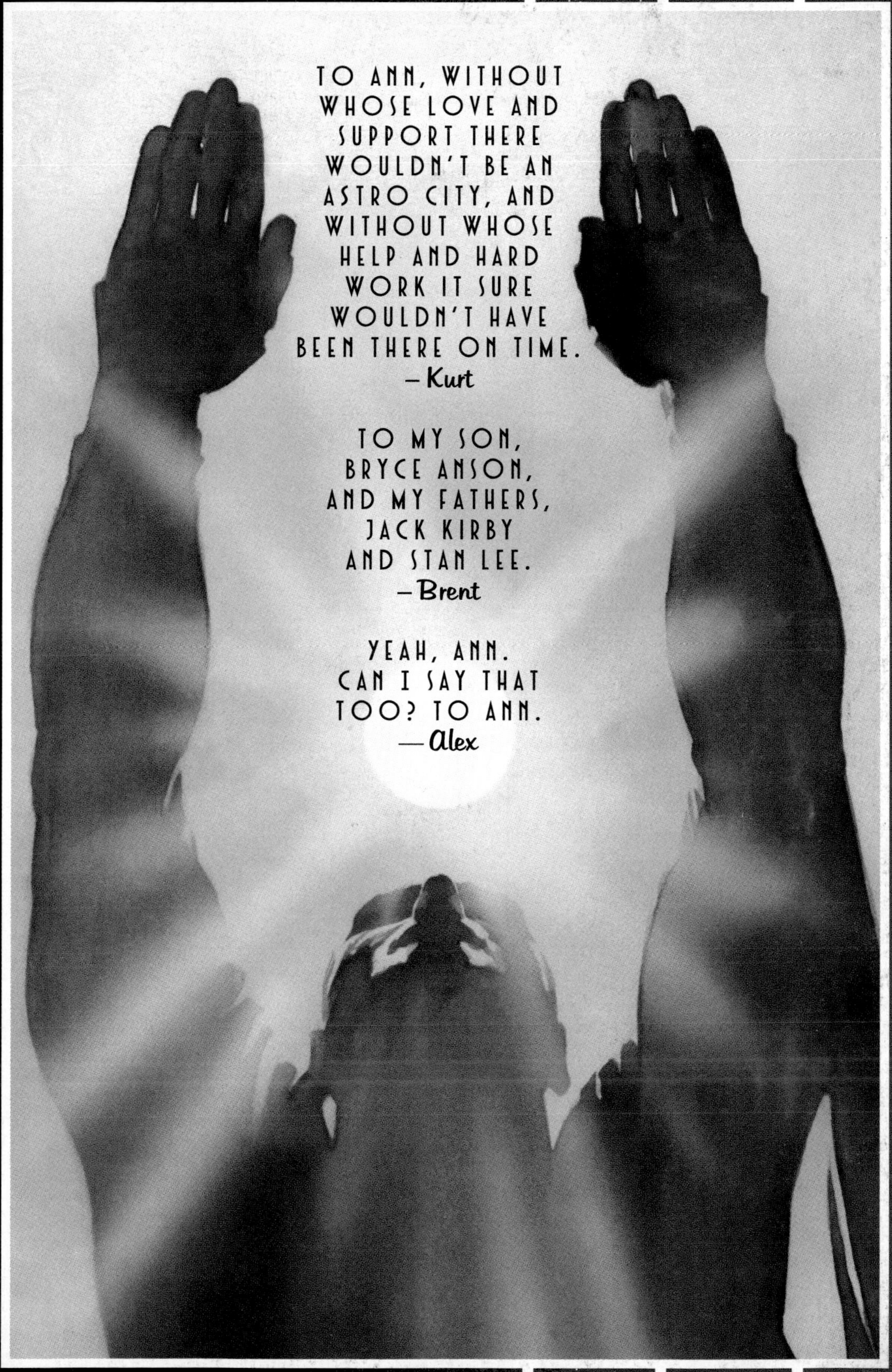

TO ANN, WITHOUT
WHOSE LOVE AND
SUPPORT THERE
WOULDN'T BE AN
ASTRO CITY, AND
WITHOUT WHOSE
HELP AND HARD
WORK IT SURE
WOULDN'T HAVE
BEEN THERE ON TIME.
–Kurt

TO MY SON,
BRYCE ANSON,
AND MY FATHERS,
JACK KIRBY
AND STAN LEE.
–Brent

YEAH, ANN.
CAN I SAY THAT
TOO? TO ANN.
—Alex

Contents

INTRODUCTION

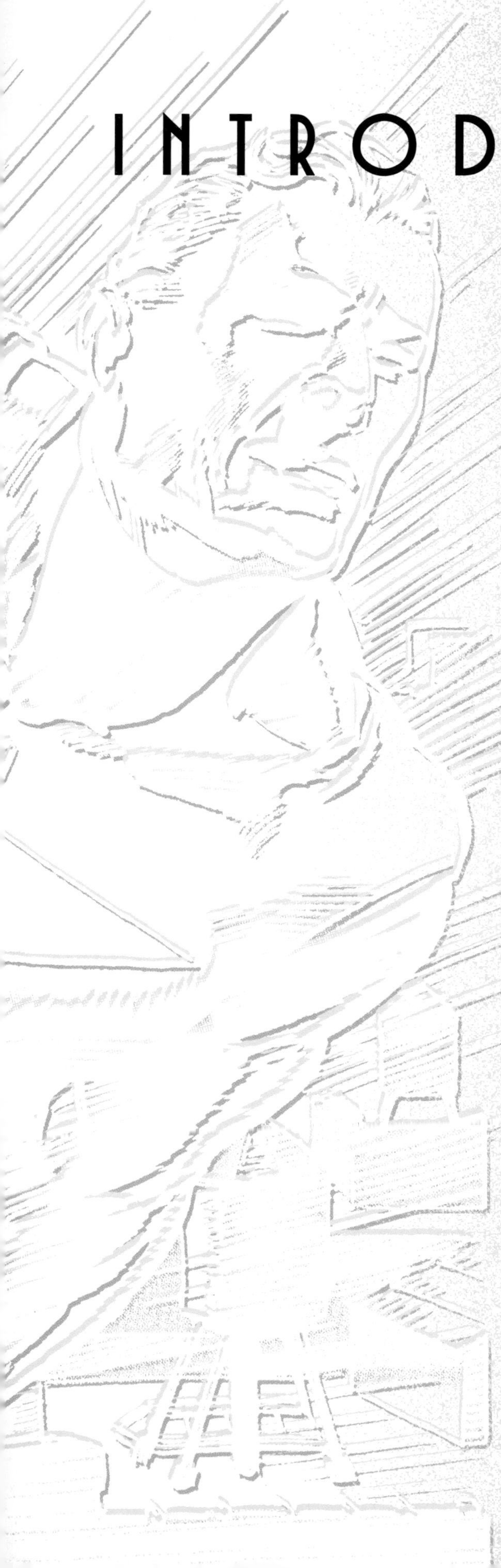

I LOVE SUPERHEROES.

This comes as no surprise to those who know me — I've been writing superhero comics professionally for well over a decade and reading them for even longer, and while superheroes haven't been all I've written (or read), there'd be no point in denying that I'm having a great time among the folks in the capes and masks, and that I have no intention of leaving them behind any time soon.

Unfortunately, at least from my perspective, the superhero is not as well regarded by many of those around me — friends, family, fellow creators and a vocal number of comics readers. I hear that there are too many superheroes, that they're choking the racks and shelves of the comic book stores, that they're the reason comics are so poorly regarded by the majority of Americans, and more. And while I could quibble with some of the above — I'd certainly like to see more diversity of the comics racks, for instance, but when I see superheroes from Batman to Superman to Spider-Man, the X-Men, the Teenage Mutant Ninja Turtles, the Mighty Morphin Power Rangers, the Crow, the Tick and more in movies, on TV, in cartoons, in books or blowing off the toy-store shelves, I wonder whether superheroes are *really* what non comics-readers are turning up their noses at when they pass up comic books — it's one specific complaint against the superhero that I want to bring up here.

The complaint, which never fails to charm me, is that superheroes are limited. They're inherently juvenile, I'm told. They're simplistic. They're just an adolescent male power fantasy, a crypto-fascist presentation of status quo values, elevated over anything strange or alien.

And sure, yeah, I can see that. Superman is adolescence personified — Clark Kent the weak child whom nobody takes seriously, turning into the powerful, respected (and sexually attractive, but nervous around women) Superman as swiftly as a teenager's voice cracks, and then back again to meek, unimportant Clark. Spider-Man is adolescence from a different angle — the teenager stumbling toward adulthood writ large, making mistakes with disastrous consequences and doing his best to remedy them as he learns to be a responsible man in an adult society. Captain America is the American ideal and self-image circa 1941 rolled into one — the biggest kid in the global playground, who's going to make the other kids play nice, even if he has to get a little rough to do it. I can absolutely see that.

However — and you knew there was going to be a however, right? — what charms me about that objection to the superhero is the way it points out, in the guise of criticism, what to me is the greatest strength of the superhero genre — the ease with which superheroes can be used as metaphor, as symbol, whether for the psychological transformation of adolescence, the self-image of a nation, or something else. A genre that can do something like that — is that really a limitation?

I don't think so.

If a superhero can be such a powerful and effective metaphor for male adolescence, then what else can you do with them? Could you build a superhero story around a metaphor for female adolescence? Around mid-life crisis? ❋ Around the changes adults go through when they become parents? Sure, why not? And if a superhero can exemplify America's self-image at the dawn of World War II, could a superhero exemplify America's self-image during the less-confident 1970s? ❋❋ How about the emerging national identity of a newly-independent African nation? Or a non-national culture, like the drug culture, or the "greed-is-good" business culture of the go-go Eighties? Of course. If it can do one, it can do the others.

I could go on, but I'll spare you. The point is, an attempt to describe how limited superheroes are quickly turns into the question, "What *can't* they do?" The possibilities of the genre are endless, and the terrain rich and inviting.

THIS IS THE SORT OF THING that was running through my head when I first started working on ASTRO CITY. The superhero genre has historically been limited to adventure thrillers, action stories that can be sold easily to boys in their teen years or younger. But that's a self-imposed, market-driven limitation, not any sort of creative limitation of the genre, and I wanted to explore the *rest* of the genre, celebrating the power it has to make ideas come to life and seeing what it can do. I've long been fascinated by the question of *what else* happens in the worlds the superheroes inhabit; what life is like for the guy who points upward and declaims, "Look! Up in the sky!"; what celebrity posters are on the walls of 13-year-old girls in the Human Torch's world; what it's like for a lawyer to go into court and argue that his client is not guilty of murder because the killer was in fact his evil twin (and trot out all the precedents for such an event). This seemed to be a perfect chance to do both — to wander off the main thoroughfares of a superhero world and see what stories have been waiting in the shadows to be told, what chords can be struck, what we can discover if we stop heeding the siren song of What Happens Next and start wondering What Else Is There? I like What Happens Next stories just fine, as it happens, and I have plenty of venues to tell those — but not many in which I can pick out an innocent bystander at a slugfest between a superhero and a super-criminal, follow him or her home and see what's worth examining about this particular life. What resonates with our own experience? What cobwebbed, dusty corners can we illuminate?

One thing I didn't want to do is take the superhero story and make it "realistic" — which is odd, since that's become the quickie shorthand description of ASTRO CITY (and of MARVELS before it) that I've heard time and again: It's what superheroes would be like in the real world.

Well, no. No, it isn't.

We've got trolls living underground in Astro City. We've got time travelers reweaving the future. We've got fantastic technology, mystical creatures, alien contact and powerful, violent, destructive beings by the double handful — and in Astro City history, they've been around for decades, without turning the world into something unrecognizable from our own perspective. The telephone and the airplane may have transformed our world, but the superhero and the sorcerer haven't had anywhere near as great an effect in the world of Astro City. And I like it that way. Making a superhero world realistic — making it a hermetically-logical alternate reality in which all the pieces make sense and work logically — that strikes me less as a superhero story per se, and more as that branch of science fiction that gets its stories out of making some change in the world, and then extrapolating from it, exploring the ramifications of a change in technology, or history, or politics on all other aspects of the world. *How would the world be different*, this type of story asks, and while it's a perfectly valid form of fiction, I'm just not interested.

One of the most charming elements of the superhero story, for me, lies in the fact that the world it all happens in is our world — that this fantastic, furious, cosmic stuff happens in what could be the skies over our heads — and sure, it should transform the world into something unrecognizable, but it doesn't, not any more than the prevalence of court wizards or of multiple intelligent humanoid races sharing the same environment changes the politics or commerce of a fairy-tale world. I *like* the absurd, unrealistic glory of the superhero genre, and I want to see it as a place of gods and aliens and super-science and talking gorillas and ordinary people like you and me, all dealing with metaphor run amok, coping not with what *logical* effect it all has, but with the *emotional* effect. Not what it would *be* like if superheroes existed in our world, but what it would *feel* like if we could wander through theirs. It's not a realistic world, but it's a fascinating one.

ANOTHER REASON I'M HAPPY to let the world of Astro City be thoroughly unrealistic is that I think it's about time. For the past decade, starting around the time of the brilliant WATCHMEN and THE DARK KNIGHT RETURNS, the prevalent mode for "serious" superhero creators has been deconstruction. The superhero has been dissected, analyzed and debunked, his irrationalities held up to the light to show them for the unworkable Rube Goldberg machines they are, that it's almost become impossible to present a superhero who does what he does without being emotionally unstable, incapable of dealing with reality without "acting out" his psychoses and obsessions. But it strikes me that the only real reason to take apart a pocket watch, or a car engine, aside from the simple delight of disassembly, is to find out how it works. To understand it, so that you can put it back together again better than before, or build a new one that goes beyond what the old model could do.

We've been taking apart the superhero for ten years or more; it's time to put it back together and wind it up, time to take it out on the road and floor it, see what it'll do. That's the prospect that excites me, that makes me eager to tell my stories to anyone who's willing to listen. Where can we go from here? What's out there to find? Come on, let's head that way — all we can see are shapes in the dark, but they sure look interesting, don't they?

I'VE BEEN EXTREMELY LUCKY in all this. Lucky to have done MARVELS at just the right time, winning me enough of an audience and a reputation to allow me to launch ASTRO CITY. Lucky to have worked with Alex Ross, whose devotion to archetype and emotional power birthed MARVELS, and whose consummate skill brought readers flocking to the project — and who brings the same commitment and skill to striking just the right image with the ASTRO CITY covers. Lucky to work with Brent Anderson, who can draw anything I throw at him, and who's willing to do whatever it takes to make the story come to life on the page. And lucky that neither Brent nor Alex is content to just "do the job" — they've contributed ideas, shaped characters and settings, argued me out of mistakes, fought for their vision and the good of the stories and been fully engaged in making ASTRO CITY a reality; without them I might have a book, but it wouldn't be anywhere near as good. The same can be said for Richard Starkings and John Gaushell of Comicraft, whose design skills and technical expertise have made ASTRO CITY a clean, crisp package; for Steve Buccellato and Electric Crayon, who gave the stories life and mood and power in their color work; and for Image Comics, who gave us a shot at telling our stories as best we could, helping us reach an audience without trying to exert any creative control.

There are no talking gorillas in the stories that follow (we'll get to them, honest). But looking back on them, I think we did what we set out to do — we told the stories we wanted to tell with as much honesty and as much skill as we could muster, and let them out into the world to fly or fall. They seem, for the most part, to have flown.

Welcome to Astro City. Whether you're getting to know the place for the first time, or are a regular commuter, I hope you enjoy wandering its streets and seeing its sights as much as we have.

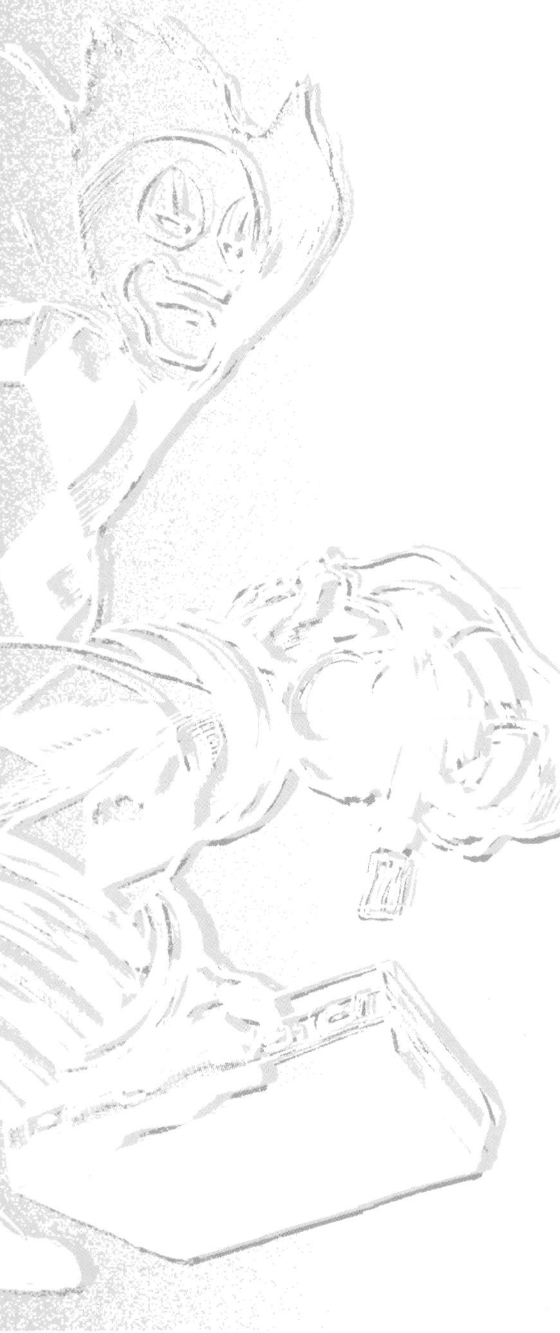

— **Kurt Busiek**
MAY 1996

⚛ IN FACT, IT'S ALREADY BEEN DONE. DO YOURSELF A FAVOR AND HUNT DOWN A COPY OF *SUPERFOLKS*, BY ROBERT N. MAYER [DIAL PRESS, 1977], A NOVEL THAT BRILLIANTLY USES SUPERHERO SYMBOLS TO TELL A SIDESPLITTINGLY FUNNY AND EMOTIONALLY AFFECTING STORY OF A MAN DEALING WITH MIDDLE AGE; IT'S LONG OUT OF PRINT BUT IT'S WELL WORTH THE TROUBLE OF FINDING IT.

⚛ ⚛ THE KINKS USE CAPTAIN AMERICA TO DO JUST THAT, IN THEIR SONG, "CATCH ME NOW I'M FALLING," ON THE ALBUM *LOW BUDGET*.

CHAPTER 1

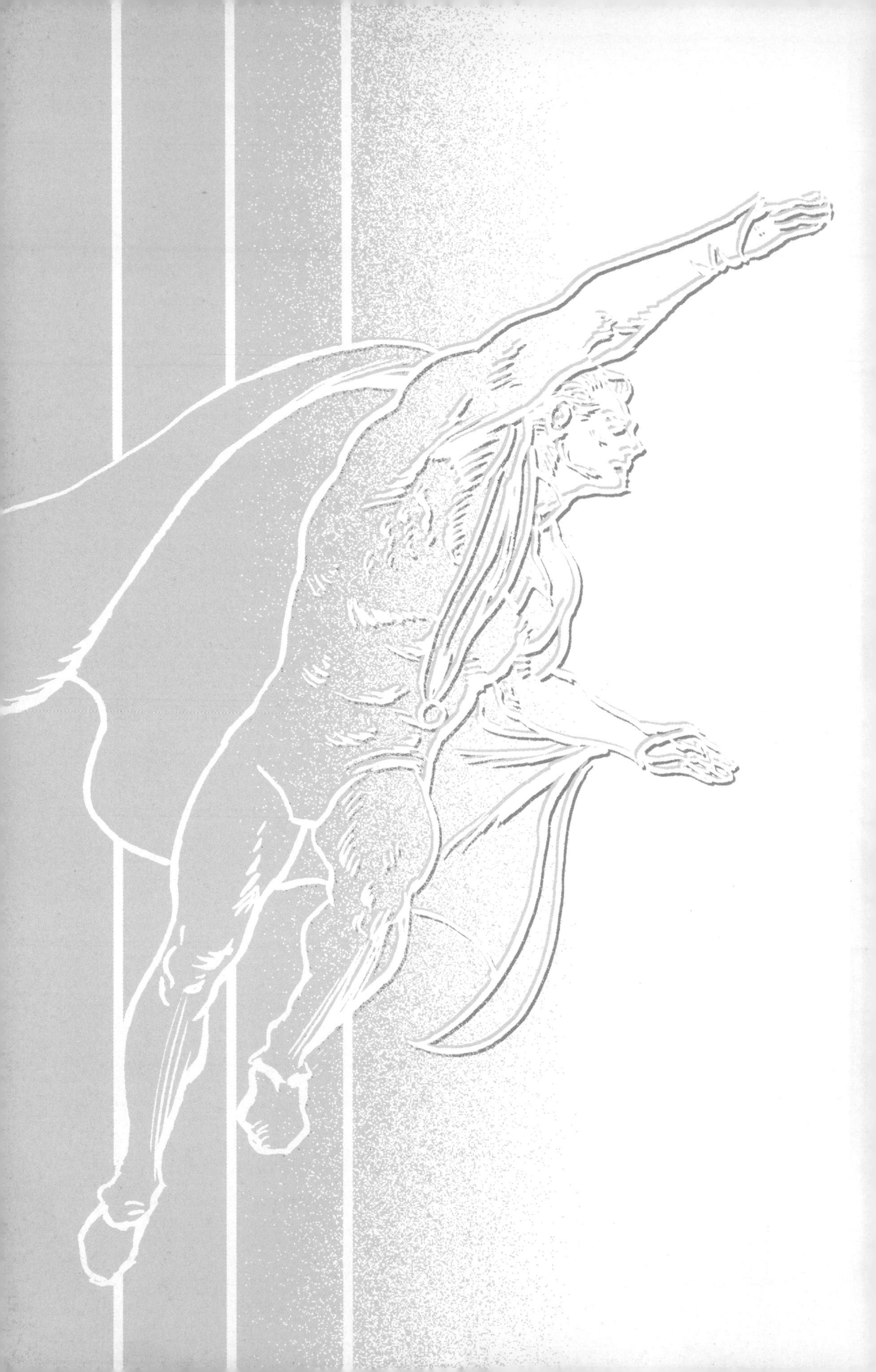

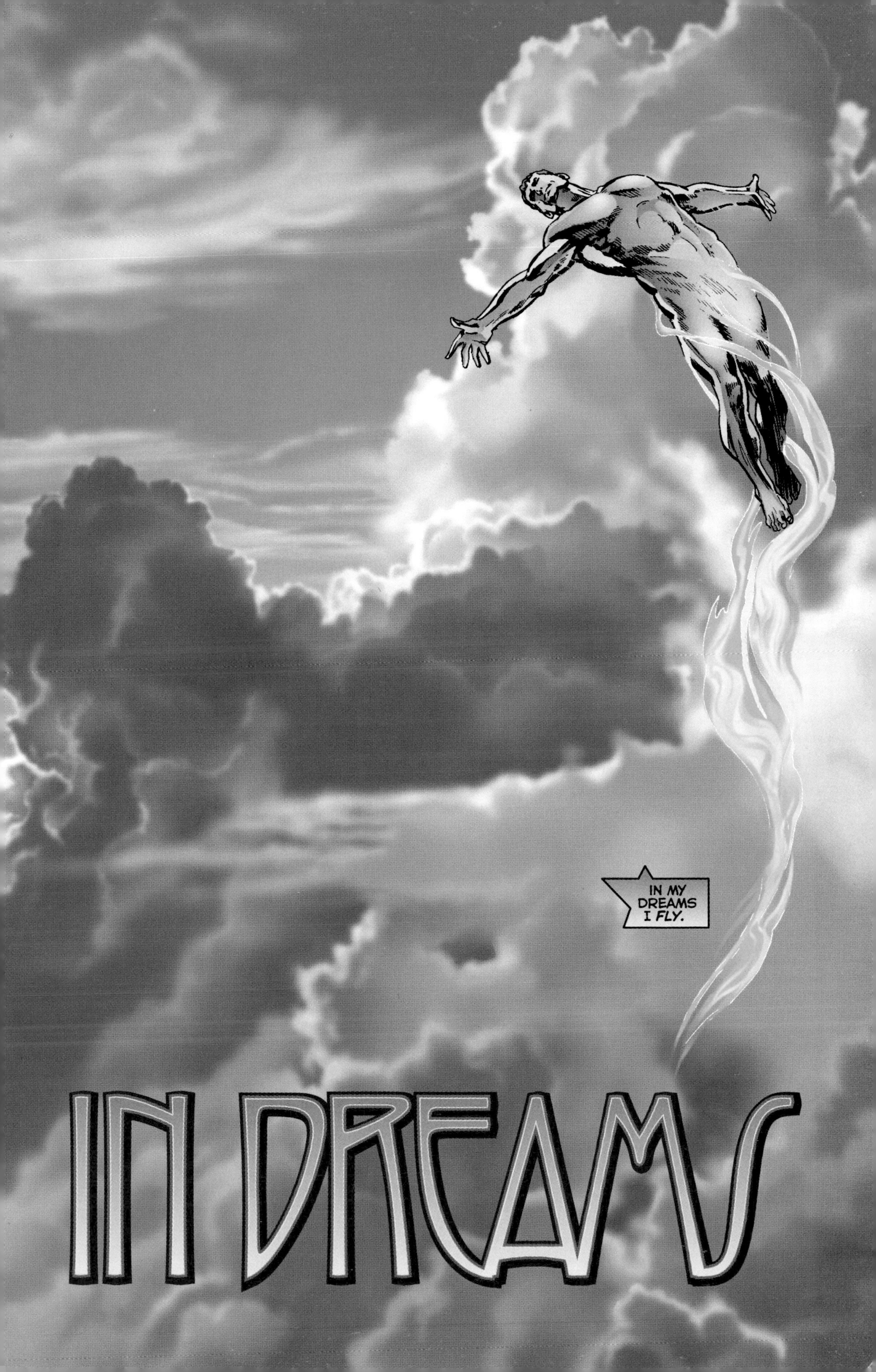
IN MY DREAMS I FLY.
IN DREAMS

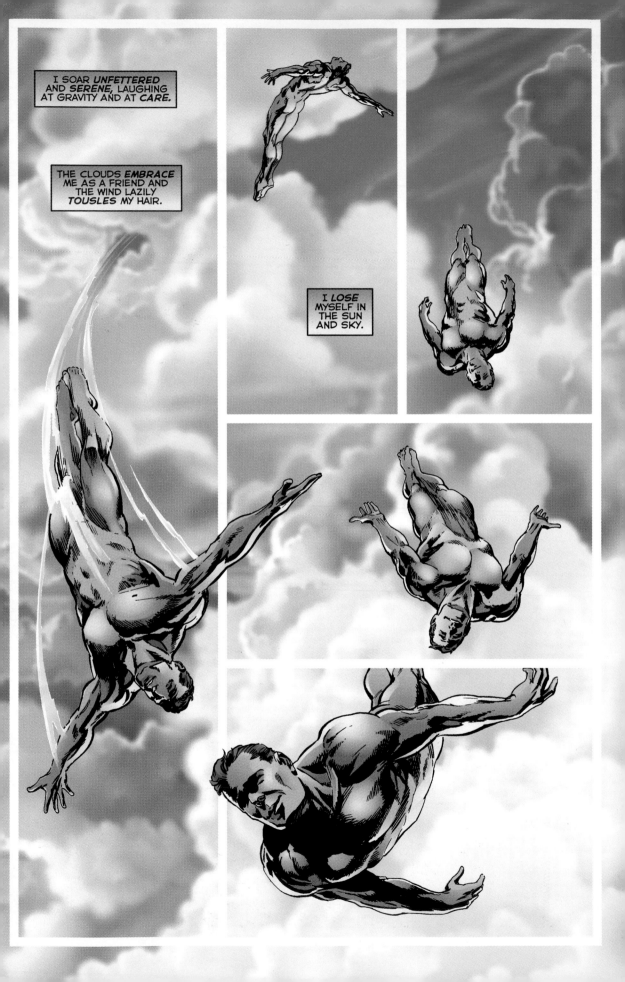

I SOAR *UNFETTERED* AND *SERENE,* LAUGHING AT GRAVITY AND AT *CARE.*

THE CLOUDS *EMBRACE* ME AS A FRIEND AND THE WIND LAZILY *TOUSLES* MY HAIR.

I *LOSE* MYSELF IN THE SUN AND SKY.

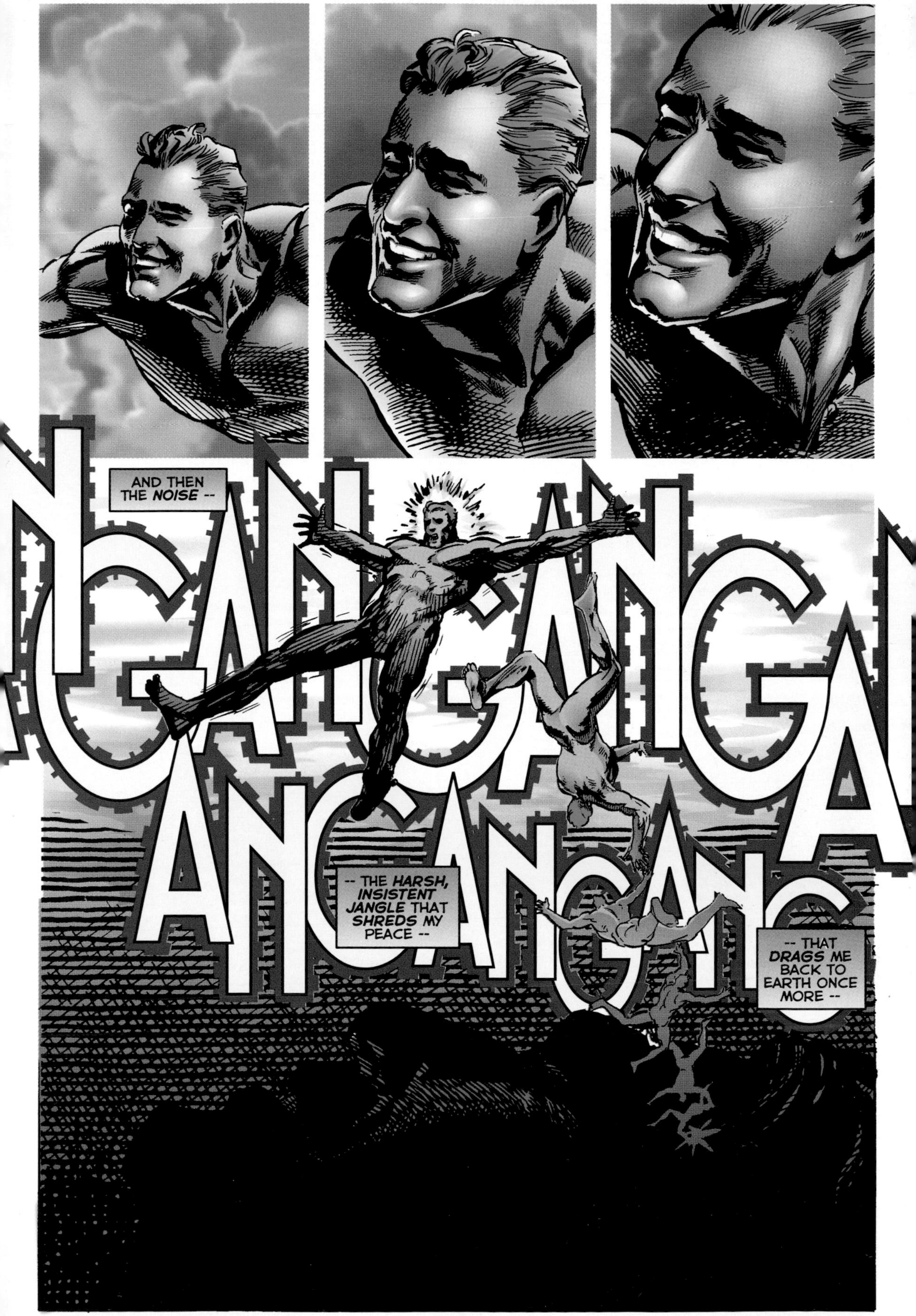
AND THEN THE *NOISE* --
-- THE *HARSH, INSISTENT JANGLE* THAT *SHREDS MY* PEACE --
-- THAT *DRAGS* ME BACK TO EARTH ONCE MORE --

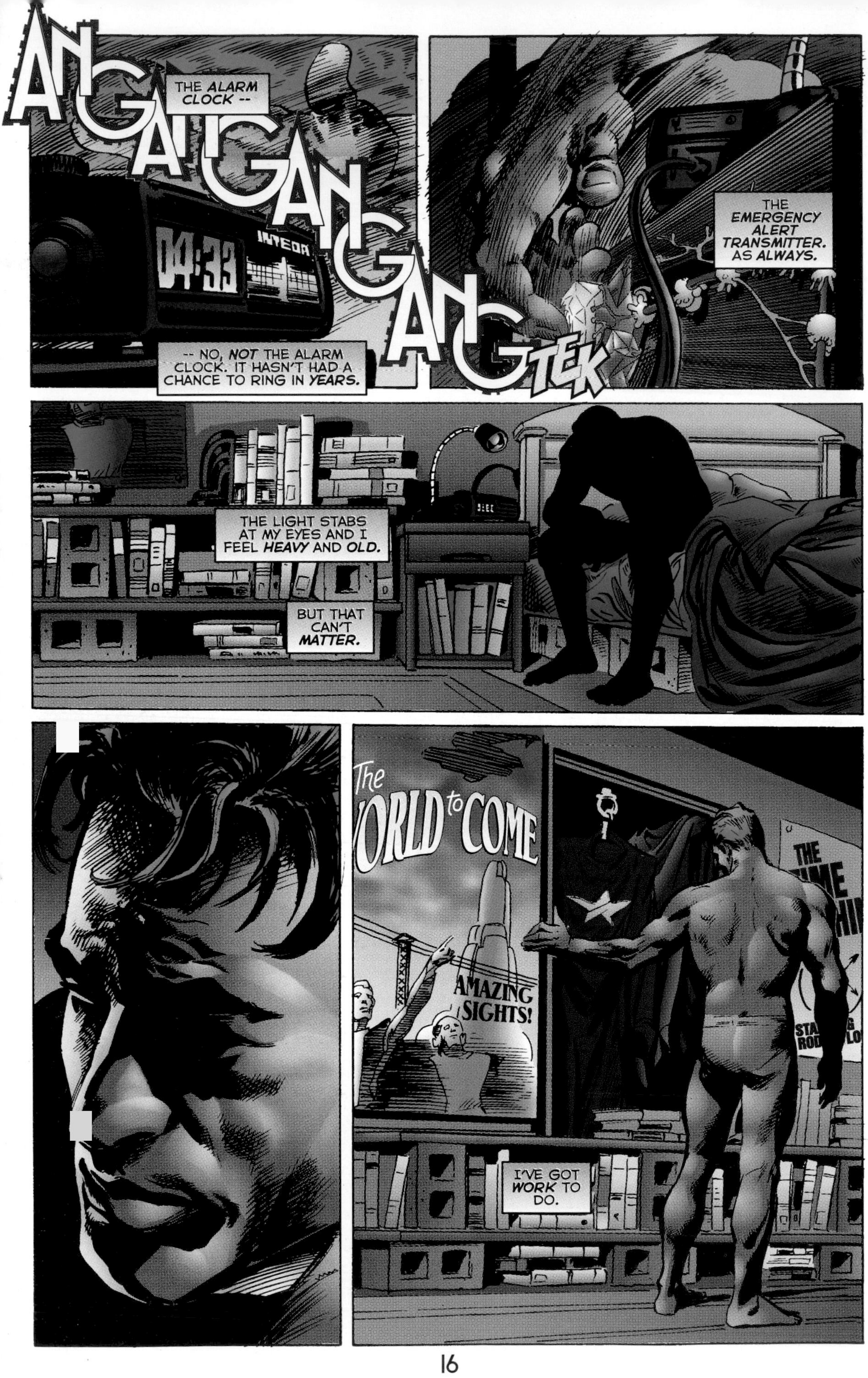
ANGANGANGANGANGTEK
THE ALARM CLOCK --
-- NO, NOT THE ALARM CLOCK. IT HASN'T HAD A CHANCE TO RING IN YEARS.
THE EMERGENCY ALERT TRANSMITTER. AS ALWAYS.
THE LIGHT STABS AT MY EYES AND I FEEL HEAVY AND OLD.
BUT THAT CAN'T MATTER.
The WORLD to COME
AMAZING SIGHTS!
I'VE GOT WORK TO DO.

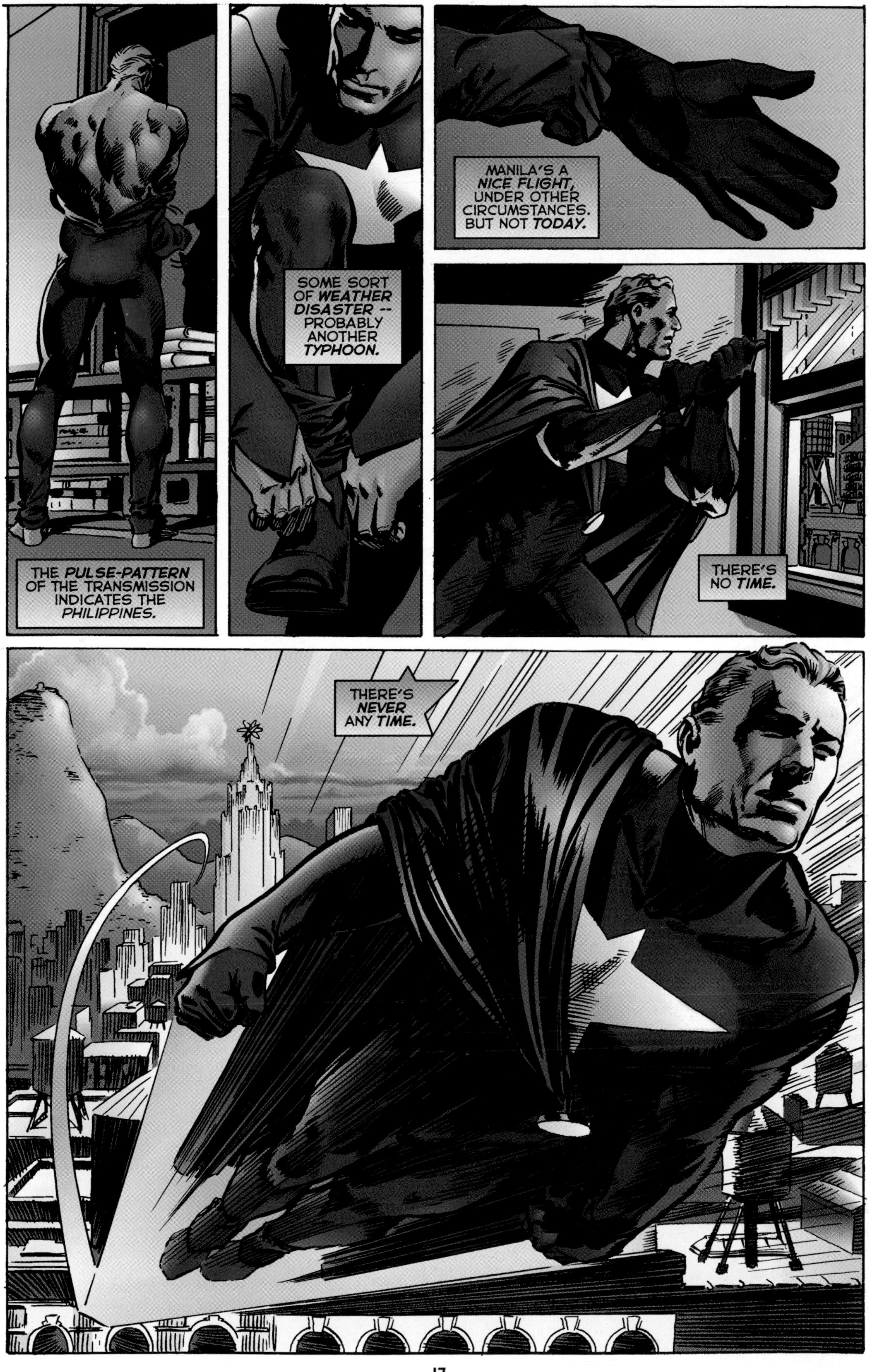
THE PULSE-PATTERN OF THE TRANSMISSION INDICATES THE PHILIPPINES.
SOME SORT OF WEATHER DISASTER -- PROBABLY ANOTHER TYPHOON.
MANILA'S A NICE FLIGHT, UNDER OTHER CIRCUMSTANCES. BUT NOT TODAY.
THERE'S NO TIME.
THERE'S NEVER ANY TIME.

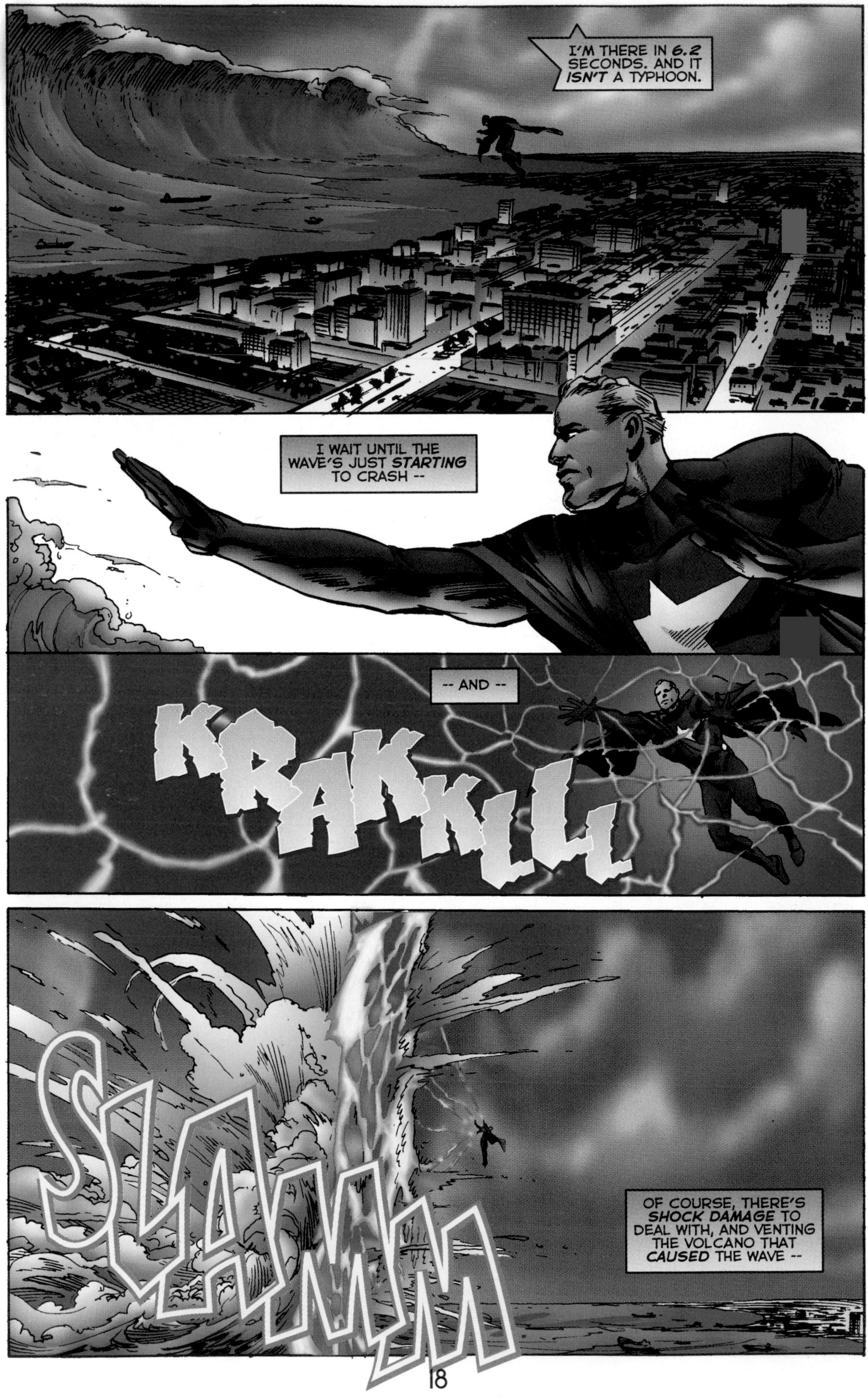
I'M THERE IN 6.2 SECONDS. AND IT ISN'T A TYPHOON.
I WAIT UNTIL THE WAVE'S JUST STARTING TO CRASH --
-- AND --
KRAKKLLL
SLAMMM
OF COURSE, THERE'S SHOCK DAMAGE TO DEAL WITH, AND VENTING THE VOLCANO THAT CAUSED THE WAVE --

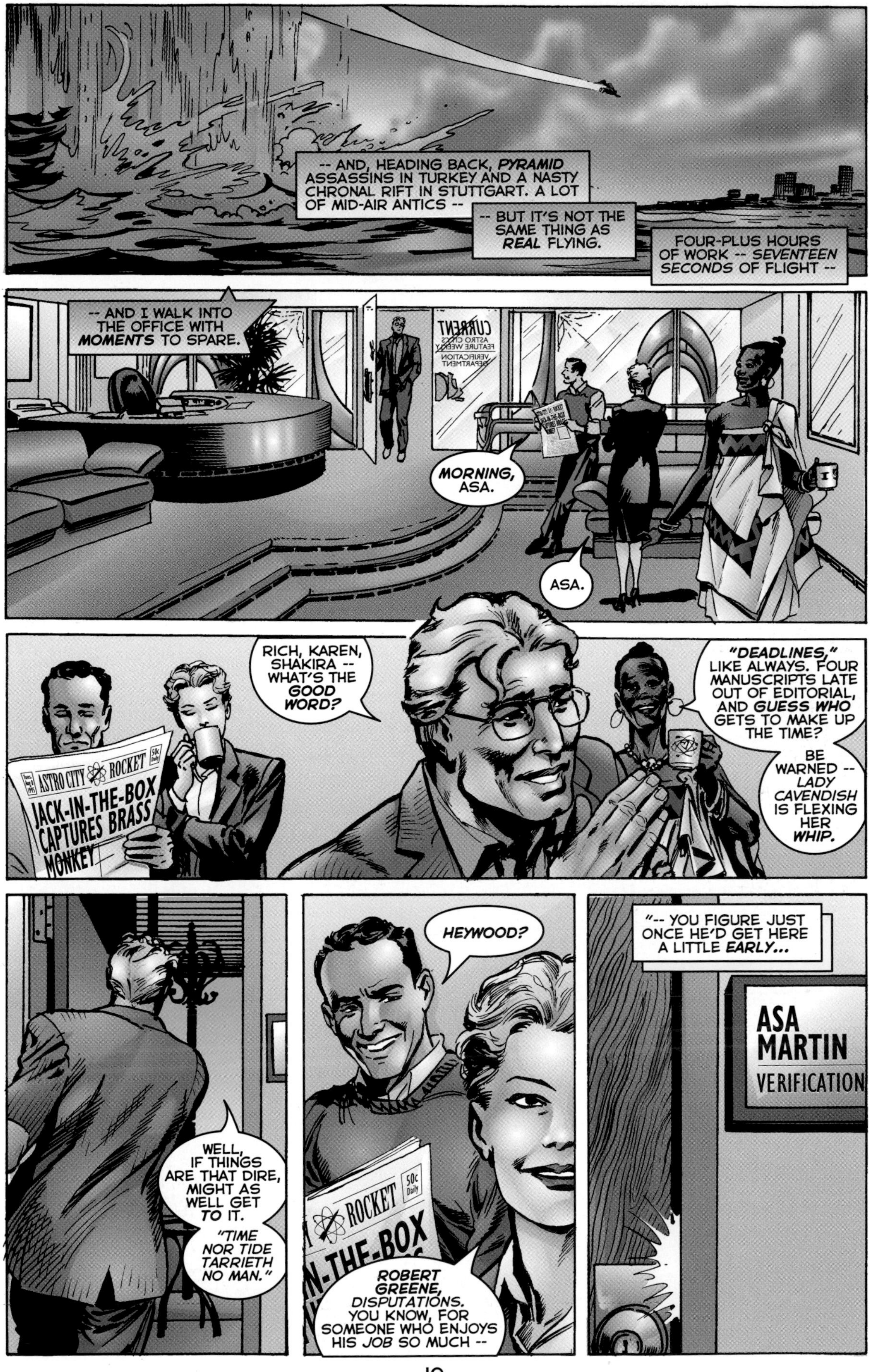
-- AND, HEADING BACK, PYRAMID ASSASSINS IN TURKEY AND A NASTY CHRONAL RIFT IN STUTTGART. A LOT OF MID-AIR ANTICS --
-- BUT IT'S NOT THE SAME THING AS REAL FLYING.
FOUR-PLUS HOURS OF WORK -- SEVENTEEN SECONDS OF FLIGHT --
-- AND I WALK INTO THE OFFICE WITH MOMENTS TO SPARE.
CURRENT
ASTRO CITY'S FEATURE WEEKLY
VERIFICATION DEPARTMENT
MORNING, ASA.
ASA.
RICH, KAREN, SHAKIRA -- WHAT'S THE GOOD WORD?
"DEADLINES," LIKE ALWAYS. FOUR MANUSCRIPTS LATE OUT OF EDITORIAL, AND GUESS WHO GETS TO MAKE UP THE TIME?
BE WARNED -- LADY CAVENDISH IS FLEXING HER WHIP.
ASTRO CITY ROCKET
50c Daily
JACK-IN-THE-BOX CAPTURES BRASS MONKEY
WELL, IF THINGS ARE THAT DIRE, MIGHT AS WELL GET TO IT.
"TIME NOR TIDE TARRIETH NO MAN."
HEYWOOD?
ROBERT GREENE, DISPUTATIONS. YOU KNOW, FOR SOMEONE WHO ENJOYS HIS JOB SO MUCH --
"-- YOU FIGURE JUST ONCE HE'D GET HERE A LITTLE EARLY...
ASA MARTIN
VERIFICATION

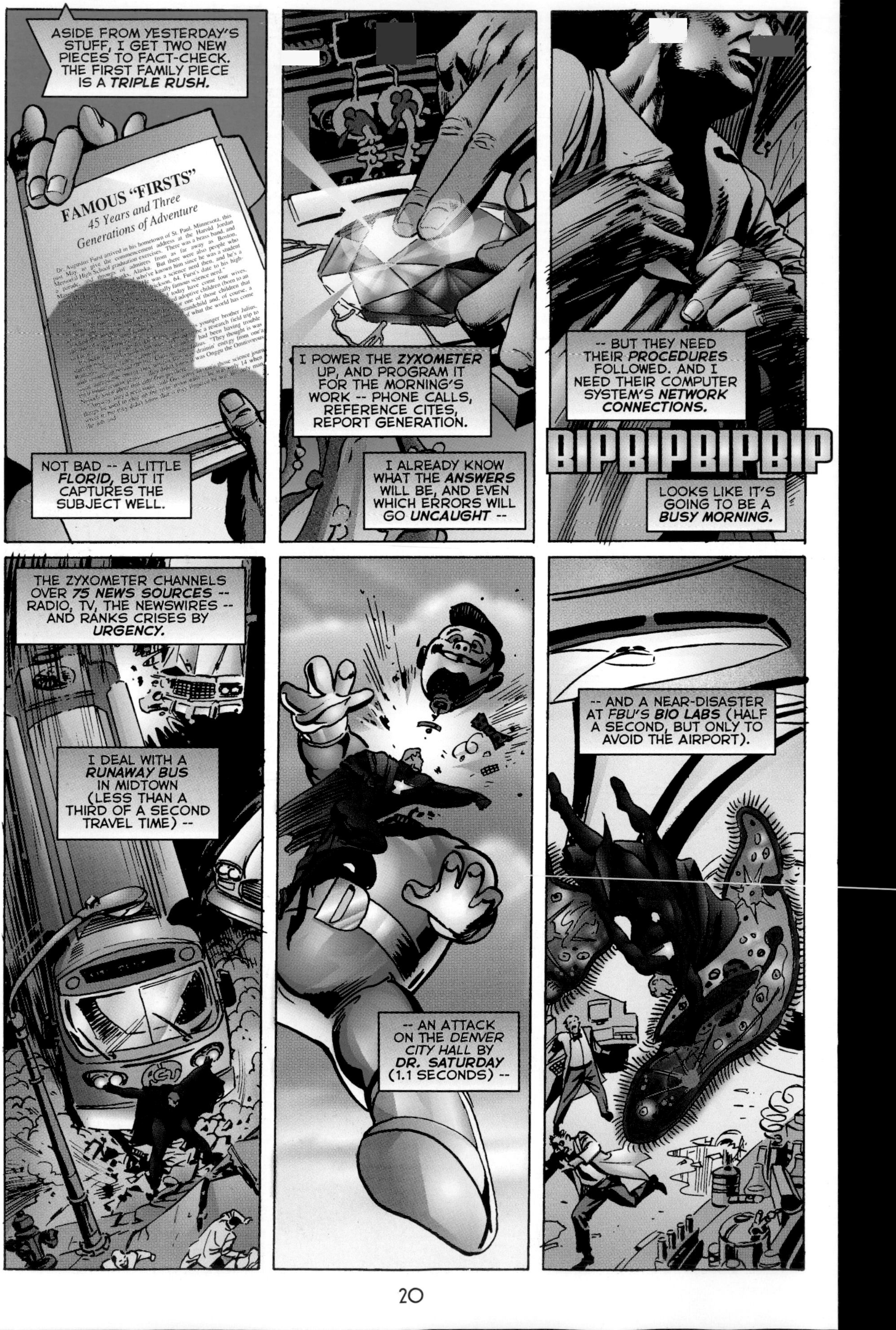
ASIDE FROM YESTERDAY'S STUFF, I GET TWO NEW PIECES TO FACT-CHECK. THE FIRST FAMILY PIECE IS A *TRIPLE RUSH.*
FAMOUS "FIRSTS"
45 Years and Three Generations of Adventure
NOT BAD -- A LITTLE *FLORID,* BUT IT CAPTURES THE SUBJECT WELL.
I POWER THE *ZYXOMETER* UP, AND PROGRAM IT FOR THE MORNING'S WORK -- PHONE CALLS, REFERENCE CITES, REPORT GENERATION.
I ALREADY KNOW WHAT THE *ANSWERS* WILL BE, AND EVEN WHICH ERRORS WILL GO *UNCAUGHT* --
-- BUT THEY NEED THEIR *PROCEDURES* FOLLOWED. AND I NEED THEIR COMPUTER SYSTEM'S *NETWORK CONNECTIONS.*
BIPBIPBIPBIP
LOOKS LIKE IT'S GOING TO BE A *BUSY MORNING.*
THE ZYXOMETER CHANNELS OVER *75 NEWS SOURCES* -- RADIO, TV, THE NEWSWIRES -- AND RANKS CRISES BY *URGENCY.*
I DEAL WITH A *RUNAWAY BUS* IN MIDTOWN (LESS THAN A THIRD OF A SECOND TRAVEL TIME) --
-- AN ATTACK ON THE *DENVER CITY HALL* BY *DR. SATURDAY* (1.1 SECONDS) --
-- AND A NEAR-DISASTER AT *FBU'S BIO LABS* (HALF A SECOND, BUT ONLY TO AVOID THE AIRPORT).

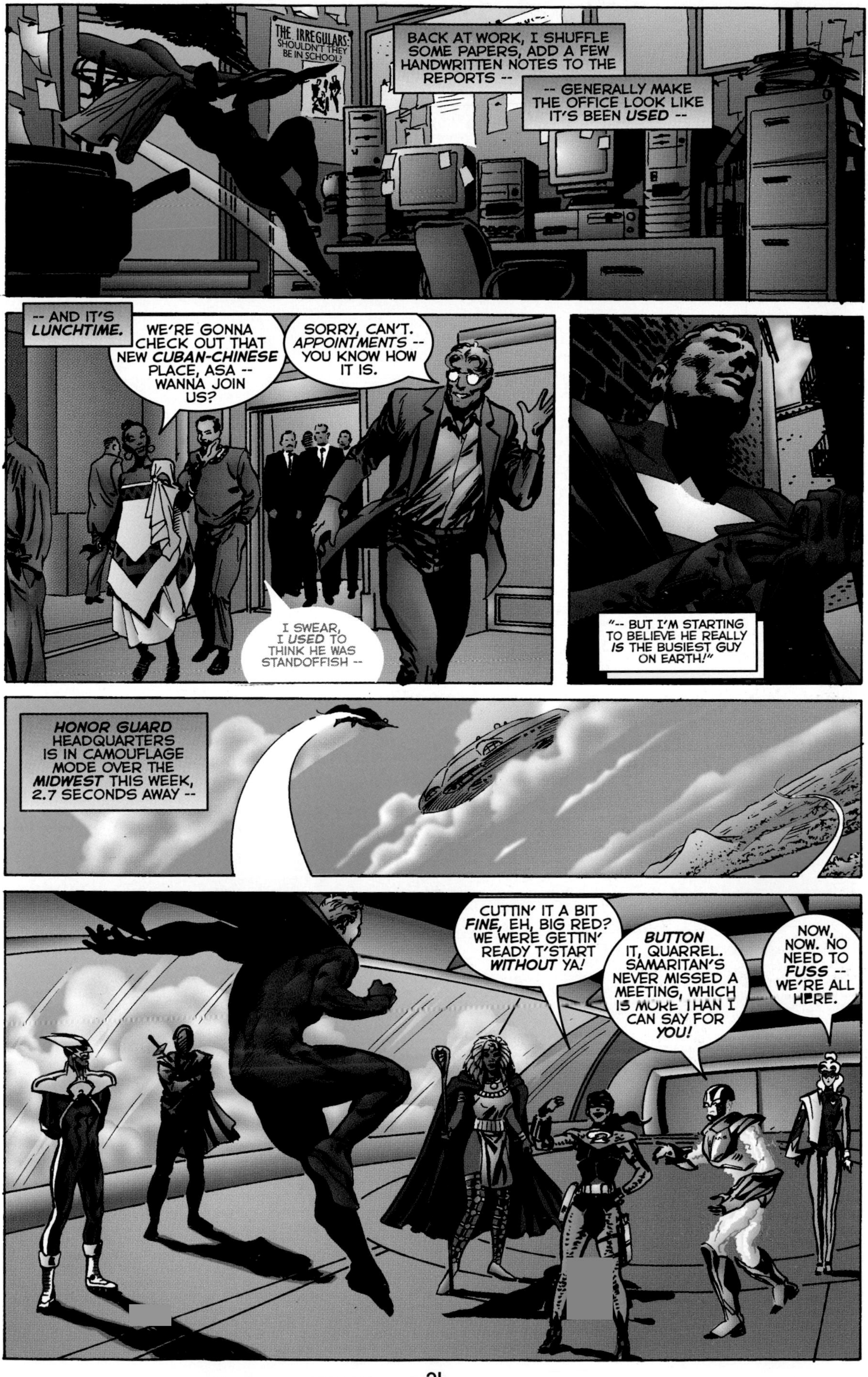
THE IRREGULARS: SHOULDN'T THEY BE IN SCHOOL?
BACK AT WORK, I SHUFFLE SOME PAPERS, ADD A FEW HANDWRITTEN NOTES TO THE REPORTS --
-- GENERALLY MAKE THE OFFICE LOOK LIKE IT'S BEEN *USED* --
-- AND IT'S *LUNCHTIME.*
WE'RE GONNA CHECK OUT THAT NEW *CUBAN-CHINESE* PLACE, ASA -- WANNA JOIN US?
SORRY, CAN'T. *APPOINTMENTS* -- YOU KNOW HOW IT IS.
I SWEAR, I *USED* TO THINK HE WAS STANDOFFISH --
"-- BUT I'M STARTING TO BELIEVE HE REALLY *IS* THE BUSIEST GUY ON EARTH!"
HONOR GUARD HEADQUARTERS IS IN CAMOUFLAGE MODE OVER THE *MIDWEST* THIS WEEK, 2.7 SECONDS AWAY --
CUTTIN' IT A BIT *FINE*, EH, BIG RED? WE WERE GETTIN' READY T'START *WITHOUT* YA!
BUTTON IT, QUARREL. SAMARITAN'S NEVER MISSED A MEETING, WHICH IS MORE THAN I CAN SAY FOR *YOU!*
NOW, NOW. NO NEED TO *FUSS* -- WE'RE ALL HERE.

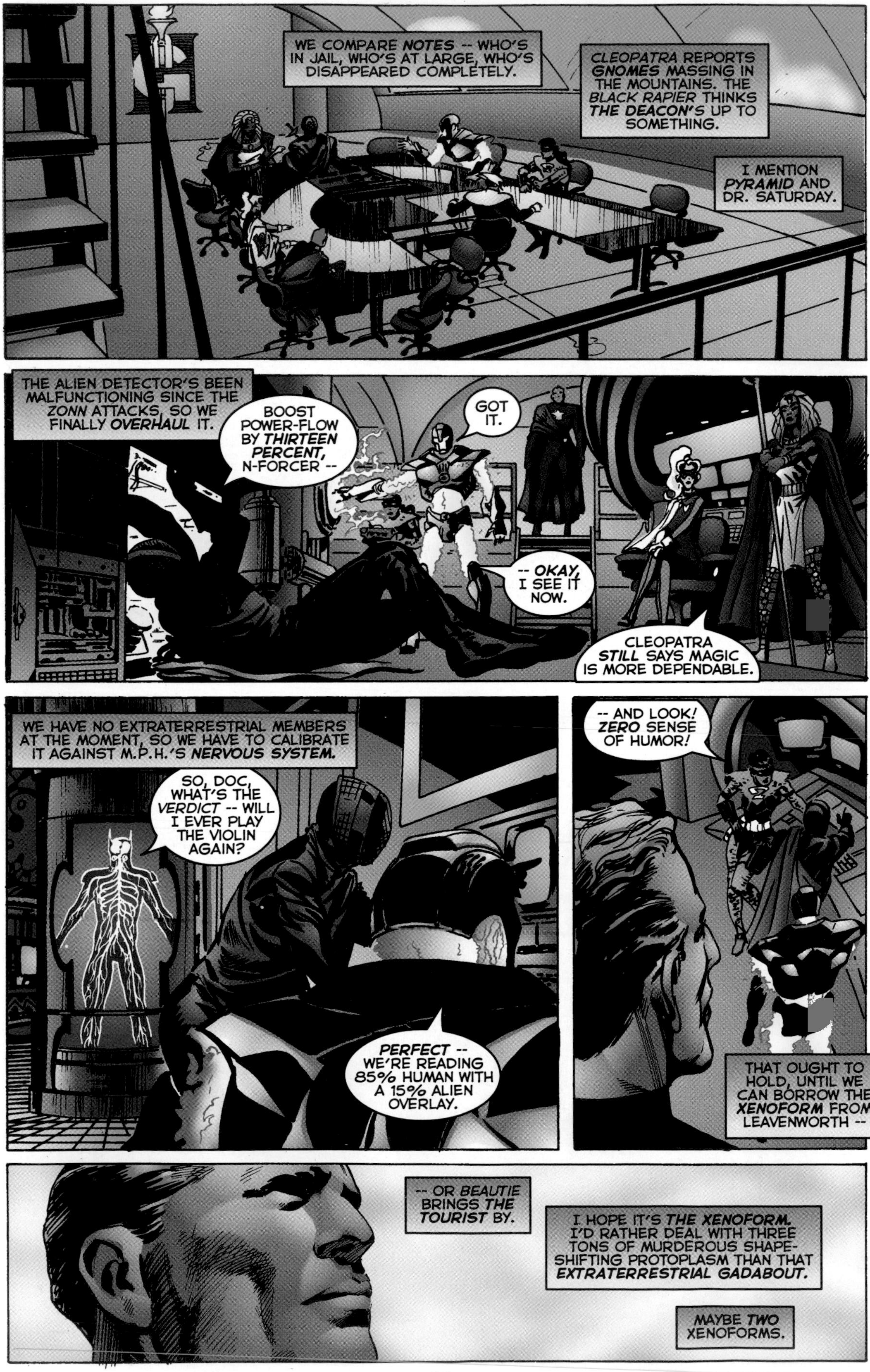
WE COMPARE NOTES -- WHO'S IN JAIL, WHO'S AT LARGE, WHO'S DISAPPEARED COMPLETELY.
CLEOPATRA REPORTS GNOMES MASSING IN THE MOUNTAINS. THE BLACK RAPIER THINKS THE DEACON'S UP TO SOMETHING.
I MENTION PYRAMID AND DR. SATURDAY.
THE ALIEN DETECTOR'S BEEN MALFUNCTIONING SINCE THE ZONN ATTACKS, SO WE FINALLY OVERHAUL IT.
BOOST POWER-FLOW BY THIRTEEN PERCENT, N-FORCER --
GOT IT.
-- OKAY, I SEE IT NOW.
CLEOPATRA STILL SAYS MAGIC IS MORE DEPENDABLE.
WE HAVE NO EXTRATERRESTRIAL MEMBERS AT THE MOMENT, SO WE HAVE TO CALIBRATE IT AGAINST M.P.H.'S NERVOUS SYSTEM.
SO, DOC, WHAT'S THE VERDICT -- WILL I EVER PLAY THE VIOLIN AGAIN?
PERFECT -- WE'RE READING 85% HUMAN WITH A 15% ALIEN OVERLAY.
-- AND LOOK! ZERO SENSE OF HUMOR!
THAT OUGHT TO HOLD, UNTIL WE CAN BORROW THE XENOFORM FROM LEAVENWORTH --
-- OR BEAUTIE BRINGS THE TOURIST BY.
I HOPE IT'S THE XENOFORM. I'D RATHER DEAL WITH THREE TONS OF MURDEROUS SHAPE-SHIFTING PROTOPLASM THAN THAT EXTRATERRESTRIAL GADABOUT.
MAYBE TWO XENOFORMS.

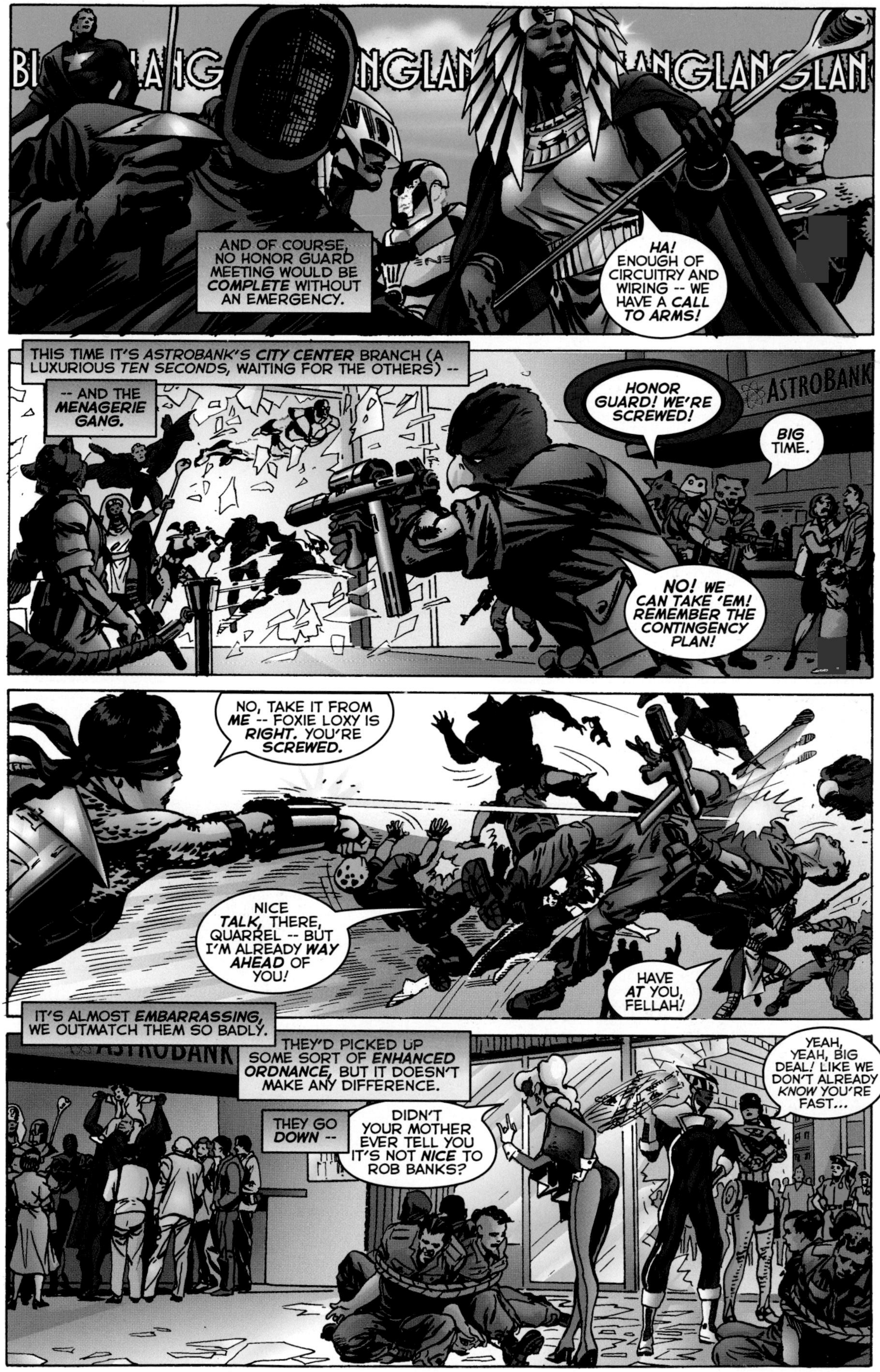
AND OF COURSE, NO HONOR GUARD MEETING WOULD BE COMPLETE WITHOUT AN EMERGENCY.
HA! ENOUGH OF CIRCUITRY AND WIRING -- WE HAVE A CALL TO ARMS!
THIS TIME IT'S ASTROBANK'S CITY CENTER BRANCH (A LUXURIOUS TEN SECONDS, WAITING FOR THE OTHERS) --
-- AND THE MENAGERIE GANG.
ASTROBANK
HONOR GUARD! WE'RE SCREWED!
BIG TIME.
NO! WE CAN TAKE 'EM! REMEMBER THE CONTINGENCY PLAN!
NO, TAKE IT FROM ME -- FOXIE LOXY IS RIGHT. YOU'RE SCREWED.
NICE TALK, THERE, QUARREL -- BUT I'M ALREADY WAY AHEAD OF YOU!
HAVE AT YOU, FELLAH!
IT'S ALMOST EMBARRASSING, WE OUTMATCH THEM SO BADLY.
THEY'D PICKED UP SOME SORT OF ENHANCED ORDNANCE, BUT IT DOESN'T MAKE ANY DIFFERENCE.
YEAH, YEAH, BIG DEAL! LIKE WE DON'T ALREADY KNOW YOU'RE FAST...
THEY GO DOWN --
DIDN'T YOUR MOTHER EVER TELL YOU IT'S NOT NICE TO ROB BANKS?

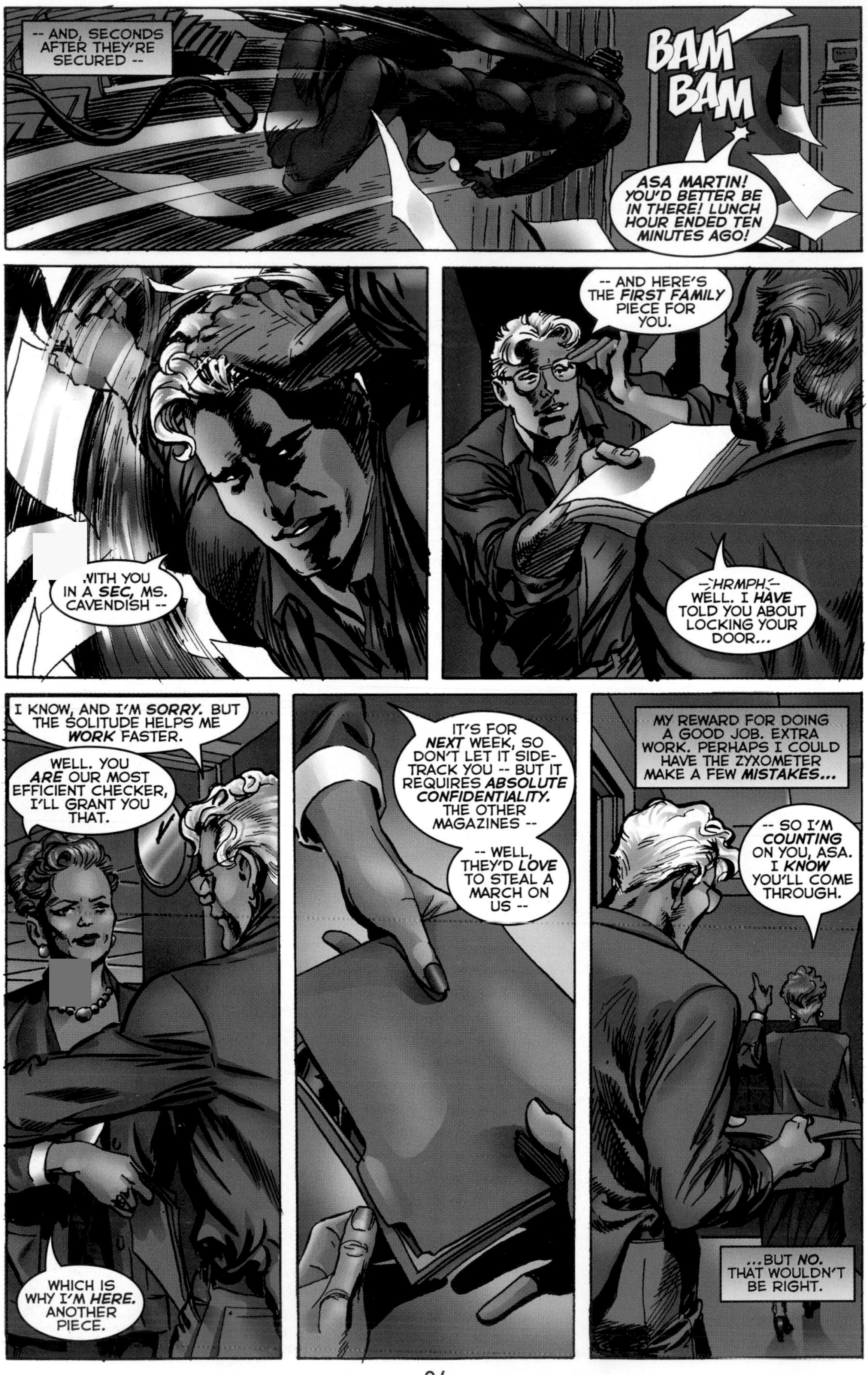

-- AND, SECONDS AFTER THEY'RE SECURED --
BAM BAM
ASA MARTIN! YOU'D BETTER BE IN THERE! LUNCH HOUR ENDED TEN MINUTES AGO!
WITH YOU IN A SEC, MS. CAVENDISH --
-- AND HERE'S THE FIRST FAMILY PIECE FOR YOU.
-HRMPH- WELL. I HAVE TOLD YOU ABOUT LOCKING YOUR DOOR...
I KNOW, AND I'M SORRY. BUT THE SOLITUDE HELPS ME WORK FASTER.
WELL. YOU ARE OUR MOST EFFICIENT CHECKER, I'LL GRANT YOU THAT.
WHICH IS WHY I'M HERE. ANOTHER PIECE.
IT'S FOR NEXT WEEK, SO DON'T LET IT SIDE-TRACK YOU -- BUT IT REQUIRES ABSOLUTE CONFIDENTIALITY. THE OTHER MAGAZINES --
-- WELL, THEY'D LOVE TO STEAL A MARCH ON US --
MY REWARD FOR DOING A GOOD JOB. EXTRA WORK. PERHAPS I COULD HAVE THE ZYXOMETER MAKE A FEW MISTAKES...
-- SO I'M COUNTING ON YOU, ASA. I KNOW YOU'LL COME THROUGH.
...BUT NO. THAT WOULDN'T BE RIGHT.

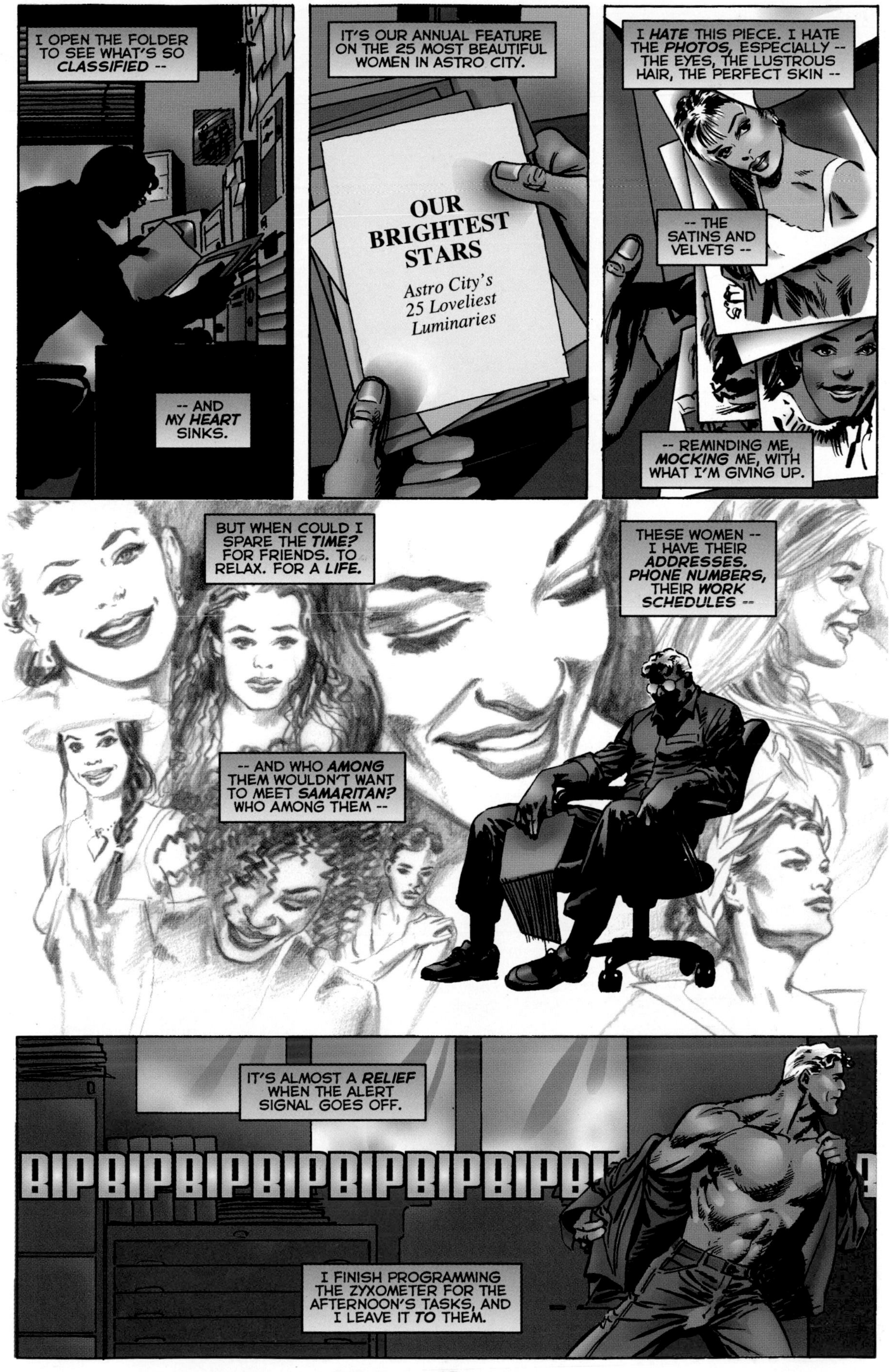
I OPEN THE FOLDER TO SEE WHAT'S SO CLASSIFIED --
-- AND MY HEART SINKS.
IT'S OUR ANNUAL FEATURE ON THE 25 MOST BEAUTIFUL WOMEN IN ASTRO CITY.
OUR BRIGHTEST STARS
Astro City's 25 Loveliest Luminaries
I HATE THIS PIECE. I HATE THE PHOTOS, ESPECIALLY -- THE EYES, THE LUSTROUS HAIR, THE PERFECT SKIN --
-- THE SATINS AND VELVETS --
-- REMINDING ME, MOCKING ME, WITH WHAT I'M GIVING UP.
BUT WHEN COULD I SPARE THE TIME? FOR FRIENDS. TO RELAX. FOR A LIFE.
THESE WOMEN -- I HAVE THEIR ADDRESSES. PHONE NUMBERS, THEIR WORK SCHEDULES --
-- AND WHO AMONG THEM WOULDN'T WANT TO MEET SAMARITAN? WHO AMONG THEM --
IT'S ALMOST A RELIEF WHEN THE ALERT SIGNAL GOES OFF.
BIPBIPBIPBIPBIPBIPBIPBIPB
I FINISH PROGRAMMING THE ZYXOMETER FOR THE AFTERNOON'S TASKS, AND I LEAVE IT TO THEM.

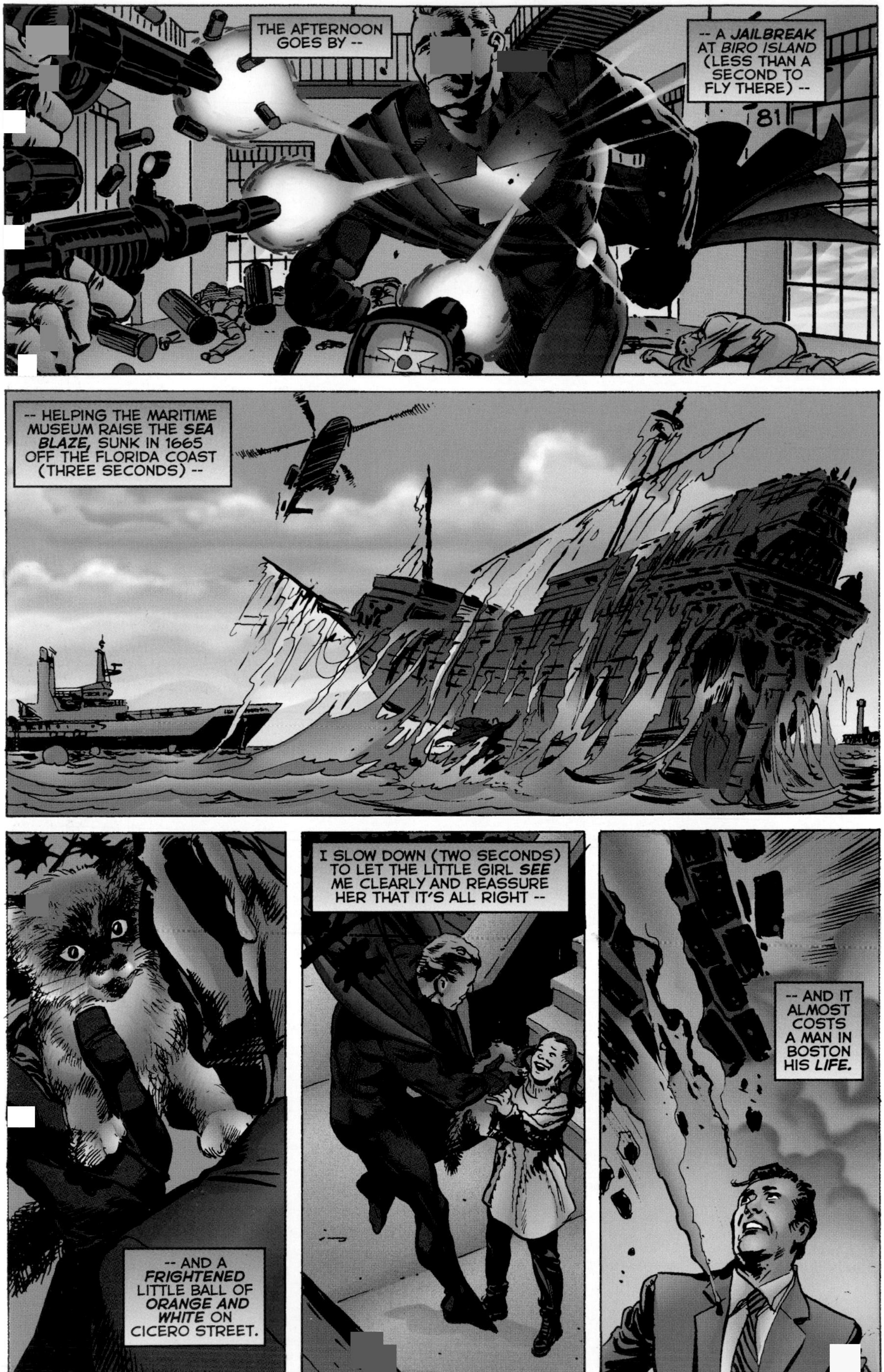
THE AFTERNOON GOES BY --
-- A JAILBREAK AT BIRO ISLAND (LESS THAN A SECOND TO FLY THERE) --
81
-- HELPING THE MARITIME MUSEUM RAISE THE SEA BLAZE, SUNK IN 1665 OFF THE FLORIDA COAST (THREE SECONDS) --
-- AND A FRIGHTENED LITTLE BALL OF ORANGE AND WHITE ON CICERO STREET.
I SLOW DOWN (TWO SECONDS) TO LET THE LITTLE GIRL SEE ME CLEARLY AND REASSURE HER THAT IT'S ALL RIGHT --
-- AND IT ALMOST COSTS A MAN IN BOSTON HIS LIFE.

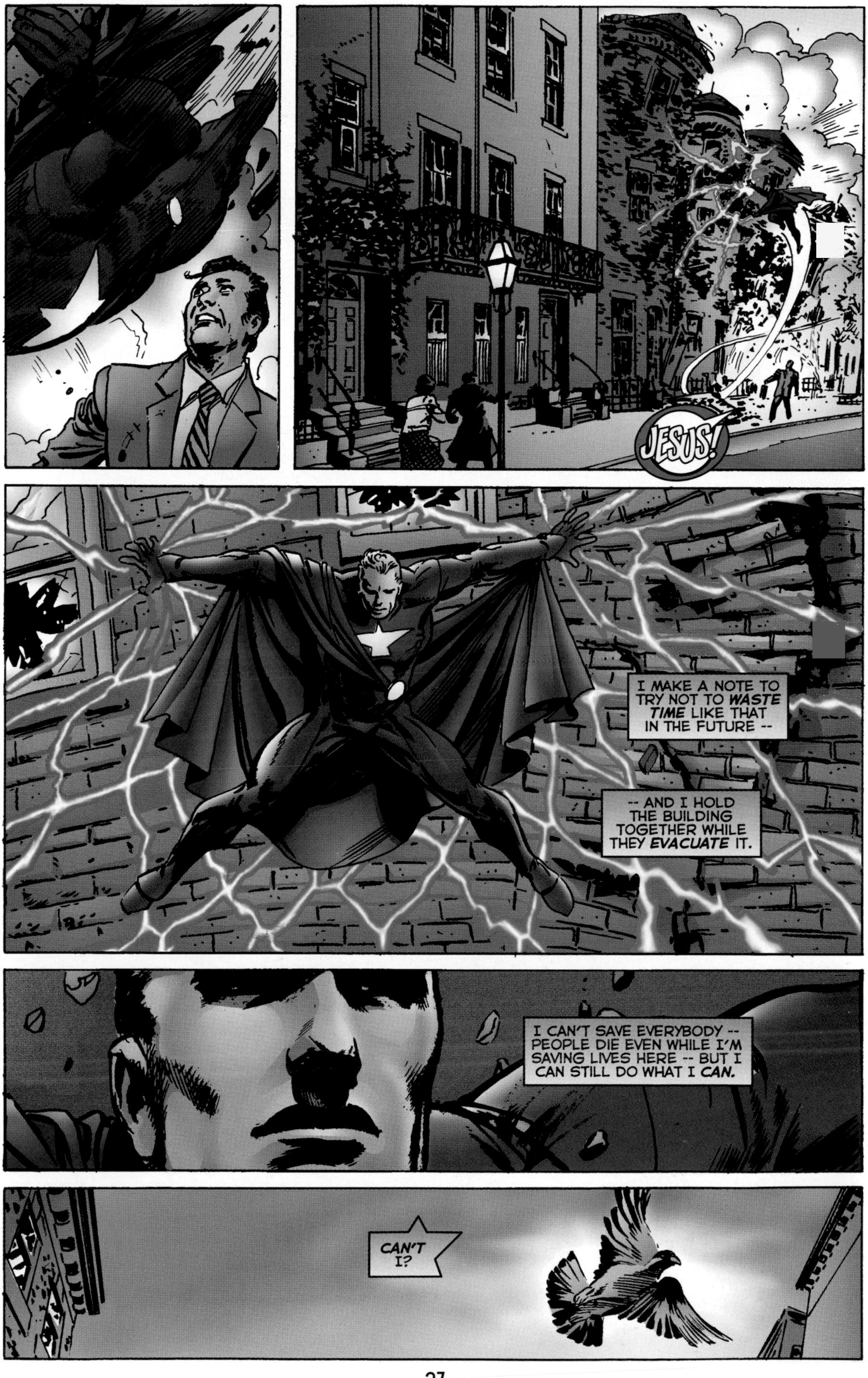
JESUS!
I MAKE A NOTE TO TRY NOT TO WASTE TIME LIKE THAT IN THE FUTURE --
-- AND I HOLD THE BUILDING TOGETHER WHILE THEY EVACUATE IT.
I CAN'T SAVE EVERYBODY -- PEOPLE DIE EVEN WHILE I'M SAVING LIVES HERE -- BUT I CAN STILL DO WHAT I CAN.
CAN'T I?

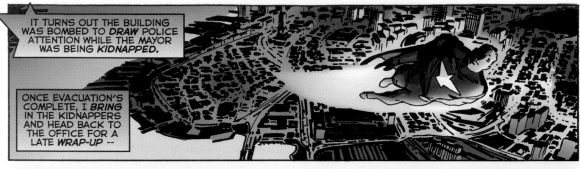

IT TURNS OUT THE BUILDING WAS BOMBED TO *DRAW* POLICE ATTENTION WHILE THE MAYOR WAS BEING *KIDNAPPED.*

ONCE EVACUATION'S COMPLETE, I *BRING* IN THE KIDNAPPERS AND HEAD BACK TO THE OFFICE FOR A LATE *WRAP-UP* --

-- AND IN TIME TO GET READY FOR *DINNER.*

TONIGHT, IT'S THE *FIREFIGHTERS* ASSOCIATION.

-- WITH THE *GREATEST HONOR,* AND *DEEPEST* SENSE OF *GRATITUDE,* THAT I *PRESENT* THIS TOKEN OF OUR ESTEEM TO THE MAN WHO --

ACFA
PRESENTED BY THE
ASTRO CITY
FIREFIGHTERS ASSOCIATION
WITH GRATITUDE AND RESPECT, TO
SAMARITAN
AUGUST 8, 1995

I TRIED ONCE TO SIMPLY *IGNORE* THESE EVENTS, BUT IT OFFENDED PEOPLE --

-- GREAT HONOR. I *THANK* YOU, AND WILL CONTINUE TO DO MY BEST, FOR THE PEOPLE OF *ASTRO CITY* AND THE ENTIRE --

-- AS IF I WAS SAYING I WAS *TOO GOOD* FOR THEM.

ACFA

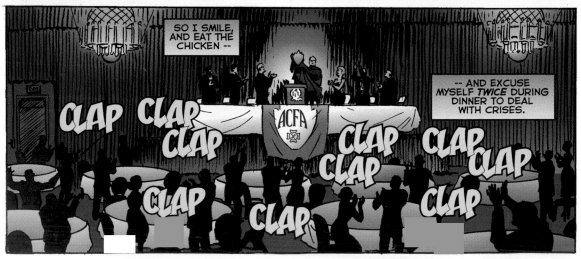

SO I SMILE, AND EAT THE CHICKEN --

-- AND EXCUSE MYSELF *TWICE* DURING DINNER TO DEAL WITH CRISES.

CLAP CLAP CLAP CLAP CLAP CLAP CLAP CLAP CLAP CLAP

ACFA

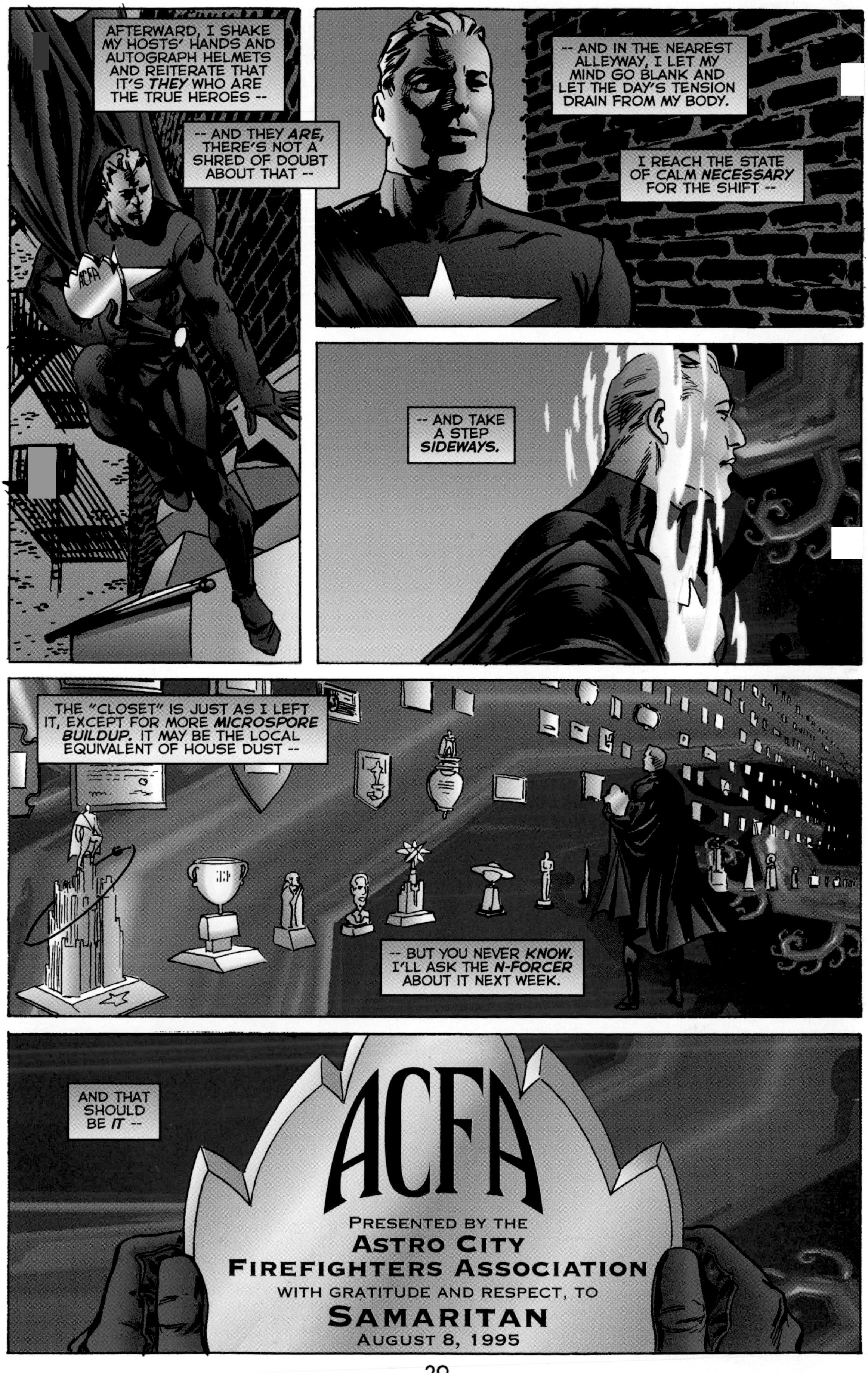
AFTERWARD, I SHAKE MY HOSTS' HANDS AND AUTOGRAPH HELMETS AND REITERATE THAT IT'S *THEY* WHO ARE THE TRUE HEROES --
-- AND THEY *ARE,* THERE'S NOT A SHRED OF DOUBT ABOUT THAT --
ACFA
-- AND IN THE NEAREST ALLEYWAY, I LET MY MIND GO BLANK AND LET THE DAY'S TENSION DRAIN FROM MY BODY.
I REACH THE STATE OF CALM *NECESSARY* FOR THE SHIFT --
-- AND TAKE A STEP *SIDEWAYS.*
THE "CLOSET" IS JUST AS I LEFT IT, EXCEPT FOR MORE *MICROSPORE BUILDUP.* IT MAY BE THE LOCAL EQUIVALENT OF HOUSE DUST --
-- BUT YOU NEVER *KNOW.* I'LL ASK THE *N-FORCER* ABOUT IT NEXT WEEK.
AND THAT SHOULD BE *IT* --
ACFA
PRESENTED BY THE
ASTRO CITY
FIREFIGHTERS ASSOCIATION
WITH GRATITUDE AND RESPECT, TO
SAMARITAN
AUGUST 8, 1995

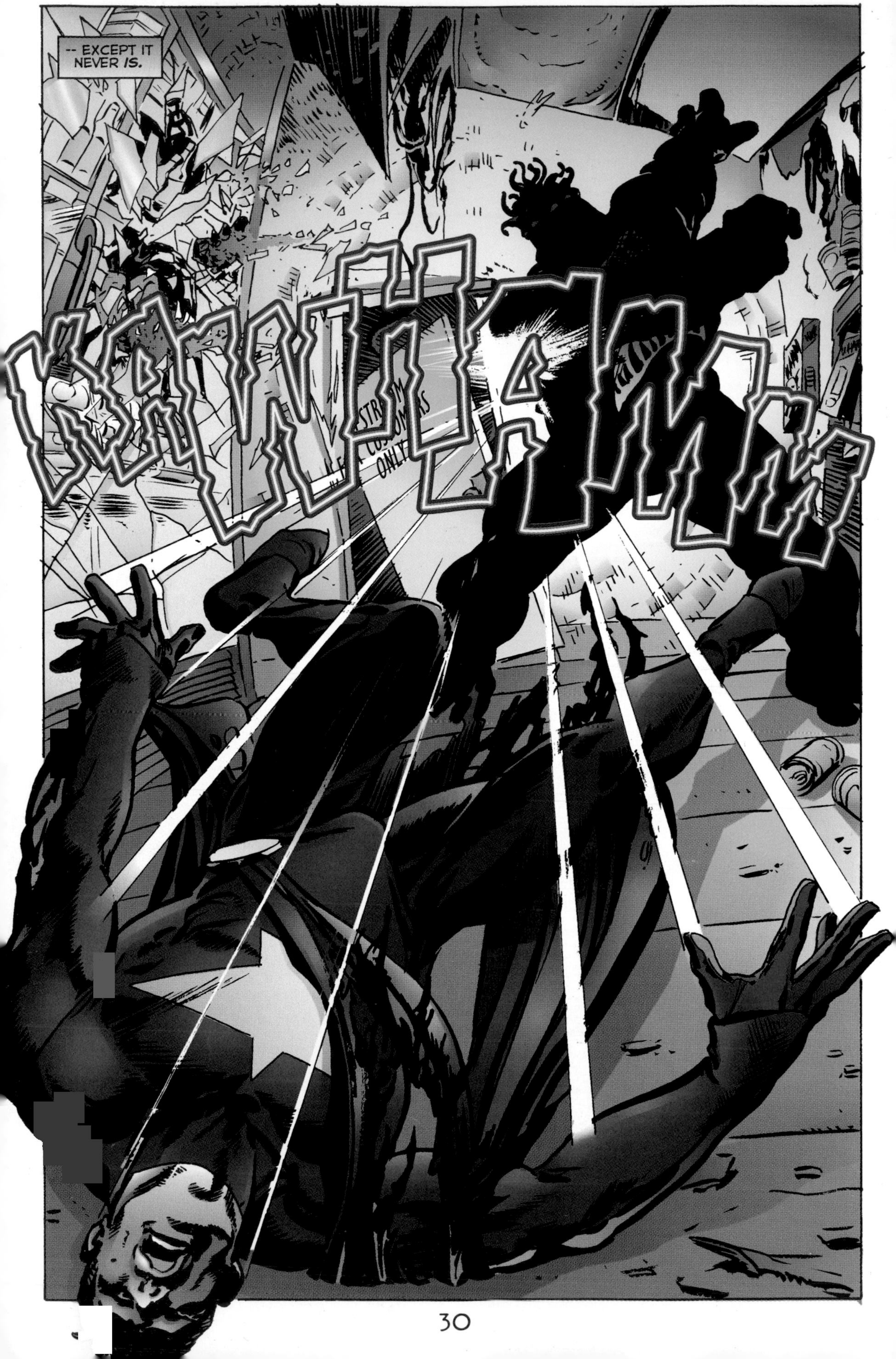
-- EXCEPT IT NEVER IS.

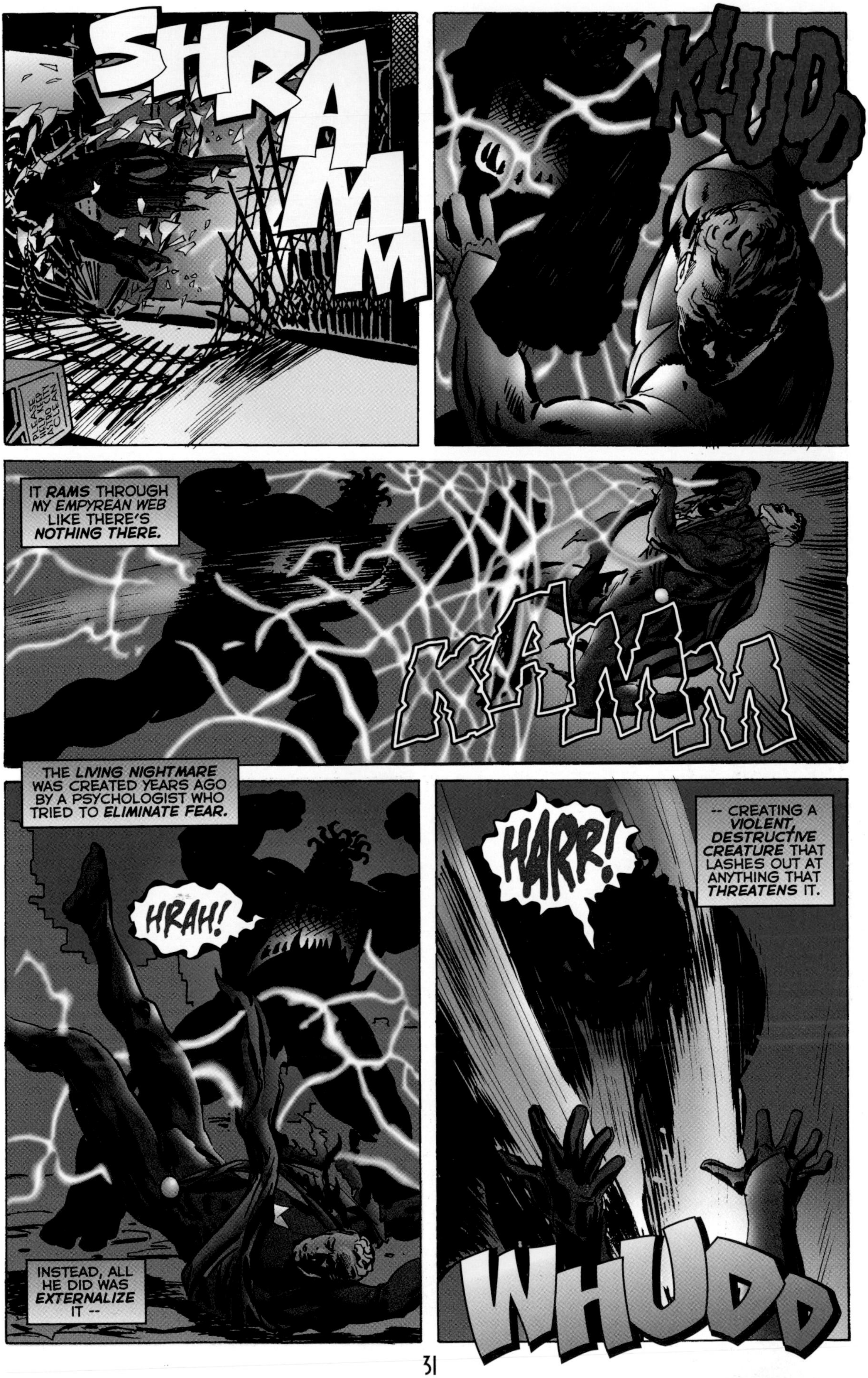
SHRAMM
PLEASE HELP KEEP ASTRO CITY CLEAN
KLUDD
IT RAMS THROUGH MY EMPYREAN WEB LIKE THERE'S NOTHING THERE.
KAMM
THE LIVING NIGHTMARE WAS CREATED YEARS AGO BY A PSYCHOLOGIST WHO TRIED TO ELIMINATE FEAR.
HRAH!
INSTEAD, ALL HE DID WAS EXTERNALIZE IT --
HARR!
-- CREATING A VIOLENT, DESTRUCTIVE CREATURE THAT LASHES OUT AT ANYTHING THAT THREATENS IT.
WHUDD

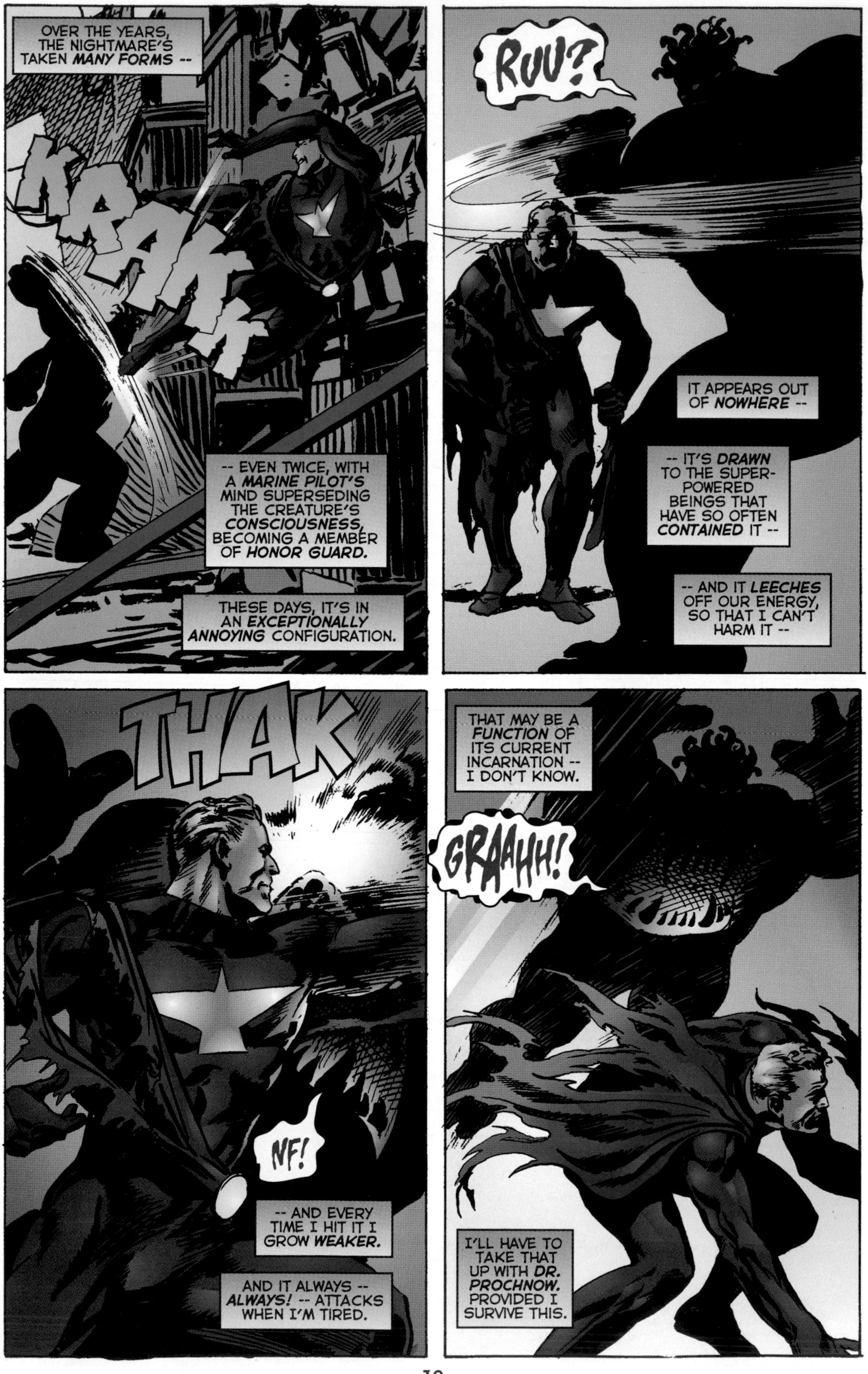
OVER THE YEARS, THE NIGHTMARE'S TAKEN MANY FORMS --
KRAKK
-- EVEN TWICE, WITH A MARINE PILOT'S MIND SUPERSEDING THE CREATURE'S CONSCIOUSNESS, BECOMING A MEMBER OF HONOR GUARD.
THESE DAYS, IT'S IN AN EXCEPTIONALLY ANNOYING CONFIGURATION.
RUU?
IT APPEARS OUT OF NOWHERE --
-- IT'S DRAWN TO THE SUPER-POWERED BEINGS THAT HAVE SO OFTEN CONTAINED IT --
-- AND IT LEECHES OFF OUR ENERGY, SO THAT I CAN'T HARM IT --
THAK
NF!
-- AND EVERY TIME I HIT IT I GROW WEAKER.
AND IT ALWAYS -- ALWAYS! -- ATTACKS WHEN I'M TIRED.
THAT MAY BE A FUNCTION OF ITS CURRENT INCARNATION -- I DON'T KNOW.
GRAAHH!
I'LL HAVE TO TAKE THAT UP WITH DR. PROCHNOW. PROVIDED I SURVIVE THIS.

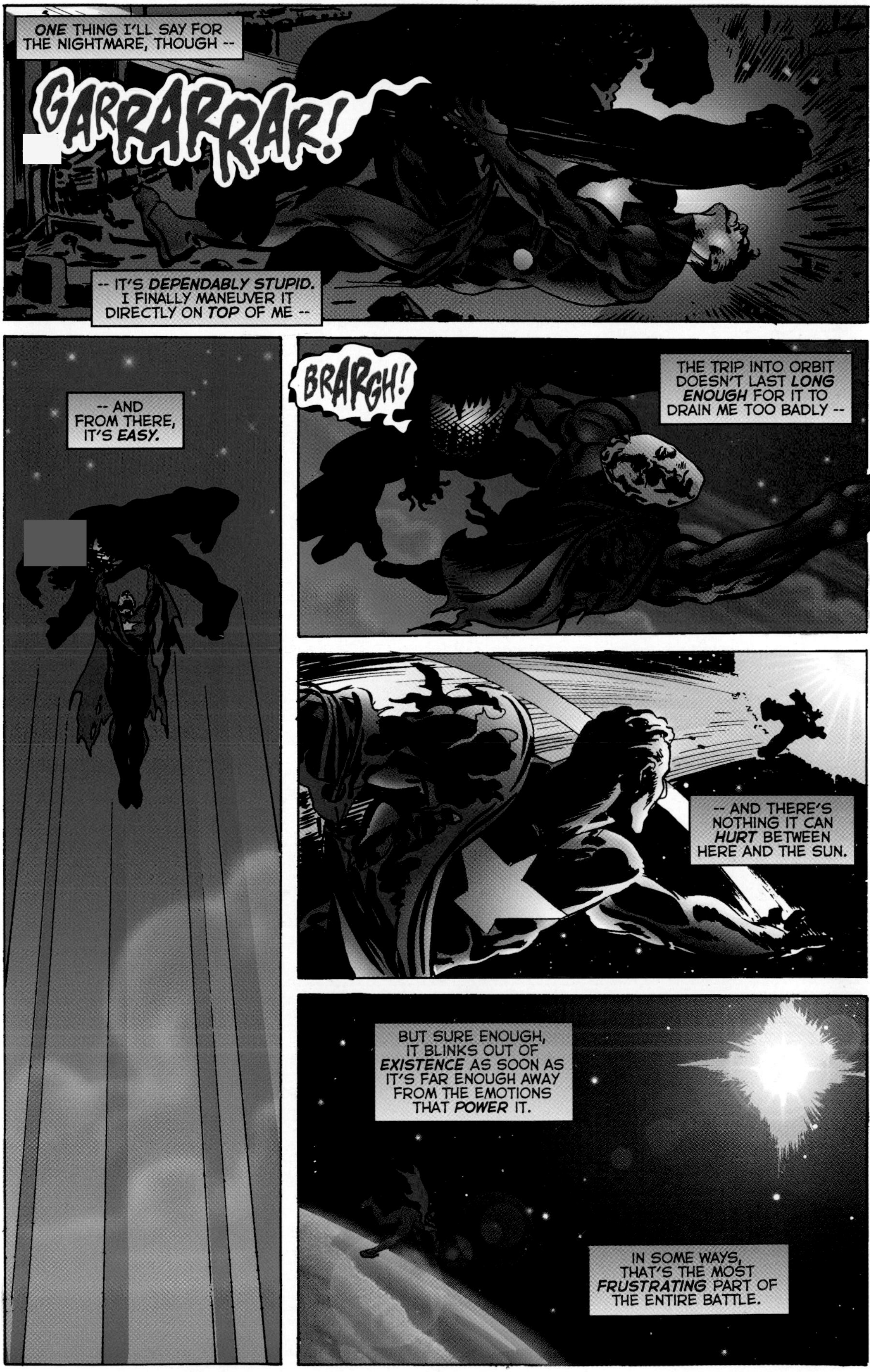
ONE THING I'LL SAY FOR THE NIGHTMARE, THOUGH --
GARRARRAR!
-- IT'S DEPENDABLY STUPID. I FINALLY MANEUVER IT DIRECTLY ON TOP OF ME --
-- AND FROM THERE, IT'S EASY.
BRARGH!
THE TRIP INTO ORBIT DOESN'T LAST LONG ENOUGH FOR IT TO DRAIN ME TOO BADLY --
-- AND THERE'S NOTHING IT CAN HURT BETWEEN HERE AND THE SUN.
BUT SURE ENOUGH, IT BLINKS OUT OF EXISTENCE AS SOON AS IT'S FAR ENOUGH AWAY FROM THE EMOTIONS THAT POWER IT.
IN SOME WAYS, THAT'S THE MOST FRUSTRATING PART OF THE ENTIRE BATTLE.

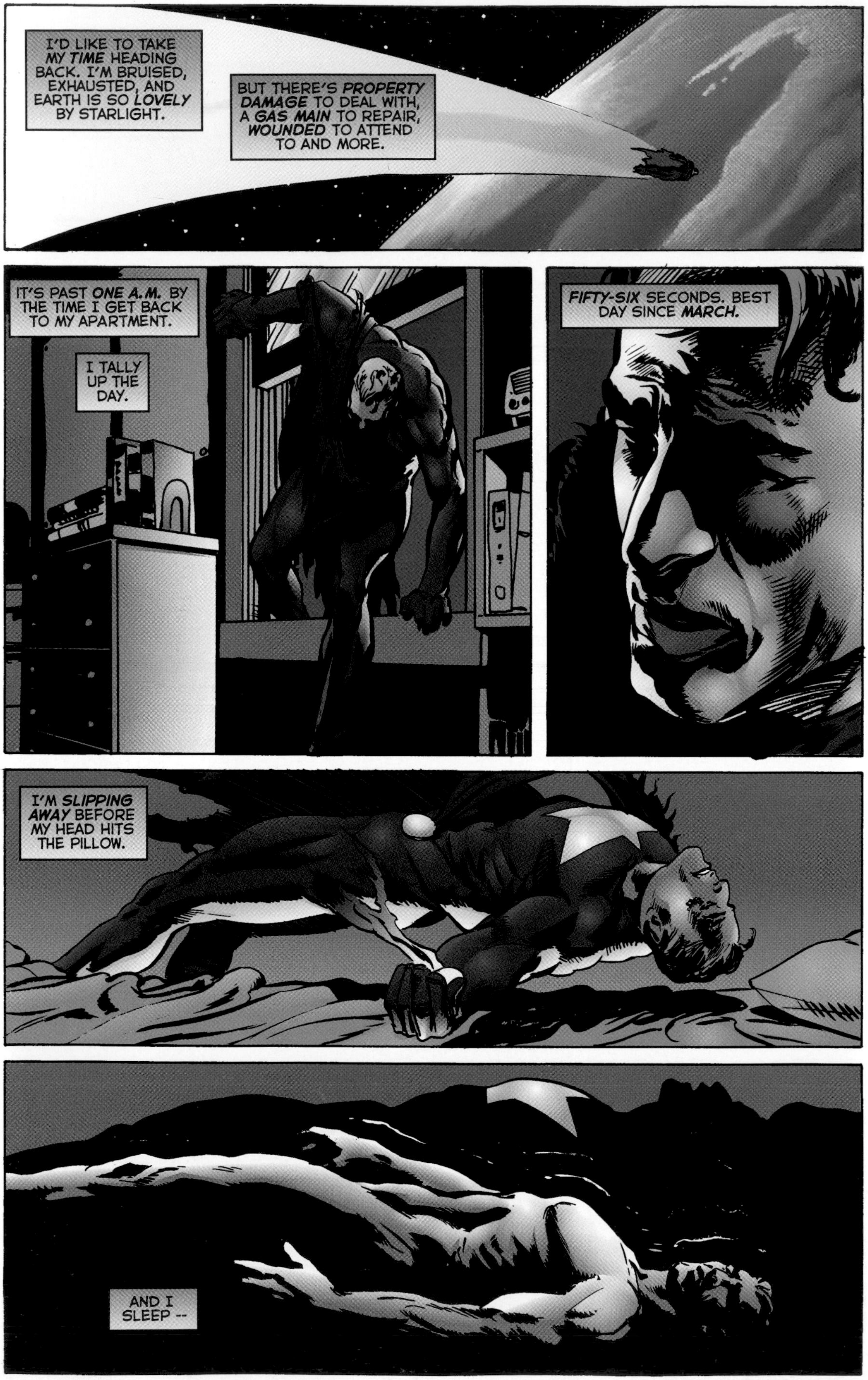
I'D LIKE TO TAKE MY TIME HEADING BACK. I'M BRUISED, EXHAUSTED, AND EARTH IS SO LOVELY BY STARLIGHT.
BUT THERE'S PROPERTY DAMAGE TO DEAL WITH, A GAS MAIN TO REPAIR, WOUNDED TO ATTEND TO AND MORE.
IT'S PAST ONE A.M. BY THE TIME I GET BACK TO MY APARTMENT.
I TALLY UP THE DAY.
FIFTY-SIX SECONDS. BEST DAY SINCE MARCH.
I'M SLIPPING AWAY BEFORE MY HEAD HITS THE PILLOW.
AND I SLEEP --

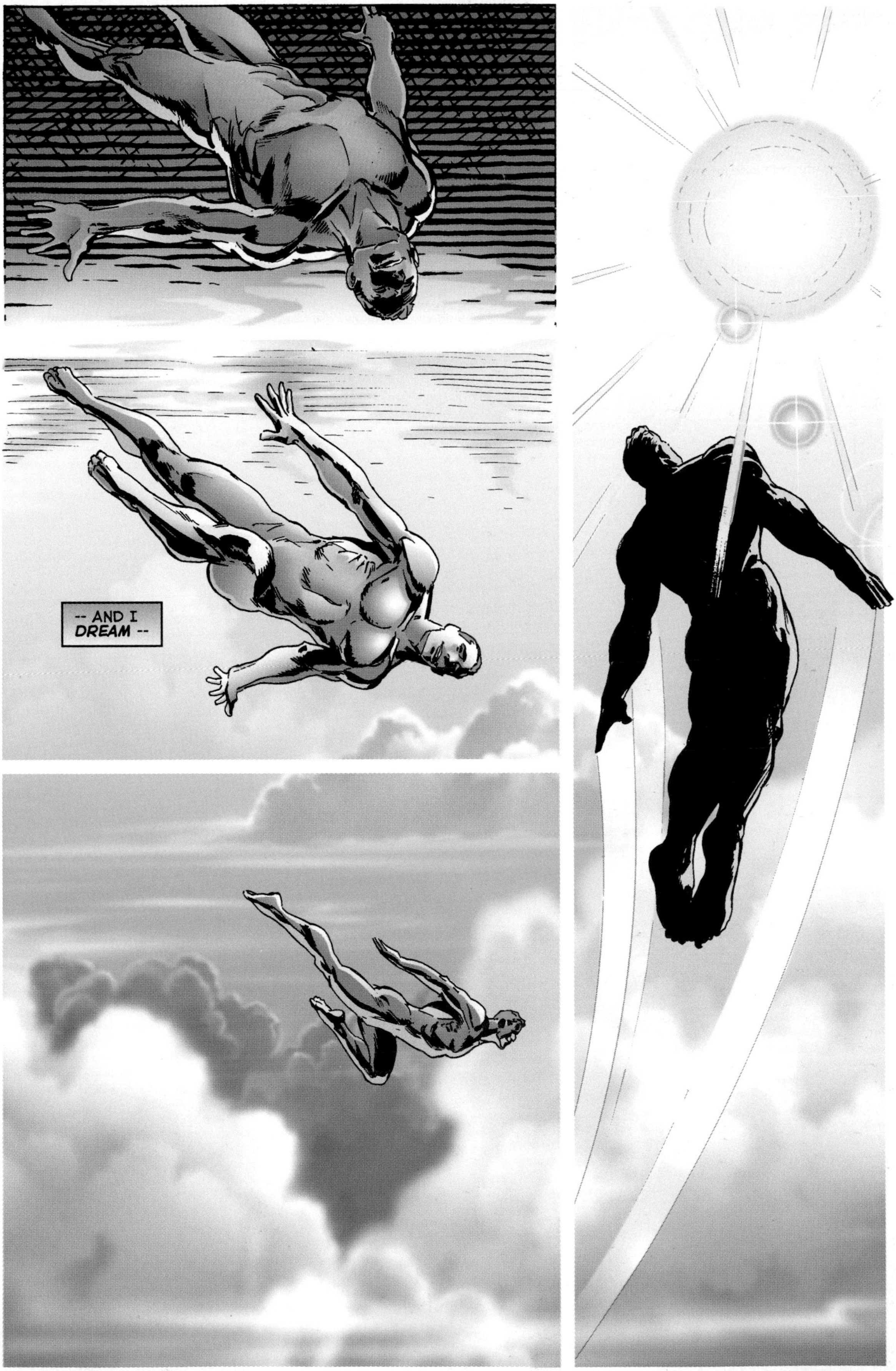
-- AND I DREAM --

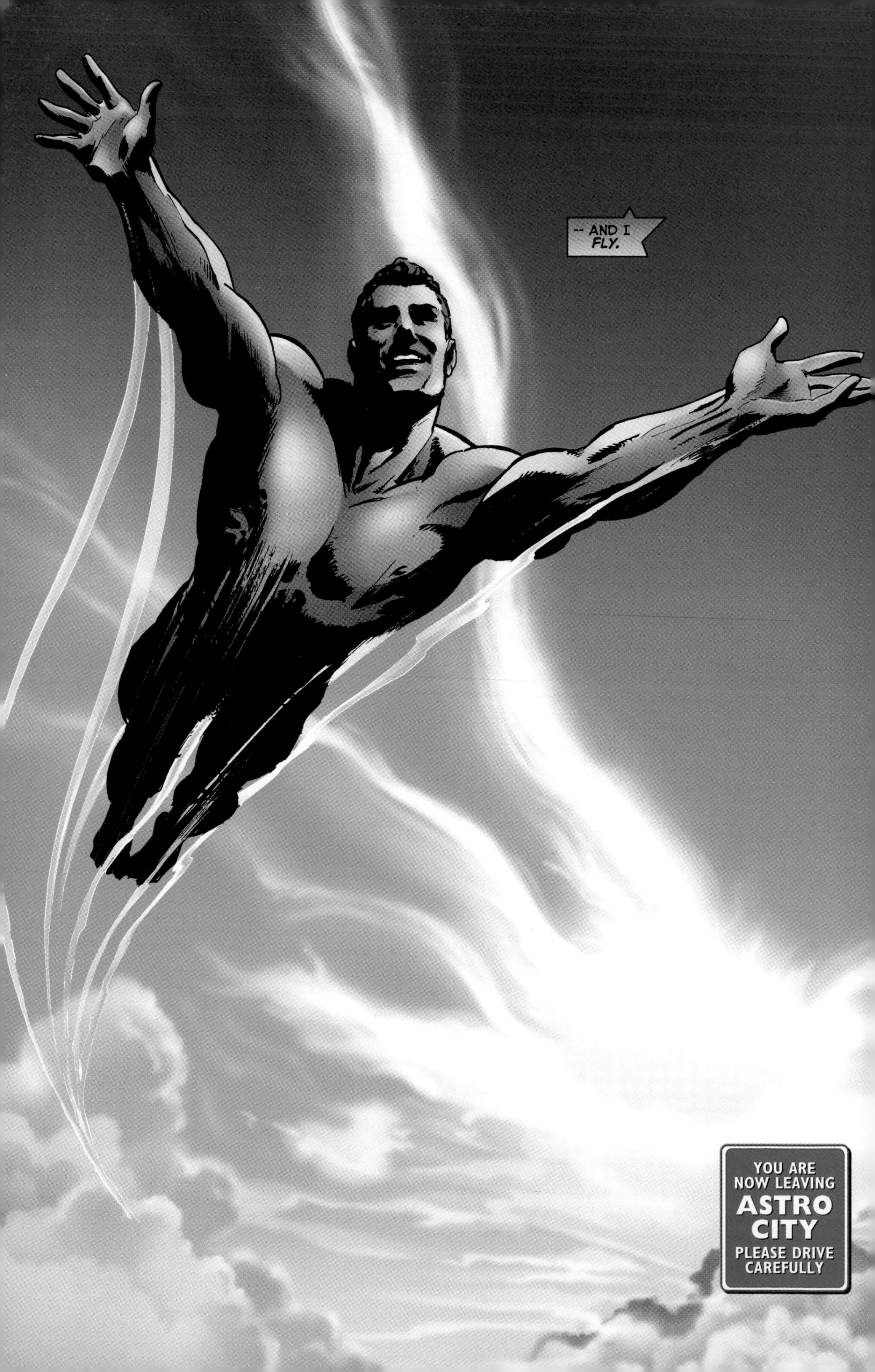
-- AND I FLY.
YOU ARE NOW LEAVING ASTRO CITY PLEASE DRIVE CAREFULLY

CHAPTER 2

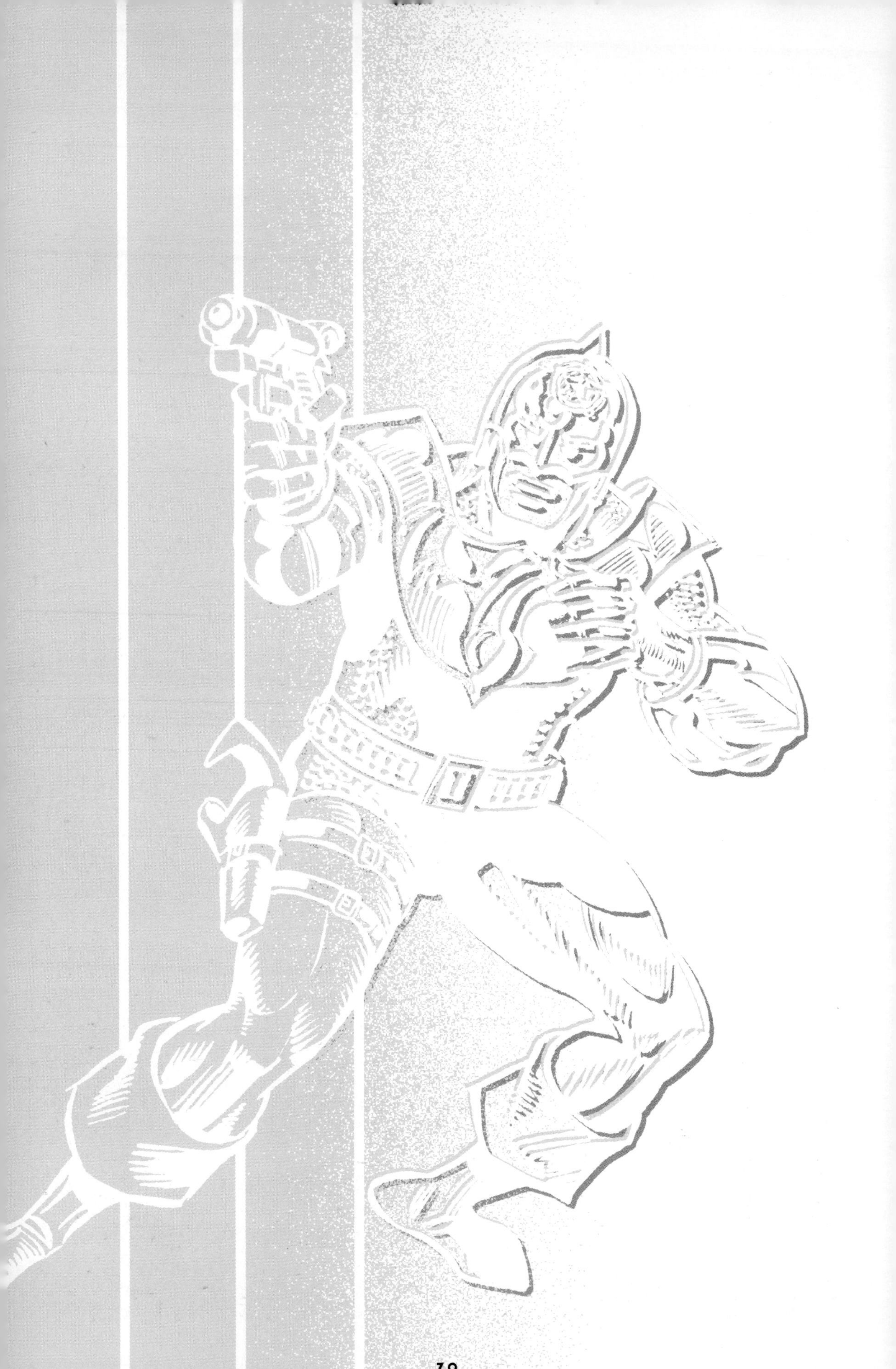

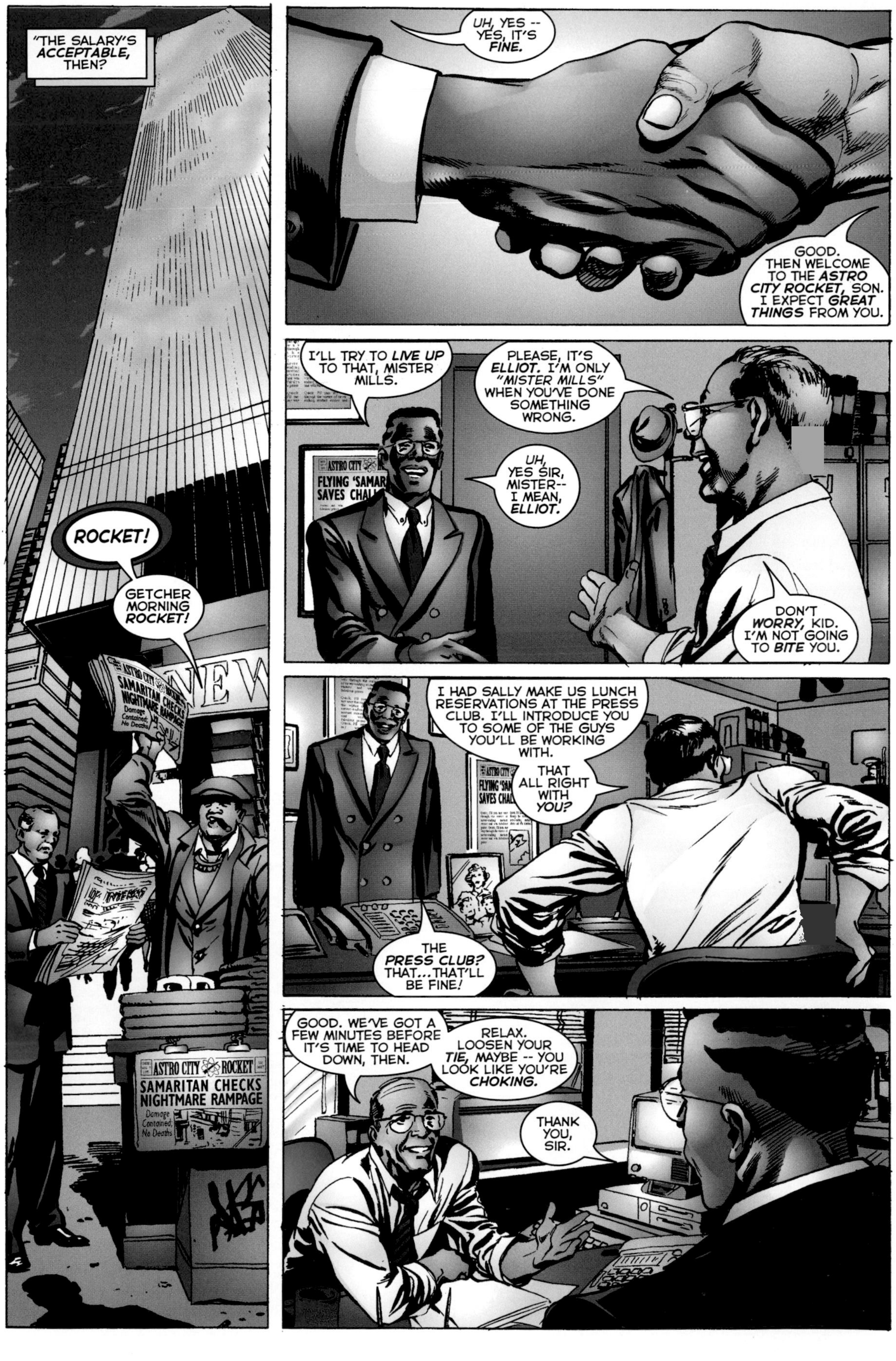
"THE SALARY'S ACCEPTABLE, THEN?
ROCKET!
GETCHER MORNING ROCKET!
ASTRO CITY ROCKET
SAMARITAN CHECKS NIGHTMARE RAMPAGE
Damage Contained; No Deaths
UH, YES -- YES, IT'S FINE.
GOOD. THEN WELCOME TO THE ASTRO CITY ROCKET, SON. I EXPECT GREAT THINGS FROM YOU.
I'LL TRY TO LIVE UP TO THAT, MISTER MILLS.
PLEASE, IT'S ELLIOT. I'M ONLY "MISTER MILLS" WHEN YOU'VE DONE SOMETHING WRONG.
UH, YES SIR, MISTER-- I MEAN, ELLIOT.
DON'T WORRY, KID. I'M NOT GOING TO BITE YOU.
I HAD SALLY MAKE US LUNCH RESERVATIONS AT THE PRESS CLUB. I'LL INTRODUCE YOU TO SOME OF THE GUYS YOU'LL BE WORKING WITH.
THAT ALL RIGHT WITH YOU?
THE PRESS CLUB? THAT... THAT'LL BE FINE!
GOOD. WE'VE GOT A FEW MINUTES BEFORE IT'S TIME TO HEAD DOWN, THEN.
RELAX. LOOSEN YOUR TIE, MAYBE -- YOU LOOK LIKE YOU'RE CHOKING.
THANK YOU, SIR.

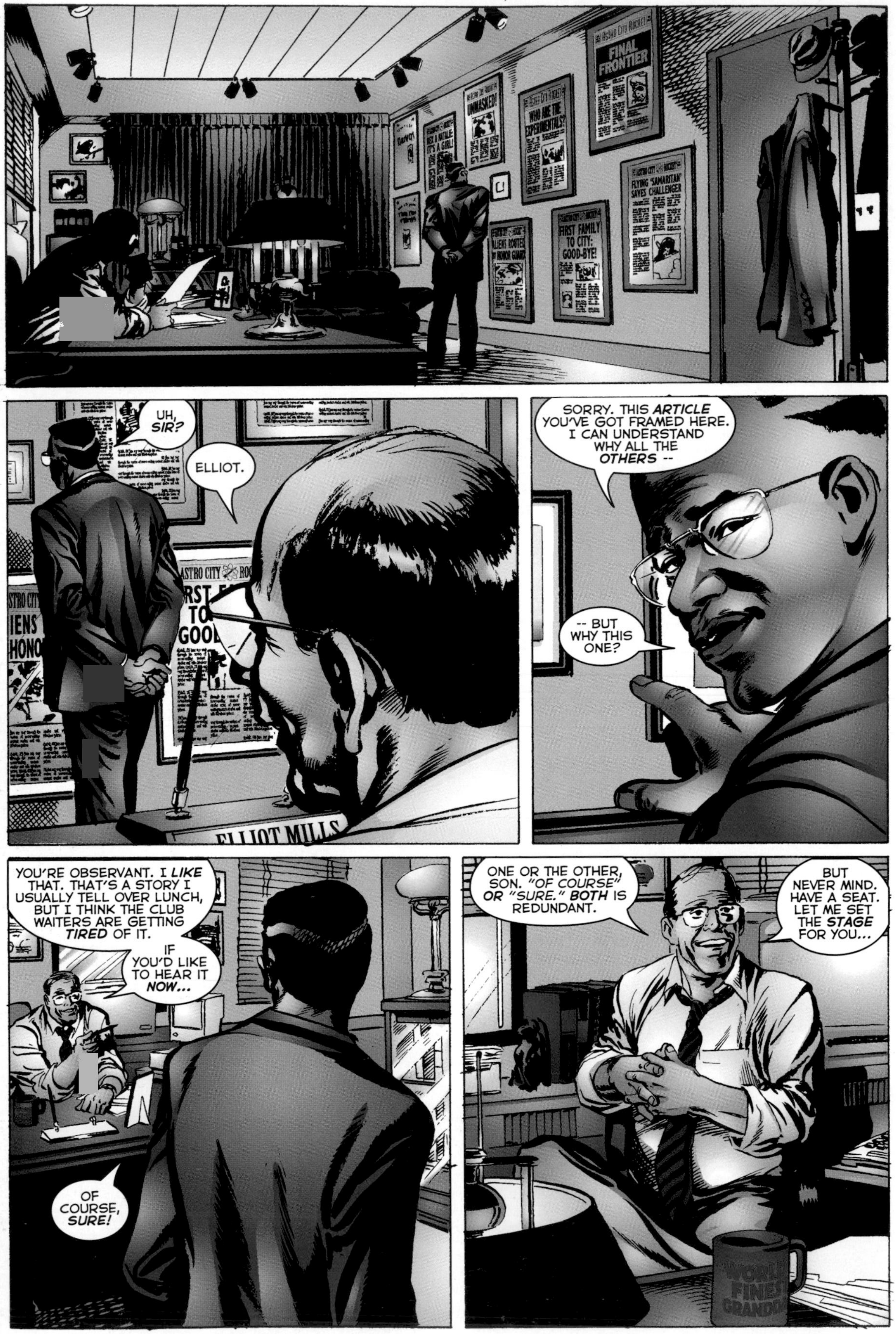

ASTRO CITY ROCKET
FINAL FRONTIER
UNMASKED!
WHO ARE THE EXPERIMENTALS?
FLYING 'SAMARITAN' SAVES CHALLENGER
FIRST FAMILY TO CITY: GOOD-BYE!
UH, SIR?
ELLIOT.
ELLIOT MILLS
SORRY. THIS ARTICLE YOU'VE GOT FRAMED HERE. I CAN UNDERSTAND WHY ALL THE OTHERS --
-- BUT WHY THIS ONE?
YOU'RE OBSERVANT. I LIKE THAT. THAT'S A STORY I USUALLY TELL OVER LUNCH, BUT I THINK THE CLUB WAITERS ARE GETTING TIRED OF IT.
IF YOU'D LIKE TO HEAR IT NOW...
OF COURSE, SURE!
ONE OR THE OTHER, SON. "OF COURSE" OR "SURE." BOTH IS REDUNDANT.
BUT NEVER MIND. HAVE A SEAT. LET ME SET THE STAGE FOR YOU...

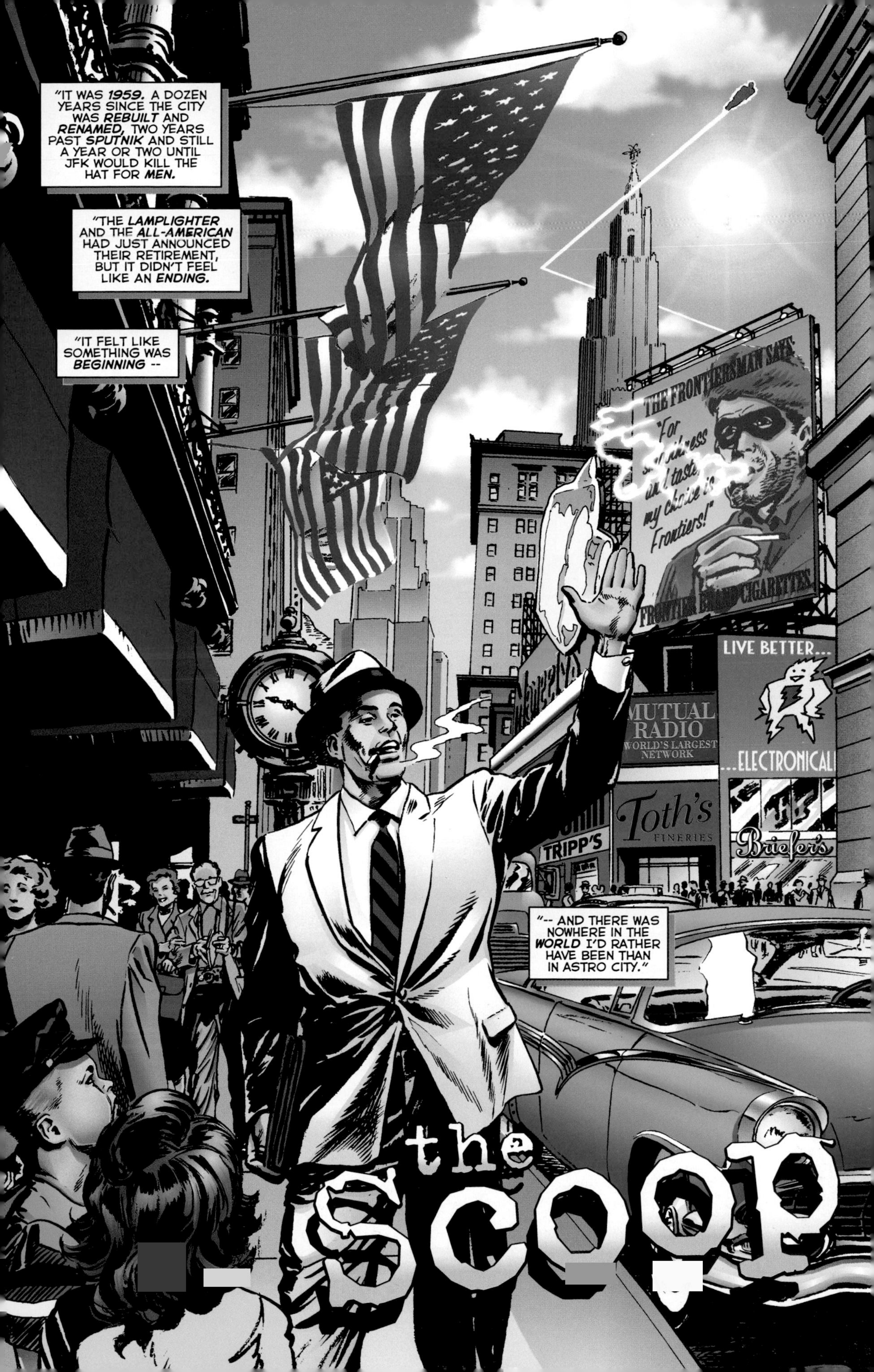
"IT WAS *1959.* A DOZEN YEARS SINCE THE CITY WAS *REBUILT* AND *RENAMED,* TWO YEARS PAST *SPUTNIK* AND STILL A YEAR OR TWO UNTIL JFK WOULD KILL THE HAT FOR *MEN.*
"THE *LAMPLIGHTER* AND THE *ALL-AMERICAN* HAD JUST ANNOUNCED THEIR RETIREMENT, BUT IT DIDN'T FEEL LIKE AN *ENDING.*
"IT FELT LIKE SOMETHING WAS *BEGINNING* --
THE FRONTIERSMAN SAYS
LIVE BETTER...
...ELECTRONICALLY
MUTUAL RADIO
WORLD'S LARGEST NETWORK
Toth's
FINERIES
TRIPP'S
Briefer's
"-- AND THERE WAS NOWHERE IN THE *WORLD* I'D RATHER HAVE BEEN THAN IN ASTRO CITY."
the SCOOP

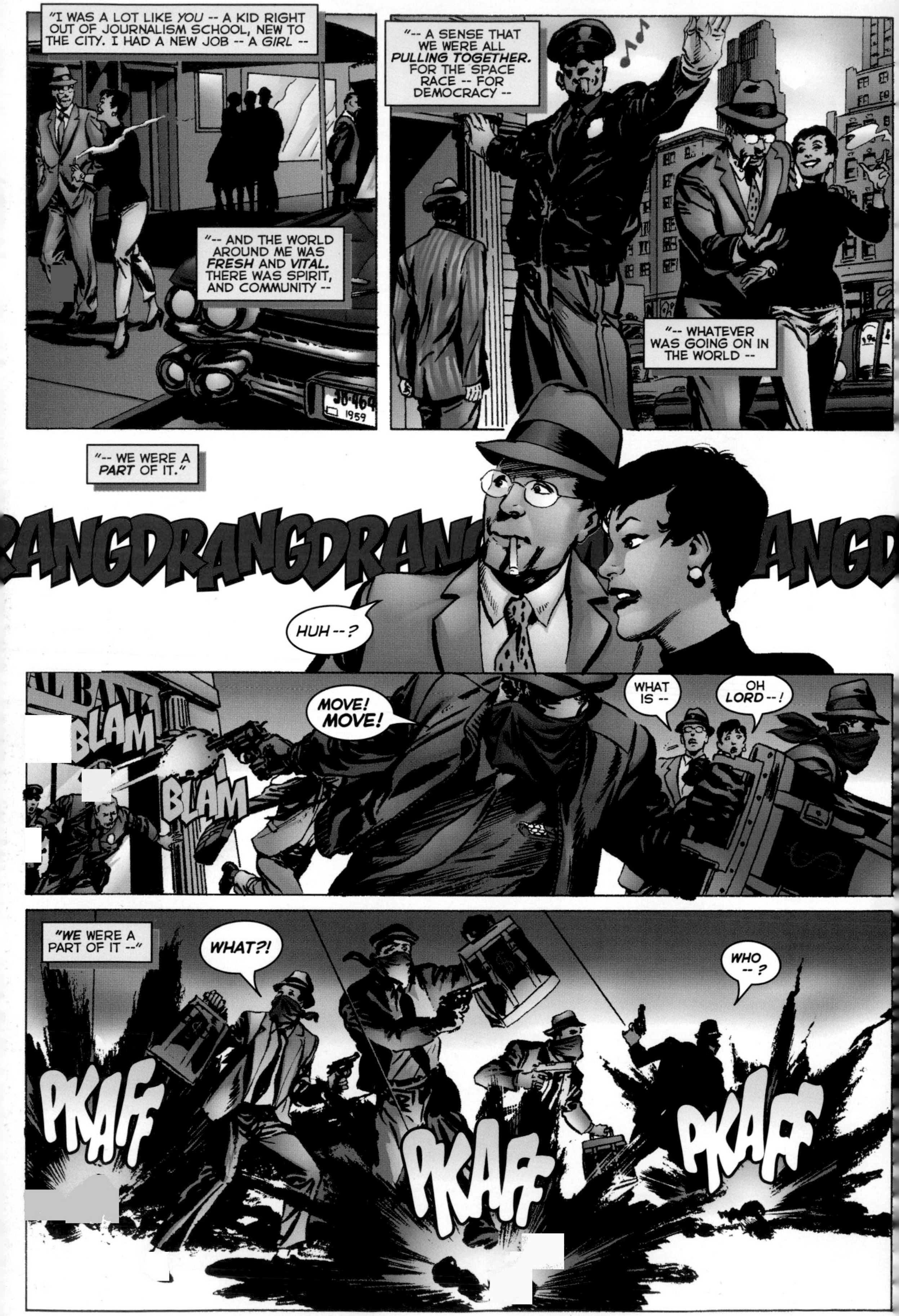
"I WAS A LOT LIKE *YOU* -- A KID RIGHT OUT OF JOURNALISM SCHOOL, NEW TO THE CITY. I HAD A NEW JOB -- A *GIRL* --
"-- AND THE WORLD AROUND ME WAS ***FRESH*** AND ***VITAL.*** THERE WAS SPIRIT, AND COMMUNITY --
JU-464
1959
"-- A SENSE THAT WE WERE ALL ***PULLING TOGETHER.*** FOR THE SPACE RACE -- FOR DEMOCRACY --
"-- WHATEVER WAS GOING ON IN THE WORLD --
"-- WE WERE A ***PART*** OF IT."
RANGDRANGDRANG
RANGD
HUH --?
AL BANK
BLAM
BLAM
MOVE! MOVE!
WHAT IS --
OH ***LORD*** --!
"***WE*** WERE A PART OF IT --"
WHAT?!
WHO -- ?
PKAFF
PKAFF
PKAFF

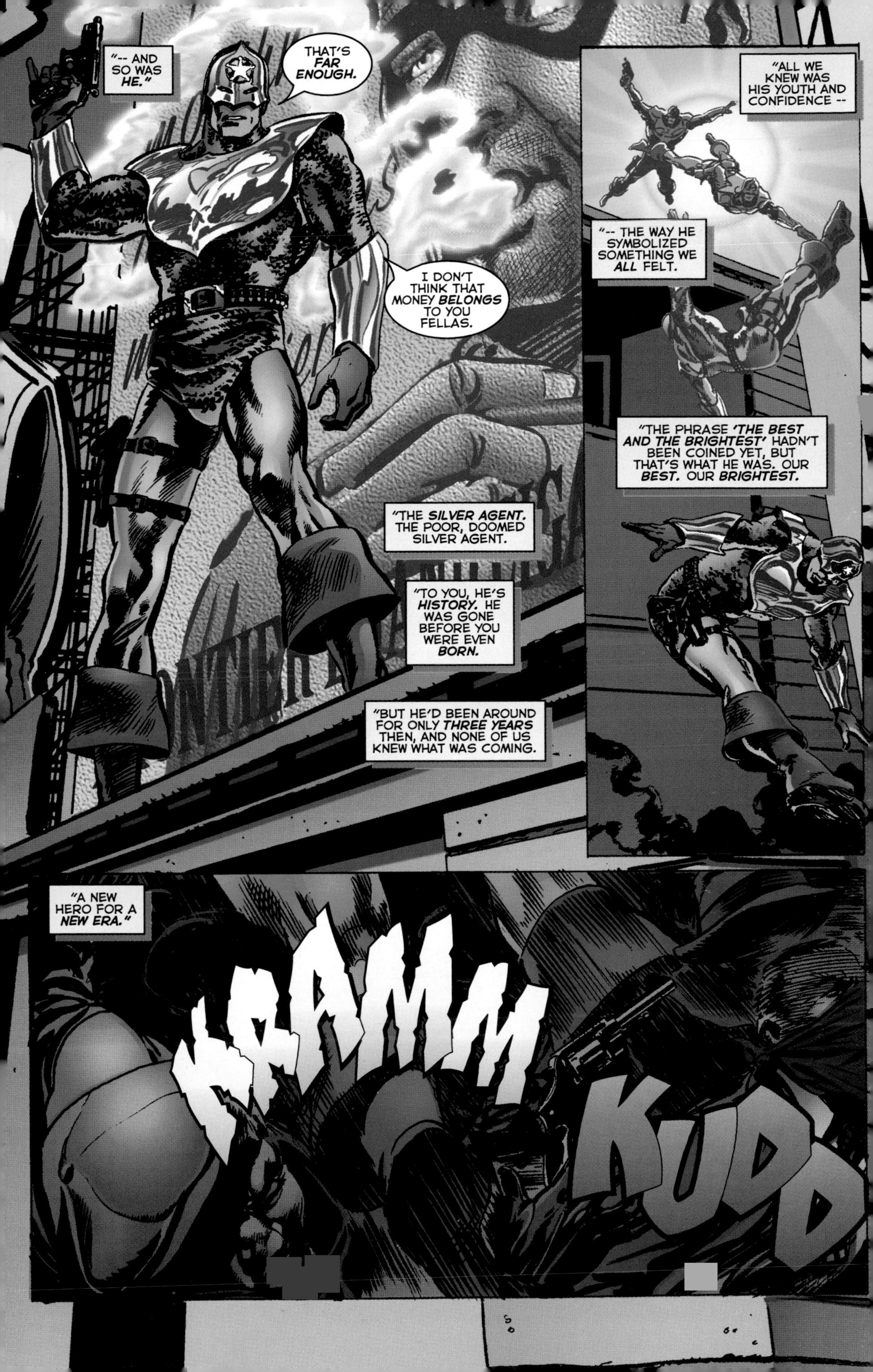
"-- AND SO WAS *HE.*"
THAT'S *FAR ENOUGH.*
I DON'T THINK THAT MONEY *BELONGS* TO YOU FELLAS.
"THE *SILVER AGENT.* THE POOR, DOOMED SILVER AGENT.
"TO YOU, HE'S *HISTORY.* HE WAS GONE BEFORE YOU WERE EVEN *BORN.*
"BUT HE'D BEEN AROUND FOR ONLY *THREE YEARS* THEN, AND NONE OF US KNEW WHAT WAS COMING.
"ALL WE KNEW WAS HIS YOUTH AND CONFIDENCE --
"-- THE WAY HE SYMBOLIZED SOMETHING WE *ALL* FELT.
"THE PHRASE *'THE BEST AND THE BRIGHTEST'* HADN'T BEEN COINED YET, BUT THAT'S WHAT HE WAS. OUR *BEST.* OUR *BRIGHTEST.*
"A NEW HERO FOR A *NEW ERA.*"

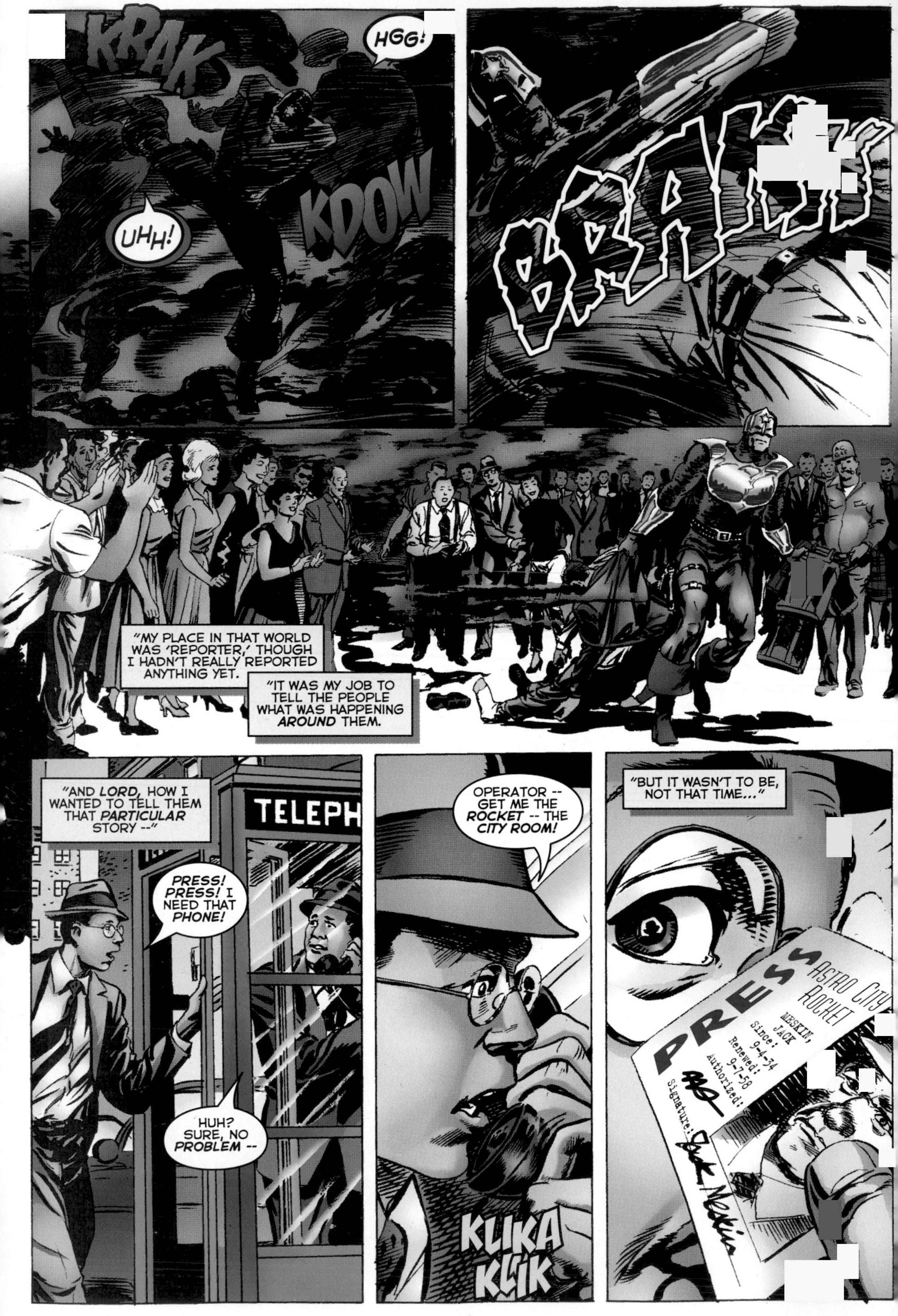
KRAK
HGG!
UHH!
KDOW
BRAKOOM
"MY PLACE IN THAT WORLD WAS 'REPORTER,' THOUGH I HADN'T REALLY REPORTED ANYTHING YET.
"IT WAS MY JOB TO TELL THE PEOPLE WHAT WAS HAPPENING AROUND THEM.
"AND LORD, HOW I WANTED TO TELL THEM THAT PARTICULAR STORY --"
TELEPH
PRESS! PRESS! I NEED THAT PHONE!
HUH? SURE, NO PROBLEM --
OPERATOR -- GET ME THE ROCKET -- THE CITY ROOM!
KLIKA KLIK
"BUT IT WASN'T TO BE, NOT THAT TIME..."
PRESS
ASTRO CITY ROCKET
MESKIN, JACK
Since: 9-4-54
Renewed: 9-7-58
Authorized:
Signature: Jack Meskin

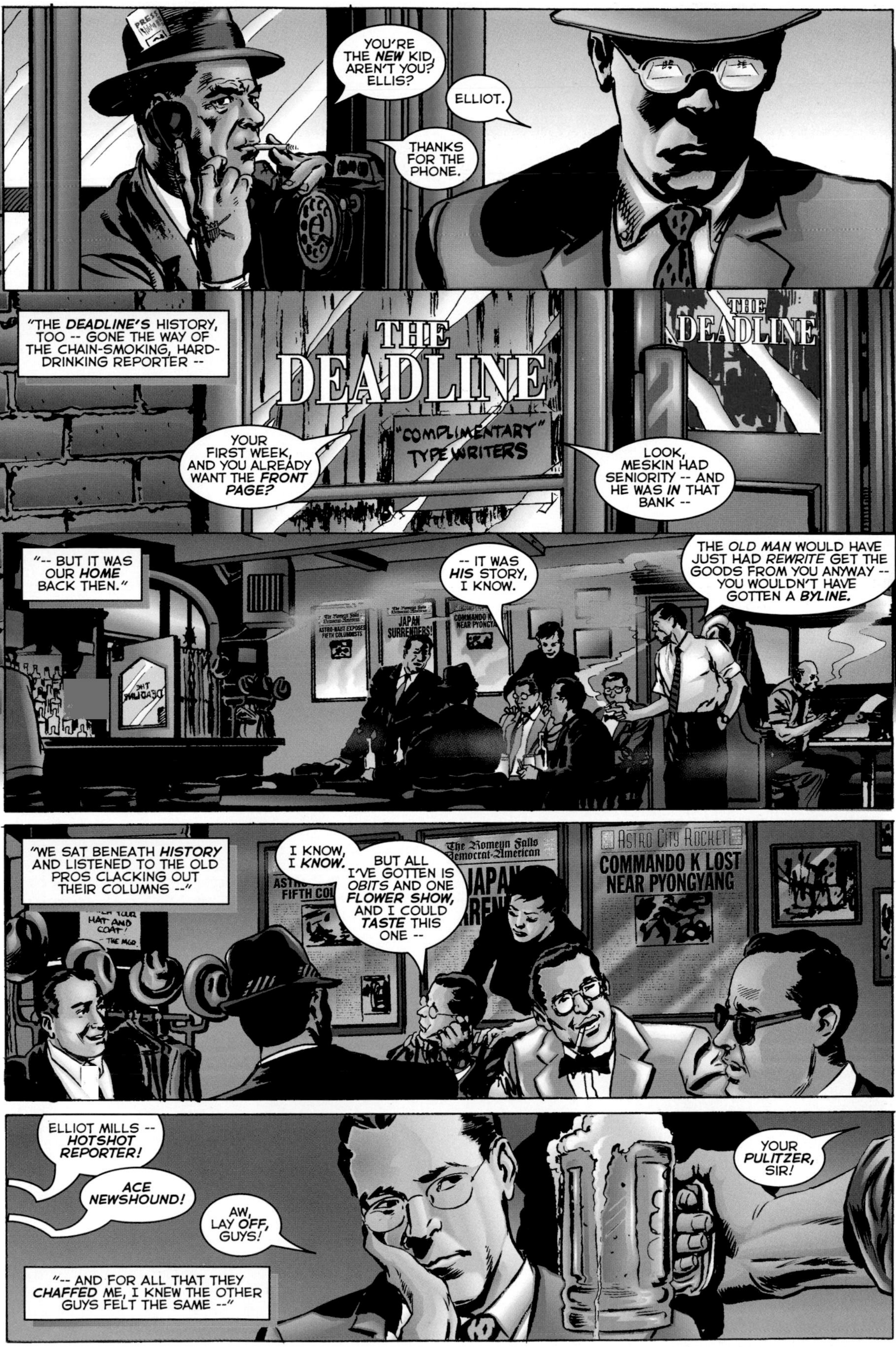
YOU'RE THE NEW KID, AREN'T YOU? ELLIS?
ELLIOT.
THANKS FOR THE PHONE.
"THE DEADLINE'S HISTORY, TOO -- GONE THE WAY OF THE CHAIN-SMOKING, HARD-DRINKING REPORTER --
THE DEADLINE
"COMPLIMENTARY" TYPEWRITERS
THE DEADLINE
YOUR FIRST WEEK, AND YOU ALREADY WANT THE FRONT PAGE?
LOOK, MESKIN HAD SENIORITY -- AND HE WAS IN THAT BANK --
"-- BUT IT WAS OUR HOME BACK THEN."
-- IT WAS HIS STORY, I KNOW.
THE OLD MAN WOULD HAVE JUST HAD REWRITE GET THE GOODS FROM YOU ANYWAY -- YOU WOULDN'T HAVE GOTTEN A BYLINE.
JAPAN SURRENDERS!
"WE SAT BENEATH HISTORY AND LISTENED TO THE OLD PROS CLACKING OUT THEIR COLUMNS --"
I KNOW, I KNOW.
BUT ALL I'VE GOTTEN IS OBITS AND ONE FLOWER SHOW, AND I COULD TASTE THIS ONE --
The Romeyn Falls Democrat-American
Astro City Rocket
COMMANDO K LOST NEAR PYONGYANG
ELLIOT MILLS -- HOTSHOT REPORTER!
ACE NEWSHOUND!
AW, LAY OFF, GUYS!
YOUR PULITZER, SIR!
"-- AND FOR ALL THAT THEY CHAFFED ME, I KNEW THE OTHER GUYS FELT THE SAME --"

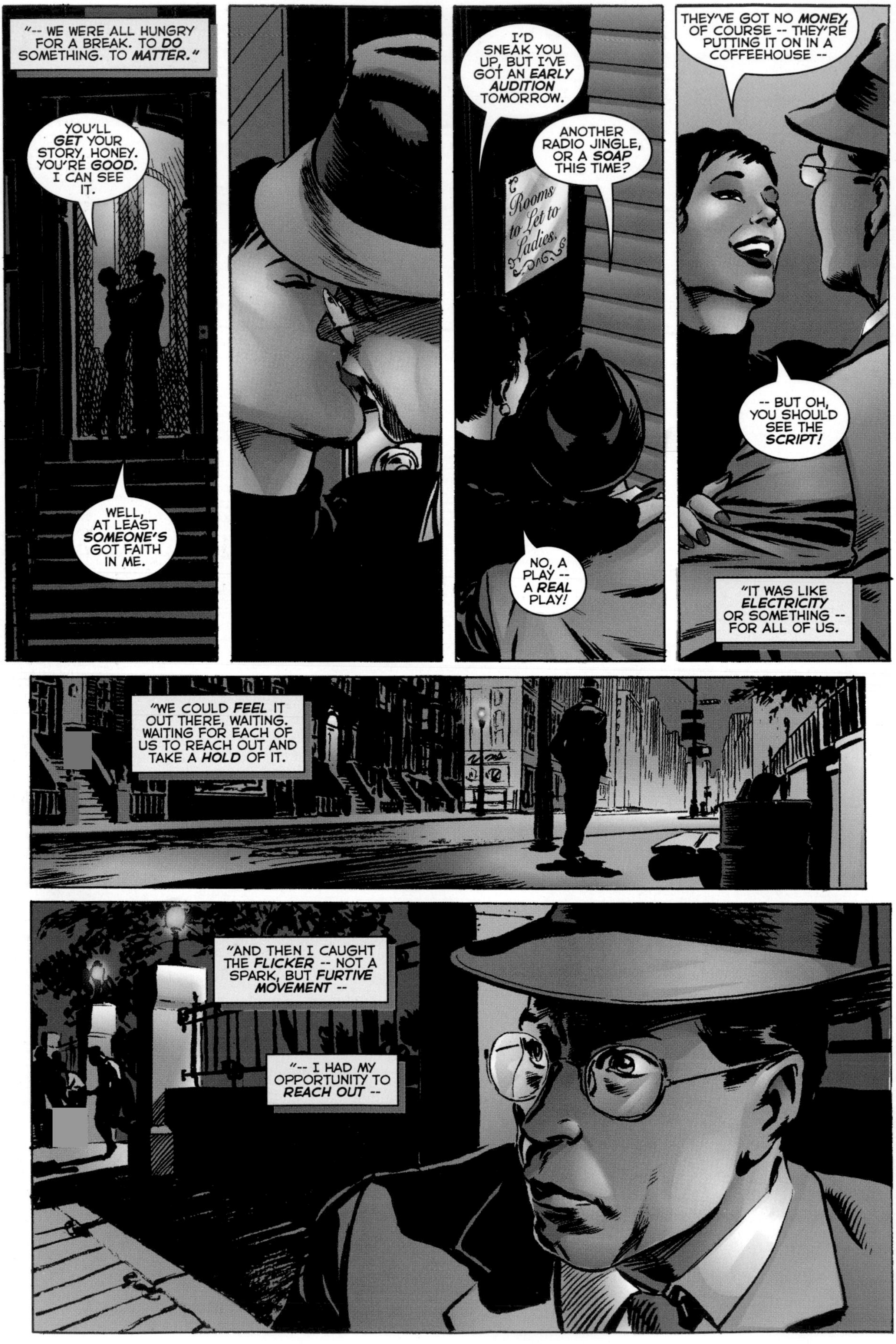
"-- WE WERE ALL HUNGRY FOR A BREAK. TO DO SOMETHING. TO MATTER."
YOU'LL GET YOUR STORY, HONEY. YOU'RE GOOD. I CAN SEE IT.
WELL, AT LEAST SOMEONE'S GOT FAITH IN ME.
I'D SNEAK YOU UP, BUT I'VE GOT AN EARLY AUDITION TOMORROW.
ANOTHER RADIO JINGLE, OR A SOAP THIS TIME?
Rooms to Let to Ladies.
NO, A PLAY -- A REAL PLAY!
THEY'VE GOT NO MONEY, OF COURSE -- THEY'RE PUTTING IT ON IN A COFFEEHOUSE --
-- BUT OH, YOU SHOULD SEE THE SCRIPT!
"IT WAS LIKE ELECTRICITY OR SOMETHING -- FOR ALL OF US.
"WE COULD FEEL IT OUT THERE, WAITING. WAITING FOR EACH OF US TO REACH OUT AND TAKE A HOLD OF IT.
"AND THEN I CAUGHT THE FLICKER -- NOT A SPARK, BUT FURTIVE MOVEMENT --
"-- I HAD MY OPPORTUNITY TO REACH OUT --

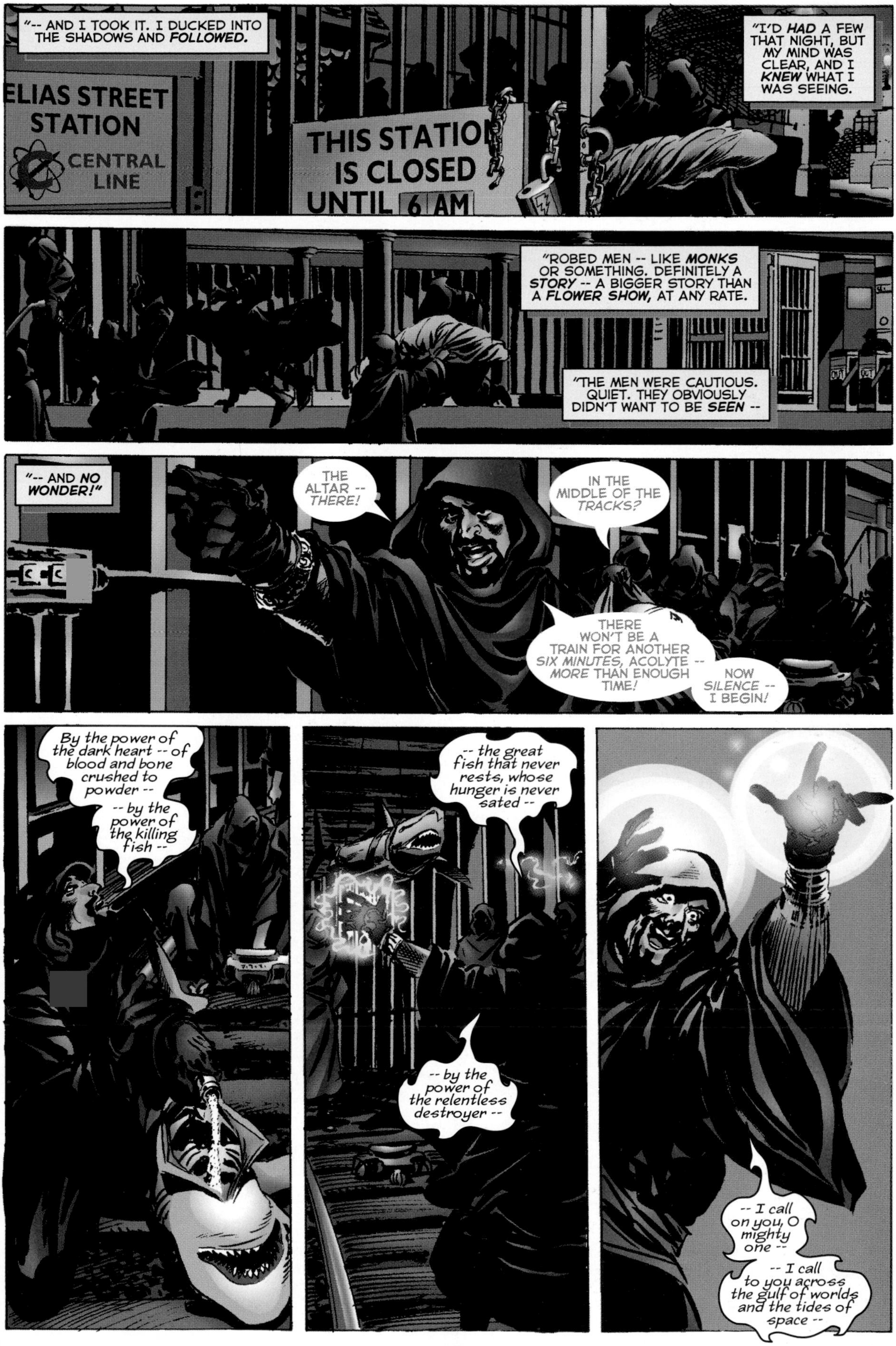
"-- AND I TOOK IT. I DUCKED INTO THE SHADOWS AND FOLLOWED.
ELIAS STREET STATION
CENTRAL LINE
THIS STATIO IS CLOSED UNTIL 6 AM
"I'D HAD A FEW THAT NIGHT, BUT MY MIND WAS CLEAR, AND I KNEW WHAT I WAS SEEING.
"ROBED MEN -- LIKE MONKS OR SOMETHING. DEFINITELY A STORY -- A BIGGER STORY THAN A FLOWER SHOW, AT ANY RATE.
"THE MEN WERE CAUTIOUS. QUIET. THEY OBVIOUSLY DIDN'T WANT TO BE SEEN --
"-- AND NO WONDER!"
THE ALTAR -- THERE!
IN THE MIDDLE OF THE TRACKS?
THERE WON'T BE A TRAIN FOR ANOTHER SIX MINUTES, ACOLYTE -- MORE THAN ENOUGH TIME!
NOW SILENCE -- I BEGIN!
By the power of the dark heart -- of blood and bone crushed to powder --
-- by the power of the killing fish --
-- the great fish that never rests, whose hunger is never sated --
-- by the power of the relentless destroyer --
-- I call on you, O mighty one --
-- I call to you across the gulf of worlds and the tides of space --

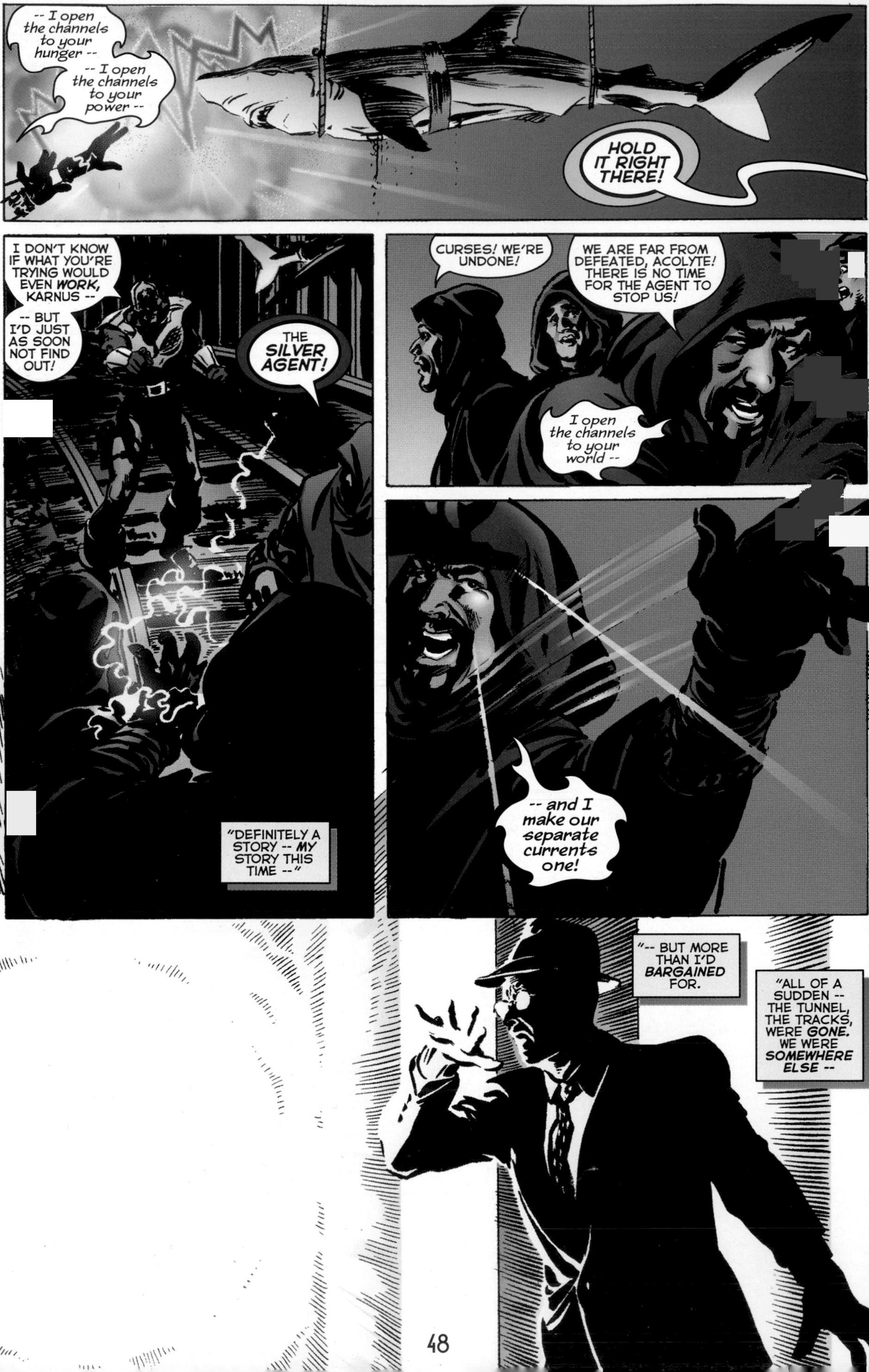
-- I open the channels to your hunger --
-- I open the channels to your power --
HOLD IT RIGHT THERE!
I DON'T KNOW IF WHAT YOU'RE TRYING WOULD EVEN WORK, KARNUS --
-- BUT I'D JUST AS SOON NOT FIND OUT!
THE SILVER AGENT!
"DEFINITELY A STORY -- MY STORY THIS TIME --"
CURSES! WE'RE UNDONE!
WE ARE FAR FROM DEFEATED, ACOLYTE! THERE IS NO TIME FOR THE AGENT TO STOP US!
I open the channels to your world --
-- and I make our separate currents one!
"-- BUT MORE THAN I'D BARGAINED FOR.
"ALL OF A SUDDEN -- THE TUNNEL, THE TRACKS, WERE GONE. WE WERE SOMEWHERE ELSE --

"-- AND IN THE PRESENCE OF *SOMETHING ELSE* "

I THANK YOU, KARNUS. YOUR WORLD IS NOW WITHIN STRIKING DISTANCE.

YOU AND YOUR MINNOWS HAVE SERVED ME WELL --

-- AND YOU SHALL NOT GO UNREWARDED!

TAKE MY POWER UNTO YOU -- TAKE MY HUNGER AS YOUR OWN --

-- AND *RISE* --

-- RISE AS THE NEWEST RAVAGERS IN THE ARMY OF **SHIRAK** THE **DEVOURER!**

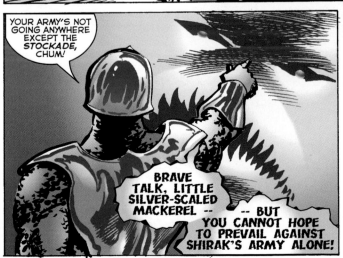

YOUR ARMY'S NOT GOING ANYWHERE EXCEPT THE *STOCKADE,* CHUM!

BRAVE TALK, LITTLE *SILVER-SCALED MACKEREL* --

-- BUT YOU CANNOT HOPE TO PREVAIL AGAINST SHIRAK'S ARMY ALONE!

COULD BE YOU'RE *RIGHT,* SHIRAK --

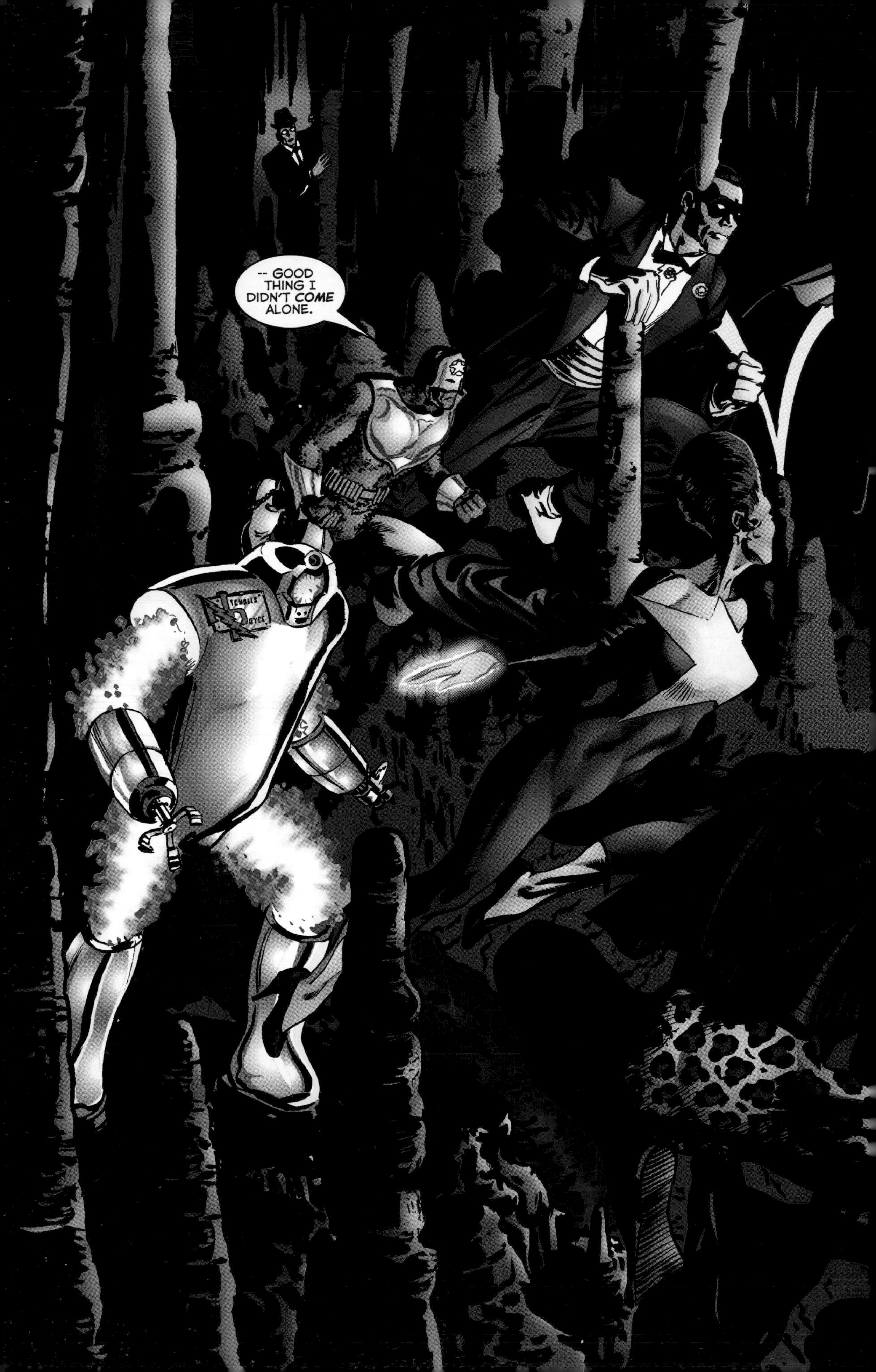
-- GOOD THING I DIDN'T COME ALONE.

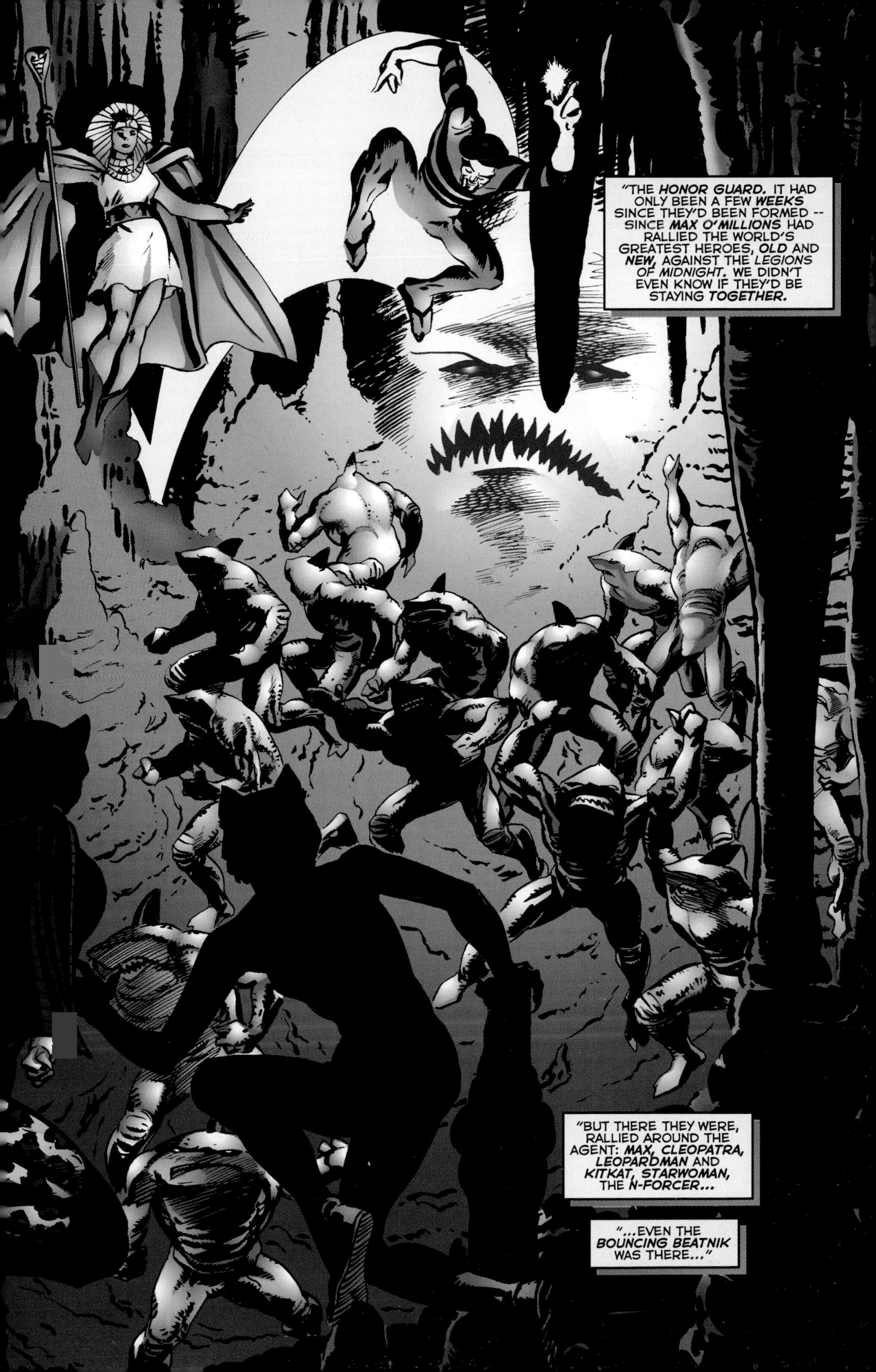
"THE HONOR GUARD. IT HAD ONLY BEEN A FEW WEEKS SINCE THEY'D BEEN FORMED -- SINCE MAX O'MILLIONS HAD RALLIED THE WORLD'S GREATEST HEROES, OLD AND NEW, AGAINST THE LEGIONS OF MIDNIGHT. WE DIDN'T EVEN KNOW IF THEY'D BE STAYING TOGETHER.
"BUT THERE THEY WERE, RALLIED AROUND THE AGENT: MAX, CLEOPATRA, LEOPARDMAN AND KITKAT, STARWOMAN, THE N-FORCER...
"...EVEN THE BOUNCING BEATNIK WAS THERE..."

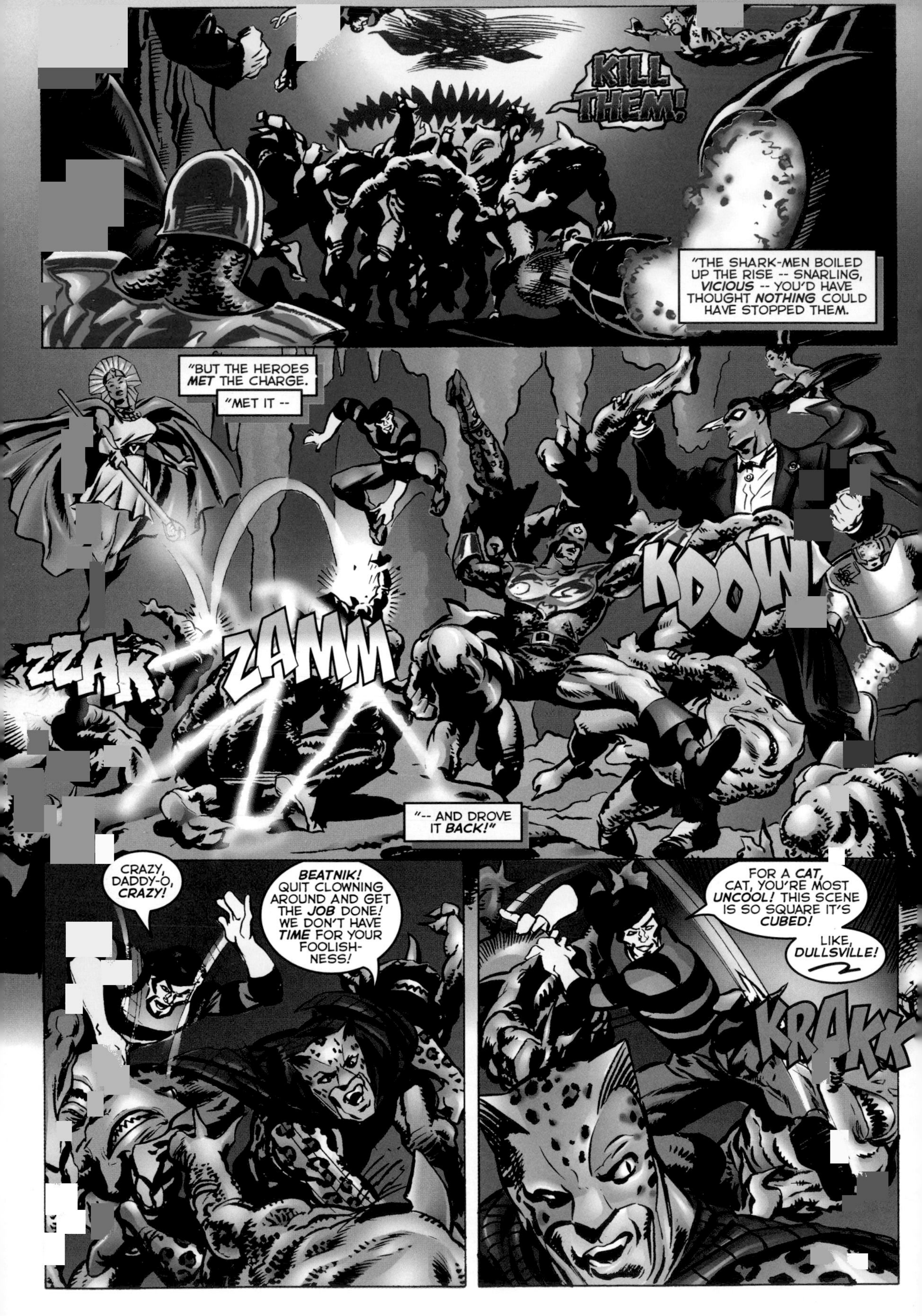
KILL THEM!
"THE SHARK-MEN BOILED UP THE RISE -- SNARLING, VICIOUS -- YOU'D HAVE THOUGHT NOTHING COULD HAVE STOPPED THEM.
"BUT THE HEROES MET THE CHARGE.
"MET IT --
KDOW
ZZAK
ZAMM
"-- AND DROVE IT BACK!"
CRAZY, DADDY-O, CRAZY!
BEATNIK! QUIT CLOWNING AROUND AND GET THE JOB DONE! WE DON'T HAVE TIME FOR YOUR FOOLISH-NESS!
FOR A CAT, CAT, YOU'RE MOST UNCOOL! THIS SCENE IS SO SQUARE IT'S CUBED!
LIKE, DULLSVILLE!
KRAKK

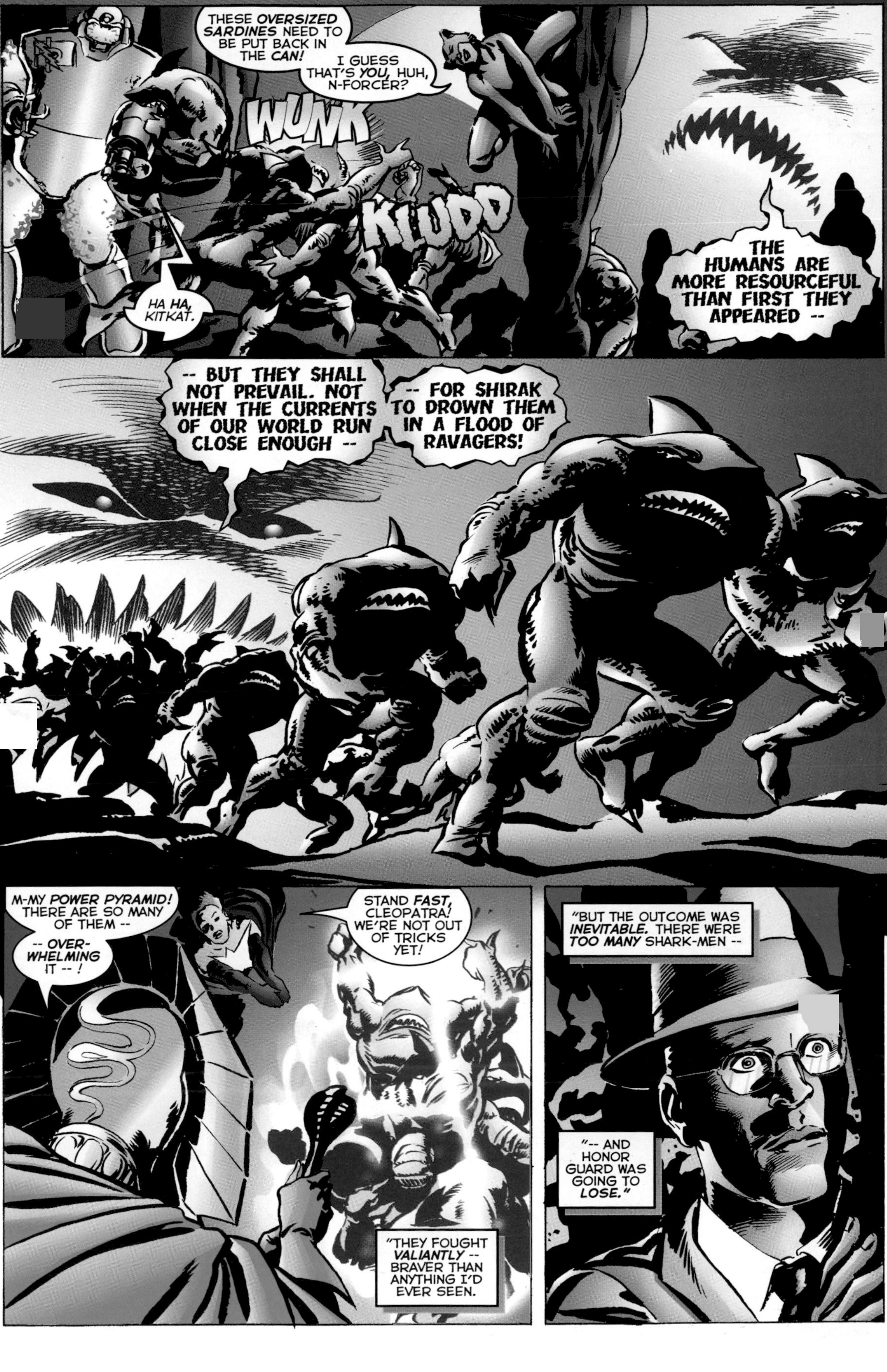
THESE OVERSIZED SARDINES NEED TO BE PUT BACK IN THE CAN!
I GUESS THAT'S YOU, HUH, N-FORCER?
WUNK
KLUDD
HA HA, KITKAT.
THE HUMANS ARE MORE RESOURCEFUL THAN FIRST THEY APPEARED --
-- BUT THEY SHALL NOT PREVAIL. NOT WHEN THE CURRENTS OF OUR WORLD RUN CLOSE ENOUGH --
-- FOR SHIRAK TO DROWN THEM IN A FLOOD OF RAVAGERS!
M-MY POWER PYRAMID! THERE ARE SO MANY OF THEM --
-- OVER-WHELMING IT -- !
STAND FAST, CLEOPATRA! WE'RE NOT OUT OF TRICKS YET!
"THEY FOUGHT VALIANTLY -- BRAVER THAN ANYTHING I'D EVER SEEN.
"BUT THE OUTCOME WAS INEVITABLE. THERE WERE TOO MANY SHARK-MEN --
"-- AND HONOR GUARD WAS GOING TO LOSE."

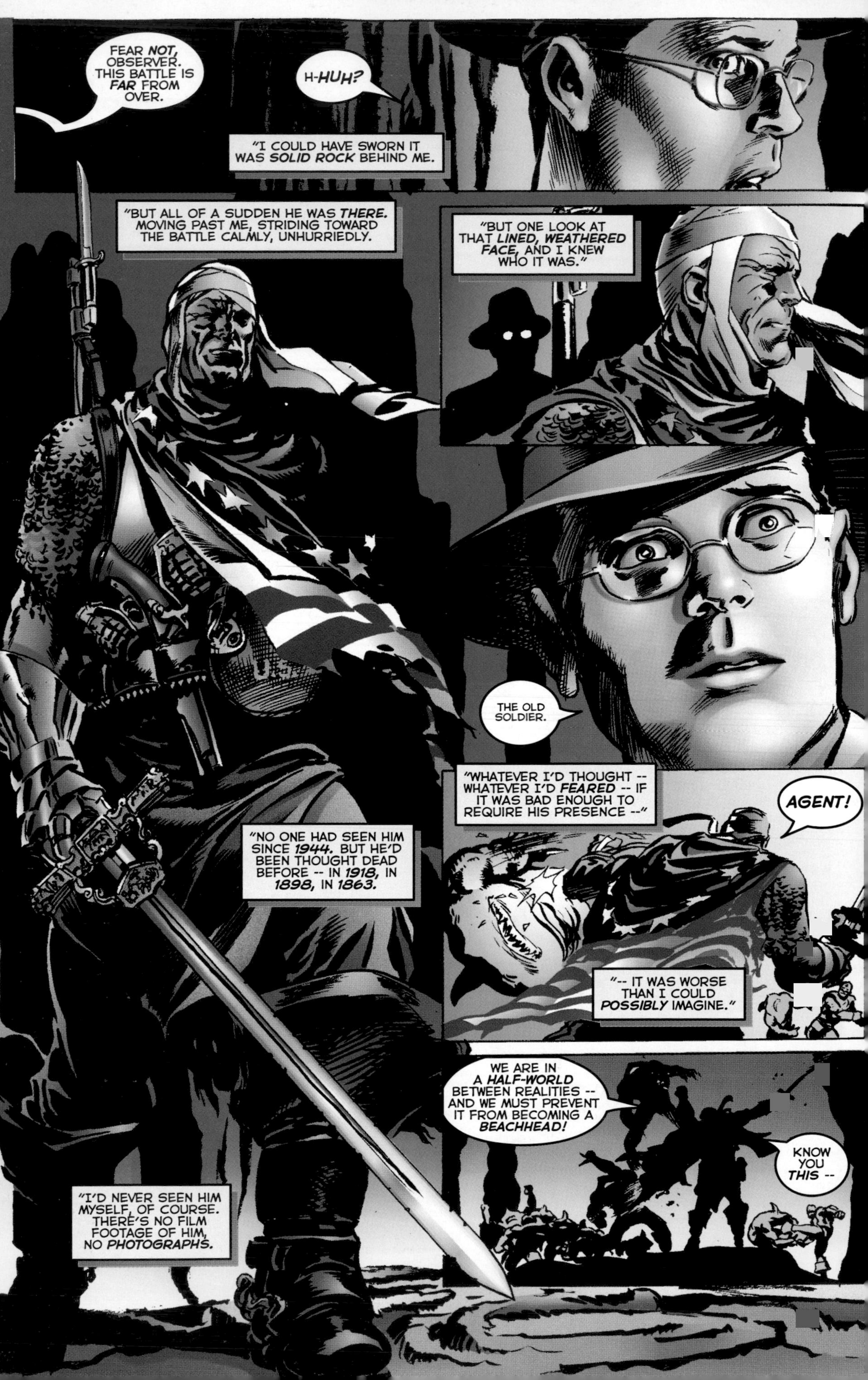

FEAR NOT, OBSERVER. THIS BATTLE IS FAR FROM OVER.
H-HUH?
"I COULD HAVE SWORN IT WAS SOLID ROCK BEHIND ME.
"BUT ALL OF A SUDDEN HE WAS THERE. MOVING PAST ME, STRIDING TOWARD THE BATTLE CALMLY, UNHURRIEDLY.
"BUT ONE LOOK AT THAT LINED, WEATHERED FACE, AND I KNEW WHO IT WAS."
THE OLD SOLDIER.
"NO ONE HAD SEEN HIM SINCE 1944. BUT HE'D BEEN THOUGHT DEAD BEFORE -- IN 1918, IN 1898, IN 1863.
"WHATEVER I'D THOUGHT -- WHATEVER I'D FEARED -- IF IT WAS BAD ENOUGH TO REQUIRE HIS PRESENCE --"
AGENT!
"-- IT WAS WORSE THAN I COULD POSSIBLY IMAGINE."
"I'D NEVER SEEN HIM MYSELF, OF COURSE. THERE'S NO FILM FOOTAGE OF HIM, NO PHOTOGRAPHS.
WE ARE IN A HALF-WORLD BETWEEN REALITIES -- AND WE MUST PREVENT IT FROM BECOMING A BEACHHEAD!
KNOW YOU THIS --

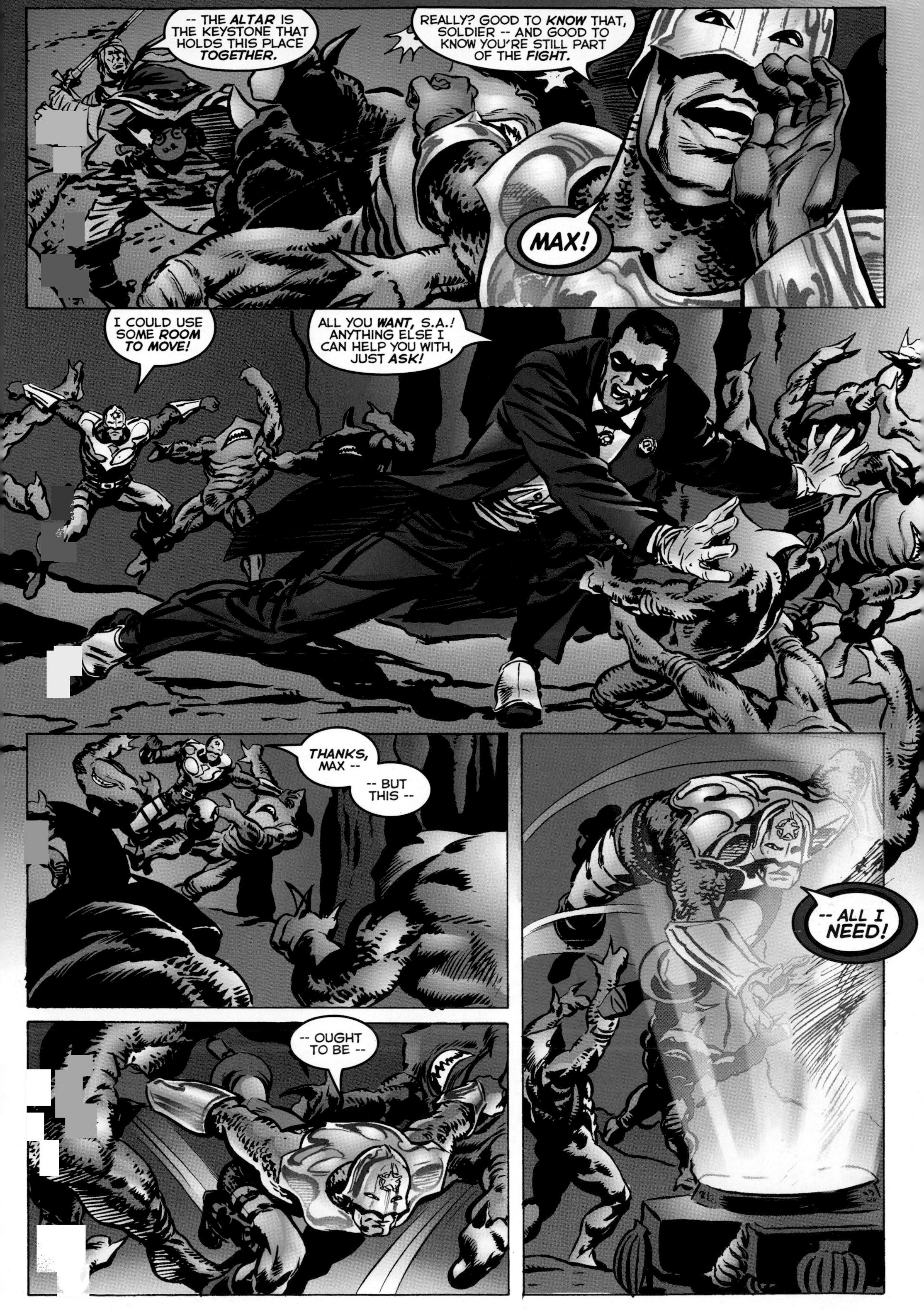

-- THE ALTAR IS THE KEYSTONE THAT HOLDS THIS PLACE TOGETHER.
REALLY? GOOD TO KNOW THAT, SOLDIER -- AND GOOD TO KNOW YOU'RE STILL PART OF THE FIGHT.
MAX!
I COULD USE SOME ROOM TO MOVE!
ALL YOU WANT, S.A.! ANYTHING ELSE I CAN HELP YOU WITH, JUST ASK!
THANKS, MAX --
-- BUT THIS --
-- OUGHT TO BE --
-- ALL I NEED!

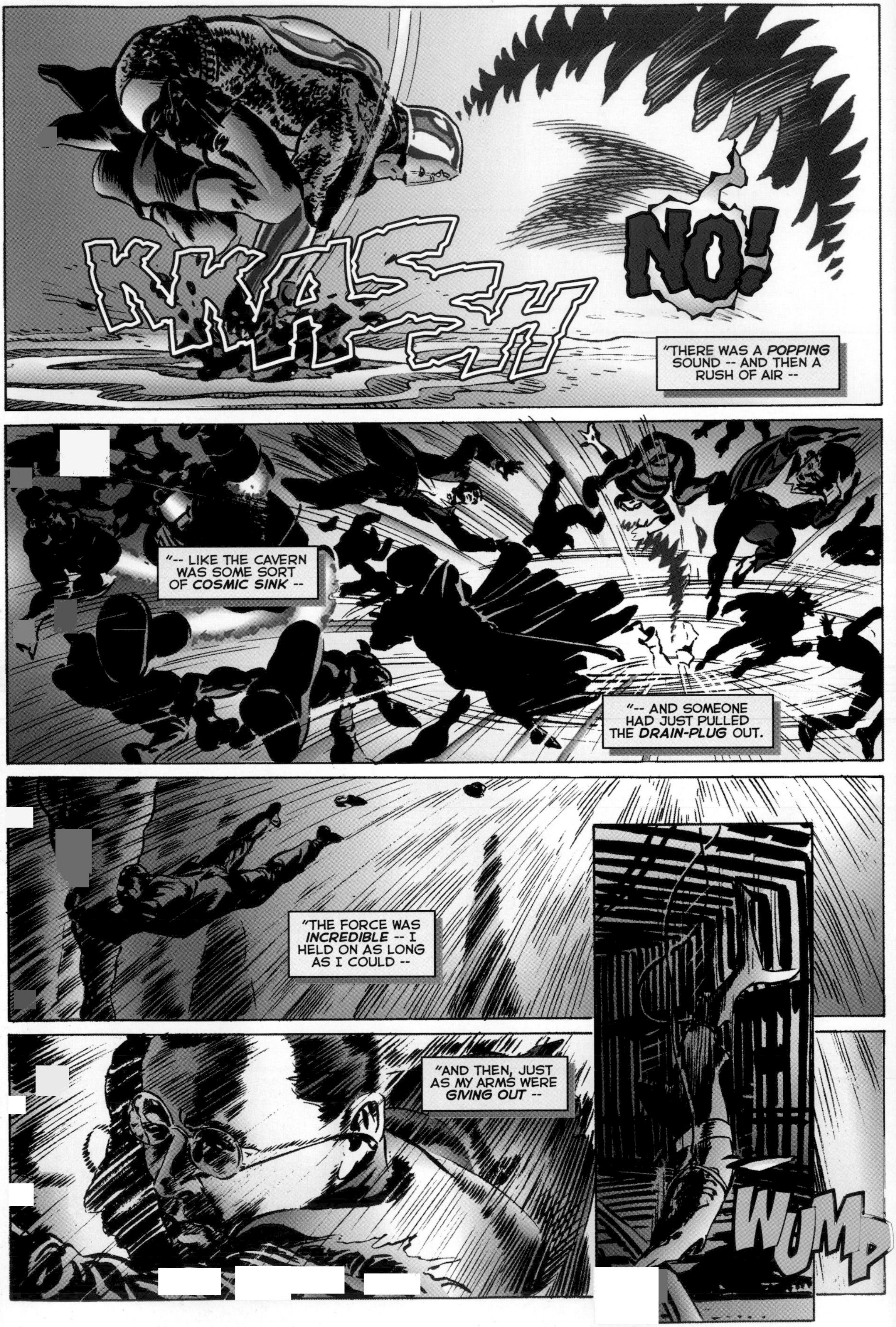
KKKASSHH
NO!
"THERE WAS A POPPING SOUND -- AND THEN A RUSH OF AIR --
"-- LIKE THE CAVERN WAS SOME SORT OF COSMIC SINK --
"-- AND SOMEONE HAD JUST PULLED THE DRAIN-PLUG OUT.
"THE FORCE WAS INCREDIBLE -- I HELD ON AS LONG AS I COULD --
"AND THEN, JUST AS MY ARMS WERE GIVING OUT --
WUMP

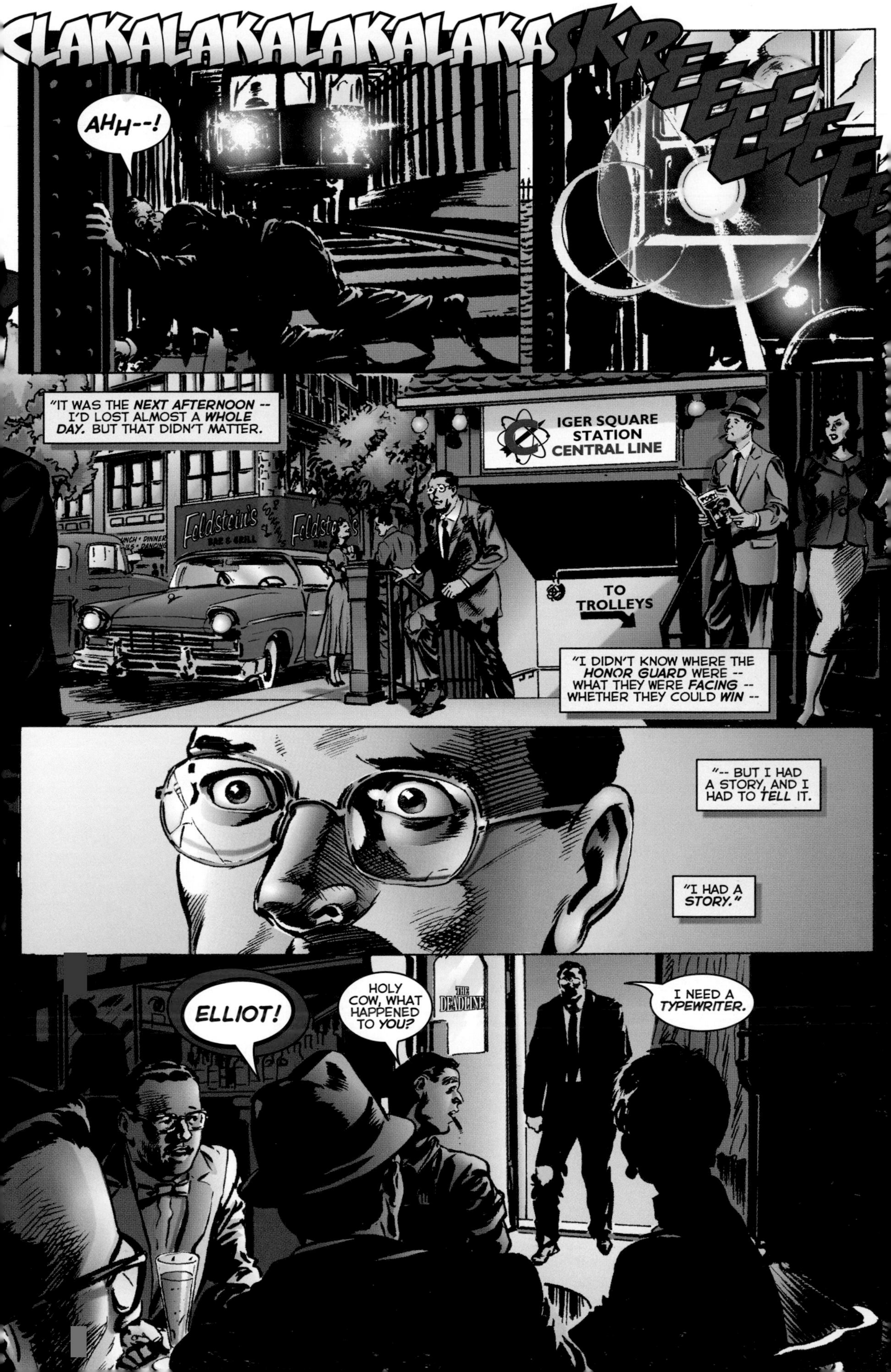
CLAKALAKALAKALAKA
SKREEEEEEEEE
AHH--!
"IT WAS THE NEXT AFTERNOON -- I'D LOST ALMOST A WHOLE DAY. BUT THAT DIDN'T MATTER.
IGER SQUARE STATION CENTRAL LINE
Feldstein's
TO TROLLEYS
"I DIDN'T KNOW WHERE THE HONOR GUARD WERE -- WHAT THEY WERE FACING -- WHETHER THEY COULD WIN --
"-- BUT I HAD A STORY, AND I HAD TO TELL IT.
"I HAD A STORY."
ELLIOT!
HOLY COW, WHAT HAPPENED TO YOU?
THE DEADLINE
I NEED A TYPEWRITER.

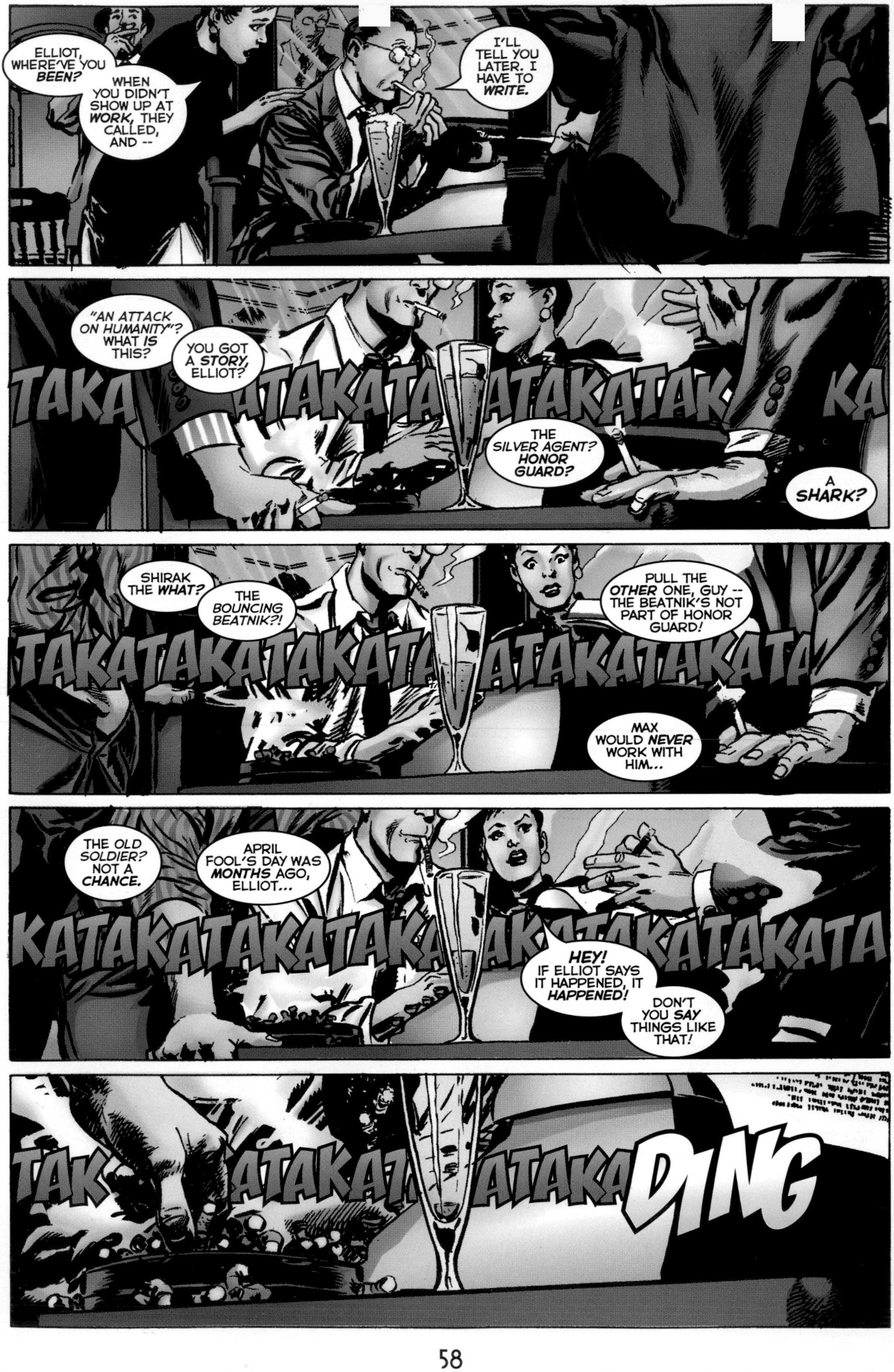
ELLIOT, WHERE'VE YOU BEEN?
WHEN YOU DIDN'T SHOW UP AT WORK, THEY CALLED, AND --
I'LL TELL YOU LATER. I HAVE TO WRITE.
"AN ATTACK ON HUMANITY"? WHAT IS THIS?
YOU GOT A STORY, ELLIOT?
TAKA ATAKATA ATAKATAK KA
THE SILVER AGENT? HONOR GUARD?
A SHARK?
SHIRAK THE WHAT?
THE BOUNCING BEATNIK?!
PULL THE OTHER ONE, GUY -- THE BEATNIK'S NOT PART OF HONOR GUARD!
TAKATAKATAKATA ATAKATAKATA
MAX WOULD NEVER WORK WITH HIM...
THE OLD SOLDIER? NOT A CHANCE.
APRIL FOOL'S DAY WAS MONTHS AGO, ELLIOT...
KATAKATAKATAKA AKATAKATAKATA
HEY! IF ELLIOT SAYS IT HAPPENED, IT HAPPENED!
DON'T YOU SAY THINGS LIKE THAT!
TAK ATAKAT ATAKADING

I *CAN'T*, ELLIOT. IT'S UNSUPPORTABLE.

BUT -- IT *HAPPENED!* WE WERE UNDER *ATTACK* -- THEY WOULD HAVE *INVADED* US --

WHAT?!

WHAT DO YOU *MEAN* YOU'RE NOT RUNNING IT!

I'VE *READ* IT, I'VE *READ* IT. BUT IT'S COMPLETELY *UNSOURCED.* YOU HAVE NO *WITNESSES.*

I WAS *THERE!* I SAW IT *ALL!*

THE AGENT, THE SHARK-MEN, THE OLD SOLDIER -- HE WAS CLOSE ENOUGH FOR ME TO *TOUCH!*

I WAS *THERE!*

NO OFFENSE, ELLIOT. BUT A *NEOPHYTE REPORTER,* HIS FIRST WEEK ON THE JOB, BRINGING IN A *WILD STORY* LIKE THIS --

-- EXTRA-DIMENSIONAL ATTACK, MYSTIC HALF-WORLDS, THE *OLD SOLDIER...*

...WOULD *YOU* BELIEVE IT, IN MY SHOES?

BUT -- BUT --

REWRITE IT, ELLIOT. REWRITE IT --

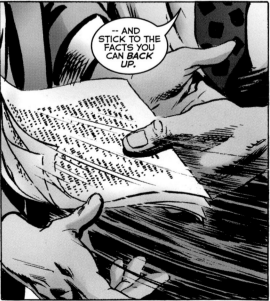

-- AND STICK TO THE FACTS YOU CAN *BACK* UP.

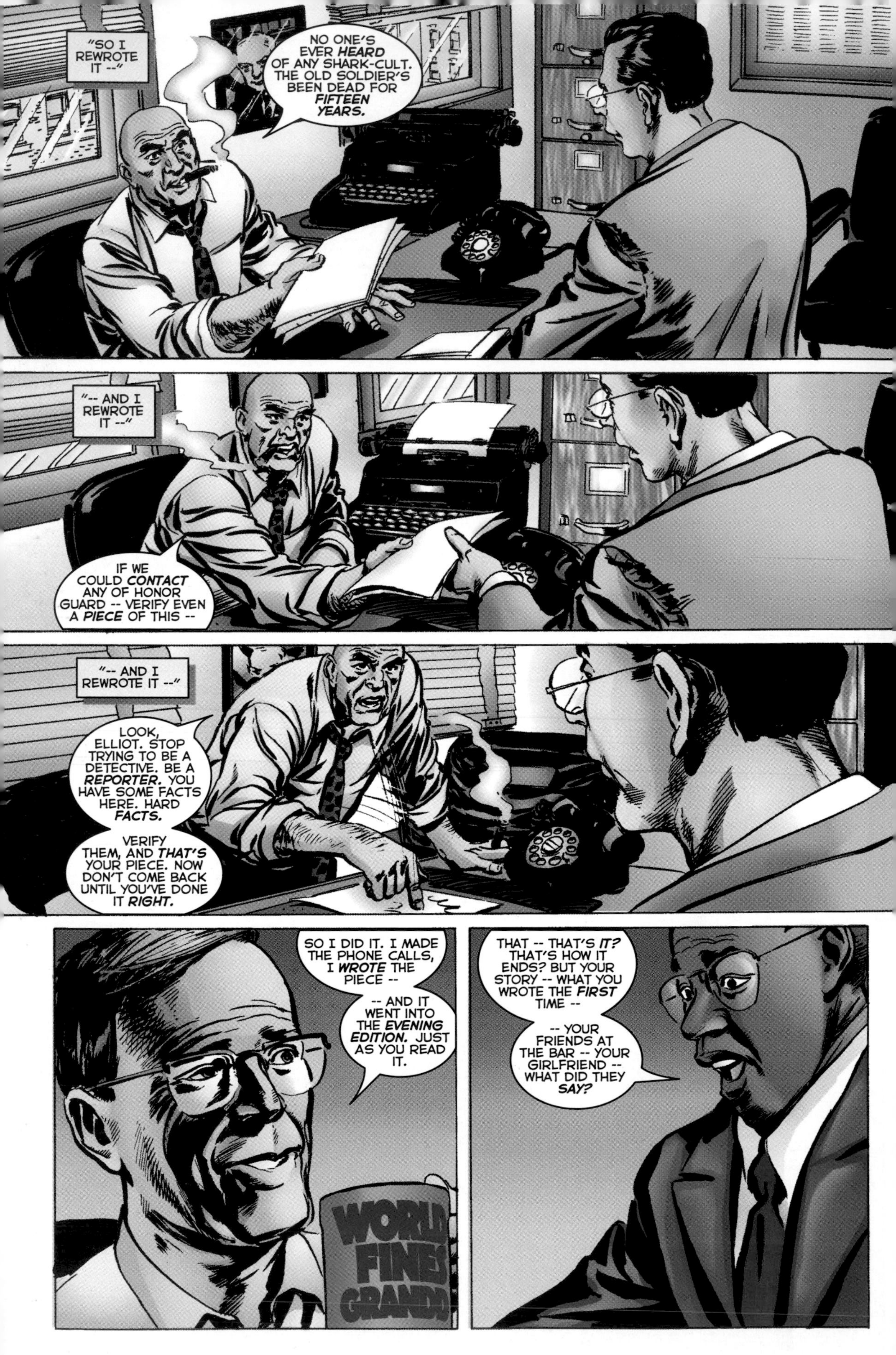
"SO I REWROTE IT --"
NO ONE'S EVER **HEARD** OF ANY SHARK-CULT. THE OLD SOLDIER'S BEEN DEAD FOR **FIFTEEN YEARS.**
"-- AND I REWROTE IT --"
IF WE COULD **CONTACT** ANY OF HONOR GUARD -- VERIFY EVEN A **PIECE** OF THIS --
"-- AND I REWROTE IT --"
LOOK, ELLIOT. STOP TRYING TO BE A DETECTIVE. BE A **REPORTER.** YOU HAVE SOME FACTS HERE. HARD **FACTS.**
VERIFY THEM, AND **THAT'S** YOUR PIECE. NOW DON'T COME BACK UNTIL YOU'VE DONE IT **RIGHT.**
SO I DID IT. I MADE THE PHONE CALLS, I **WROTE** THE PIECE --
-- AND IT WENT INTO THE **EVENING EDITION.** JUST AS YOU READ IT.
THAT -- THAT'S **IT?** THAT'S HOW IT ENDS? BUT YOUR STORY -- WHAT YOU WROTE THE **FIRST** TIME --
-- YOUR FRIENDS AT THE BAR -- YOUR GIRLFRIEND -- WHAT DID THEY **SAY?**

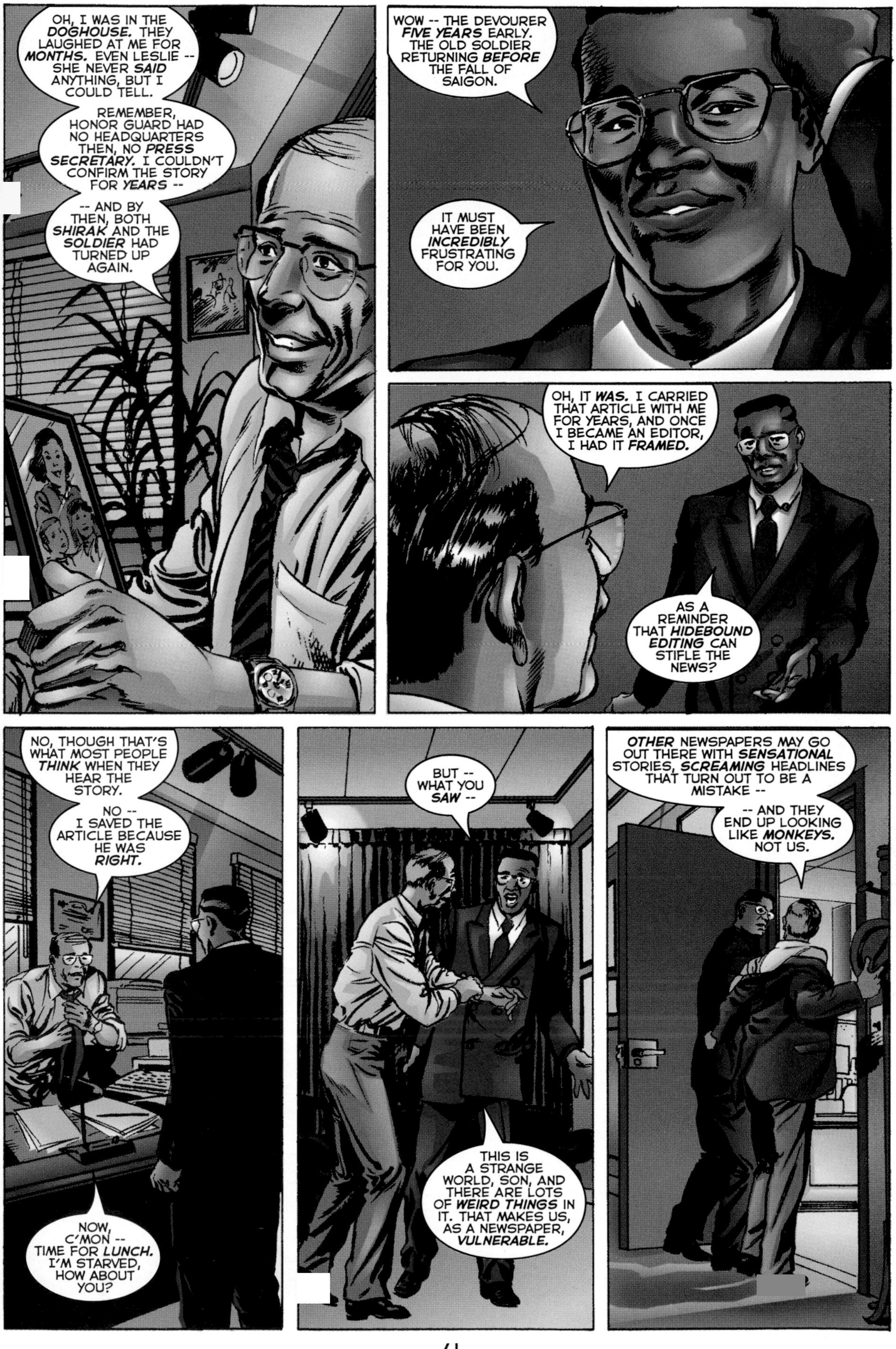

OH, I WAS IN THE DOGHOUSE. THEY LAUGHED AT ME FOR MONTHS. EVEN LESLIE -- SHE NEVER SAID ANYTHING, BUT I COULD TELL.
REMEMBER, HONOR GUARD HAD NO HEADQUARTERS THEN, NO PRESS SECRETARY. I COULDN'T CONFIRM THE STORY FOR YEARS --
-- AND BY THEN, BOTH SHIRAK AND THE SOLDIER HAD TURNED UP AGAIN.
WOW -- THE DEVOURER FIVE YEARS EARLY. THE OLD SOLDIER RETURNING BEFORE THE FALL OF SAIGON.
IT MUST HAVE BEEN INCREDIBLY FRUSTRATING FOR YOU.
OH, IT WAS. I CARRIED THAT ARTICLE WITH ME FOR YEARS, AND ONCE I BECAME AN EDITOR, I HAD IT FRAMED.
AS A REMINDER THAT HIDEBOUND EDITING CAN STIFLE THE NEWS?
NO, THOUGH THAT'S WHAT MOST PEOPLE THINK WHEN THEY HEAR THE STORY.
NO -- I SAVED THE ARTICLE BECAUSE HE WAS RIGHT.
NOW, C'MON -- TIME FOR LUNCH. I'M STARVED, HOW ABOUT YOU?
BUT -- WHAT YOU SAW --
THIS IS A STRANGE WORLD, SON, AND THERE ARE LOTS OF WEIRD THINGS IN IT. THAT MAKES US, AS A NEWSPAPER, VULNERABLE.
OTHER NEWSPAPERS MAY GO OUT THERE WITH SENSATIONAL STORIES, SCREAMING HEADLINES THAT TURN OUT TO BE A MISTAKE --
-- AND THEY END UP LOOKING LIKE MONKEYS. NOT US.

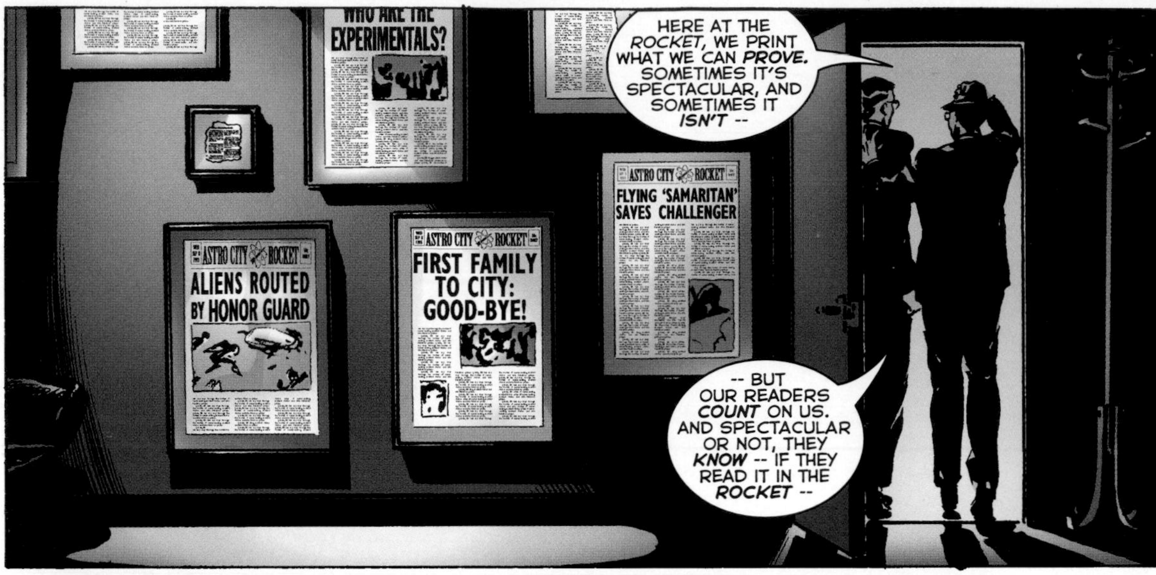
EXPERIMENTALS?
ASTRO CITY ROCKET
ALIENS ROUTED BY HONOR GUARD
ASTRO CITY ROCKET
FIRST FAMILY TO CITY: GOOD-BYE!
ASTRO CITY ROCKET
FLYING 'SAMARITAN' SAVES CHALLENGER
HERE AT THE *ROCKET,* WE PRINT WHAT WE CAN *PROVE.* SOMETIMES IT'S SPECTACULAR, AND SOMETIMES IT *ISN'T* --
-- BUT OUR READERS *COUNT* ON US. AND SPECTACULAR OR NOT, THEY *KNOW* -- IF THEY READ IT IN THE *ROCKET* --

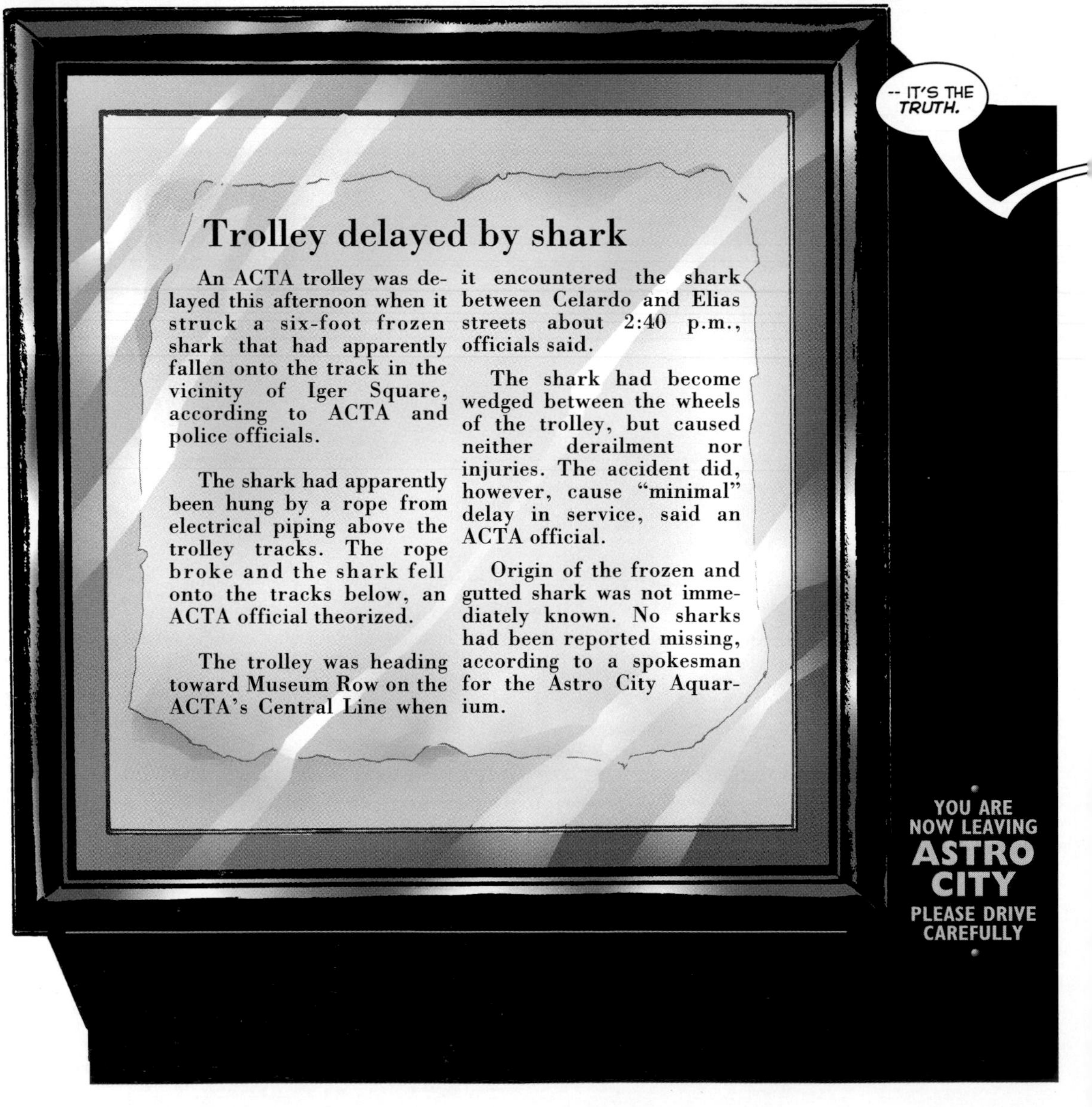

Trolley delayed by shark

An ACTA trolley was delayed this afternoon when it struck a six-foot frozen shark that had apparently fallen onto the track in the vicinity of Iger Square, according to ACTA and police officials.

The shark had apparently been hung by a rope from electrical piping above the trolley tracks. The rope broke and the shark fell onto the tracks below, an ACTA official theorized.

The trolley was heading toward Museum Row on the ACTA's Central Line when it encountered the shark between Celardo and Elias streets about 2:40 p.m., officials said.

The shark had become wedged between the wheels of the trolley, but caused neither derailment nor injuries. The accident did, however, cause "minimal" delay in service, said an ACTA official.

Origin of the frozen and gutted shark was not immediately known. No sharks had been reported missing, according to a spokesman for the Astro City Aquarium.

-- IT'S THE *TRUTH.*
YOU ARE NOW LEAVING
ASTRO CITY
PLEASE DRIVE CAREFULLY

CHAPTER 3

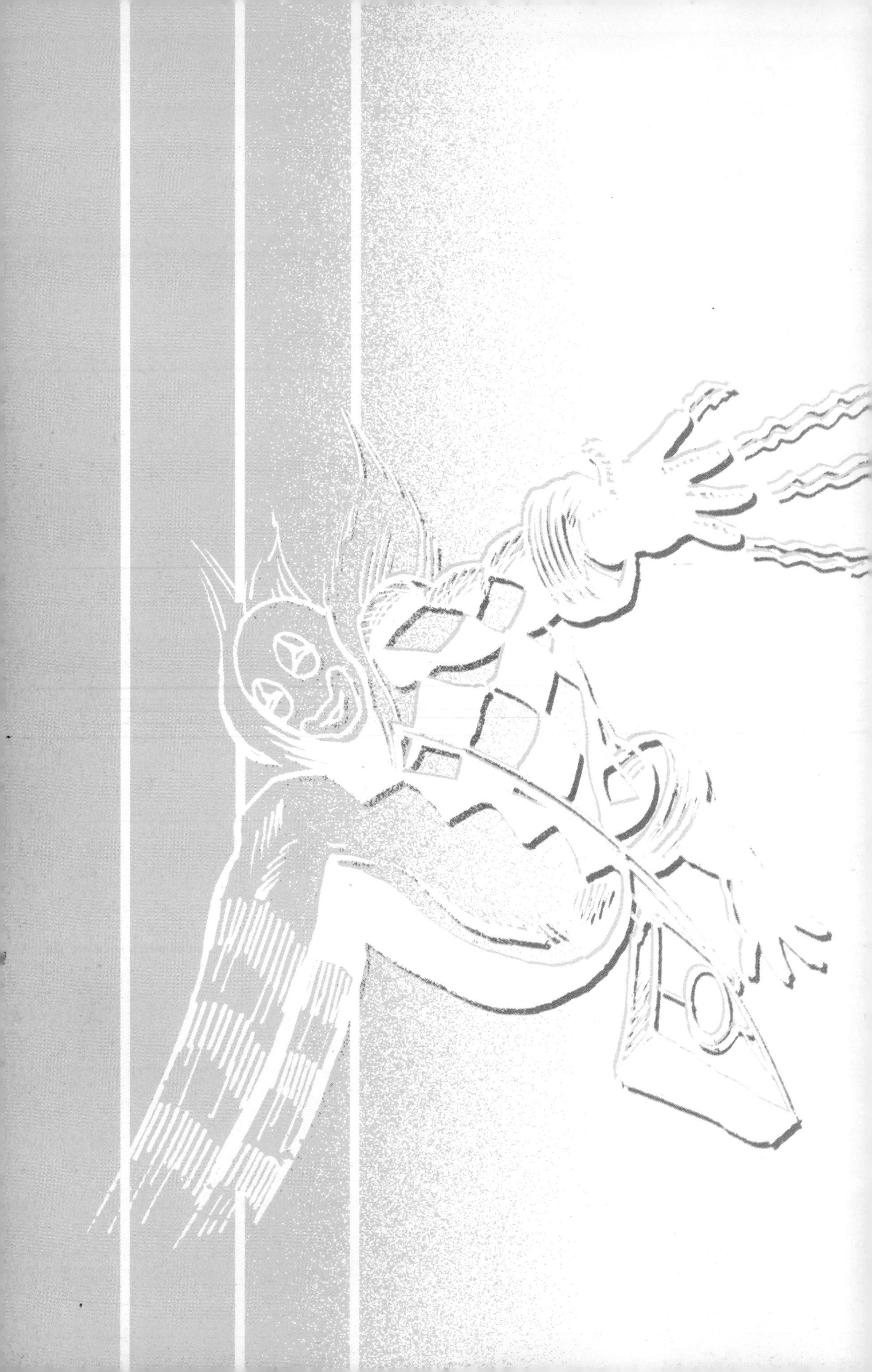

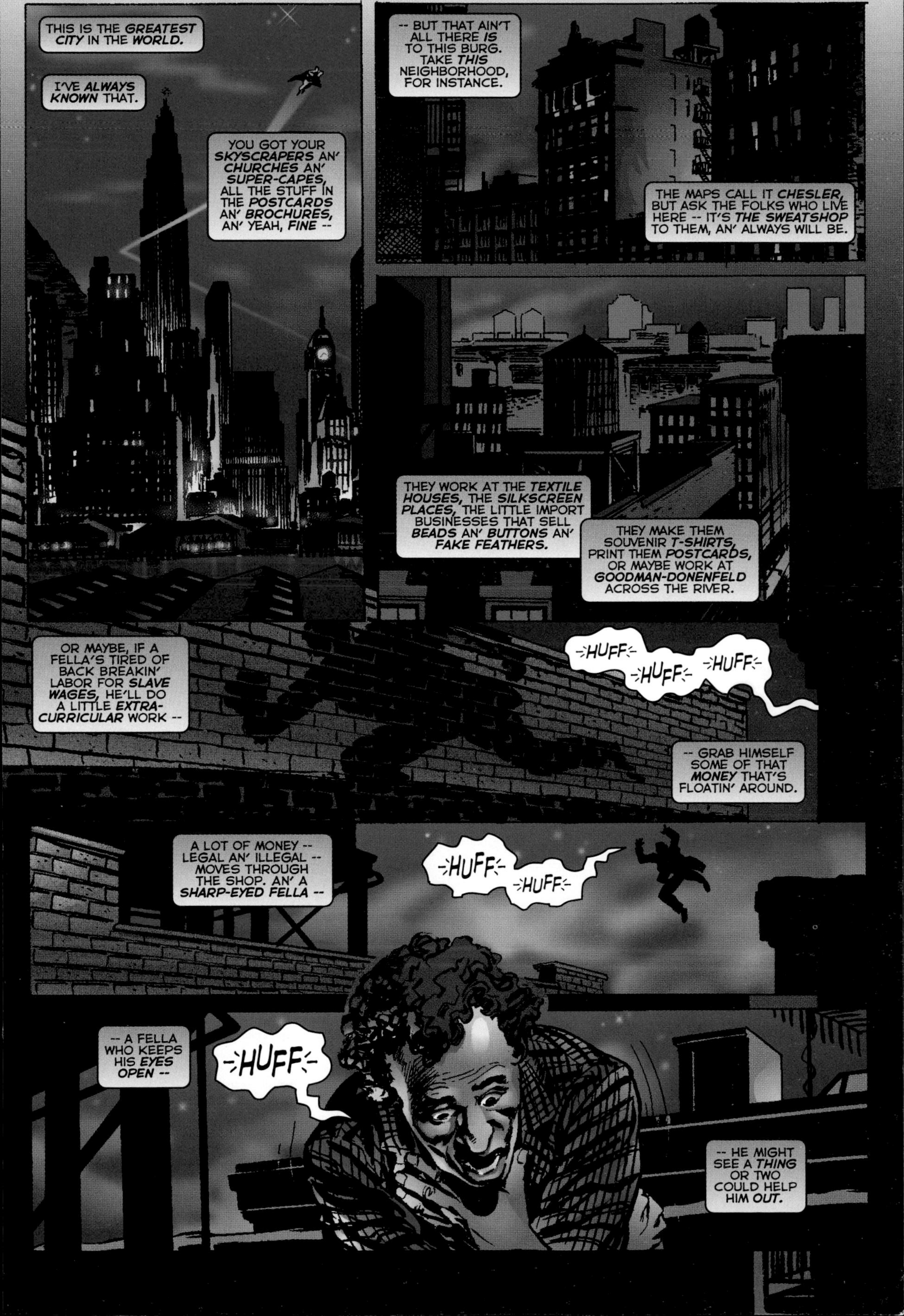
THIS IS THE GREATEST CITY IN THE WORLD.
I'VE ALWAYS KNOWN THAT.
YOU GOT YOUR SKYSCRAPERS AN' CHURCHES AN' SUPER-CAPES, ALL THE STUFF IN THE POSTCARDS AN' BROCHURES, AN' YEAH, FINE --
-- BUT THAT AIN'T ALL THERE IS TO THIS BURG. TAKE THIS NEIGHBORHOOD, FOR INSTANCE.
THE MAPS CALL IT CHESLER, BUT ASK THE FOLKS WHO LIVE HERE -- IT'S THE SWEATSHOP TO THEM, AN' ALWAYS WILL BE.
THEY WORK AT THE TEXTILE HOUSES, THE SILKSCREEN PLACES, THE LITTLE IMPORT BUSINESSES THAT SELL BEADS AN' BUTTONS AN' FAKE FEATHERS.
THEY MAKE THEM SOUVENIR T-SHIRTS, PRINT THEM POSTCARDS, OR MAYBE WORK AT GOODMAN-DONENFELD ACROSS THE RIVER.
OR MAYBE, IF A FELLA'S TIRED OF BACK BREAKIN' LABOR FOR SLAVE WAGES, HE'LL DO A LITTLE EXTRA-CURRICULAR WORK --
HUFF HUFF HUFF
-- GRAB HIMSELF SOME OF THAT MONEY THAT'S FLOATIN' AROUND.
A LOT OF MONEY -- LEGAL AN' ILLEGAL -- MOVES THROUGH THE SHOP. AN' A SHARP-EYED FELLA --
HUFF HUFF
-- A FELLA WHO KEEPS HIS EYES OPEN --
HUFF
-- HE MIGHT SEE A THING OR TWO COULD HELP HIM OUT.

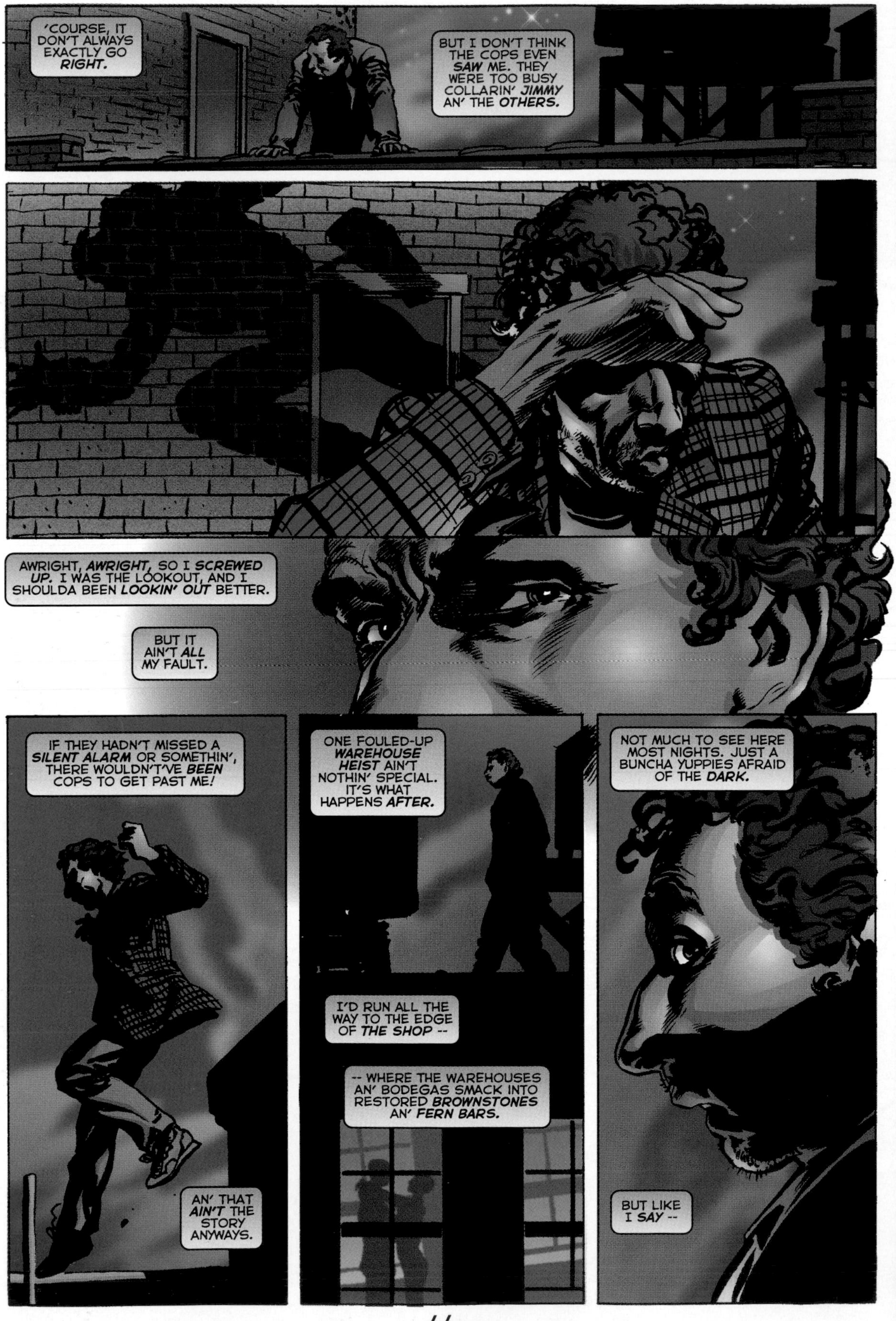

'COURSE, IT DON'T ALWAYS EXACTLY GO *RIGHT.*
BUT I DON'T THINK THE COPS EVEN *SAW* ME. THEY WERE TOO BUSY COLLARIN' *JIMMY* AN' THE *OTHERS.*
AWRIGHT, *AWRIGHT,* SO I *SCREWED UP.* I WAS THE LOOKOUT, AND I SHOULDA BEEN *LOOKIN' OUT* BETTER.
BUT IT AIN'T *ALL* MY FAULT.
IF THEY HADN'T MISSED A *SILENT ALARM* OR SOMETHIN', THERE WOULDN'T'VE *BEEN* COPS TO GET PAST ME!
AN' THAT *AIN'T* THE STORY ANYWAYS.
ONE FOULED-UP *WAREHOUSE HEIST* AIN'T NOTHIN' SPECIAL. IT'S WHAT HAPPENS *AFTER.*
I'D RUN ALL THE WAY TO THE EDGE OF *THE SHOP* --
-- WHERE THE WAREHOUSES AN' BODEGAS SMACK INTO RESTORED *BROWNSTONES* AN' *FERN BARS.*
NOT MUCH TO SEE HERE MOST NIGHTS. JUST A BUNCHA YUPPIES AFRAID OF THE *DARK.*
BUT LIKE I *SAY* --

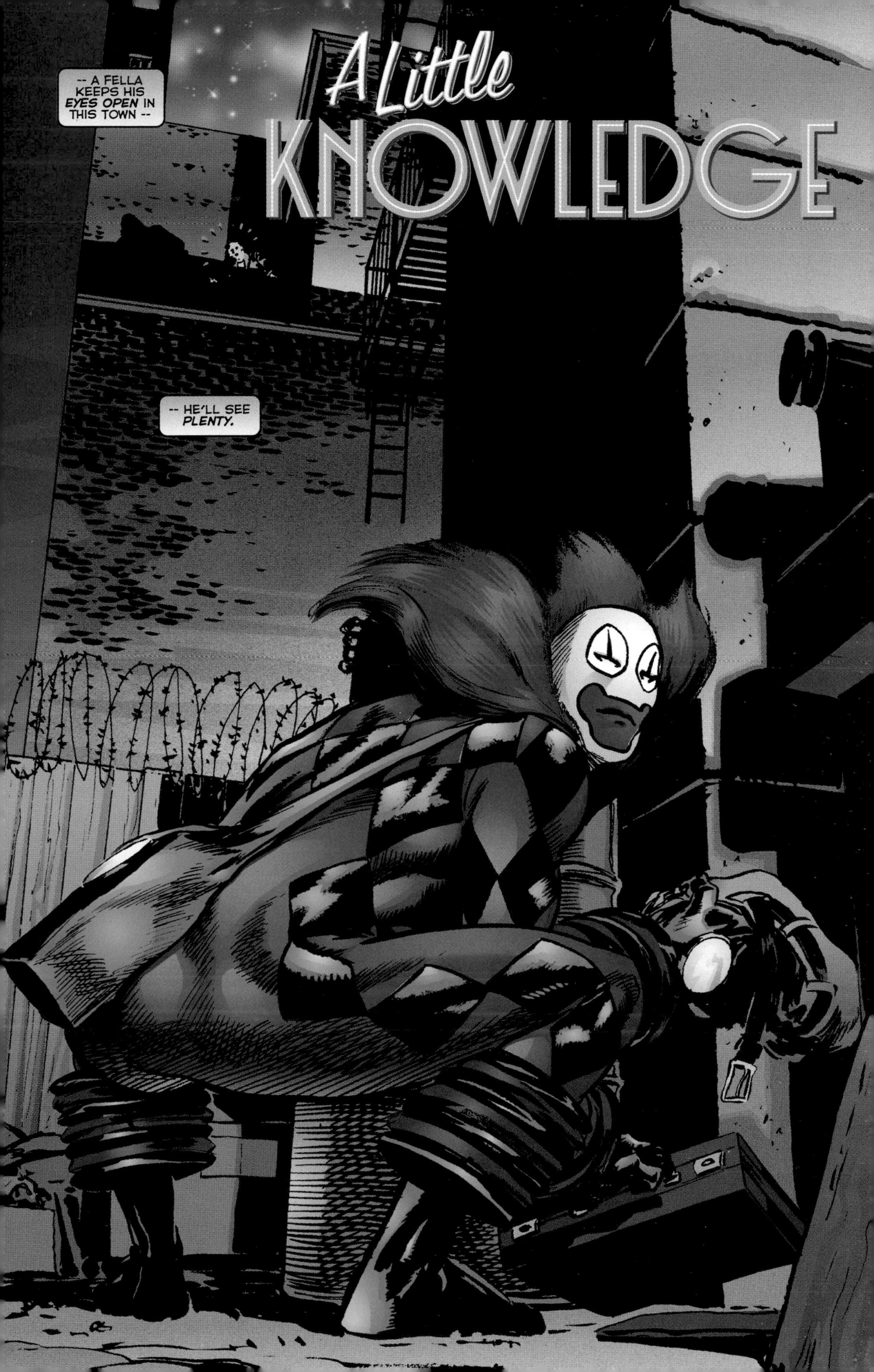
-- A FELLA KEEPS HIS EYES OPEN IN THIS TOWN --
A Little
KNOWLEDGE
-- HE'LL SEE PLENTY.

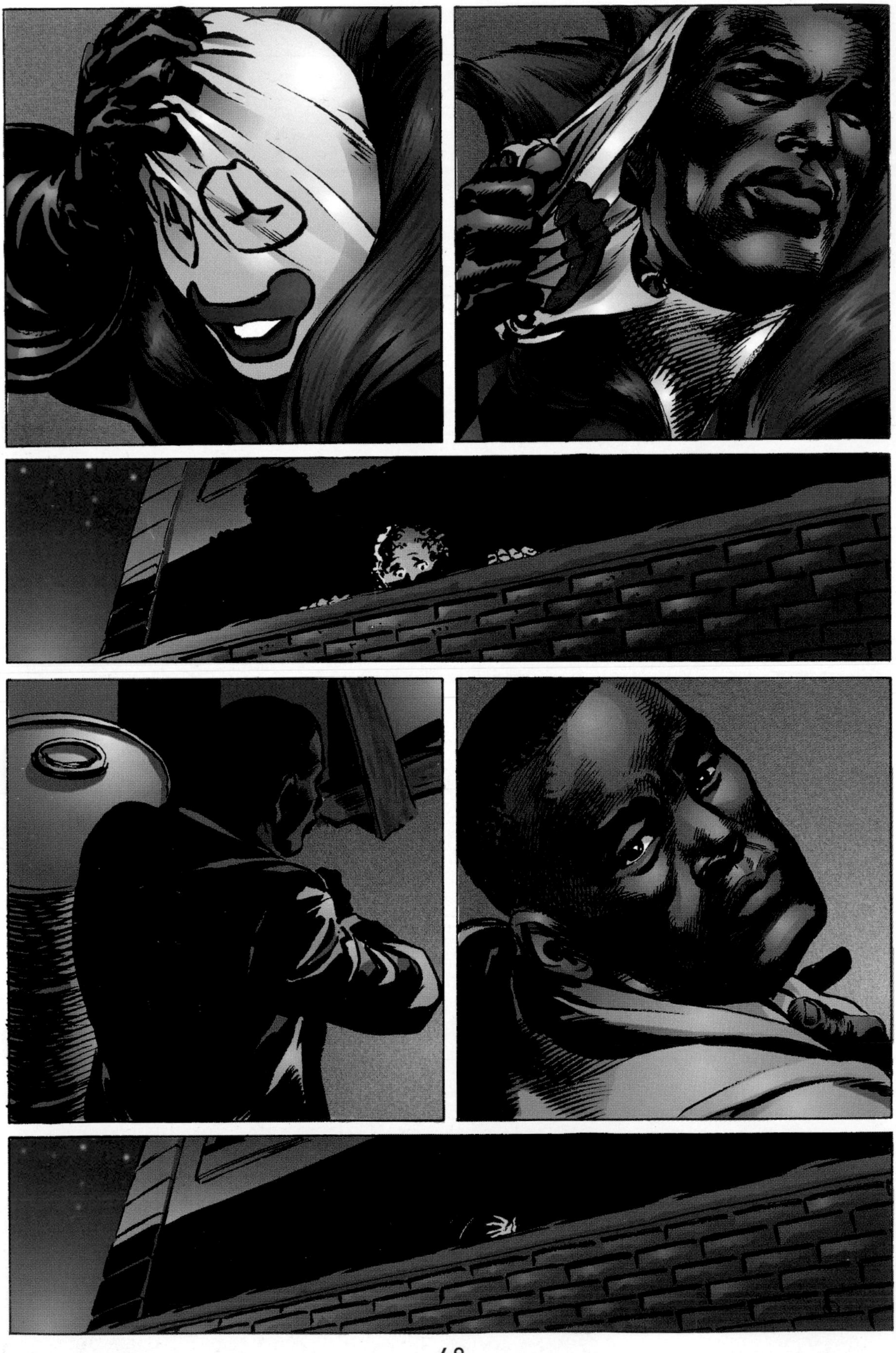

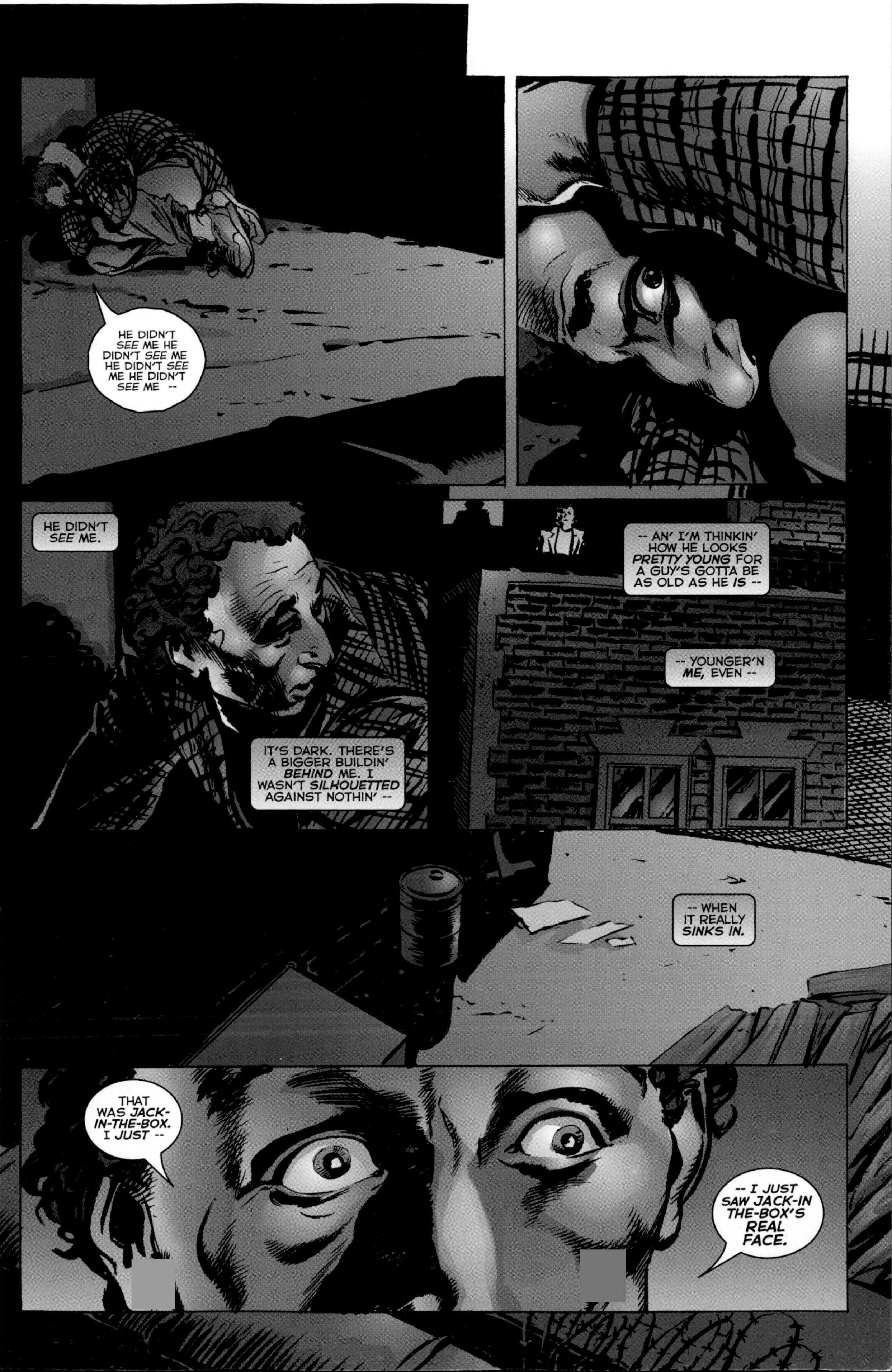
HE DIDN'T SEE ME HE DIDN'T SEE ME HE DIDN'T SEE ME HE DIDN'T SEE ME --
HE DIDN'T SEE ME.
IT'S DARK. THERE'S A BIGGER BUILDIN' BEHIND ME. I WASN'T SILHOUETTED AGAINST NOTHIN' --
-- AN' I'M THINKIN' HOW HE LOOKS PRETTY YOUNG FOR A GUY'S GOTTA BE AS OLD AS HE IS --
-- YOUNGER'N ME, EVEN --
-- WHEN IT REALLY SINKS IN.
THAT WAS JACK-IN-THE-BOX. I JUST --
-- I JUST SAW JACK-IN THE-BOX'S REAL FACE.

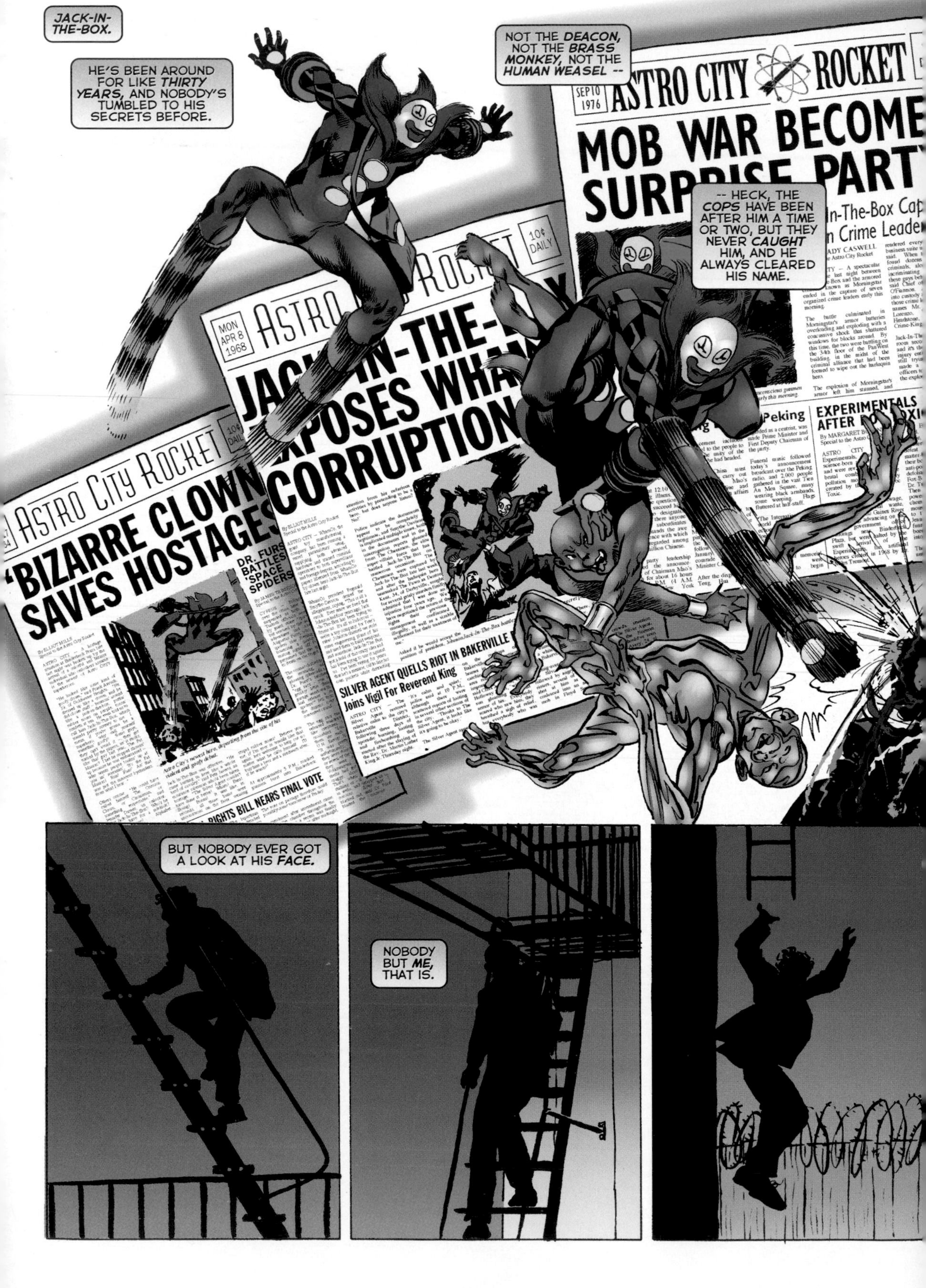

JACK-IN-THE-BOX.
HE'S BEEN AROUND FOR LIKE *THIRTY YEARS,* AND NOBODY'S TUMBLED TO HIS SECRETS BEFORE.
NOT THE *DEACON,* NOT THE *BRASS MONKEY,* NOT THE *HUMAN WEASEL* --
-- HECK, THE *COPS* HAVE BEEN AFTER HIM A TIME OR TWO, BUT THEY NEVER *CAUGHT* HIM, AND HE ALWAYS CLEARED HIS NAME.
ASTRO CITY ROCKET
SEP 10 1976
MOB WAR BECOME
SURPRISE PART
ASTRO CITY ROCKET
MON APR 8 1968
EXPOSES WHA
CORRUPTION
SILVER AGENT QUELLS RIOT IN BAKERVILLE
Joins Vigil For Reverend King
ASTRO CITY ROCKET
'BIZARRE CLOWN
SAVES HOSTAGES
DR. FURS BATTLES 'SPACE SPIDERS'
RIGHTS BILL NEARS FINAL VOTE
Peking
EXPERIMENTALS AFTER
BUT NOBODY EVER GOT A LOOK AT HIS *FACE.*
NOBODY BUT *ME,* THAT IS.

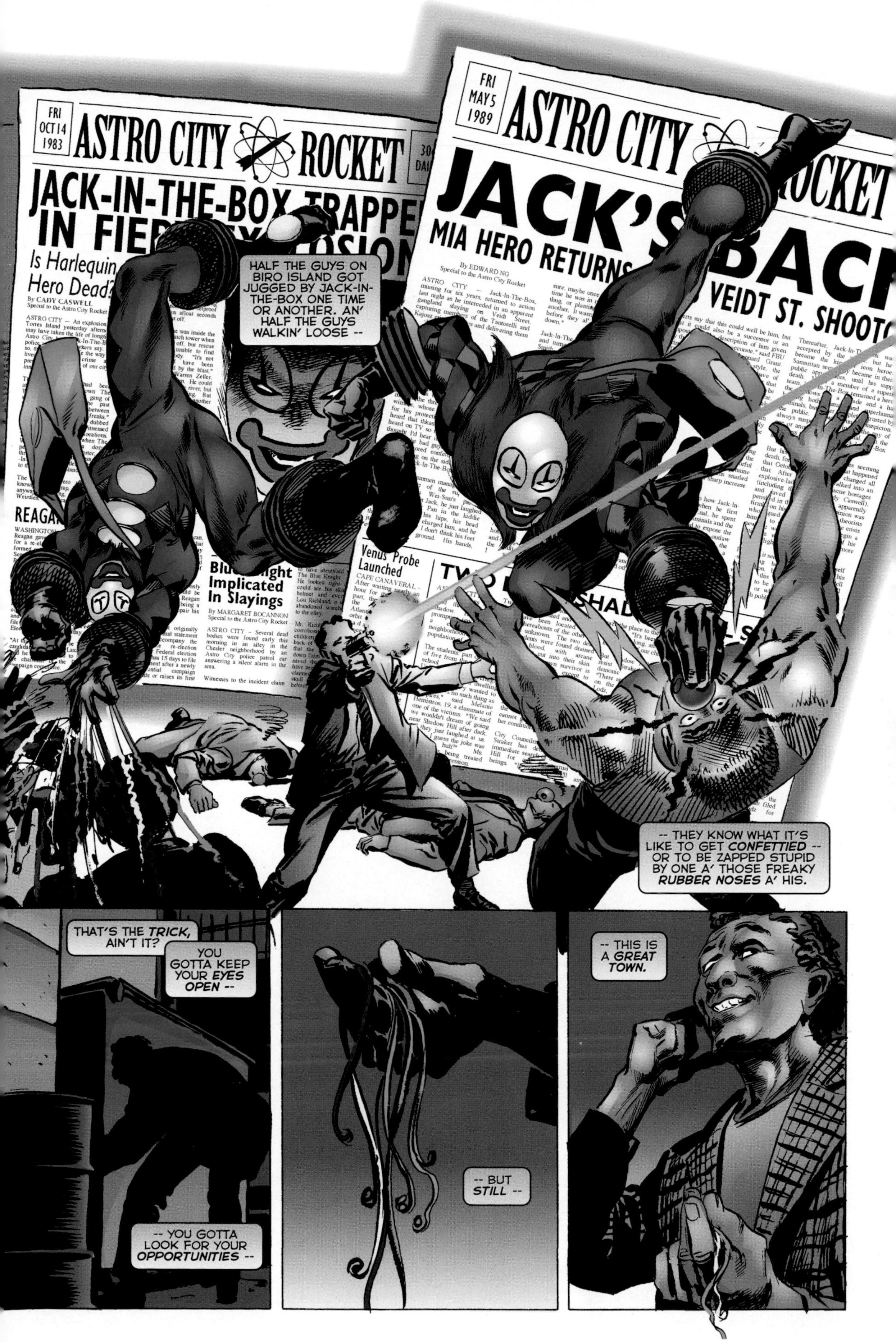
FRI OCT 14 1983
ASTRO CITY ROCKET
JACK-IN-THE-BOX TRAPPE
IN FIE
Is Harlequin
Hero Dead?
By CADY CASWELL
FRI MAY 5 1989
ASTRO CITY
JACK'S
MIA HERO RETURNS
By EDWARD NG
VEIDT ST. SHOOT
Venus Probe Launched
Implicated In Slayings
By MARGARET BOCANNON
HALF THE GUYS ON BIRO ISLAND GOT JUGGED BY JACK-IN-THE-BOX ONE TIME OR ANOTHER. AN' HALF THE GUYS WALKIN' LOOSE --
-- THEY KNOW WHAT IT'S LIKE TO GET CONFETTIED -- OR TO BE ZAPPED STUPID BY ONE A' THOSE FREAKY RUBBER NOSES A' HIS.
THAT'S THE TRICK, AIN'T IT?
YOU GOTTA KEEP YOUR EYES OPEN --
-- YOU GOTTA LOOK FOR YOUR OPPORTUNITIES --
-- BUT STILL --
-- THIS IS A GREAT TOWN.

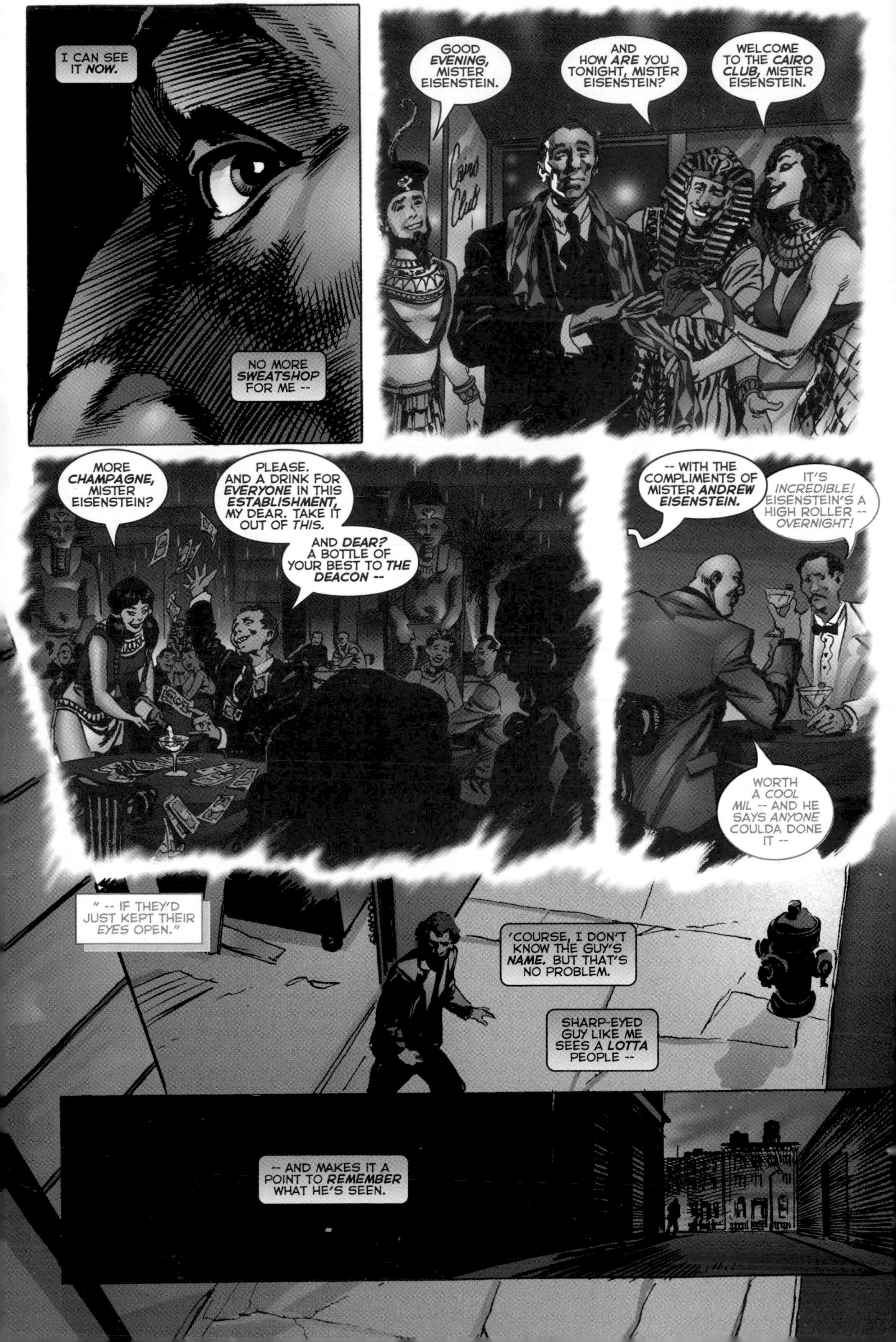
I CAN SEE IT NOW.
NO MORE SWEATSHOP FOR ME --
GOOD EVENING, MISTER EISENSTEIN.
AND HOW ARE YOU TONIGHT, MISTER EISENSTEIN?
WELCOME TO THE CAIRO CLUB, MISTER EISENSTEIN.
Cairo Club
MORE CHAMPAGNE, MISTER EISENSTEIN?
PLEASE. AND A DRINK FOR EVERYONE IN THIS ESTABLISHMENT, MY DEAR. TAKE IT OUT OF THIS.
AND DEAR? A BOTTLE OF YOUR BEST TO THE DEACON --
-- WITH THE COMPLIMENTS OF MISTER ANDREW EISENSTEIN.
IT'S INCREDIBLE! EISENSTEIN'S A HIGH ROLLER -- OVERNIGHT!
WORTH A COOL MIL -- AND HE SAYS ANYONE COULDA DONE IT --
" -- IF THEY'D JUST KEPT THEIR EYES OPEN."
'COURSE, I DON'T KNOW THE GUY'S NAME. BUT THAT'S NO PROBLEM.
SHARP-EYED GUY LIKE ME SEES A LOTTA PEOPLE --
-- AND MAKES IT A POINT TO REMEMBER WHAT HE'S SEEN.

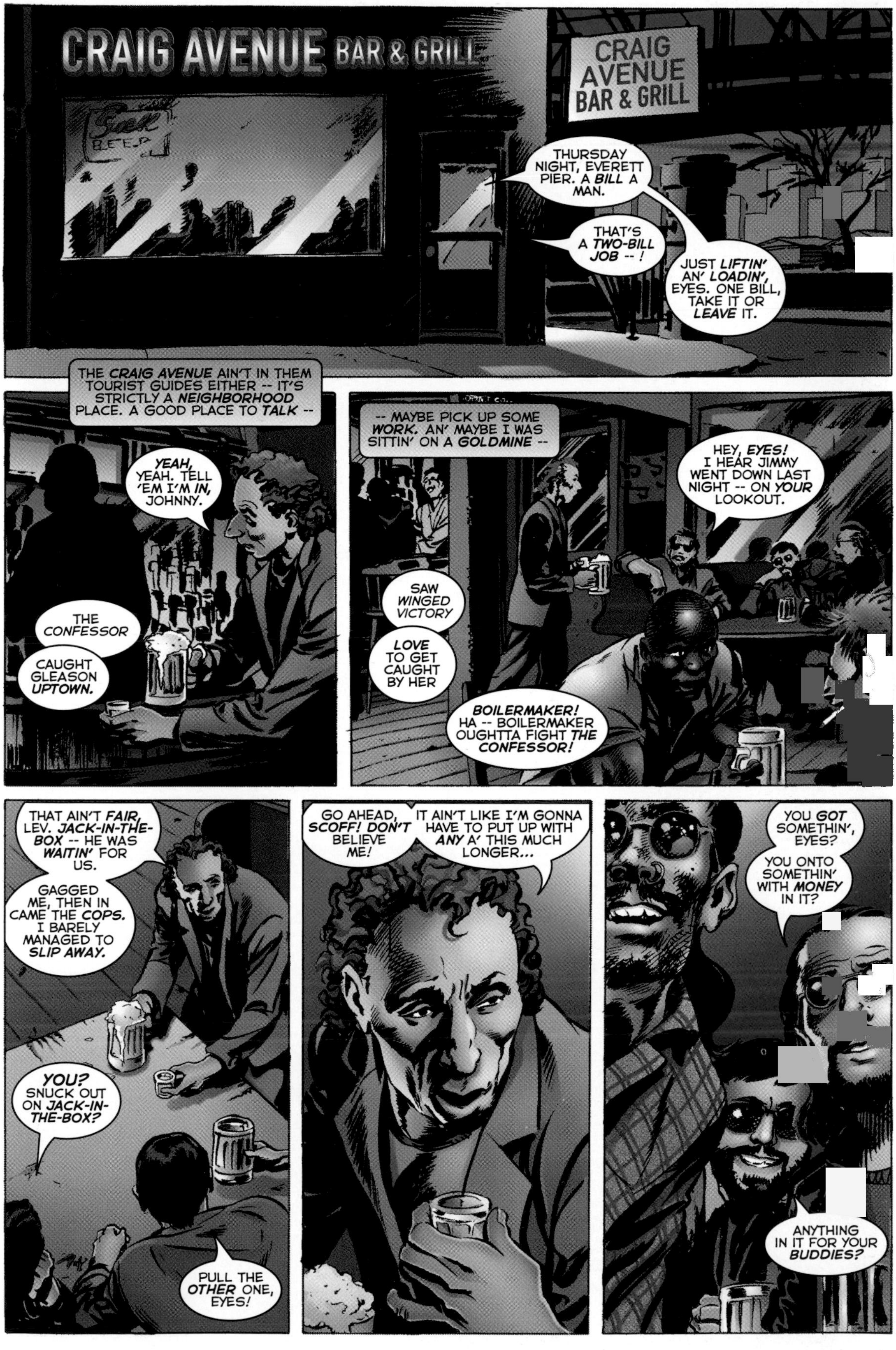
CRAIG AVENUE BAR & GRILL
CRAIG AVENUE BAR & GRILL
THURSDAY NIGHT, EVERETT PIER. A BILL A MAN.
THAT'S A TWO-BILL JOB -- !
JUST LIFTIN' AN' LOADIN', EYES. ONE BILL, TAKE IT OR LEAVE IT.
THE CRAIG AVENUE AIN'T IN THEM TOURIST GUIDES EITHER -- IT'S STRICTLY A NEIGHBORHOOD PLACE. A GOOD PLACE TO TALK --
YEAH, YEAH. TELL 'EM I'M IN, JOHNNY.
THE CONFESSOR
CAUGHT GLEASON UPTOWN.
-- MAYBE PICK UP SOME WORK. AN' MAYBE I WAS SITTIN' ON A GOLDMINE --
HEY, EYES! I HEAR JIMMY WENT DOWN LAST NIGHT -- ON YOUR LOOKOUT.
SAW WINGED VICTORY
LOVE TO GET CAUGHT BY HER
BOILERMAKER! HA -- BOILERMAKER OUGHTTA FIGHT THE CONFESSOR!
THAT AIN'T FAIR, LEV. JACK-IN-THE-BOX -- HE WAS WAITIN' FOR US.
GAGGED ME, THEN IN CAME THE COPS. I BARELY MANAGED TO SLIP AWAY.
YOU? SNUCK OUT ON JACK-IN-THE-BOX?
PULL THE OTHER ONE, EYES!
GO AHEAD, SCOFF! DON'T BELIEVE ME!
IT AIN'T LIKE I'M GONNA HAVE TO PUT UP WITH ANY A' THIS MUCH LONGER...
YOU GOT SOMETHIN', EYES?
YOU ONTO SOMETHIN' WITH MONEY IN IT?
ANYTHING IN IT FOR YOUR BUDDIES?

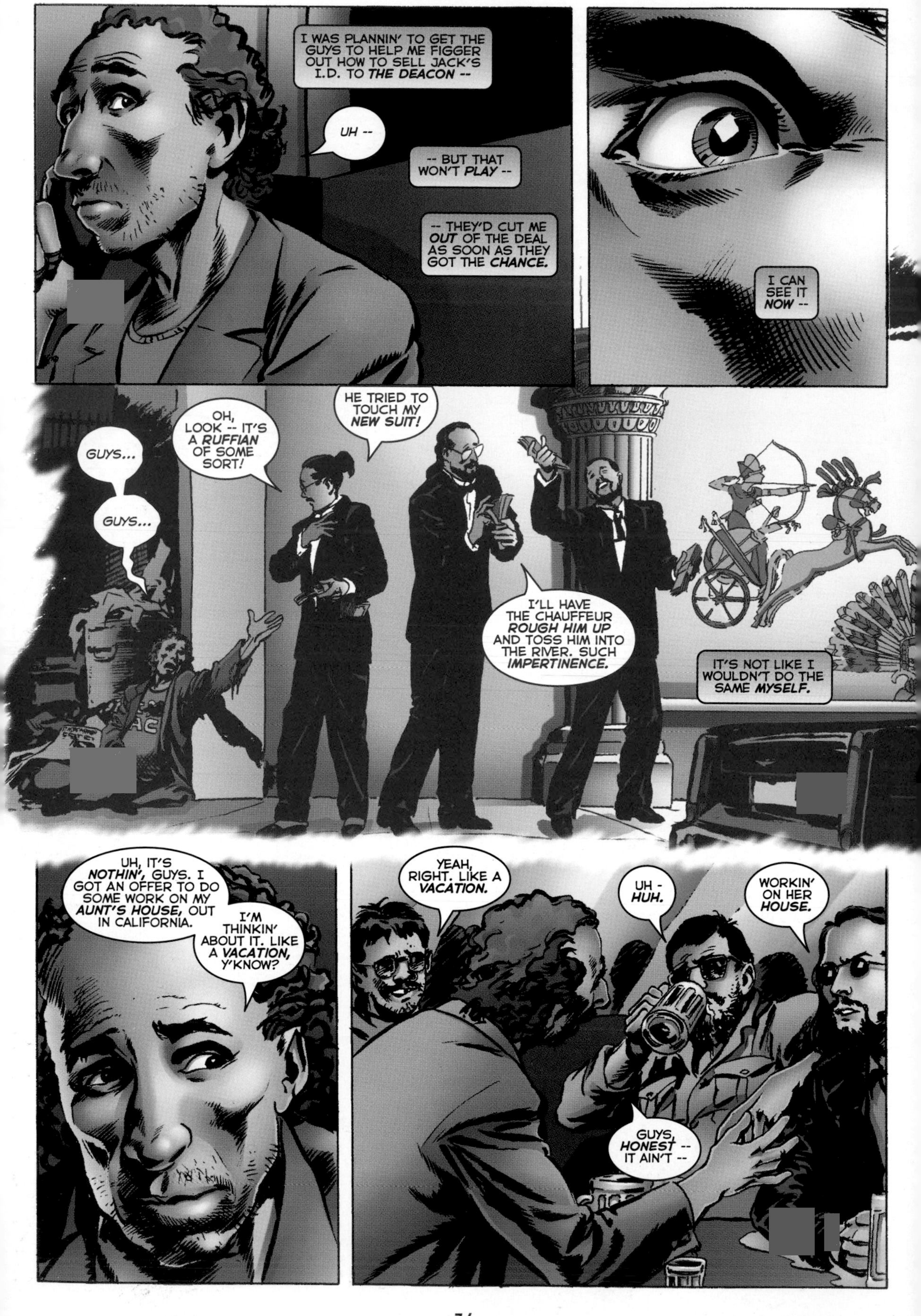
I WAS PLANNIN' TO GET THE GUYS TO HELP ME FIGGER OUT HOW TO SELL JACK'S I.D. TO THE DEACON --
UH --
-- BUT THAT WON'T PLAY --
-- THEY'D CUT ME OUT OF THE DEAL AS SOON AS THEY GOT THE CHANCE.
I CAN SEE IT NOW --
GUYS...
GUYS...
OH, LOOK -- IT'S A RUFFIAN OF SOME SORT!
HE TRIED TO TOUCH MY NEW SUIT!
I'LL HAVE THE CHAUFFEUR ROUGH HIM UP AND TOSS HIM INTO THE RIVER. SUCH IMPERTINENCE.
IT'S NOT LIKE I WOULDN'T DO THE SAME MYSELF.
UH, IT'S NOTHIN', GUYS. I GOT AN OFFER TO DO SOME WORK ON MY AUNT'S HOUSE, OUT IN CALIFORNIA.
I'M THINKIN' ABOUT IT. LIKE A VACATION, Y'KNOW?
YEAH, RIGHT. LIKE A VACATION.
UH - HUH.
WORKIN' ON HER HOUSE.
GUYS, HONEST -- IT AIN'T --

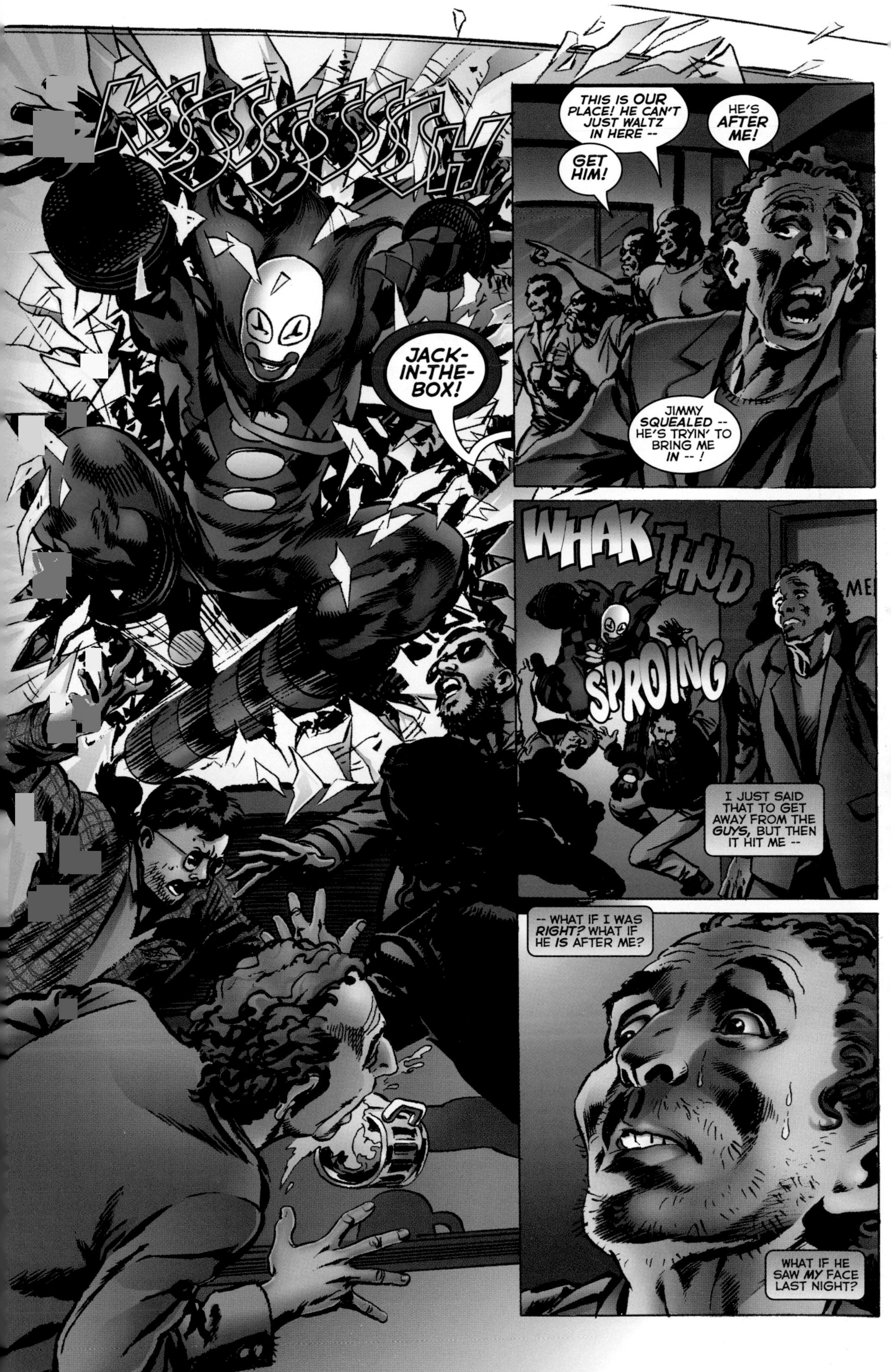
KRSSSSSSSH
JACK-IN-THE-BOX!
THIS IS OUR PLACE! HE CAN'T JUST WALTZ IN HERE --
GET HIM!
HE'S AFTER ME!
JIMMY SQUEALED -- HE'S TRYIN' TO BRING ME IN -- !
WHAK
THUD
SPROING
I JUST SAID THAT TO GET AWAY FROM THE GUYS, BUT THEN IT HIT ME --
-- WHAT IF I WAS RIGHT? WHAT IF HE IS AFTER ME?
WHAT IF HE SAW MY FACE LAST NIGHT?

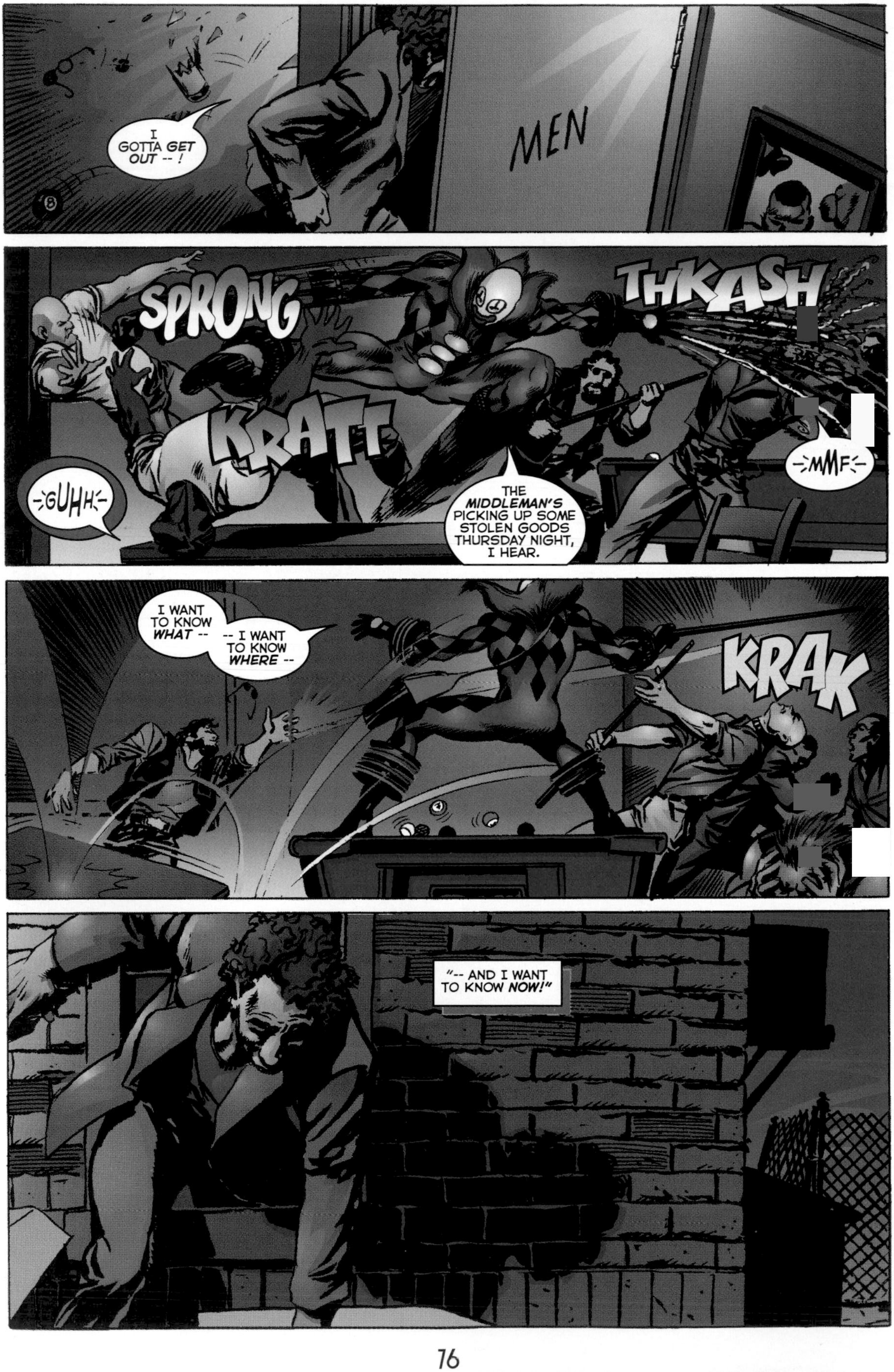
MEN
I GOTTA GET OUT -- !
SPRONG
THKASH
KRATT
-GUHH-
THE MIDDLEMAN'S PICKING UP SOME STOLEN GOODS THURSDAY NIGHT, I HEAR.
-MMF-
I WANT TO KNOW WHAT --
-- I WANT TO KNOW WHERE --
KRAK
"-- AND I WANT TO KNOW NOW!"

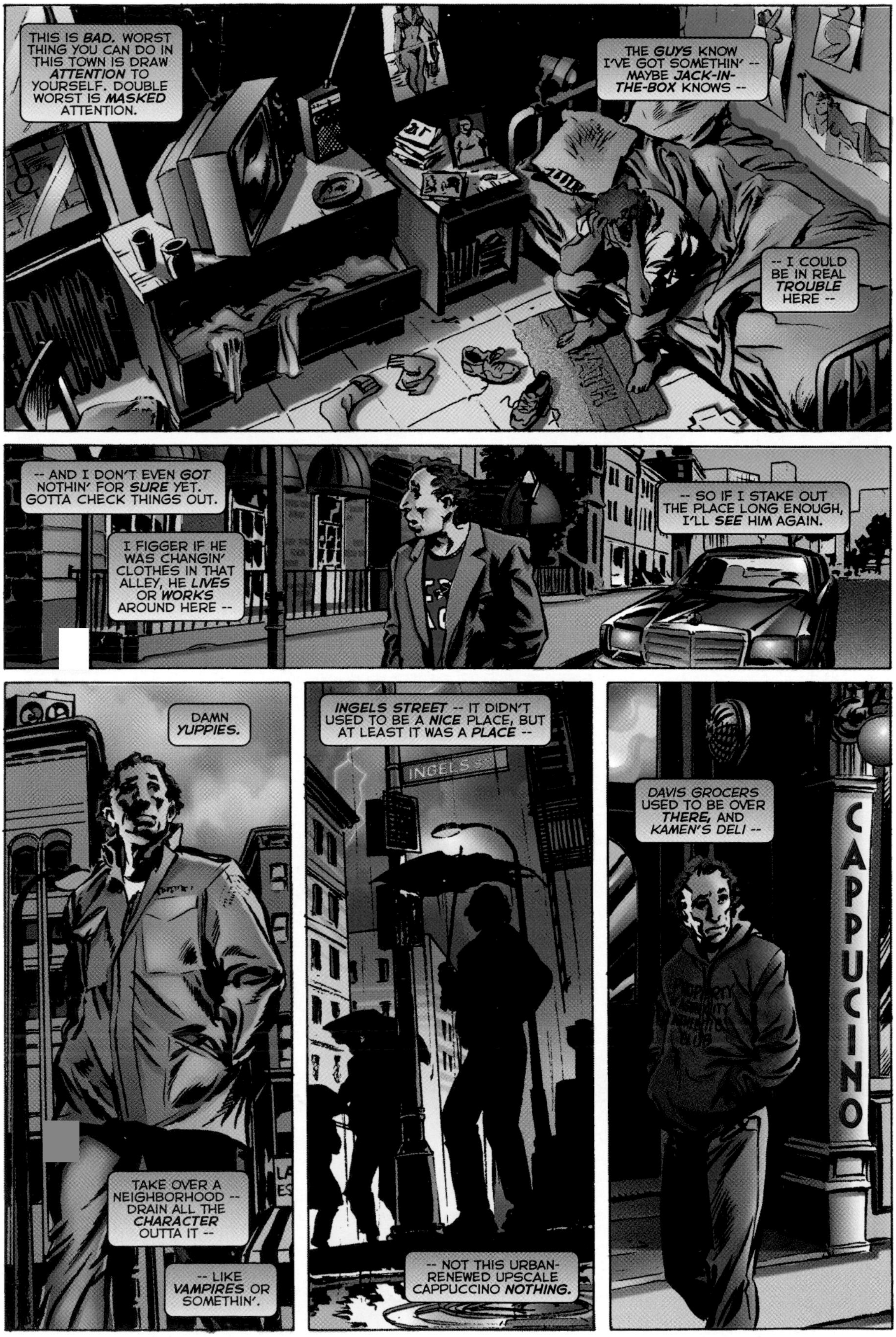
THIS IS BAD. WORST THING YOU CAN DO IN THIS TOWN IS DRAW ATTENTION TO YOURSELF. DOUBLE WORST IS MASKED ATTENTION.
THE GUYS KNOW I'VE GOT SOMETHIN' -- MAYBE JACK-IN-THE-BOX KNOWS --
-- I COULD BE IN REAL TROUBLE HERE --
-- AND I DON'T EVEN GOT NOTHIN' FOR SURE YET. GOTTA CHECK THINGS OUT.
I FIGGER IF HE WAS CHANGIN' CLOTHES IN THAT ALLEY, HE LIVES OR WORKS AROUND HERE --
-- SO IF I STAKE OUT THE PLACE LONG ENOUGH, I'LL SEE HIM AGAIN.
DAMN YUPPIES.
TAKE OVER A NEIGHBORHOOD -- DRAIN ALL THE CHARACTER OUTTA IT --
-- LIKE VAMPIRES OR SOMETHIN'.
INGELS STREET -- IT DIDN'T USED TO BE A NICE PLACE, BUT AT LEAST IT WAS A PLACE --
INGELS ST.
-- NOT THIS URBAN-RENEWED UPSCALE CAPPUCCINO NOTHING.
DAVIS GROCERS USED TO BE OVER THERE, AND KAMEN'S DELI --
CAPPUCINO

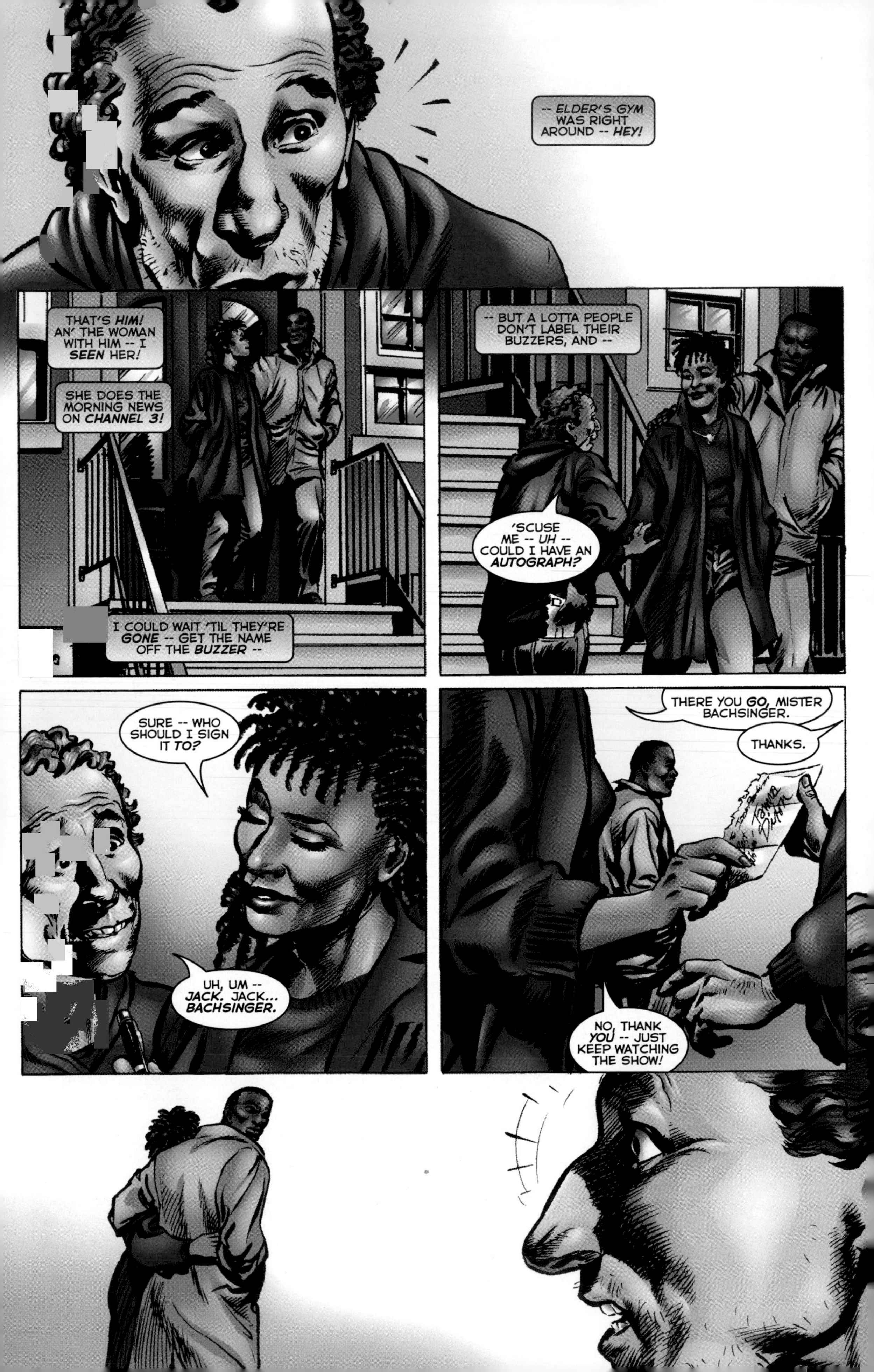
-- ELDER'S GYM WAS RIGHT AROUND -- HEY!
THAT'S HIM! AN' THE WOMAN WITH HIM -- I SEEN HER!
SHE DOES THE MORNING NEWS ON CHANNEL 3!
I COULD WAIT 'TIL THEY'RE GONE -- GET THE NAME OFF THE BUZZER --
-- BUT A LOTTA PEOPLE DON'T LABEL THEIR BUZZERS, AND --
'SCUSE ME -- UH -- COULD I HAVE AN AUTOGRAPH?
SURE -- WHO SHOULD I SIGN IT TO?
UH, UM -- JACK. JACK... BACHSINGER.
THERE YOU GO, MISTER BACHSINGER.
THANKS.
NO, THANK YOU -- JUST KEEP WATCHING THE SHOW!

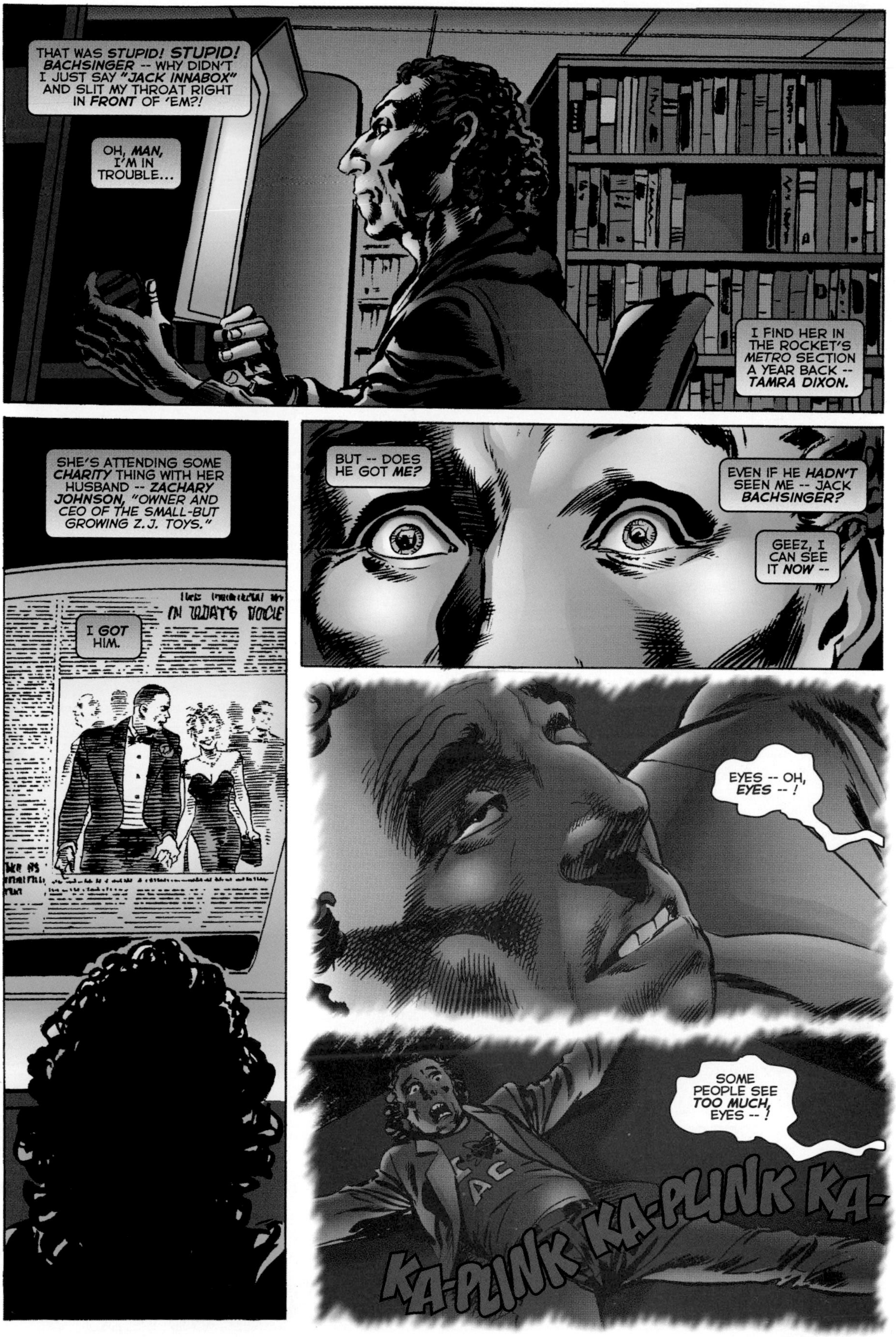
THAT WAS STUPID! STUPID! BACHSINGER -- WHY DIDN'T I JUST SAY "JACK INNABOX" AND SLIT MY THROAT RIGHT IN FRONT OF 'EM?!
OH, MAN, I'M IN TROUBLE...
I FIND HER IN THE ROCKET'S METRO SECTION A YEAR BACK -- TAMRA DIXON.
SHE'S ATTENDING SOME CHARITY THING WITH HER HUSBAND -- ZACHARY JOHNSON, "OWNER AND CEO OF THE SMALL-BUT GROWING Z.J. TOYS."
I GOT HIM.
BUT -- DOES HE GOT ME?
EVEN IF HE HADN'T SEEN ME -- JACK BACHSINGER?
GEEZ, I CAN SEE IT NOW --
EYES -- OH, EYES -- !
SOME PEOPLE SEE TOO MUCH, EYES -- !
KA-PLINK KA-PLINK KA-

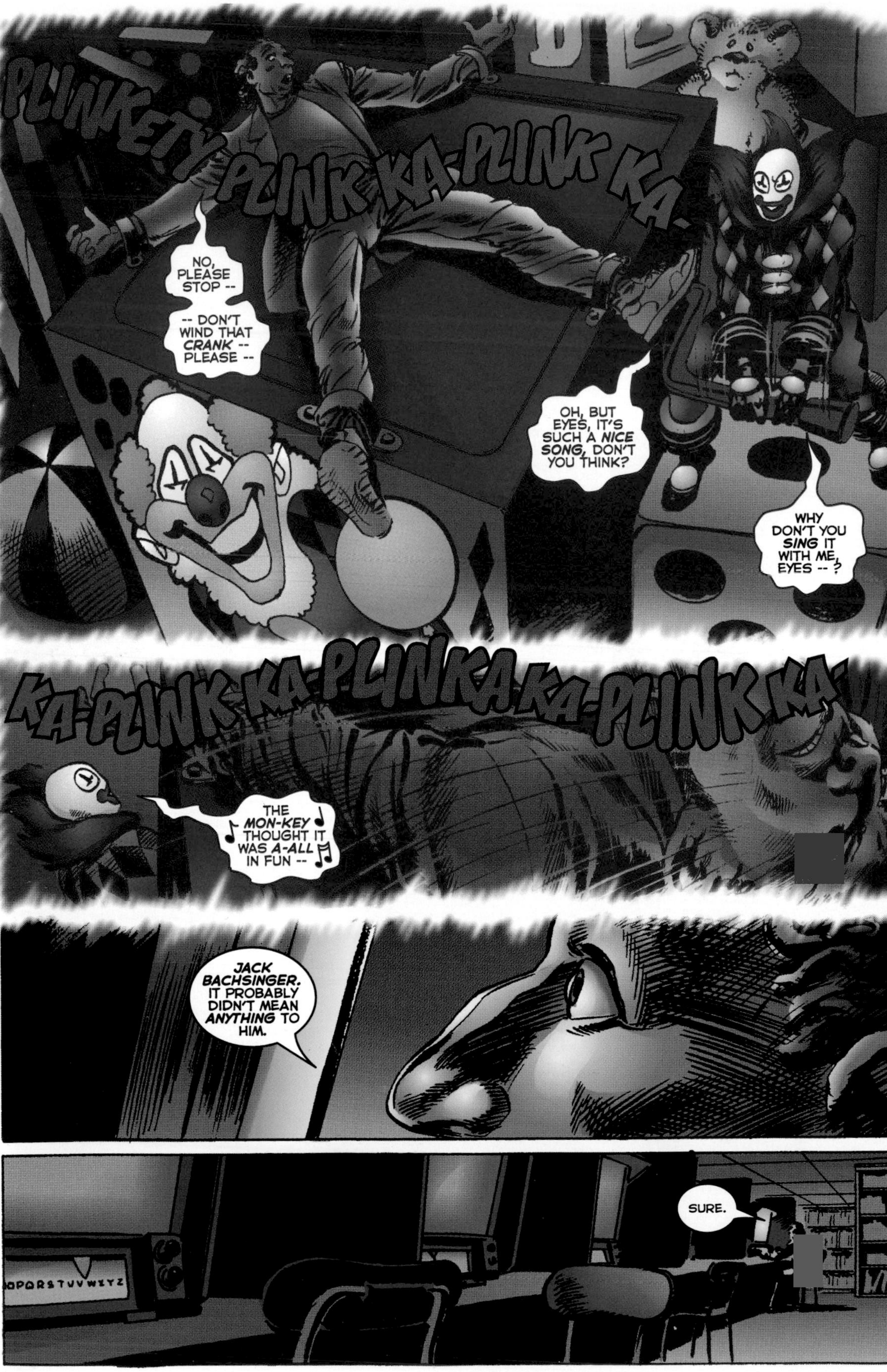
PLINKETY PLINK KA-PLINK KA-
NO, PLEASE STOP --
-- DON'T WIND THAT CRANK -- PLEASE --
OH, BUT EYES, IT'S SUCH A NICE SONG, DON'T YOU THINK?
WHY DON'T YOU SING IT WITH ME, EYES -- ?
KA-PLINK KA-PLINKA KA-PLINK KA-
THE MON-KEY THOUGHT IT WAS A-ALL IN FUN --
JACK BACHSINGER. IT PROBABLY DIDN'T MEAN ANYTHING TO HIM.
SURE.
OPQRSTUVWXYZ

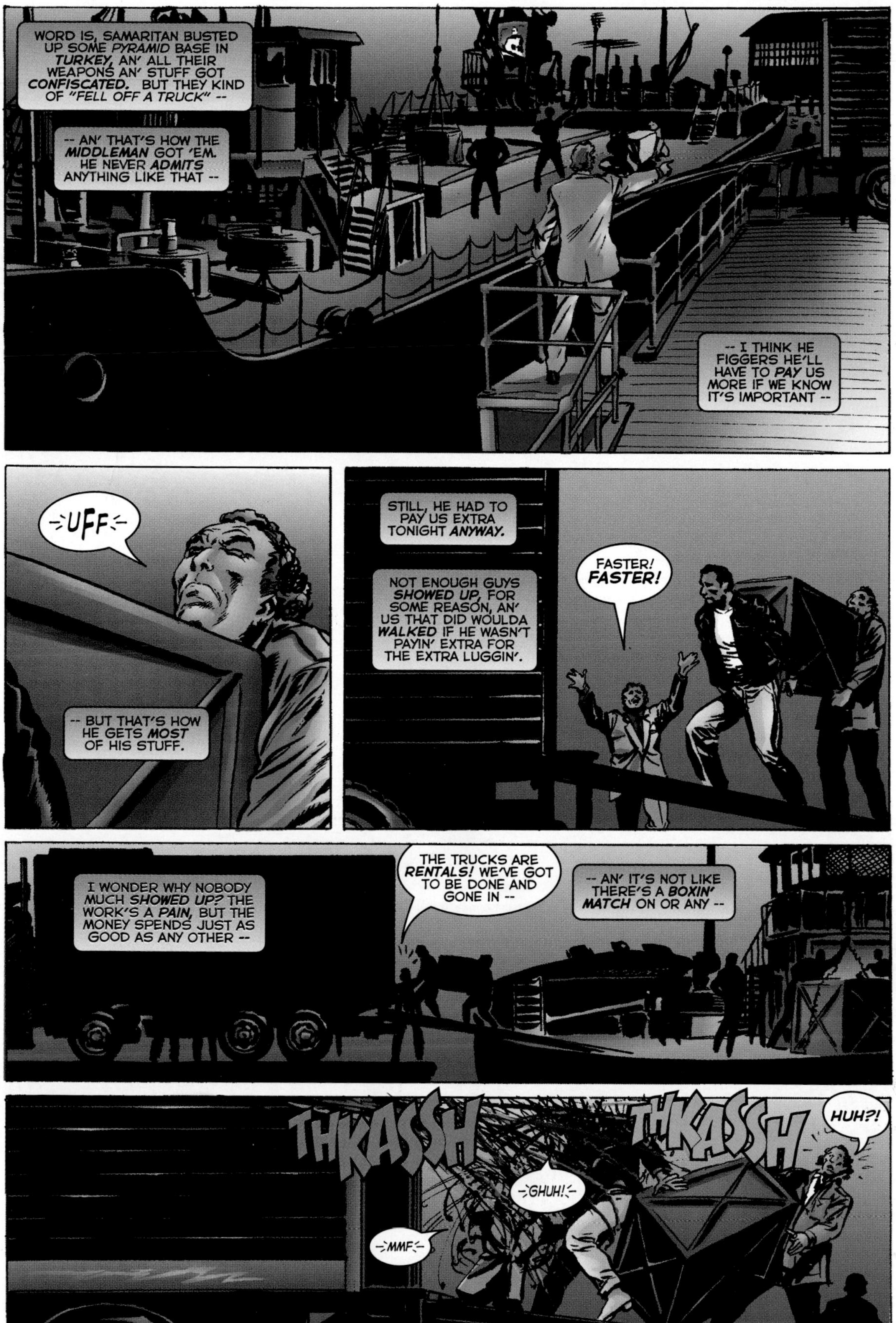
WORD IS, SAMARITAN BUSTED UP SOME *PYRAMID* BASE IN *TURKEY,* AN' ALL THEIR WEAPONS AN' STUFF GOT *CONFISCATED.* BUT THEY KIND OF *"FELL OFF A TRUCK"* --
-- AN' THAT'S HOW THE *MIDDLEMAN* GOT 'EM. HE NEVER *ADMITS* ANYTHING LIKE THAT --
-- I THINK HE FIGGERS HE'LL HAVE TO *PAY* US MORE IF WE KNOW IT'S IMPORTANT --
UFF
-- BUT THAT'S HOW HE GETS *MOST* OF HIS STUFF.
STILL, HE HAD TO PAY US EXTRA TONIGHT *ANYWAY.*
NOT ENOUGH GUYS *SHOWED UP,* FOR SOME REASON, AN' US THAT DID WOULDA *WALKED* IF HE WASN'T PAYIN' EXTRA FOR THE EXTRA LUGGIN'.
FASTER! *FASTER!*
I WONDER WHY NOBODY MUCH *SHOWED UP?* THE WORK'S A *PAIN,* BUT THE MONEY SPENDS JUST AS GOOD AS ANY OTHER --
THE TRUCKS ARE *RENTALS!* WE'VE GOT TO BE DONE AND GONE IN --
-- AN' IT'S NOT LIKE THERE'S A *BOXIN' MATCH* ON OR ANY --
THKASSH
THKASSH
HUH?!
GHUH!
MMF

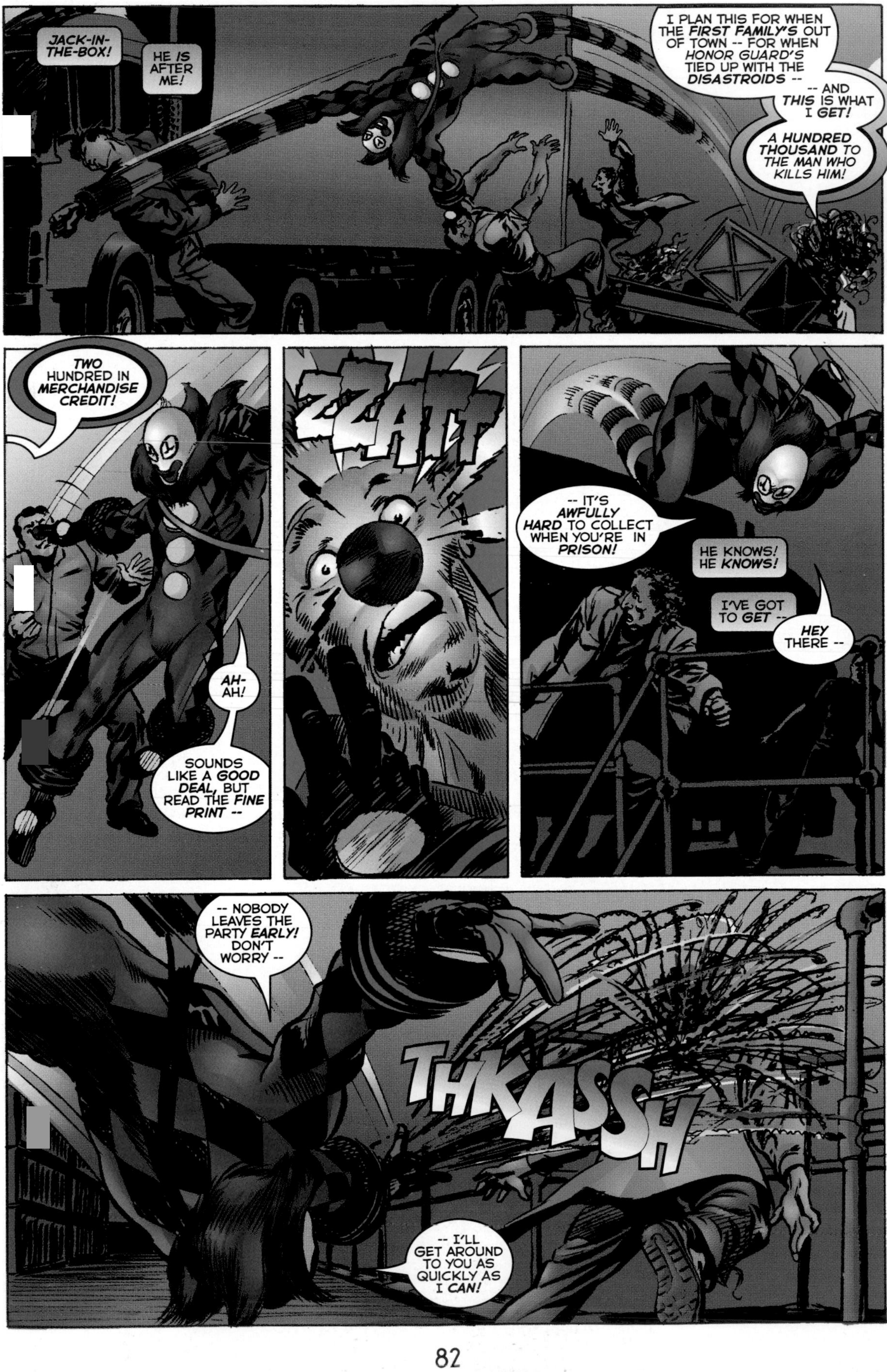

JACK-IN-THE-BOX!
HE IS AFTER ME!
I PLAN THIS FOR WHEN THE FIRST FAMILY'S OUT OF TOWN -- FOR WHEN HONOR GUARD'S TIED UP WITH THE DISASTROIDS --
-- AND THIS IS WHAT I GET!
A HUNDRED THOUSAND TO THE MAN WHO KILLS HIM!
TWO HUNDRED IN MERCHANDISE CREDIT!
AH-AH!
SOUNDS LIKE A GOOD DEAL, BUT READ THE FINE PRINT --
ZZATT
-- IT'S AWFULLY HARD TO COLLECT WHEN YOU'RE IN PRISON!
HE KNOWS! HE KNOWS!
I'VE GOT TO GET --
HEY THERE --
-- NOBODY LEAVES THE PARTY EARLY! DON'T WORRY --
THKASSH
-- I'LL GET AROUND TO YOU AS QUICKLY AS I CAN!

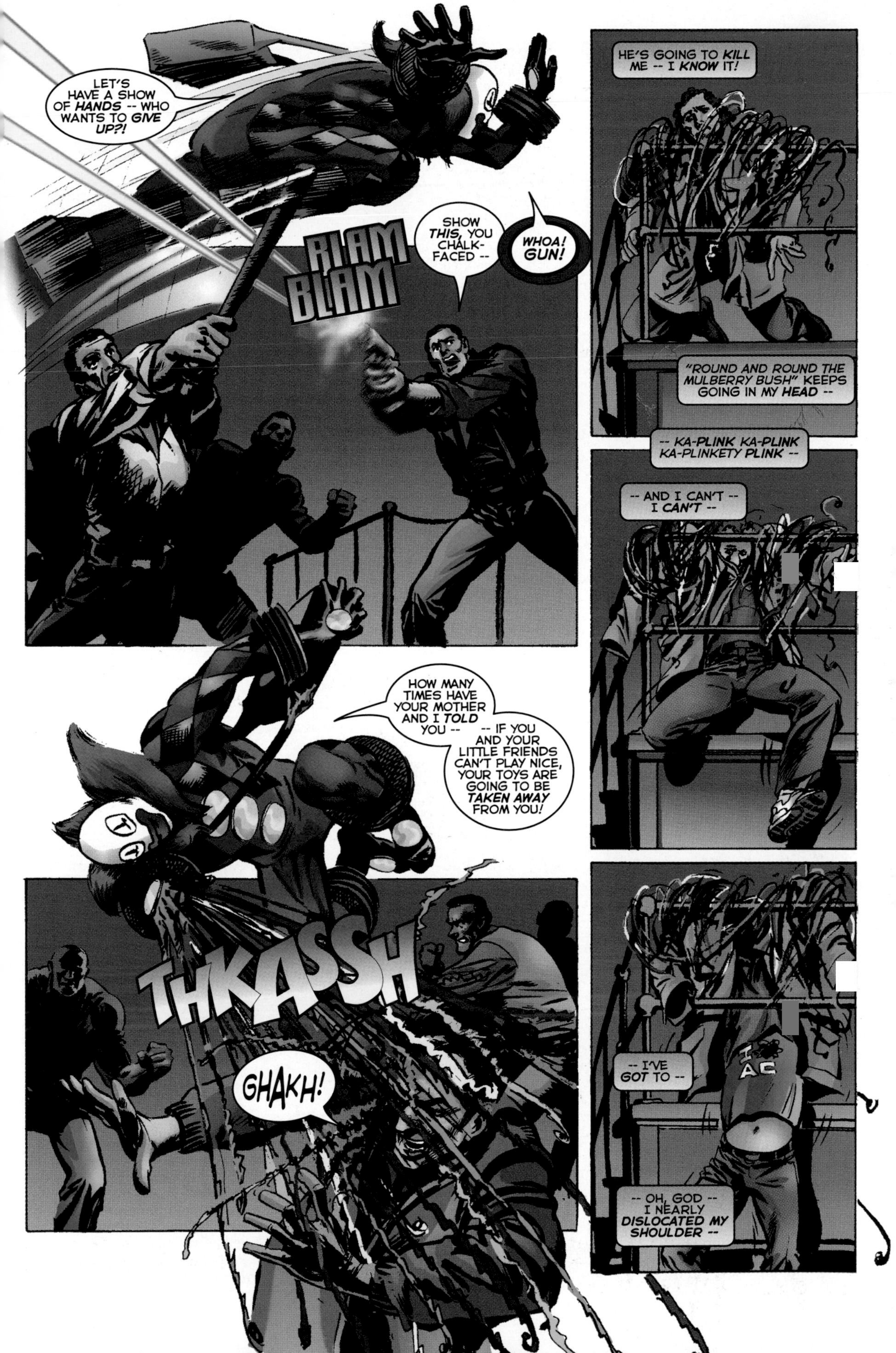
LET'S HAVE A SHOW OF HANDS -- WHO WANTS TO GIVE UP?!
SHOW THIS, YOU CHALK-FACED --
WHOA! GUN!
BLAM BLAM
HE'S GOING TO KILL ME -- I KNOW IT!
"ROUND AND ROUND THE MULBERRY BUSH" KEEPS GOING IN MY HEAD --
-- KA-PLINK KA-PLINK KA-PLINKETY PLINK --
-- AND I CAN'T -- I CAN'T --
HOW MANY TIMES HAVE YOUR MOTHER AND I TOLD YOU --
-- IF YOU AND YOUR LITTLE FRIENDS CAN'T PLAY NICE, YOUR TOYS ARE GOING TO BE TAKEN AWAY FROM YOU!
THKASSH
GHAKH!
-- I'VE GOT TO --
-- OH, GOD -- I NEARLY DISLOCATED MY SHOULDER --

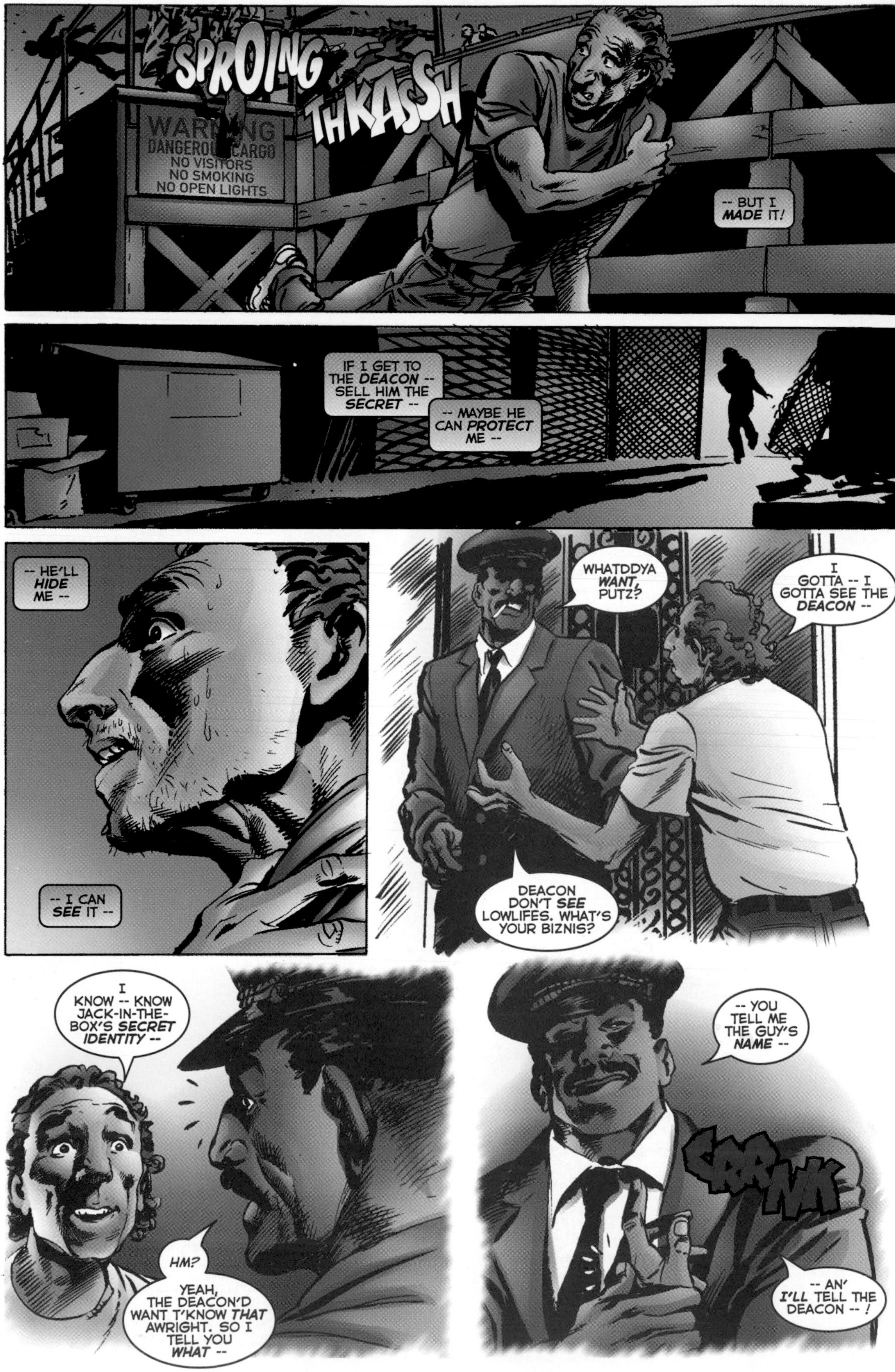
SPROING
THKASSH
WARNING
DANGEROUS CARGO
NO VISITORS
NO SMOKING
NO OPEN LIGHTS
-- BUT I MADE IT!
IF I GET TO THE DEACON -- SELL HIM THE SECRET --
-- MAYBE HE CAN PROTECT ME --
-- HE'LL HIDE ME --
-- I CAN SEE IT --
WHATDDYA WANT, PUTZ?
I GOTTA -- I GOTTA SEE THE DEACON --
DEACON DON'T SEE LOWLIFES. WHAT'S YOUR BIZNIS?
I KNOW -- KNOW JACK-IN-THE-BOX'S SECRET IDENTITY --
HM?
YEAH, THE DEACON'D WANT T'KNOW THAT AWRIGHT. SO I TELL YOU WHAT --
-- YOU TELL ME THE GUY'S NAME --
CRRUNK
-- AN' I'LL TELL THE DEACON -- !

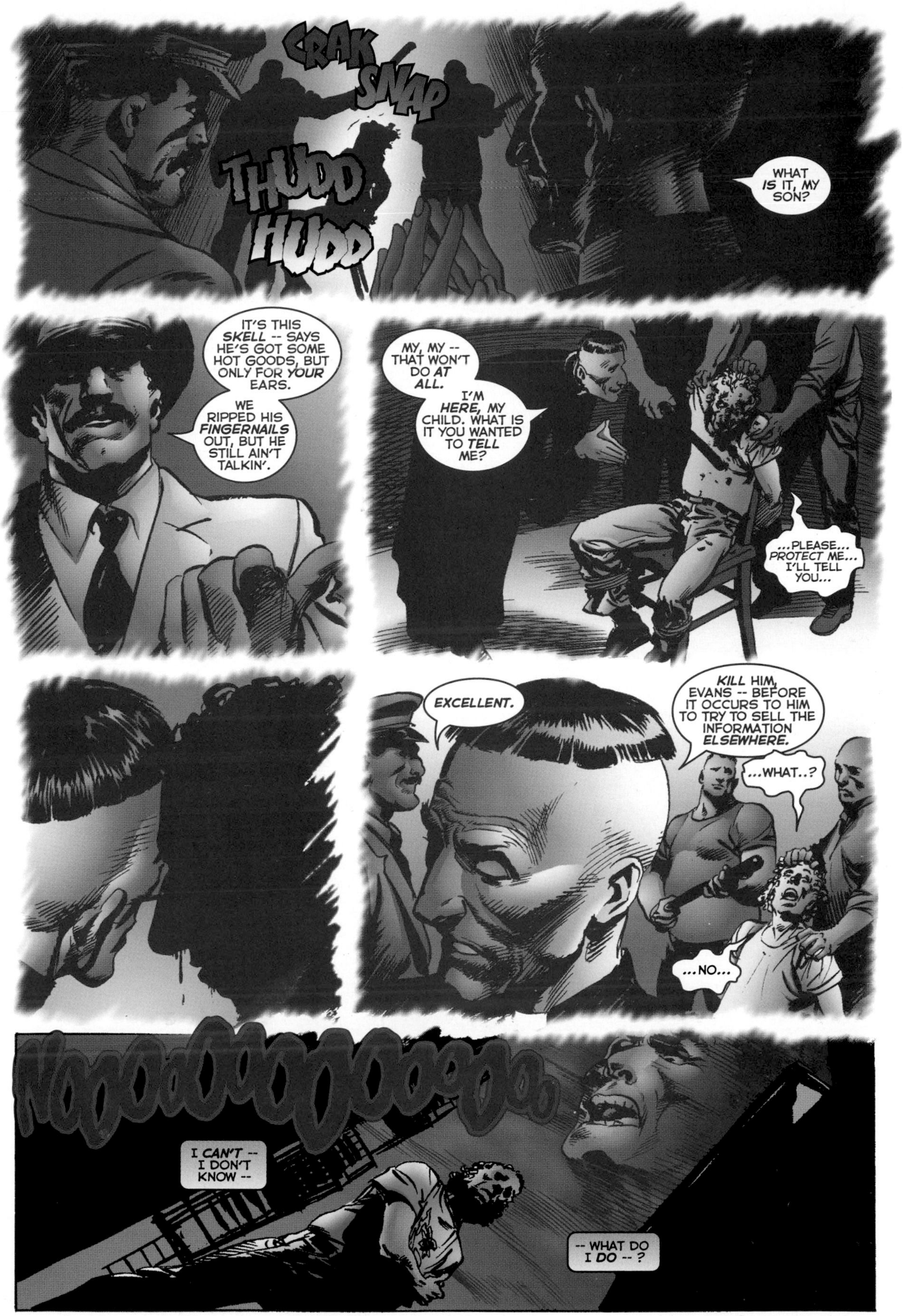
CRAK
SNAP
THUDD
HUDD
WHAT *IS* IT, MY SON?
IT'S THIS *SKELL* -- SAYS HE'S GOT SOME HOT GOODS, BUT ONLY FOR *YOUR* EARS.
WE RIPPED HIS *FINGERNAILS* OUT, BUT HE STILL AIN'T TALKIN'.
MY, MY -- THAT WON'T DO *AT ALL.*
I'M *HERE,* MY CHILD. WHAT IS IT YOU WANTED TO *TELL* ME?
...PLEASE... *PROTECT ME*... I'LL TELL YOU...
EXCELLENT.
KILL HIM, EVANS -- BEFORE IT OCCURS TO HIM TO TRY TO SELL THE INFORMATION *ELSEWHERE.*
...WHAT..?
...NO...
NOOOOOOOOOOOOOOO
I *CAN'T* -- I DON'T KNOW --
-- WHAT DO I *DO* -- ?

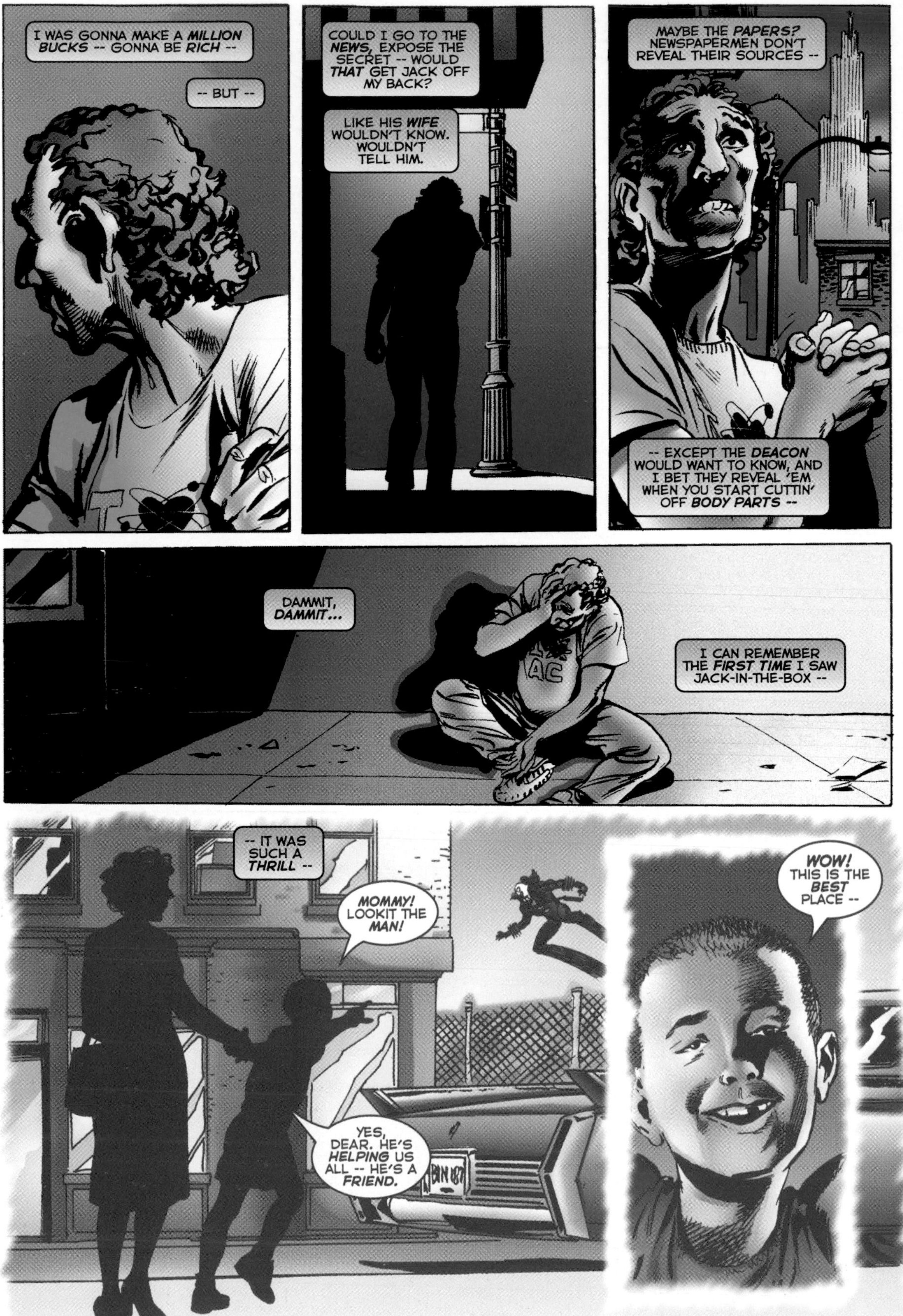
I WAS GONNA MAKE A MILLION BUCKS -- GONNA BE RICH --
-- BUT --
COULD I GO TO THE NEWS, EXPOSE THE SECRET -- WOULD THAT GET JACK OFF MY BACK?
LIKE HIS WIFE WOULDN'T KNOW. WOULDN'T TELL HIM.
MAYBE THE PAPERS? NEWSPAPERMEN DON'T REVEAL THEIR SOURCES --
-- EXCEPT THE DEACON WOULD WANT TO KNOW, AND I BET THEY REVEAL 'EM WHEN YOU START CUTTIN' OFF BODY PARTS --
DAMMIT, DAMMIT...
I CAN REMEMBER THE FIRST TIME I SAW JACK-IN-THE-BOX --
-- IT WAS SUCH A THRILL --
MOMMY! LOOKIT THE MAN!
YES, DEAR. HE'S HELPING US ALL -- HE'S A FRIEND.
WOW! THIS IS THE BEST PLACE --

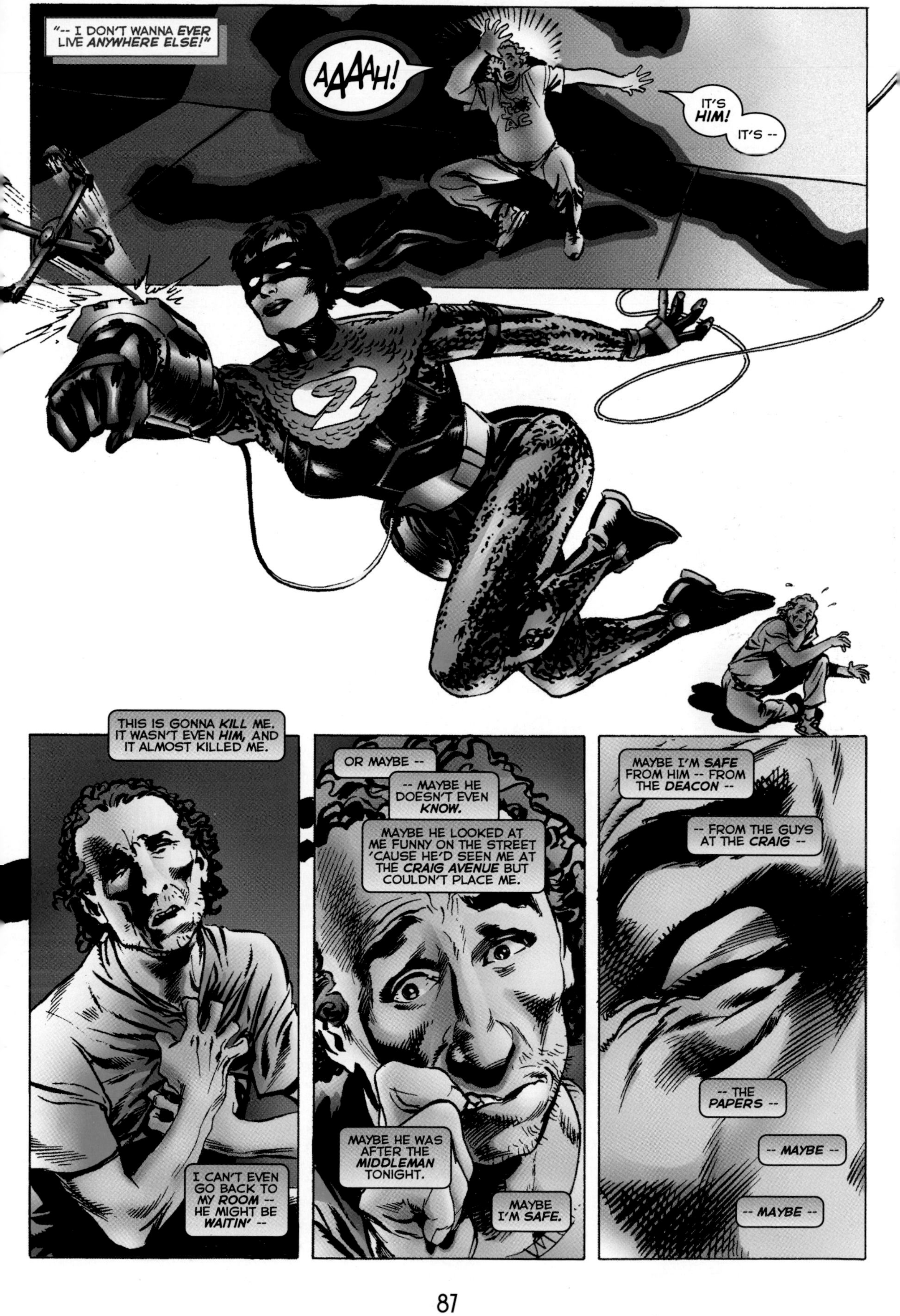
"-- I DON'T WANNA EVER LIVE ANYWHERE ELSE!"
AAAAH!
IT'S HIM!
IT'S --
THIS IS GONNA KILL ME. IT WASN'T EVEN HIM, AND IT ALMOST KILLED ME.
I CAN'T EVEN GO BACK TO MY ROOM -- HE MIGHT BE WAITIN' --
OR MAYBE --
-- MAYBE HE DOESN'T EVEN KNOW.
MAYBE HE LOOKED AT ME FUNNY ON THE STREET 'CAUSE HE'D SEEN ME AT THE CRAIG AVENUE BUT COULDN'T PLACE ME.
MAYBE HE WAS AFTER THE MIDDLEMAN TONIGHT.
MAYBE I'M SAFE.
MAYBE I'M SAFE FROM HIM -- FROM THE DEACON --
-- FROM THE GUYS AT THE CRAIG --
-- THE PAPERS --
-- MAYBE --
-- MAYBE --

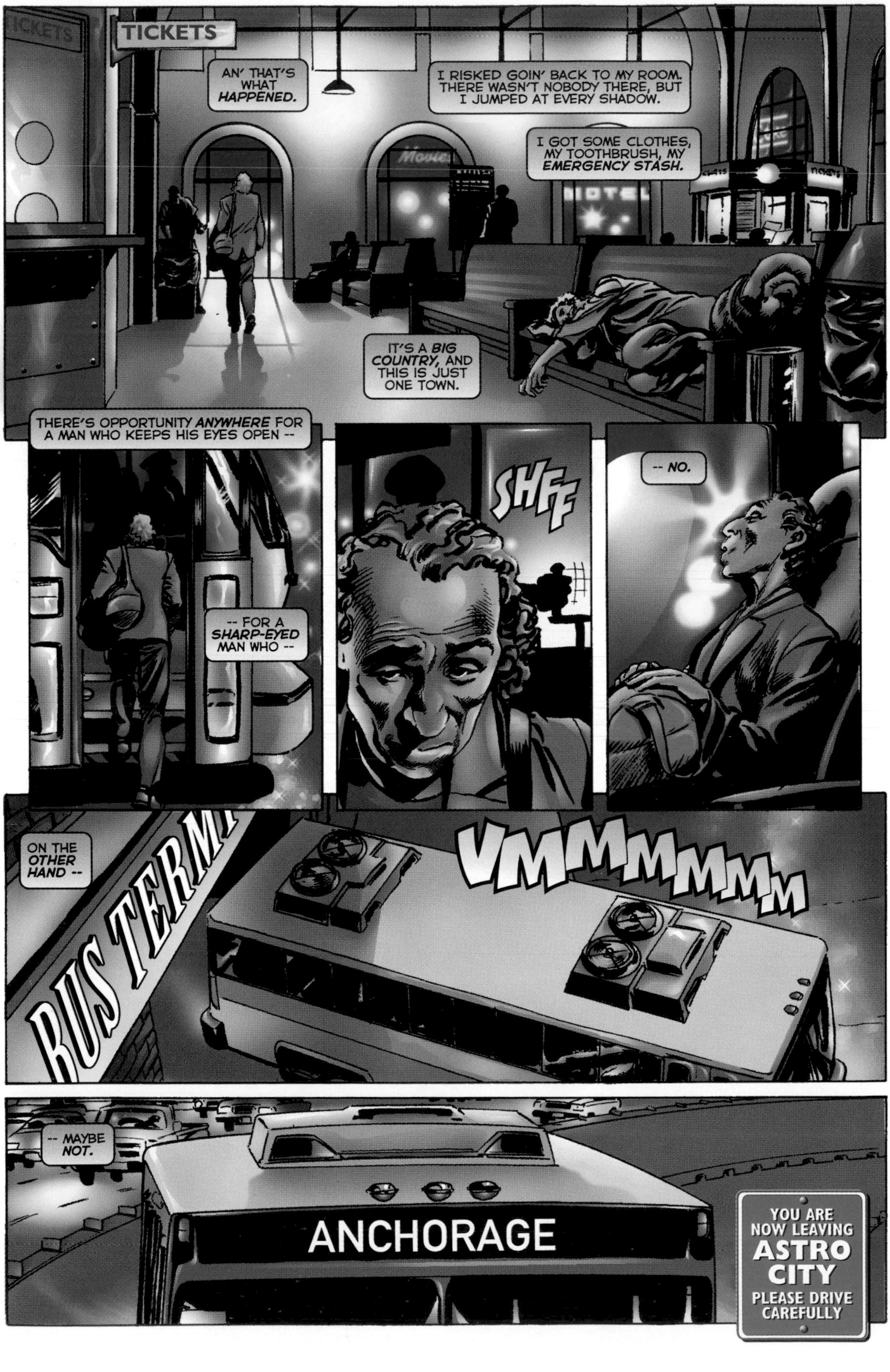
TICKETS
AN' THAT'S WHAT *HAPPENED.*
I RISKED GOIN' BACK TO MY ROOM. THERE WASN'T NOBODY THERE, BUT I JUMPED AT EVERY SHADOW.
I GOT SOME CLOTHES, MY TOOTHBRUSH, MY *EMERGENCY STASH.*
HOTEL
IT'S A *BIG COUNTRY,* AND THIS IS JUST ONE TOWN.
THERE'S OPPORTUNITY *ANYWHERE* FOR A MAN WHO KEEPS HIS EYES OPEN --
-- FOR A *SHARP-EYED* MAN WHO --
SHFF
-- *NO.*
ON THE *OTHER HAND* --
BUS TERM
VMMMMMMM
-- MAYBE *NOT.*
ANCHORAGE
YOU ARE NOW LEAVING ASTRO CITY PLEASE DRIVE CAREFULLY

CHAPTER 4

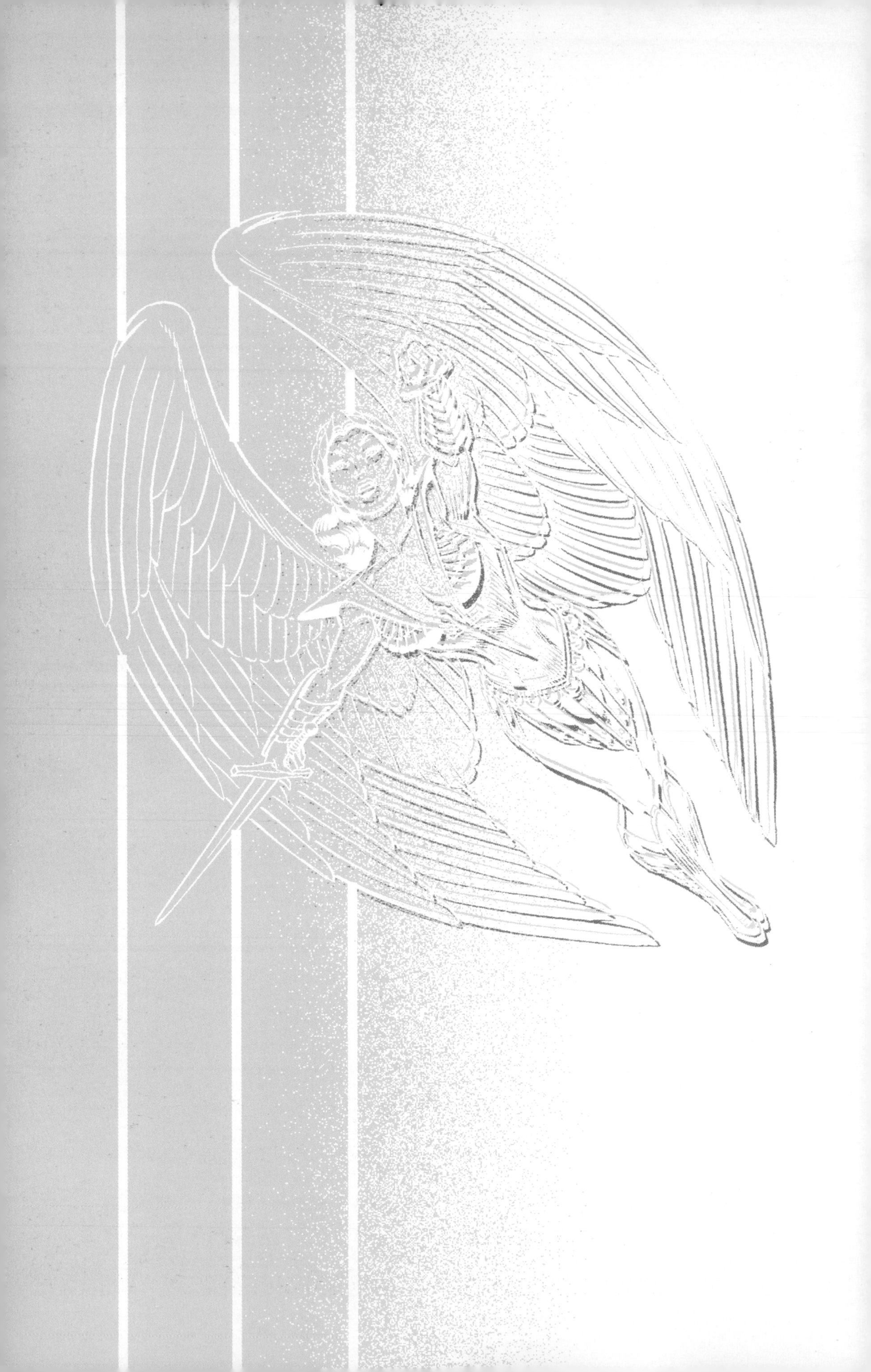

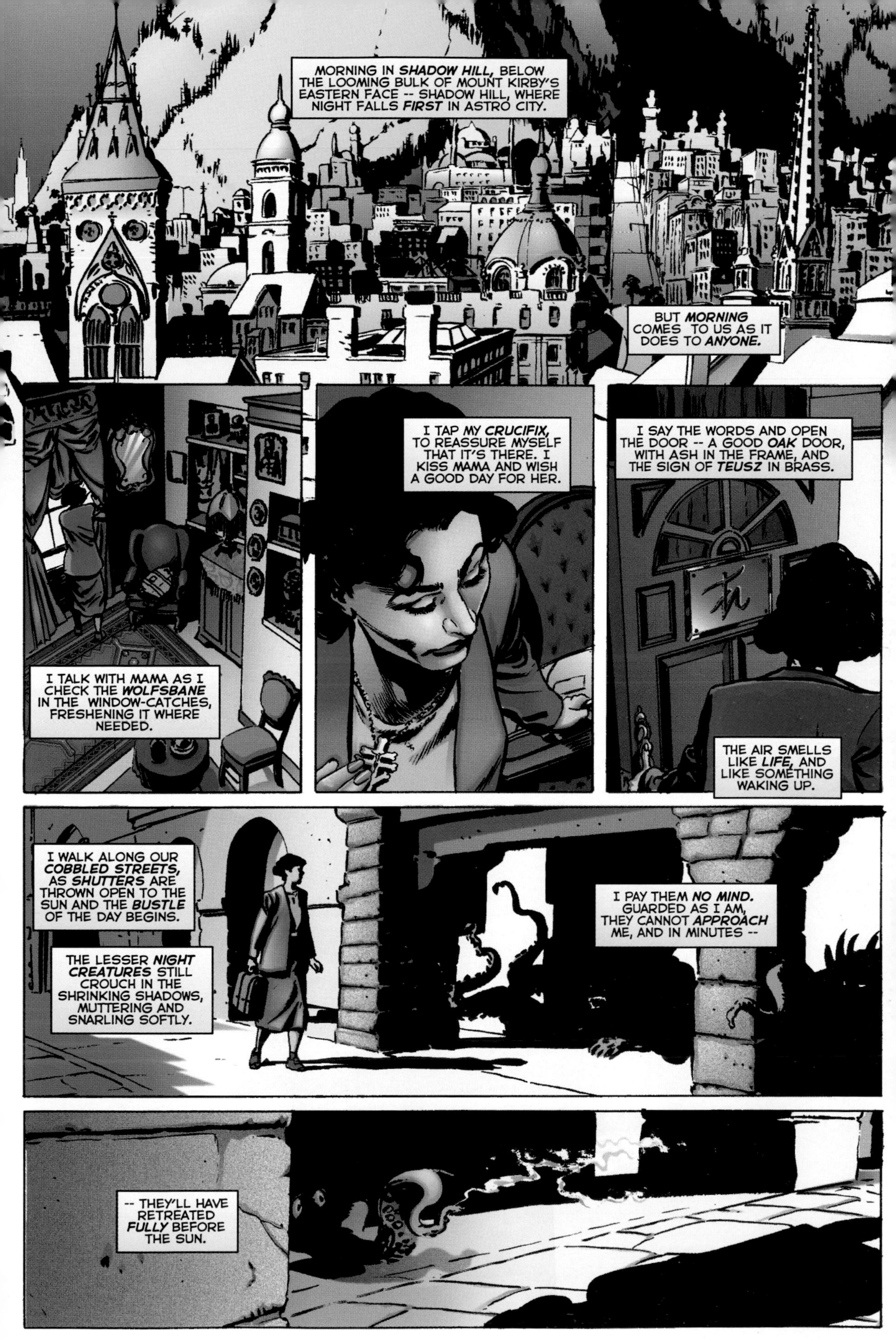
MORNING IN SHADOW HILL, BELOW THE LOOMING BULK OF MOUNT KIRBY'S EASTERN FACE -- SHADOW HILL, WHERE NIGHT FALLS FIRST IN ASTRO CITY.
BUT MORNING COMES TO US AS IT DOES TO ANYONE.
I TALK WITH MAMA AS I CHECK THE WOLFSBANE IN THE WINDOW-CATCHES, FRESHENING IT WHERE NEEDED.
I TAP MY CRUCIFIX, TO REASSURE MYSELF THAT IT'S THERE. I KISS MAMA AND WISH A GOOD DAY FOR HER.
I SAY THE WORDS AND OPEN THE DOOR -- A GOOD OAK DOOR, WITH ASH IN THE FRAME, AND THE SIGN OF TEUSZ IN BRASS.
THE AIR SMELLS LIKE LIFE, AND LIKE SOMETHING WAKING UP.
I WALK ALONG OUR COBBLED STREETS, AS SHUTTERS ARE THROWN OPEN TO THE SUN AND THE BUSTLE OF THE DAY BEGINS.
THE LESSER NIGHT CREATURES STILL CROUCH IN THE SHRINKING SHADOWS, MUTTERING AND SNARLING SOFTLY.
I PAY THEM NO MIND. GUARDED AS I AM, THEY CANNOT APPROACH ME, AND IN MINUTES --
-- THEY'LL HAVE RETREATED FULLY BEFORE THE SUN.

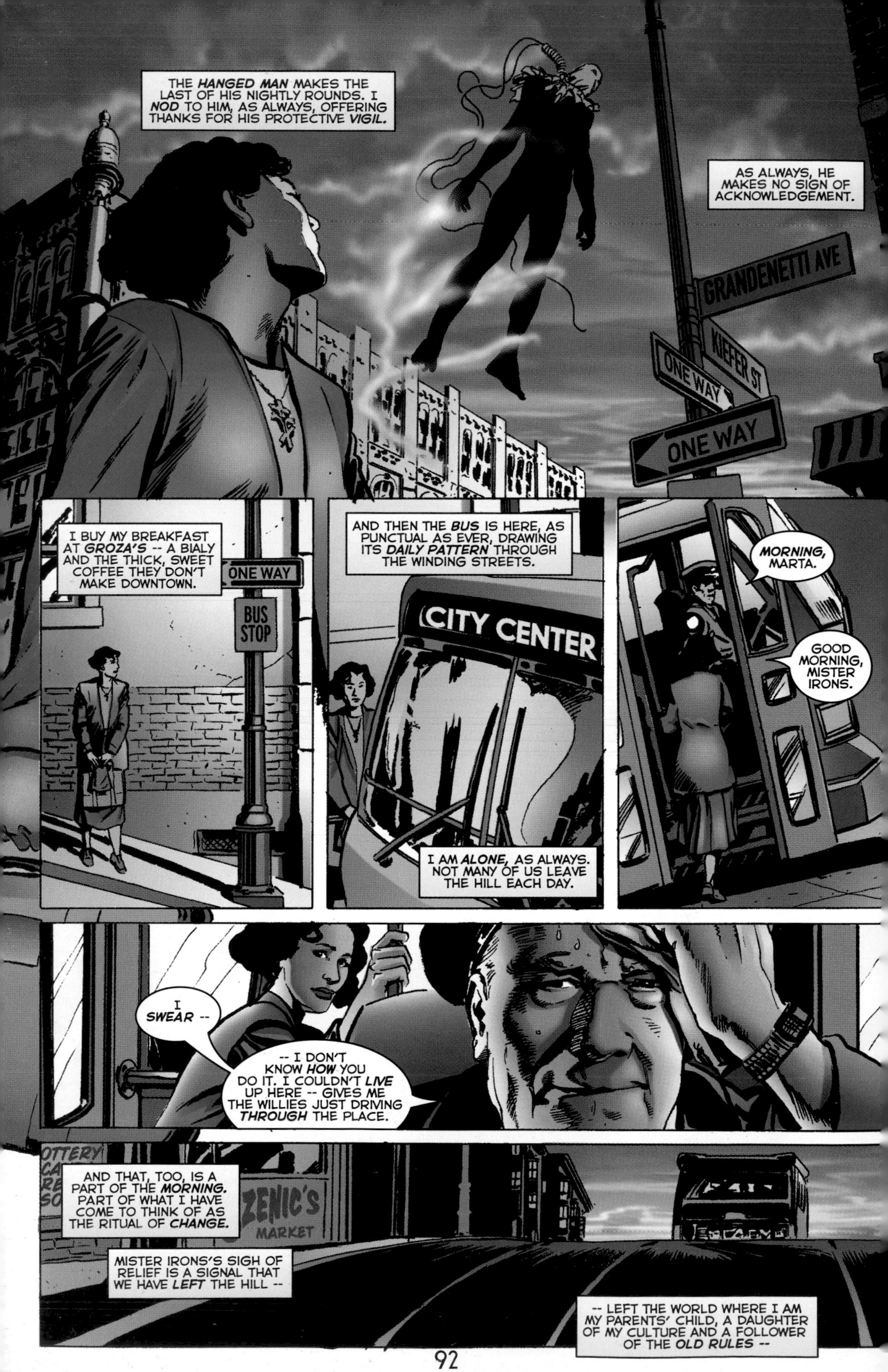
THE HANGED MAN MAKES THE LAST OF HIS NIGHTLY ROUNDS. I NOD TO HIM, AS ALWAYS, OFFERING THANKS FOR HIS PROTECTIVE VIGIL.
AS ALWAYS, HE MAKES NO SIGN OF ACKNOWLEDGEMENT.
GRANDENETTI AVE
KIEFER ST
ONE WAY
ONE WAY
I BUY MY BREAKFAST AT GROZA'S -- A BIALY AND THE THICK, SWEET COFFEE THEY DON'T MAKE DOWNTOWN.
ONE WAY
BUS STOP
AND THEN THE BUS IS HERE, AS PUNCTUAL AS EVER, DRAWING ITS DAILY PATTERN THROUGH THE WINDING STREETS.
CITY CENTER
I AM ALONE, AS ALWAYS. NOT MANY OF US LEAVE THE HILL EACH DAY.
MORNING, MARTA.
GOOD MORNING, MISTER IRONS.
I SWEAR --
-- I DON'T KNOW HOW YOU DO IT. I COULDN'T LIVE UP HERE -- GIVES ME THE WILLIES JUST DRIVING THROUGH THE PLACE.
AND THAT, TOO, IS A PART OF THE MORNING. PART OF WHAT I HAVE COME TO THINK OF AS THE RITUAL OF CHANGE.
ZENIC'S MARKET
MISTER IRONS'S SIGH OF RELIEF IS A SIGNAL THAT WE HAVE LEFT THE HILL --
-- LEFT THE WORLD WHERE I AM MY PARENTS' CHILD, A DAUGHTER OF MY CULTURE AND A FOLLOWER OF THE OLD RULES --

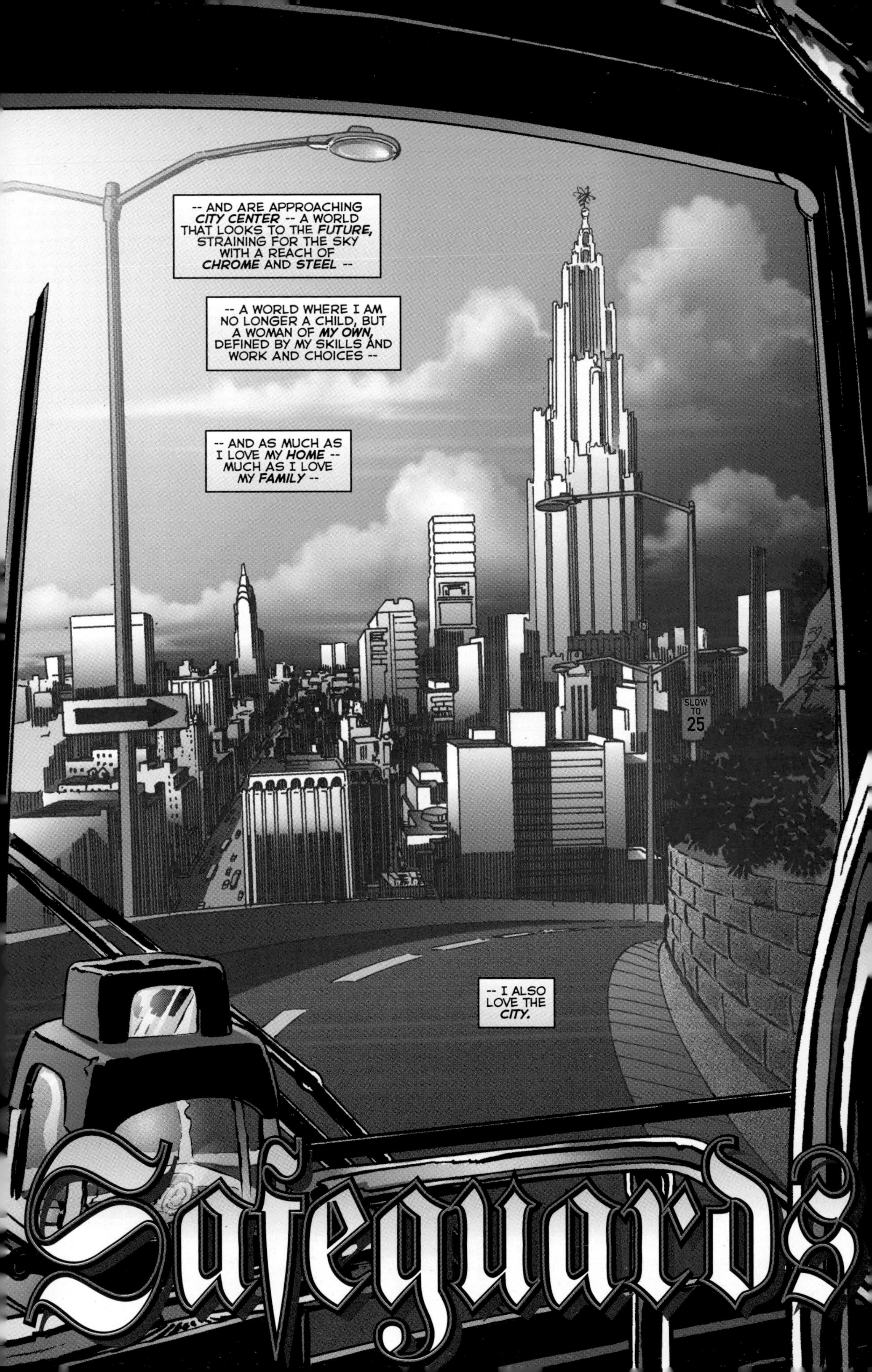
-- AND ARE APPROACHING CITY CENTER -- A WORLD THAT LOOKS TO THE FUTURE, STRAINING FOR THE SKY WITH A REACH OF CHROME AND STEEL --
-- A WORLD WHERE I AM NO LONGER A CHILD, BUT A WOMAN OF MY OWN, DEFINED BY MY SKILLS AND WORK AND CHOICES --
-- AND AS MUCH AS I LOVE MY HOME -- MUCH AS I LOVE MY FAMILY --
SLOW TO 25
-- I ALSO LOVE THE CITY.
Safeguards

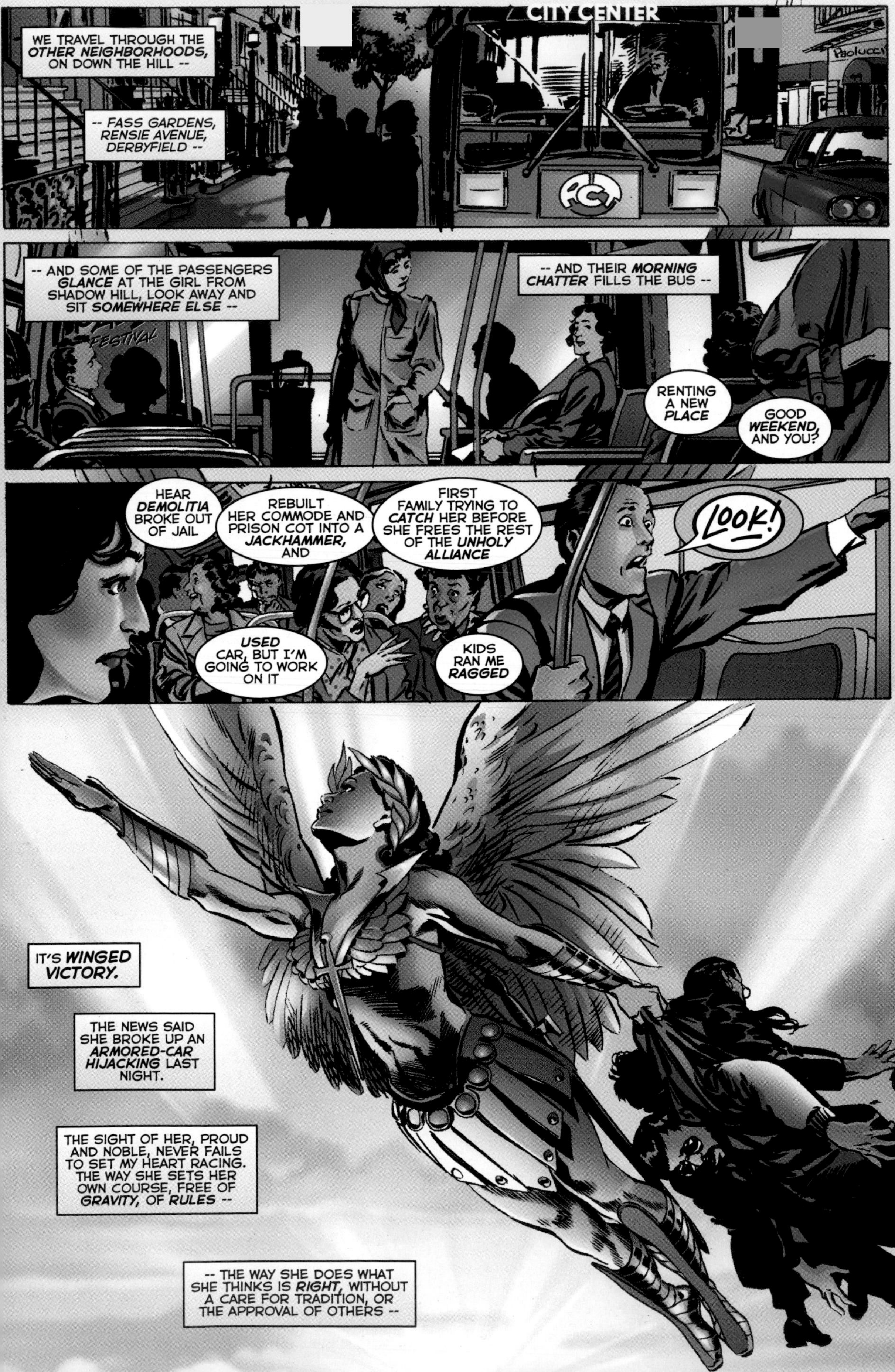
CITY CENTER
WE TRAVEL THROUGH THE OTHER NEIGHBORHOODS, ON DOWN THE HILL --
-- FASS GARDENS, RENSIE AVENUE, DERBYFIELD --
Paolucci
-- AND SOME OF THE PASSENGERS GLANCE AT THE GIRL FROM SHADOW HILL, LOOK AWAY AND SIT SOMEWHERE ELSE --
-- AND THEIR MORNING CHATTER FILLS THE BUS --
RENTING A NEW PLACE
GOOD WEEKEND, AND YOU?
HEAR DEMOLITIA BROKE OUT OF JAIL
REBUILT HER COMMODE AND PRISON COT INTO A JACKHAMMER, AND
FIRST FAMILY TRYING TO CATCH HER BEFORE SHE FREES THE REST OF THE UNHOLY ALLIANCE
LOOK!
USED CAR, BUT I'M GOING TO WORK ON IT
KIDS RAN ME RAGGED
IT'S WINGED VICTORY.
THE NEWS SAID SHE BROKE UP AN ARMORED-CAR HIJACKING LAST NIGHT.
THE SIGHT OF HER, PROUD AND NOBLE, NEVER FAILS TO SET MY HEART RACING. THE WAY SHE SETS HER OWN COURSE, FREE OF GRAVITY, OF RULES --
-- THE WAY SHE DOES WHAT SHE THINKS IS RIGHT, WITHOUT A CARE FOR TRADITION, OR THE APPROVAL OF OTHERS --

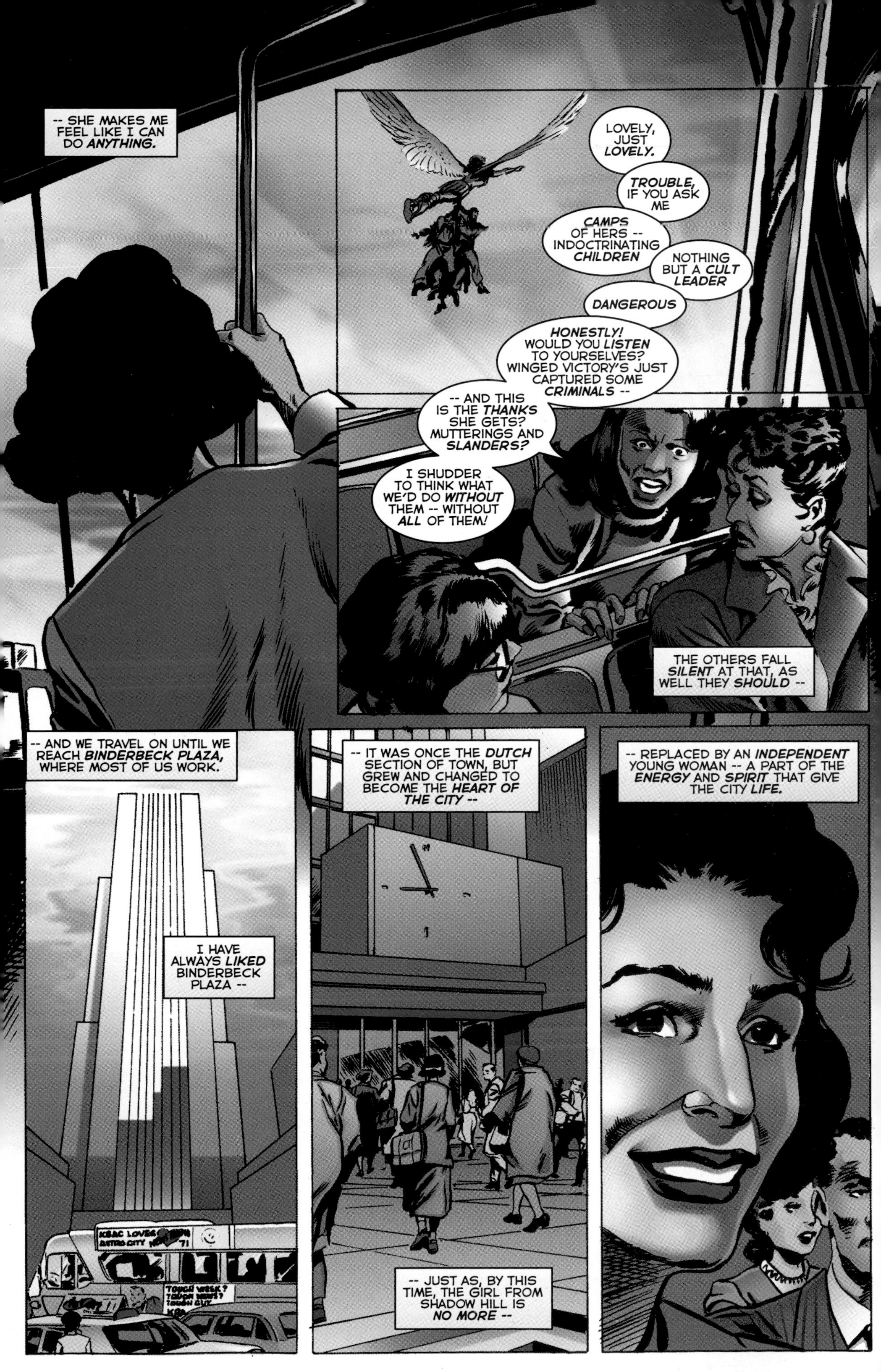

-- SHE MAKES ME FEEL LIKE I CAN DO *ANYTHING.*
LOVELY, JUST *LOVELY.*
TROUBLE, IF YOU ASK ME
CAMPS OF HERS -- INDOCTRINATING *CHILDREN*
NOTHING BUT A *CULT LEADER*
DANGEROUS
HONESTLY! WOULD YOU *LISTEN* TO YOURSELVES? WINGED VICTORY'S JUST CAPTURED SOME *CRIMINALS* --
-- AND THIS IS THE *THANKS* SHE GETS? MUTTERINGS AND *SLANDERS?*
I SHUDDER TO THINK WHAT WE'D DO *WITHOUT* THEM -- WITHOUT *ALL* OF THEM!
THE OTHERS FALL *SILENT* AT THAT, AS WELL THEY *SHOULD* --
-- AND WE TRAVEL ON UNTIL WE REACH *BINDERBECK PLAZA,* WHERE MOST OF US WORK.
I HAVE ALWAYS *LIKED* BINDERBECK PLAZA --
-- IT WAS ONCE THE *DUTCH* SECTION OF TOWN, BUT GREW AND CHANGED TO BECOME THE *HEART OF THE CITY* --
-- JUST AS, BY THIS TIME, THE GIRL FROM SHADOW HILL IS *NO MORE* --
-- REPLACED BY AN *INDEPENDENT* YOUNG WOMAN -- A PART OF THE *ENERGY* AND *SPIRIT* THAT GIVE THE CITY *LIFE.*

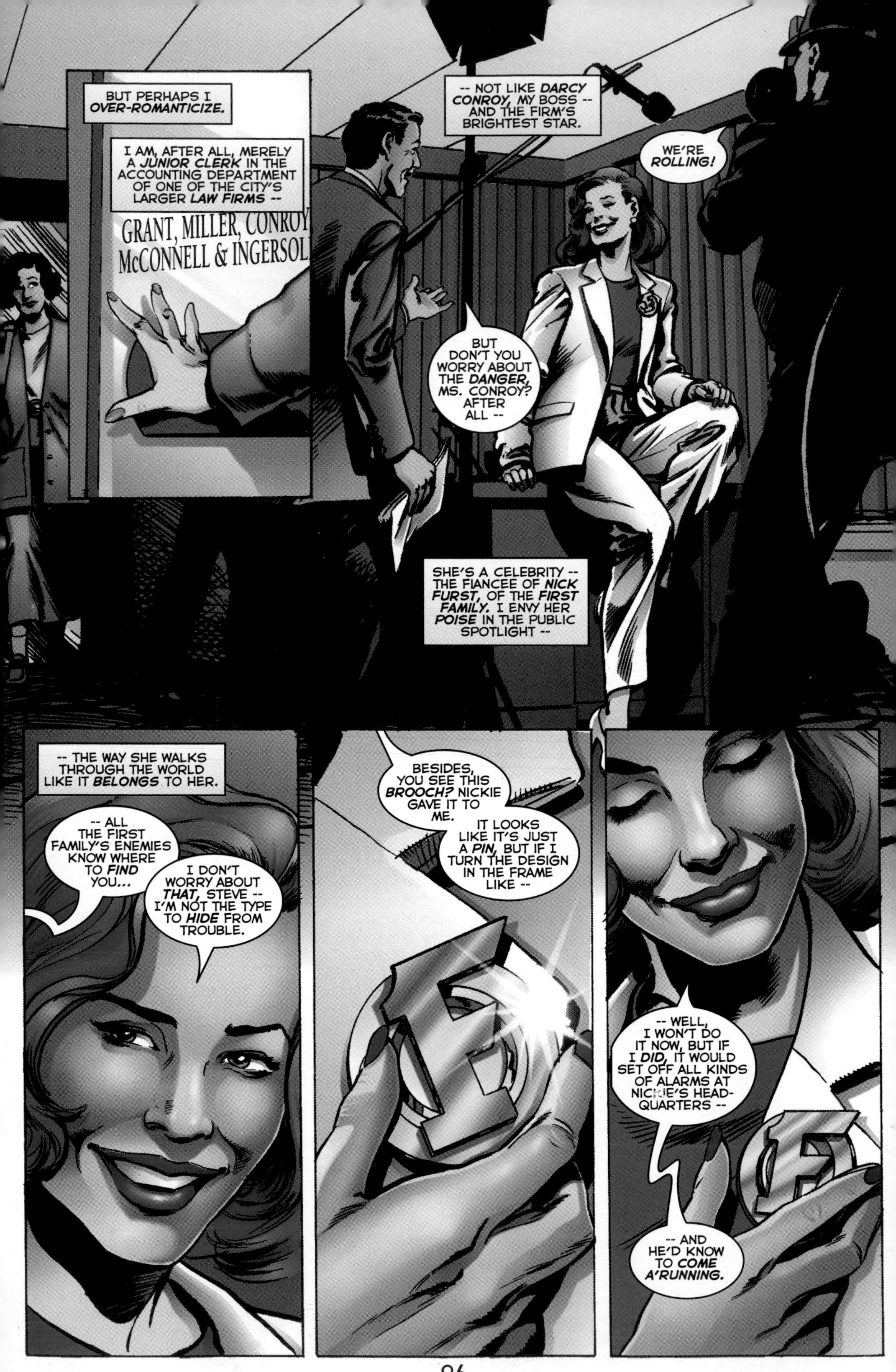
BUT PERHAPS I OVER-ROMANTICIZE.
I AM, AFTER ALL, MERELY A JUNIOR CLERK IN THE ACCOUNTING DEPARTMENT OF ONE OF THE CITY'S LARGER LAW FIRMS --
GRANT, MILLER, CONROY
McCONNELL & INGERSOL
-- NOT LIKE DARCY CONROY, MY BOSS -- AND THE FIRM'S BRIGHTEST STAR.
WE'RE ROLLING!
BUT DON'T YOU WORRY ABOUT THE DANGER, MS. CONROY? AFTER ALL --
SHE'S A CELEBRITY -- THE FIANCEE OF NICK FURST, OF THE FIRST FAMILY. I ENVY HER POISE IN THE PUBLIC SPOTLIGHT --
-- THE WAY SHE WALKS THROUGH THE WORLD LIKE IT BELONGS TO HER.
-- ALL THE FIRST FAMILY'S ENEMIES KNOW WHERE TO FIND YOU...
I DON'T WORRY ABOUT THAT, STEVE -- I'M NOT THE TYPE TO HIDE FROM TROUBLE.
BESIDES, YOU SEE THIS BROOCH? NICKIE GAVE IT TO ME.
IT LOOKS LIKE IT'S JUST A PIN, BUT IF I TURN THE DESIGN IN THE FRAME LIKE --
-- WELL, I WON'T DO IT NOW, BUT IF I DID, IT WOULD SET OFF ALL KINDS OF ALARMS AT NICKIE'S HEAD-QUARTERS --
-- AND HE'D KNOW TO COME A'RUNNING.

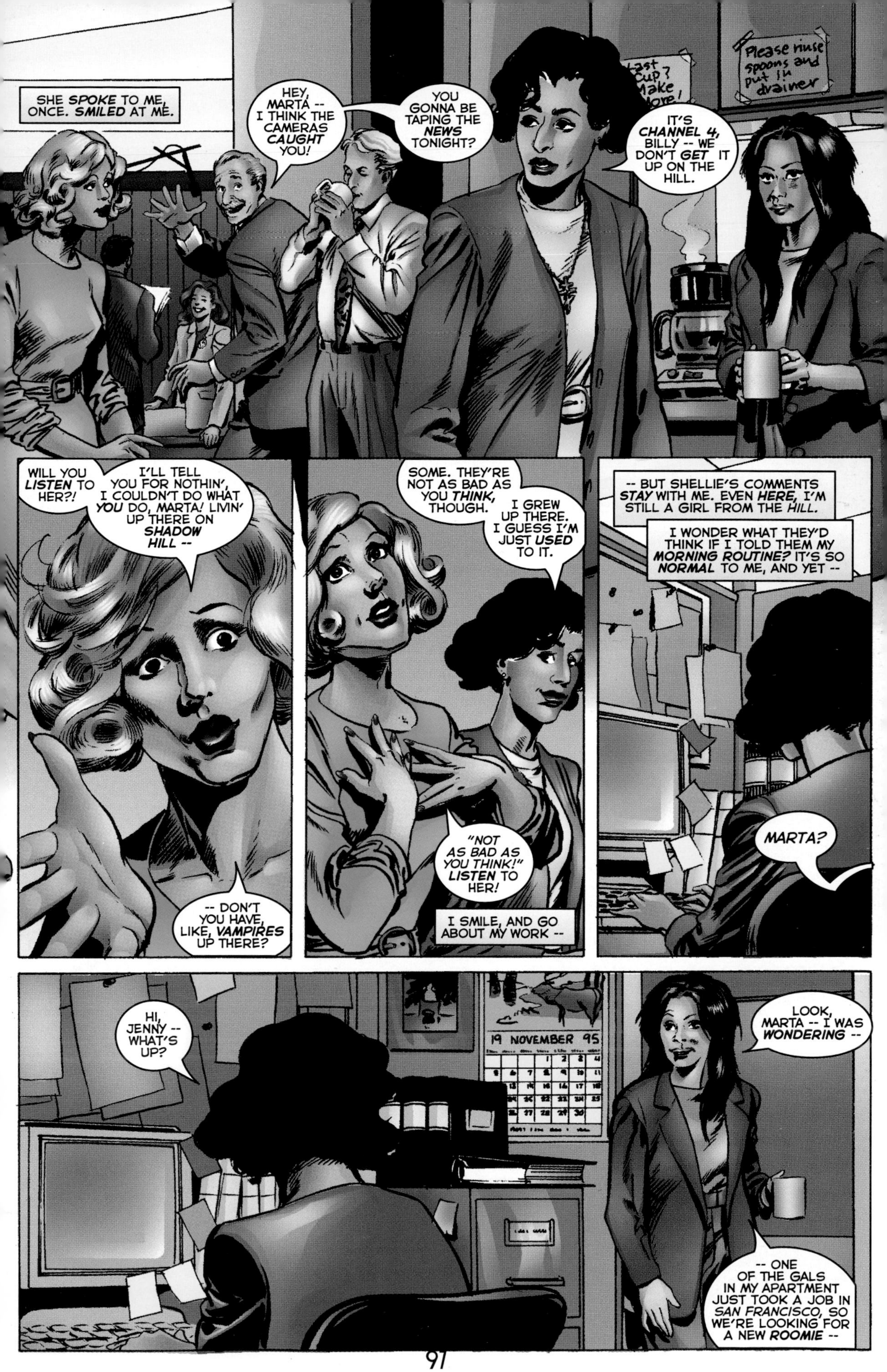
SHE SPOKE TO ME, ONCE. SMILED AT ME.
HEY, MARTA -- I THINK THE CAMERAS CAUGHT YOU!
YOU GONNA BE TAPING THE NEWS TONIGHT?
Please rinse spoons and put in drainer
IT'S CHANNEL 4, BILLY -- WE DON'T GET IT UP ON THE HILL.
WILL YOU LISTEN TO HER?!
I'LL TELL YOU FOR NOTHIN', I COULDN'T DO WHAT YOU DO, MARTA! LIVIN' UP THERE ON SHADOW HILL --
-- DON'T YOU HAVE, LIKE, VAMPIRES UP THERE?
SOME. THEY'RE NOT AS BAD AS YOU THINK, THOUGH.
I GREW UP THERE. I GUESS I'M JUST USED TO IT.
"NOT AS BAD AS YOU THINK!" LISTEN TO HER!
I SMILE, AND GO ABOUT MY WORK --
-- BUT SHELLIE'S COMMENTS STAY WITH ME. EVEN HERE, I'M STILL A GIRL FROM THE HILL.
I WONDER WHAT THEY'D THINK IF I TOLD THEM MY MORNING ROUTINE? IT'S SO NORMAL TO ME, AND YET --
MARTA?
HI, JENNY -- WHAT'S UP?
19 NOVEMBER 95
LOOK, MARTA -- I WAS WONDERING --
-- ONE OF THE GALS IN MY APARTMENT JUST TOOK A JOB IN SAN FRANCISCO, SO WE'RE LOOKING FOR A NEW ROOMIE --

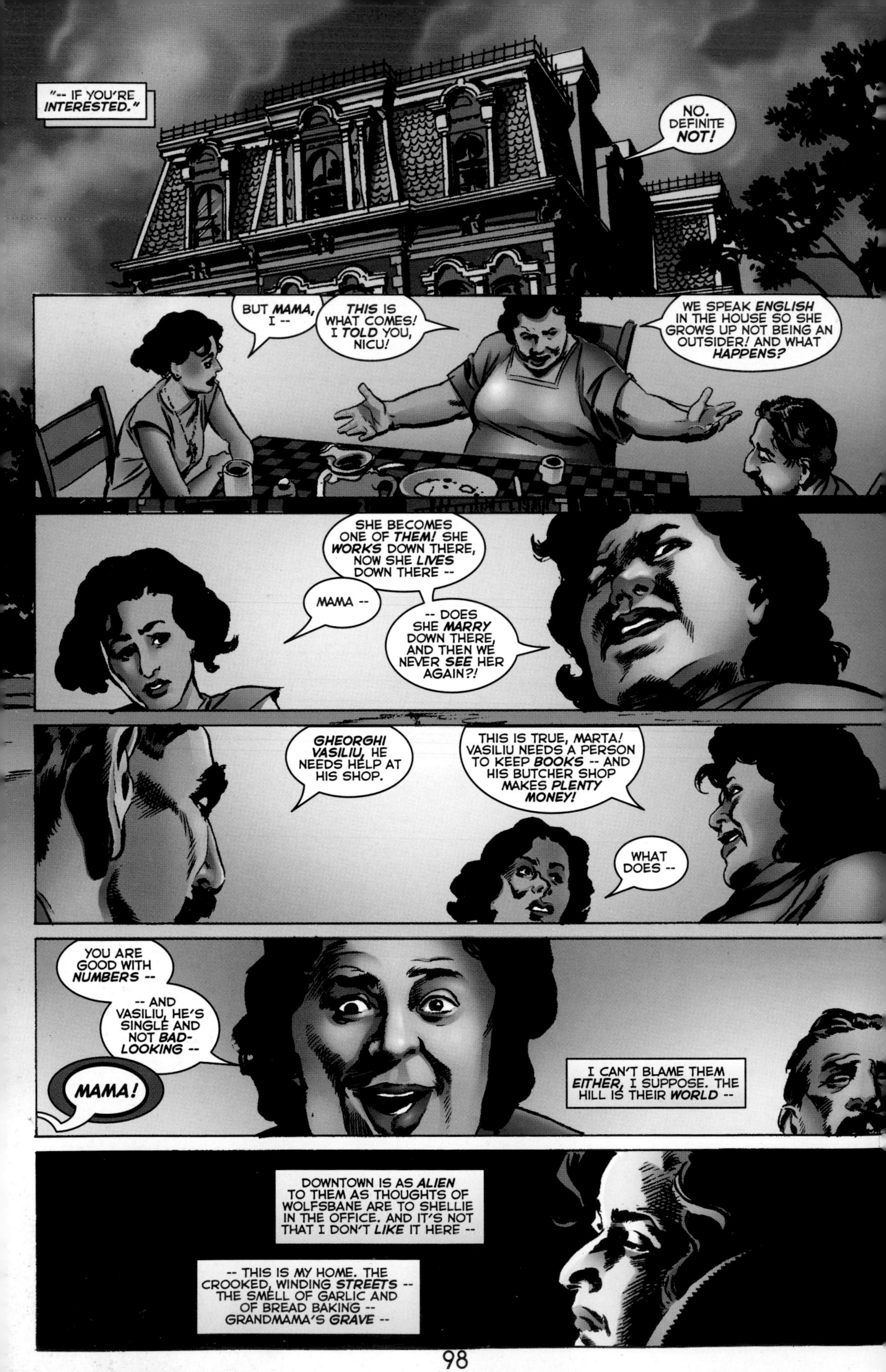
"-- IF YOU'RE INTERESTED."
NO. DEFINITE NOT!
BUT MAMA, I --
THIS IS WHAT COMES! I TOLD YOU, NICU!
WE SPEAK ENGLISH IN THE HOUSE SO SHE GROWS UP NOT BEING AN OUTSIDER! AND WHAT HAPPENS?
SHE BECOMES ONE OF THEM! SHE WORKS DOWN THERE, NOW SHE LIVES DOWN THERE --
MAMA --
-- DOES SHE MARRY DOWN THERE, AND THEN WE NEVER SEE HER AGAIN?!
GHEORGHI VASILIU, HE NEEDS HELP AT HIS SHOP.
THIS IS TRUE, MARTA! VASILIU NEEDS A PERSON TO KEEP BOOKS -- AND HIS BUTCHER SHOP MAKES PLENTY MONEY!
WHAT DOES --
YOU ARE GOOD WITH NUMBERS --
-- AND VASILIU, HE'S SINGLE AND NOT BAD-LOOKING --
MAMA!
I CAN'T BLAME THEM EITHER, I SUPPOSE. THE HILL IS THEIR WORLD --
DOWNTOWN IS AS ALIEN TO THEM AS THOUGHTS OF WOLFSBANE ARE TO SHELLIE IN THE OFFICE. AND IT'S NOT THAT I DON'T LIKE IT HERE --
-- THIS IS MY HOME. THE CROOKED, WINDING STREETS -- THE SMELL OF GARLIC AND OF BREAD BAKING -- GRANDMAMA'S GRAVE --

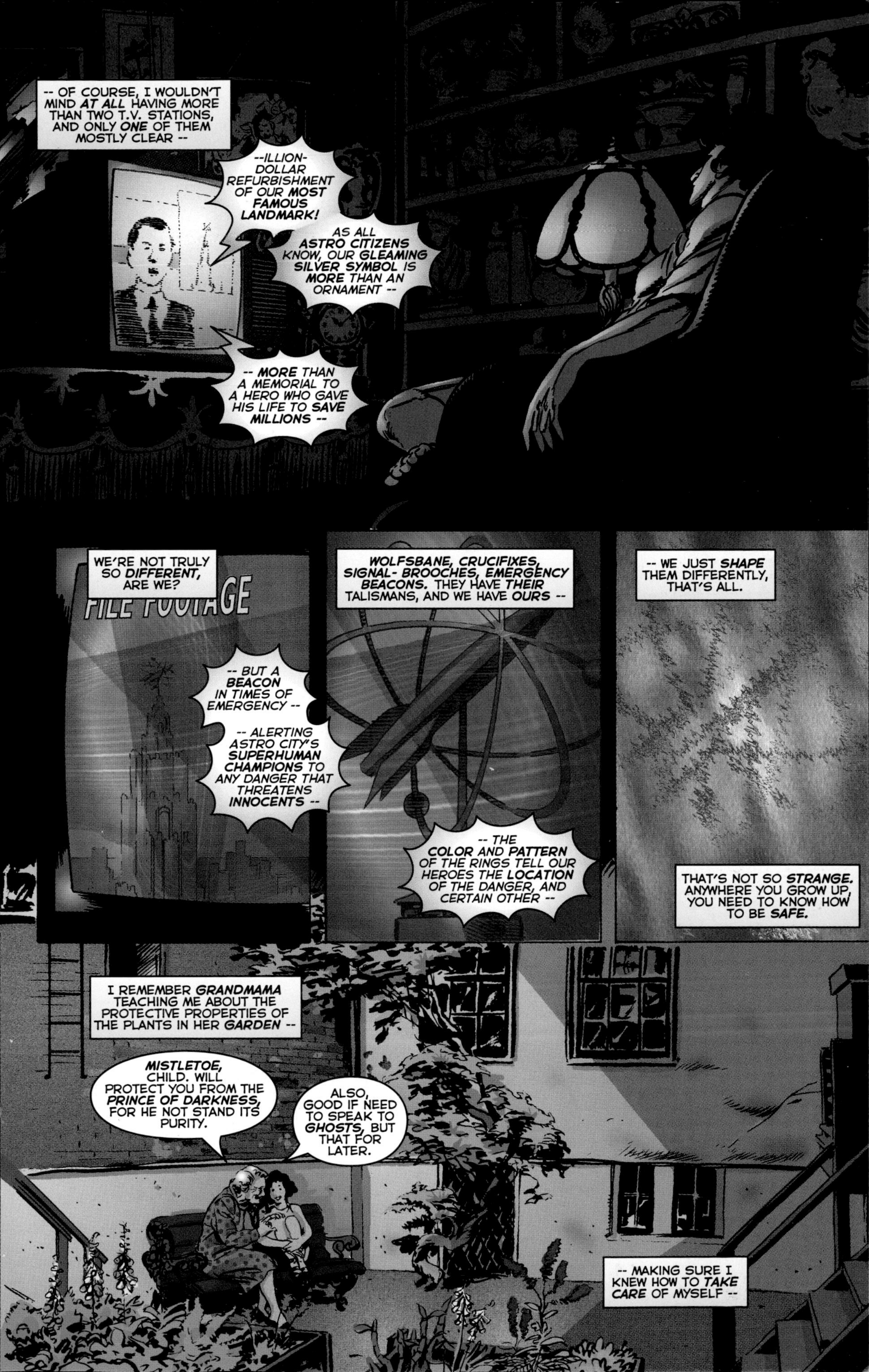

-- OF COURSE, I WOULDN'T MIND AT ALL HAVING MORE THAN TWO T.V. STATIONS, AND ONLY ONE OF THEM MOSTLY CLEAR --
--ILLION-DOLLAR REFURBISHMENT OF OUR MOST FAMOUS LANDMARK!
AS ALL ASTRO CITIZENS KNOW, OUR GLEAMING SILVER SYMBOL IS MORE THAN AN ORNAMENT --
-- MORE THAN A MEMORIAL TO A HERO WHO GAVE HIS LIFE TO SAVE MILLIONS --
WE'RE NOT TRULY SO DIFFERENT, ARE WE?
FILE FOOTAGE
-- BUT A BEACON IN TIMES OF EMERGENCY --
-- ALERTING ASTRO CITY'S SUPERHUMAN CHAMPIONS TO ANY DANGER THAT THREATENS INNOCENTS --
WOLFSBANE, CRUCIFIXES, SIGNAL- BROOCHES, EMERGENCY BEACONS. THEY HAVE THEIR TALISMANS, AND WE HAVE OURS --
-- THE COLOR AND PATTERN OF THE RINGS TELL OUR HEROES THE LOCATION OF THE DANGER, AND CERTAIN OTHER --
-- WE JUST SHAPE THEM DIFFERENTLY, THAT'S ALL.
THAT'S NOT SO STRANGE. ANYWHERE YOU GROW UP, YOU NEED TO KNOW HOW TO BE SAFE.
I REMEMBER GRANDMAMA TEACHING ME ABOUT THE PROTECTIVE PROPERTIES OF THE PLANTS IN HER GARDEN --
MISTLETOE, CHILD. WILL PROTECT YOU FROM THE PRINCE OF DARKNESS, FOR HE NOT STAND ITS PURITY.
ALSO, GOOD IF NEED TO SPEAK TO GHOSTS, BUT THAT FOR LATER.
-- MAKING SURE I KNEW HOW TO TAKE CARE OF MYSELF --

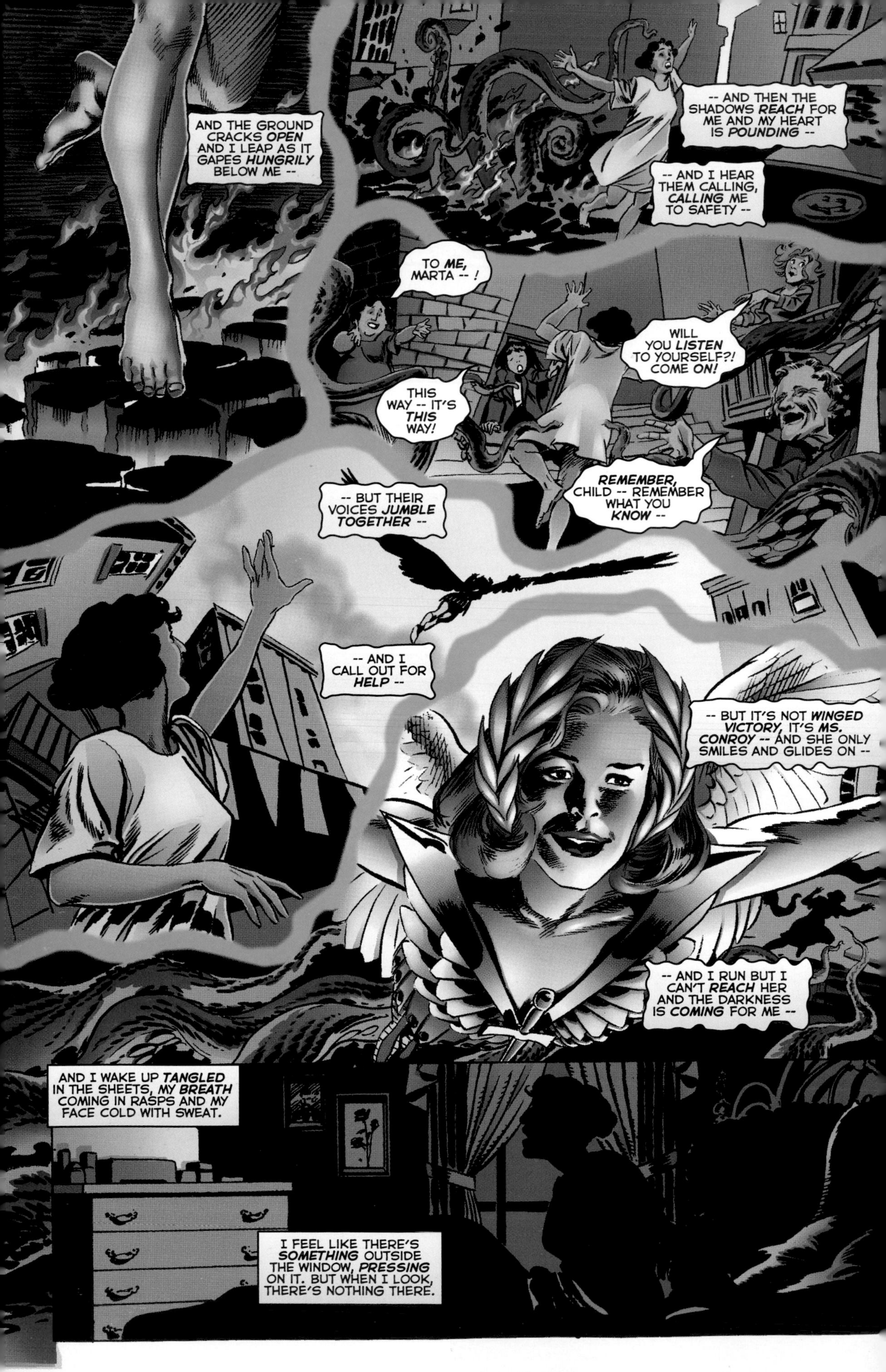
AND THE GROUND CRACKS OPEN AND I LEAP AS IT GAPES HUNGRILY BELOW ME --
-- AND THEN THE SHADOWS REACH FOR ME AND MY HEART IS POUNDING --
-- AND I HEAR THEM CALLING, CALLING ME TO SAFETY --
TO ME, MARTA -- !
WILL YOU LISTEN TO YOURSELF?! COME ON!
THIS WAY -- IT'S THIS WAY!
REMEMBER, CHILD -- REMEMBER WHAT YOU KNOW --
-- BUT THEIR VOICES JUMBLE TOGETHER --
-- AND I CALL OUT FOR HELP --
-- BUT IT'S NOT WINGED VICTORY, IT'S MS. CONROY -- AND SHE ONLY SMILES AND GLIDES ON --
-- AND I RUN BUT I CAN'T REACH HER AND THE DARKNESS IS COMING FOR ME --
AND I WAKE UP TANGLED IN THE SHEETS, MY BREATH COMING IN RASPS AND MY FACE COLD WITH SWEAT.
I FEEL LIKE THERE'S SOMETHING OUTSIDE THE WINDOW, PRESSING ON IT. BUT WHEN I LOOK, THERE'S NOTHING THERE.

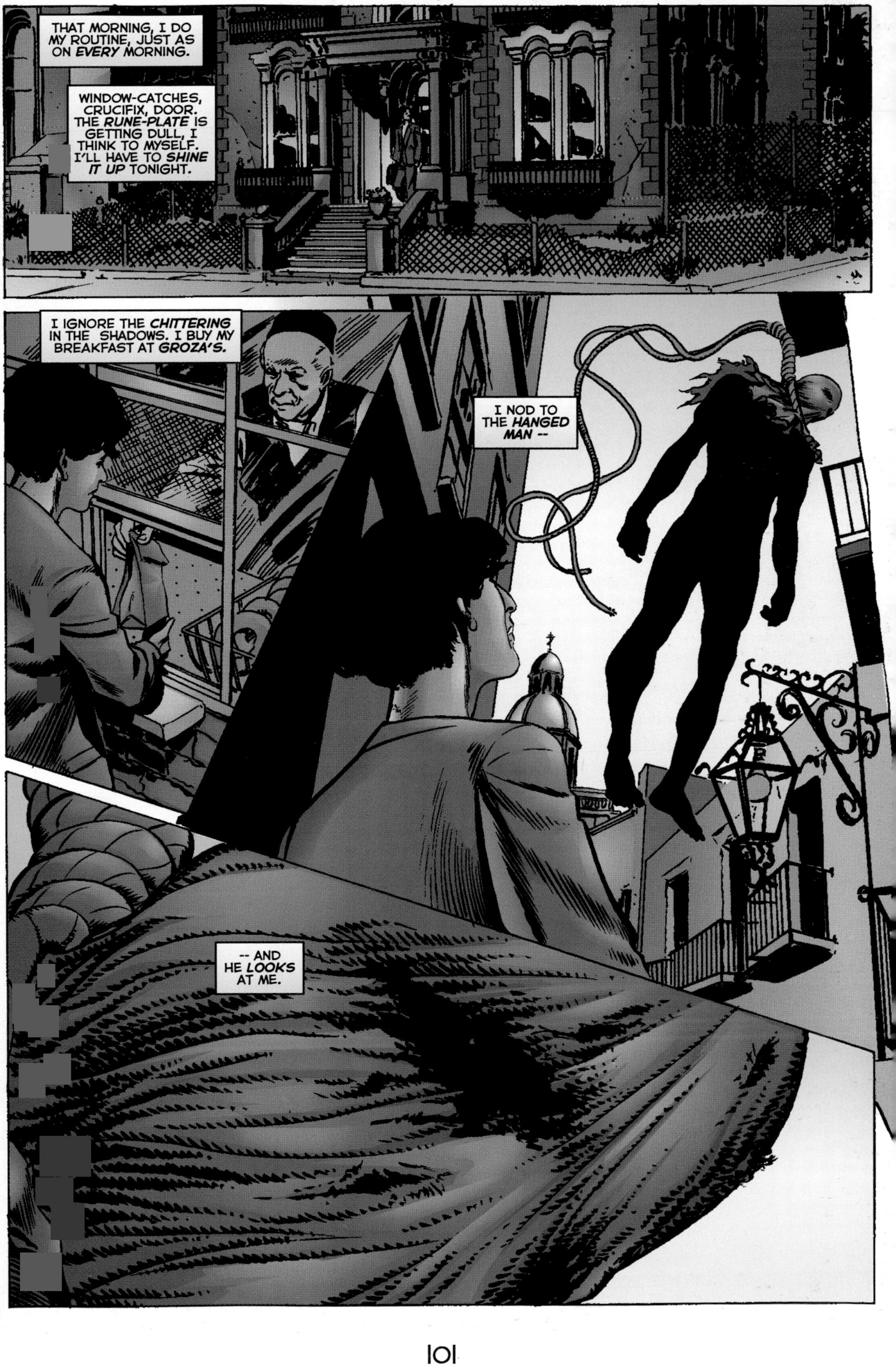
THAT MORNING, I DO MY ROUTINE, JUST AS ON *EVERY* MORNING.
WINDOW-CATCHES, CRUCIFIX, DOOR. THE *RUNE-PLATE* IS GETTING DULL, I THINK TO MYSELF. I'LL HAVE TO *SHINE IT UP* TONIGHT.
I IGNORE THE *CHITTERING* IN THE SHADOWS. I BUY MY BREAKFAST AT *GROZA'S.*
I NOD TO THE *HANGED MAN* --
-- AND HE *LOOKS* AT ME.

HE *LOOKS* AT ME!

I CAN'T SEE PAST THE RAGGED EDGES OF *BURLAP* THAT HIDE HIS EYES, BUT THERE'S SOMETHING IN THOSE *DARK SMEARS* --

-- AND I KNOW IT'S A *WARNING* --

I RACK MY BRAIN, BUT I'VE DONE *EVERYTHING* --

-- BUT A WARNING OF *WHAT?*

MARTA?

MORNING, MARTA.

-- THE LATCH CAUGHT, THE WINDOWS ARE SAFE, THE HEARTH DOESN'T NEED RE-BLESSING FOR ANOTHER MONTH --

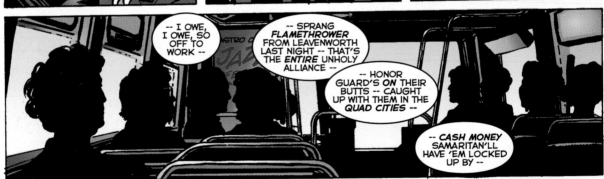

-- I OWE, I OWE, SO OFF TO WORK --

-- SPRANG *FLAMETHROWER* FROM LEAVENWORTH LAST NIGHT -- THAT'S THE *ENTIRE* UNHOLY ALLIANCE --

-- HONOR GUARD'S *ON THEIR BUTTS* -- CAUGHT UP WITH THEM IN THE *QUAD CITIES* --

-- *CASH MONEY* SAMARITAN'LL HAVE 'EM LOCKED UP BY --

AND I THINK OF MY *DREAM,* AND THE CRACKING STREETS, THE CLUTCHING *SHADOWS* --

-- AND I DON'T WANT TO BE A SCARED LITTLE GIRL ANY MORE, BUT I CAN FEEL THE BULK OF THE *HILL WEIGHING DOWN* ON ME, BURYING ME *ALIVE* --

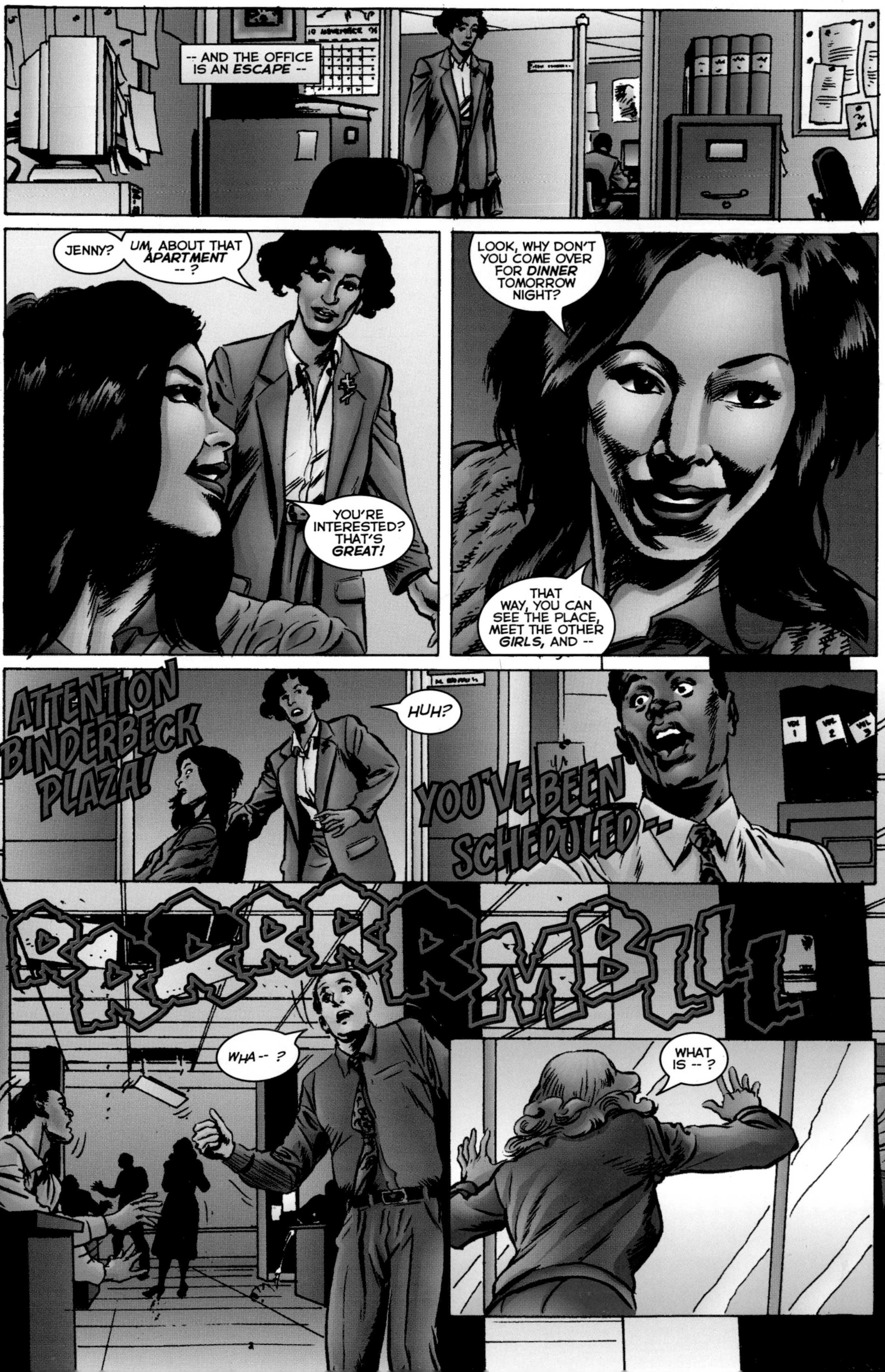

-- AND THE OFFICE IS AN ESCAPE --
JENNY?
UM, ABOUT THAT APARTMENT -- ?
YOU'RE INTERESTED? THAT'S GREAT!
LOOK, WHY DON'T YOU COME OVER FOR DINNER TOMORROW NIGHT?
THAT WAY, YOU CAN SEE THE PLACE, MEET THE OTHER GIRLS, AND --
ATTENTION BINDERBECK PLAZA!
HUH?
YOU'VE BEEN SCHEDULED --
WHA-- ?
WHAT IS -- ?

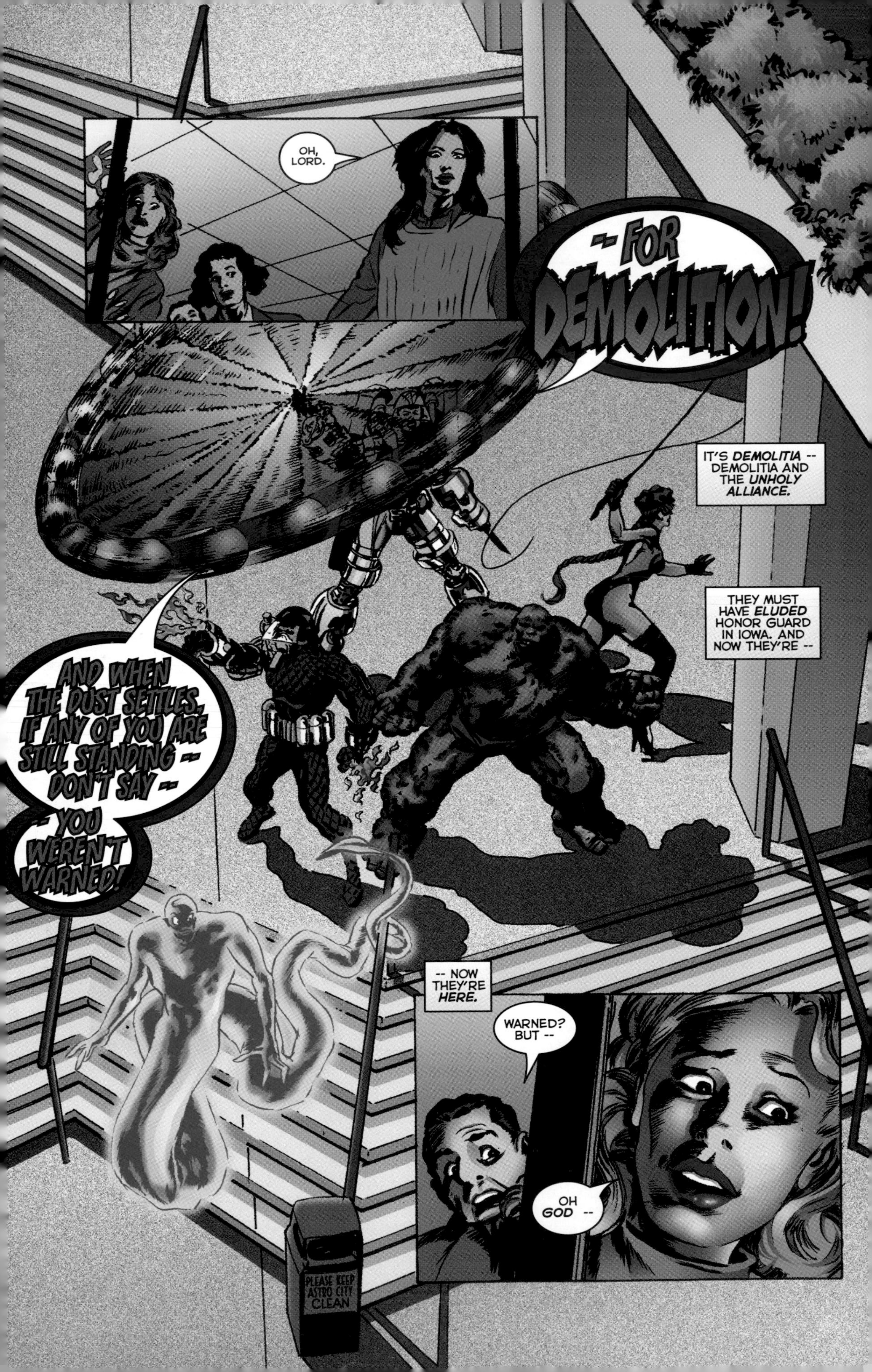
OH, LORD.
-- FOR DEMOLITION!
IT'S *DEMOLITIA* -- DEMOLITIA AND THE *UNHOLY ALLIANCE.*
THEY MUST HAVE *ELUDED* HONOR GUARD IN IOWA. AND NOW THEY'RE --
AND WHEN THE DUST SETTLES, IF ANY OF YOU ARE STILL STANDING -- DON'T SAY --
-- YOU WEREN'T WARNED!
-- NOW THEY'RE *HERE.*
WARNED? BUT --
OH *GOD* --
PLEASE KEEP ASTRO CITY CLEAN

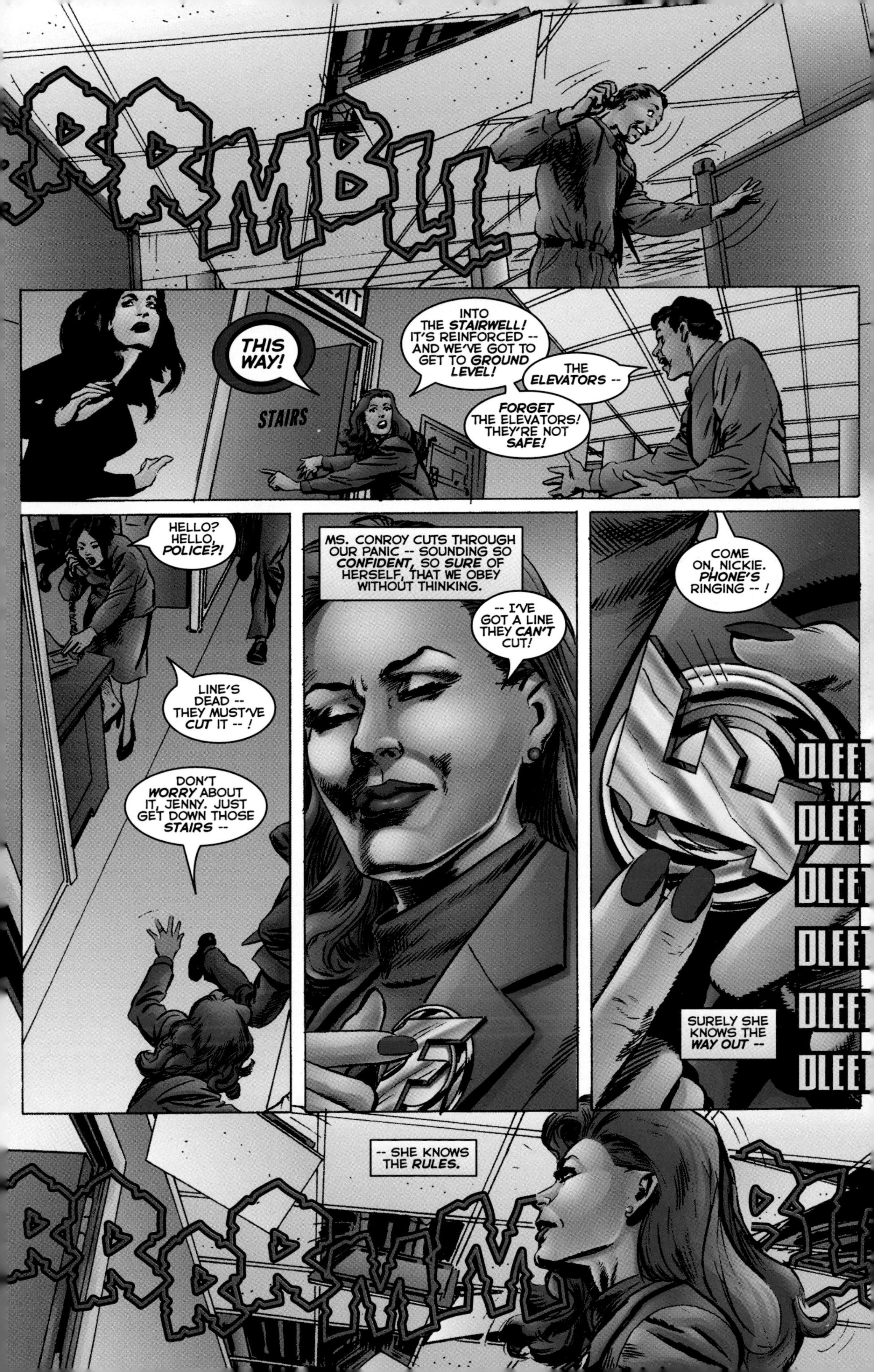RRMBLL
THIS WAY!
STAIRS
INTO THE STAIRWELL! IT'S REINFORCED -- AND WE'VE GOT TO GET TO GROUND LEVEL!
THE ELEVATORS --
FORGET THE ELEVATORS! THEY'RE NOT SAFE!
HELLO? HELLO, POLICE?!
LINE'S DEAD -- THEY MUST'VE CUT IT -- !
DON'T WORRY ABOUT IT, JENNY. JUST GET DOWN THOSE STAIRS --
MS. CONROY CUTS THROUGH OUR PANIC -- SOUNDING SO CONFIDENT, SO SURE OF HERSELF, THAT WE OBEY WITHOUT THINKING.
-- I'VE GOT A LINE THEY CAN'T CUT!
COME ON, NICKIE. PHONE'S RINGING -- !
DLEET
DLEET
DLEET
DLEET
DLEET
DLEET
SURELY SHE KNOWS THE WAY OUT --
-- SHE KNOWS THE RULES.

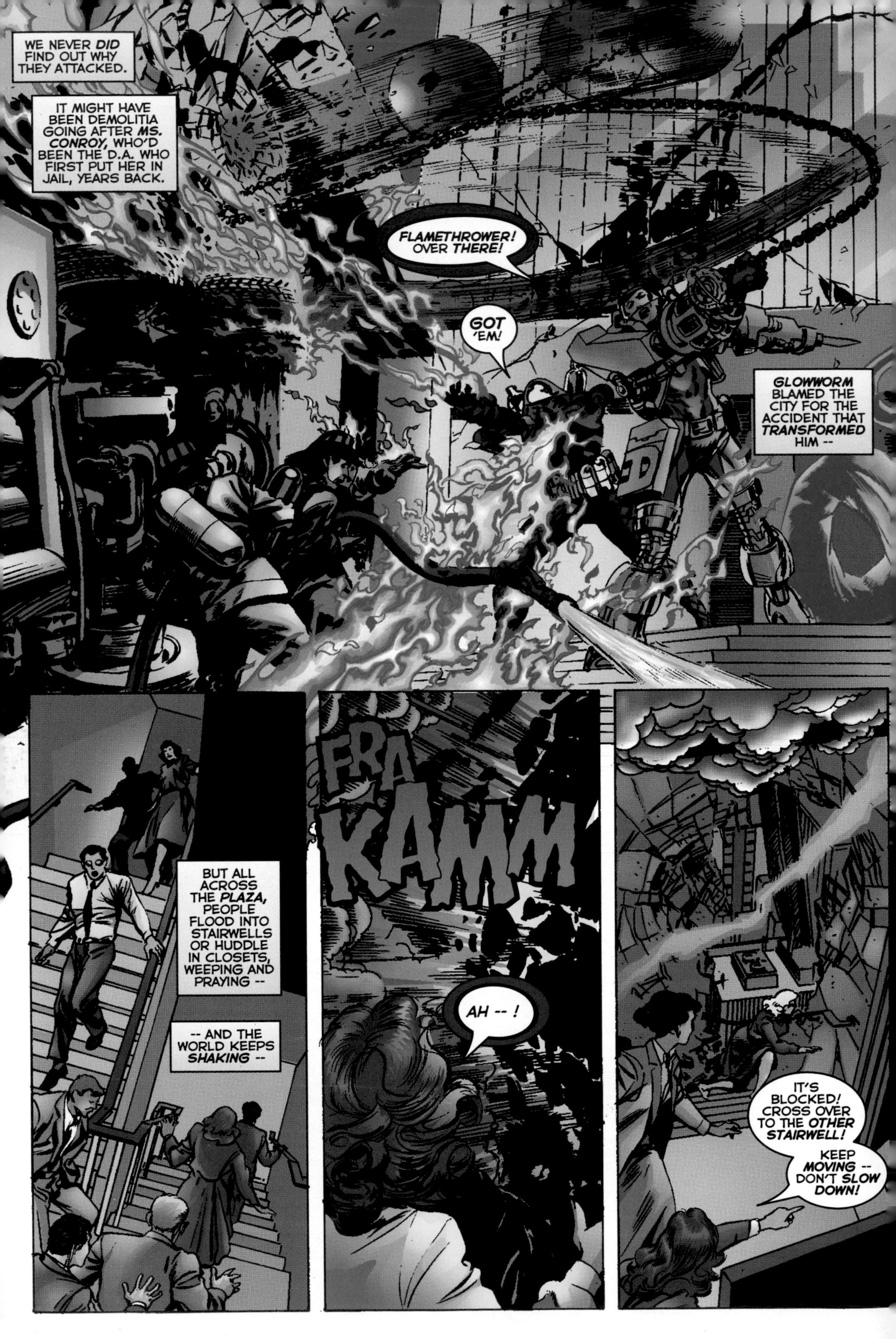
WE NEVER DID FIND OUT WHY THEY ATTACKED.
IT MIGHT HAVE BEEN DEMOLITIA GOING AFTER MS. CONROY, WHO'D BEEN THE D.A. WHO FIRST PUT HER IN JAIL, YEARS BACK.
FLAMETHROWER! OVER THERE!
GOT 'EM!
GLOWWORM BLAMED THE CITY FOR THE ACCIDENT THAT TRANSFORMED HIM --
BUT ALL ACROSS THE PLAZA, PEOPLE FLOOD INTO STAIRWELLS OR HUDDLE IN CLOSETS, WEEPING AND PRAYING --
-- AND THE WORLD KEEPS SHAKING --
FRA KAMM
AH -- !
IT'S BLOCKED! CROSS OVER TO THE OTHER STAIRWELL!
KEEP MOVING -- DON'T SLOW DOWN!

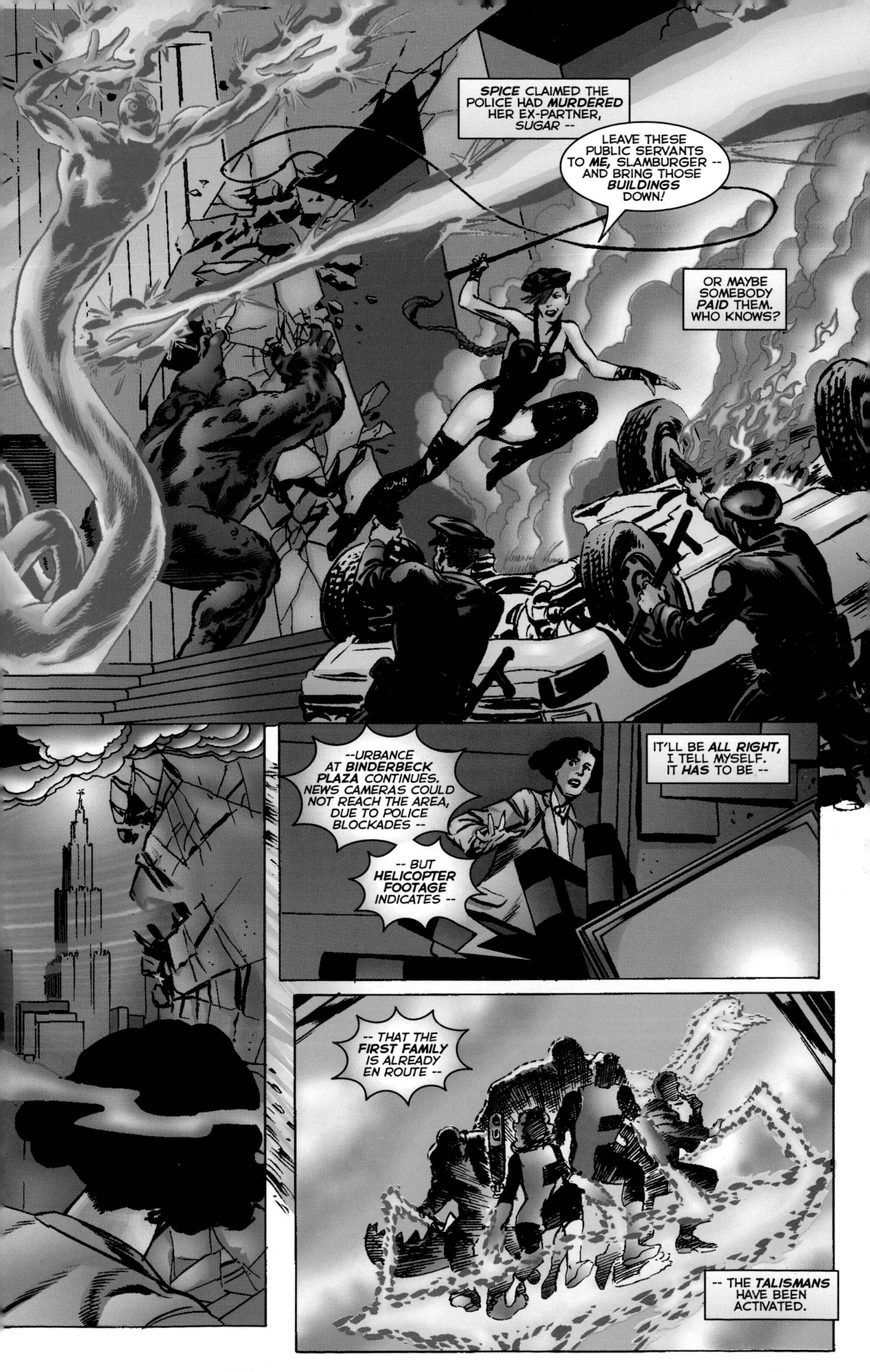
SPICE CLAIMED THE POLICE HAD MURDERED HER EX-PARTNER, SUGAR --
LEAVE THESE PUBLIC SERVANTS TO ME, SLAMBURGER -- AND BRING THOSE BUILDINGS DOWN!
OR MAYBE SOMEBODY PAID THEM. WHO KNOWS?
--URBANCE AT BINDERBECK PLAZA CONTINUES. NEWS CAMERAS COULD NOT REACH THE AREA, DUE TO POLICE BLOCKADES --
IT'LL BE ALL RIGHT, I TELL MYSELF. IT HAS TO BE --
-- BUT HELICOPTER FOOTAGE INDICATES --
-- THAT THE FIRST FAMILY IS ALREADY EN ROUTE --
-- THE TALISMANS HAVE BEEN ACTIVATED.

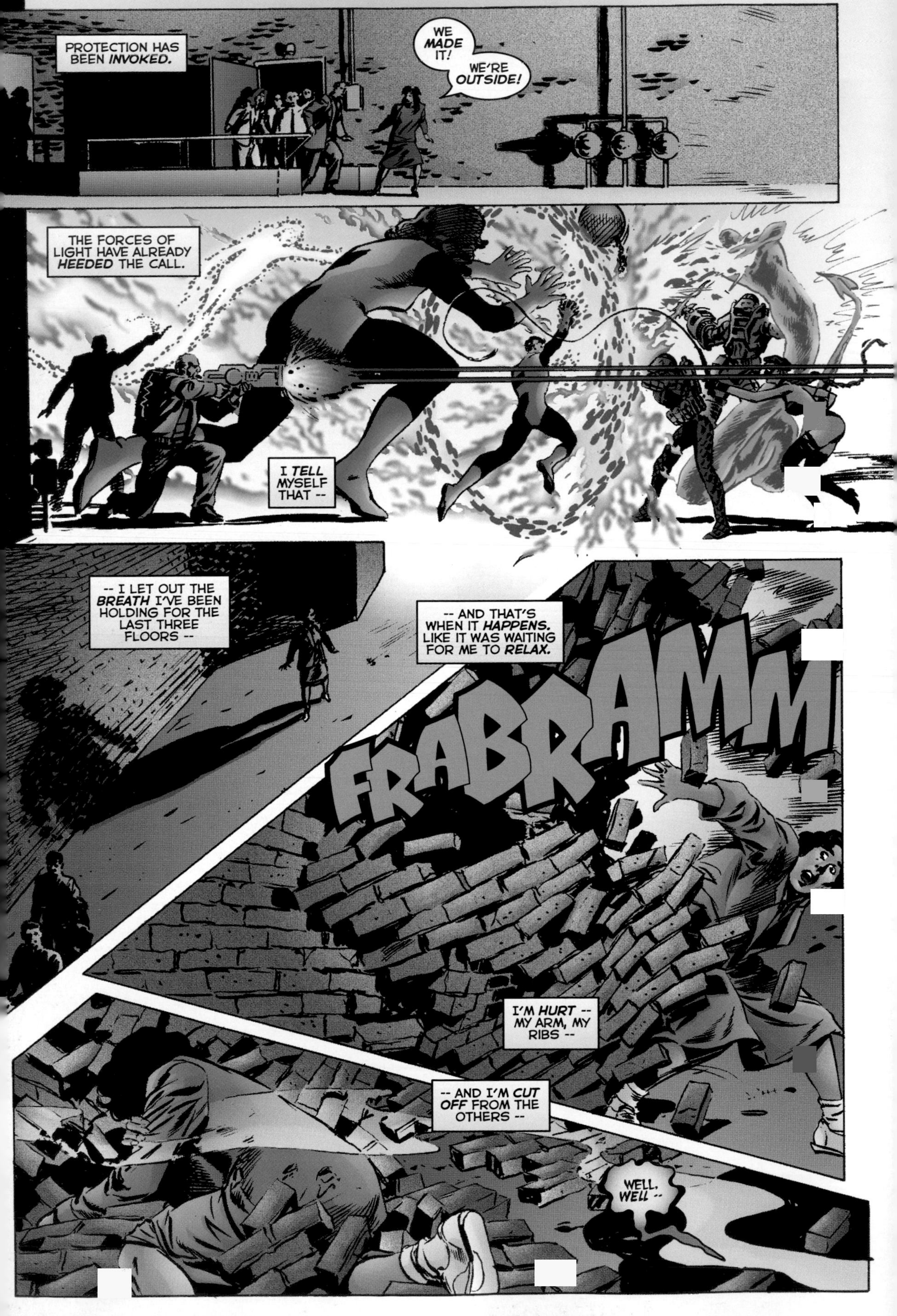
PROTECTION HAS BEEN INVOKED.
WE MADE IT!
WE'RE OUTSIDE!
THE FORCES OF LIGHT HAVE ALREADY HEEDED THE CALL.
I TELL MYSELF THAT --
-- I LET OUT THE BREATH I'VE BEEN HOLDING FOR THE LAST THREE FLOORS --
-- AND THAT'S WHEN IT HAPPENS. LIKE IT WAS WAITING FOR ME TO RELAX.
FRABRAMM
I'M HURT -- MY ARM, MY RIBS --
-- AND I'M CUT OFF FROM THE OTHERS --
WELL, WELL --

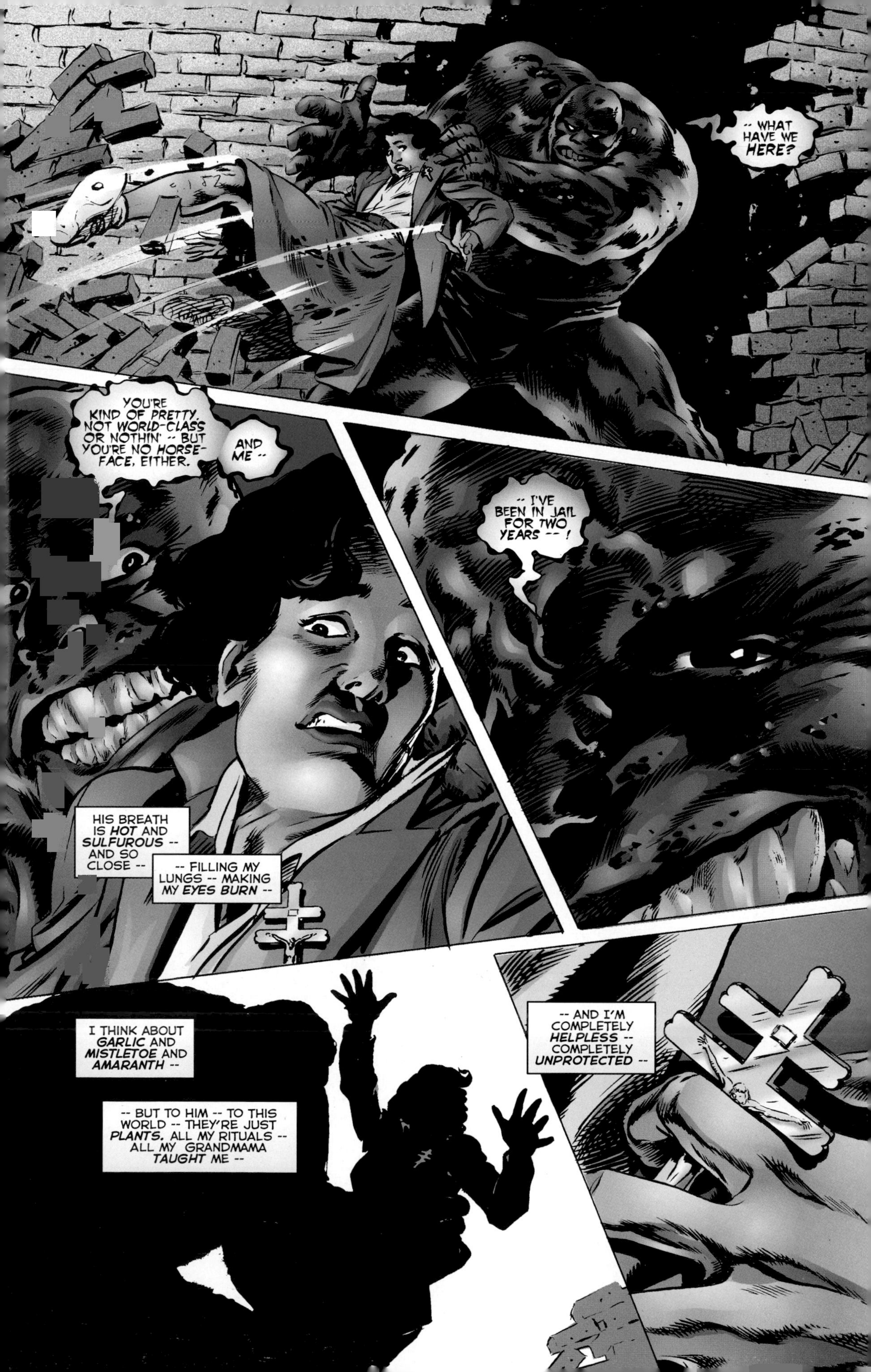
-- WHAT HAVE WE HERE?
YOU'RE KIND OF PRETTY. NOT WORLD-CLASS OR NOTHIN' -- BUT YOU'RE NO HORSE-FACE, EITHER.
AND ME --
-- I'VE BEEN IN JAIL FOR TWO YEARS -- !
HIS BREATH IS HOT AND SULFUROUS -- AND SO CLOSE --
-- FILLING MY LUNGS -- MAKING MY EYES BURN --
I THINK ABOUT GARLIC AND MISTLETOE AND AMARANTH --
-- BUT TO HIM -- TO THIS WORLD -- THEY'RE JUST PLANTS. ALL MY RITUALS -- ALL MY GRANDMAMA TAUGHT ME --
-- AND I'M COMPLETELY HELPLESS -- COMPLETELY UNPROTECTED --

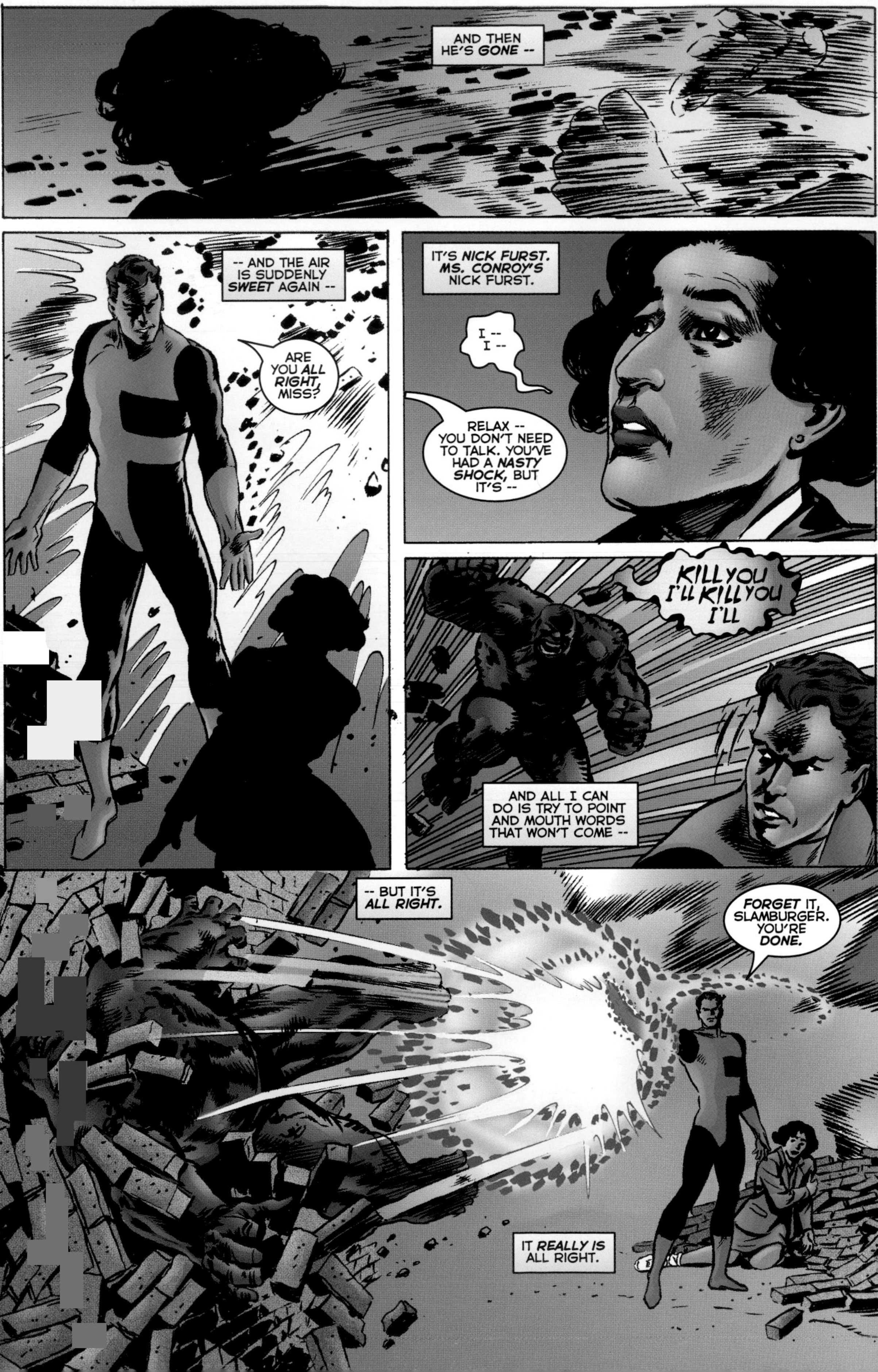
AND THEN HE'S GONE --
-- AND THE AIR IS SUDDENLY SWEET AGAIN --
ARE YOU ALL RIGHT, MISS?
IT'S NICK FURST. MS. CONROY'S NICK FURST.
I -- I --
RELAX -- YOU DON'T NEED TO TALK. YOU'VE HAD A NASTY SHOCK, BUT IT'S --
KILL YOU I'LL KILL YOU I'LL
AND ALL I CAN DO IS TRY TO POINT AND MOUTH WORDS THAT WON'T COME --
-- BUT IT'S ALL RIGHT.
FORGET IT, SLAMBURGER. YOU'RE DONE.
IT REALLY IS ALL RIGHT.

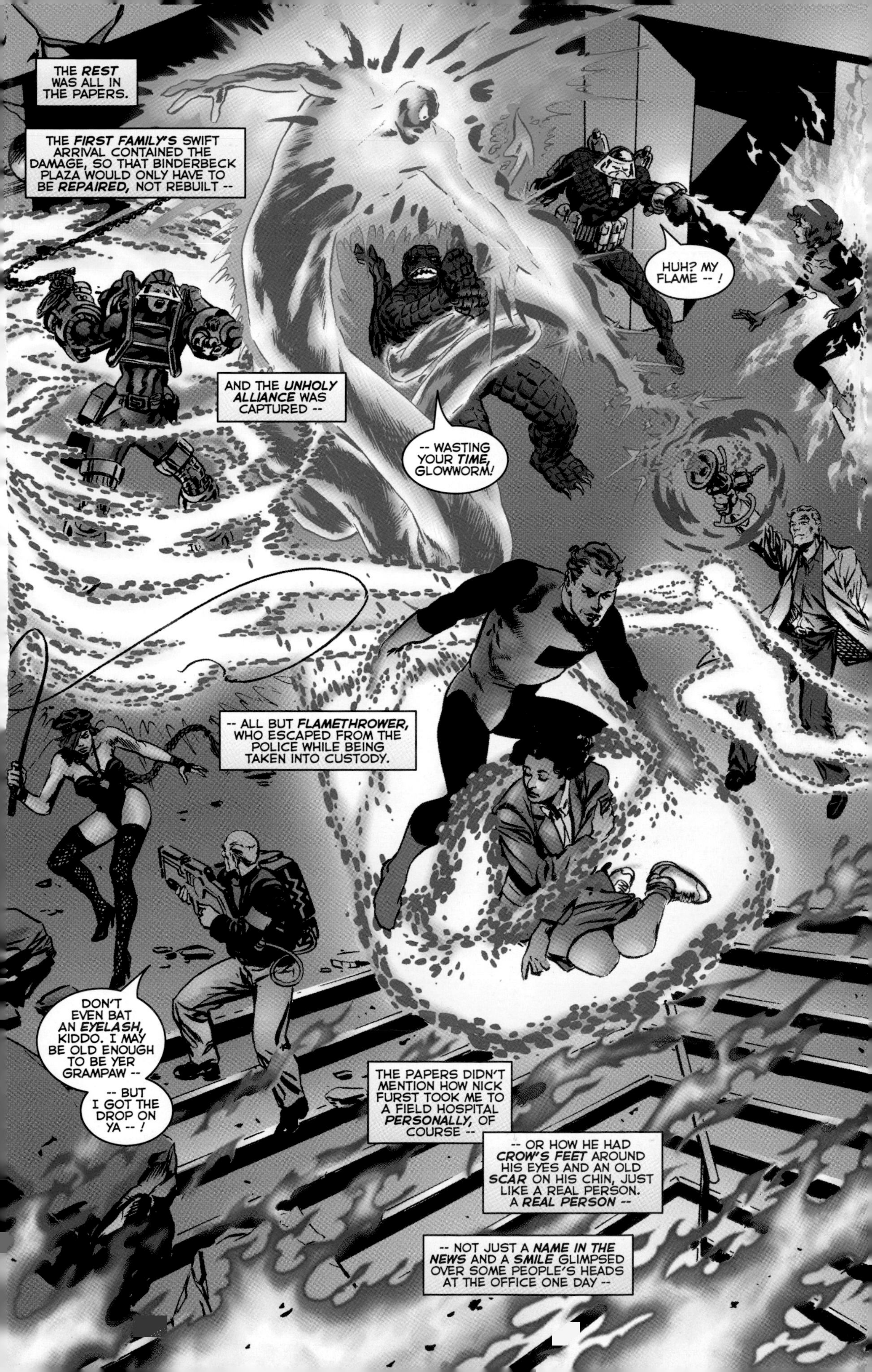
THE REST WAS ALL IN THE PAPERS.
THE FIRST FAMILY'S SWIFT ARRIVAL CONTAINED THE DAMAGE, SO THAT BINDERBECK PLAZA WOULD ONLY HAVE TO BE REPAIRED, NOT REBUILT --
HUH? MY FLAME -- !
AND THE UNHOLY ALLIANCE WAS CAPTURED --
-- WASTING YOUR TIME, GLOWWORM!
-- ALL BUT FLAMETHROWER, WHO ESCAPED FROM THE POLICE WHILE BEING TAKEN INTO CUSTODY.
DON'T EVEN BAT AN EYELASH, KIDDO. I MAY BE OLD ENOUGH TO BE YER GRAMPAW --
-- BUT I GOT THE DROP ON YA -- !
THE PAPERS DIDN'T MENTION HOW NICK FURST TOOK ME TO A FIELD HOSPITAL PERSONALLY, OF COURSE --
-- OR HOW HE HAD CROW'S FEET AROUND HIS EYES AND AN OLD SCAR ON HIS CHIN, JUST LIKE A REAL PERSON. A REAL PERSON --
-- NOT JUST A NAME IN THE NEWS AND A SMILE GLIMPSED OVER SOME PEOPLE'S HEADS AT THE OFFICE ONE DAY --

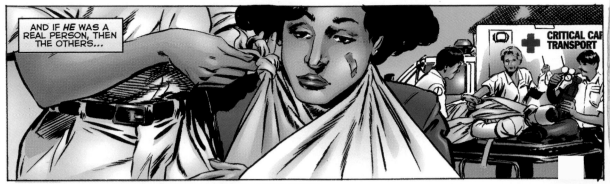

AND IF *HE* WAS A REAL PERSON, THEN THE OTHERS...

CRITICAL CARE TRANSPORT

SOMETHING *CHANGED* FOR ME THAT DAY, WATCHING THE AFTERMATH -- *RESCUE WORKERS* DOING THEIR JOBS, *T.V. NEWS CREWS* EVERYWHERE --

CITY CENTER -- IT'S JUST A *PLACE.* A DIFFERENT KIND OF PLACE FROM SHADOW HILL, BUT NOT *THAT* DIFFERENT.

THERE ARE *HEROES* AND *MONSTERS* IN BOTH PLACES. AND DOWN HERE --

MARTA?

-- THERE ARE *RULES* DOWN HERE, TOO.

MS. CONROY!

IF YOU DON'T WANT TO GO *HOME* TONIGHT -- IF YOU'RE SCARED BECAUSE FLAMETHROWER'S STILL ON THE *LOOSE* --

-- I CAN PUT YOU UP AT *MY* PLACE.

MS. CONROY IS A *GOOD* PERSON. KIND, AND SMART, AND *BRAVE.*

BUT SHE'S NOT *MAGIC* -- SHE JUST KNOWS THE RULES. SHE HAS HER TALISMAN, AND IT *WORKS* FOR HER.

I'LL BE *ALL RIGHT,* MS. CONROY. NOBODY WOULD COME UP TO SHADOW HILL AT *NIGHT* --

-- NOT IF THEY DON'T KNOW HOW TO *TAKE CARE* OF THEMSELVES.

BUT IT'S *HER* TALISMAN. THAT'S THE *REAL* DIFFERENCE.

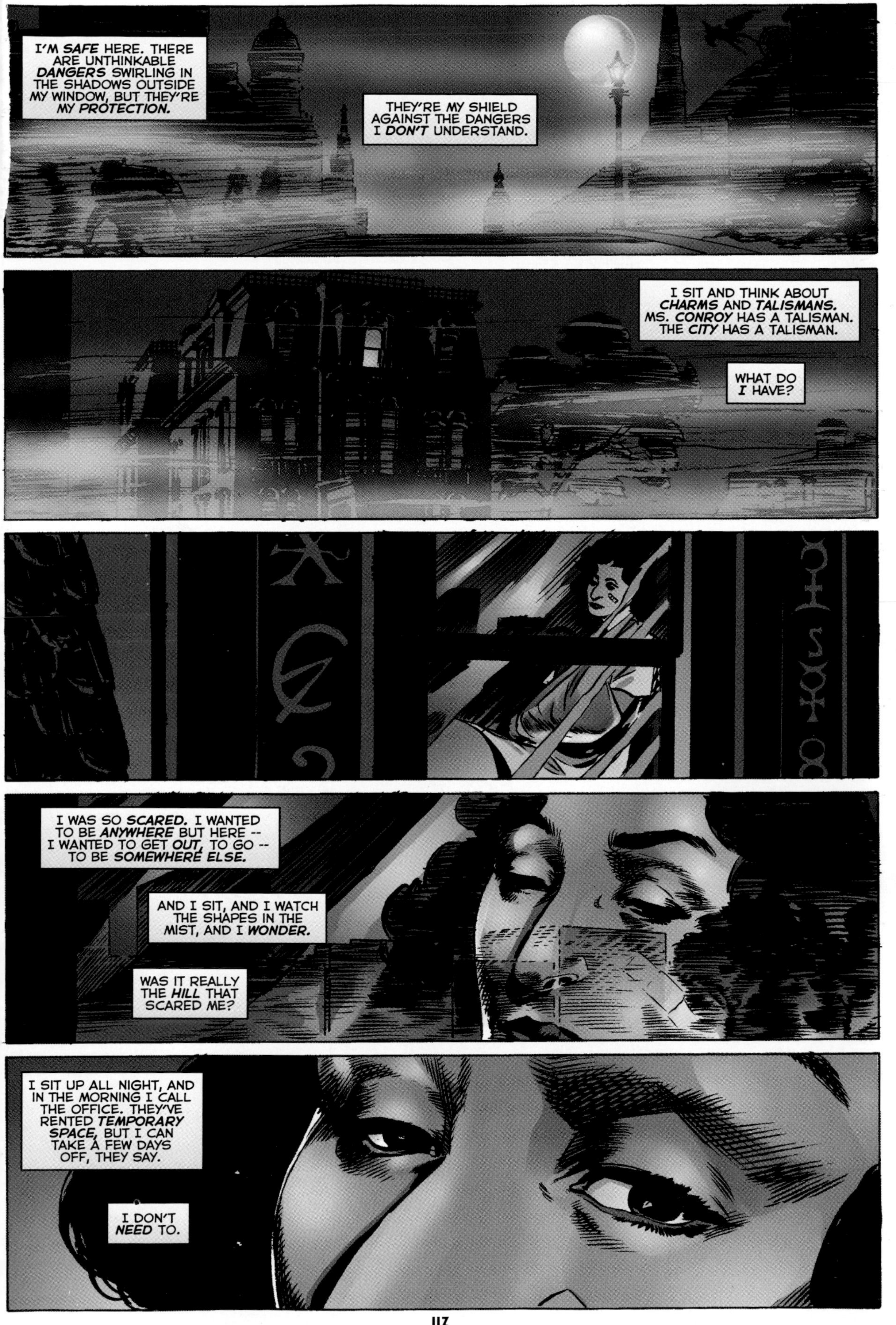
I'M SAFE HERE. THERE ARE UNTHINKABLE DANGERS SWIRLING IN THE SHADOWS OUTSIDE MY WINDOW, BUT THEY'RE MY PROTECTION.
THEY'RE MY SHIELD AGAINST THE DANGERS I DON'T UNDERSTAND.
I SIT AND THINK ABOUT CHARMS AND TALISMANS. MS. CONROY HAS A TALISMAN. THE CITY HAS A TALISMAN.
WHAT DO I HAVE?
I WAS SO SCARED. I WANTED TO BE ANYWHERE BUT HERE -- I WANTED TO GET OUT, TO GO -- TO BE SOMEWHERE ELSE.
AND I SIT, AND I WATCH THE SHAPES IN THE MIST, AND I WONDER.
WAS IT REALLY THE HILL THAT SCARED ME?
I SIT UP ALL NIGHT, AND IN THE MORNING I CALL THE OFFICE. THEY'VE RENTED TEMPORARY SPACE, BUT I CAN TAKE A FEW DAYS OFF, THEY SAY.
I DON'T NEED TO.

I CHECK THE *WINDOW-LATCHES*. I UNSEAL THE *DOOR*. I TAP MY *CRUCIFIX*.

I BUY MY BIALY AND COFFEE AT *GROZA'S*. I NOD TO THE HANGED MAN.

VASILIU BUTCHER SHOP

OPEN

HELP WANTED
COME INSIDE

ILIU BUTCHER SHOP

ILIU BUT

OPEN

HELP WANTED
COME INSIDE

SHOP

HELP WANTED

I BREATHE IN THE *SOFT MORNING AIR,* AND I EAT MY BREAKFAST IN THE WARM LIGHT OF THE *SUN*.

PERHAPS I CAN FIND AN *APARTMENT* TO RENT NEARBY. I'LL HAVE TO ASK AROUND.

YOU ARE NOW LEAVING
ASTRO CITY
PLEASE DRIVE CAREFULLY

CHAPTER 5

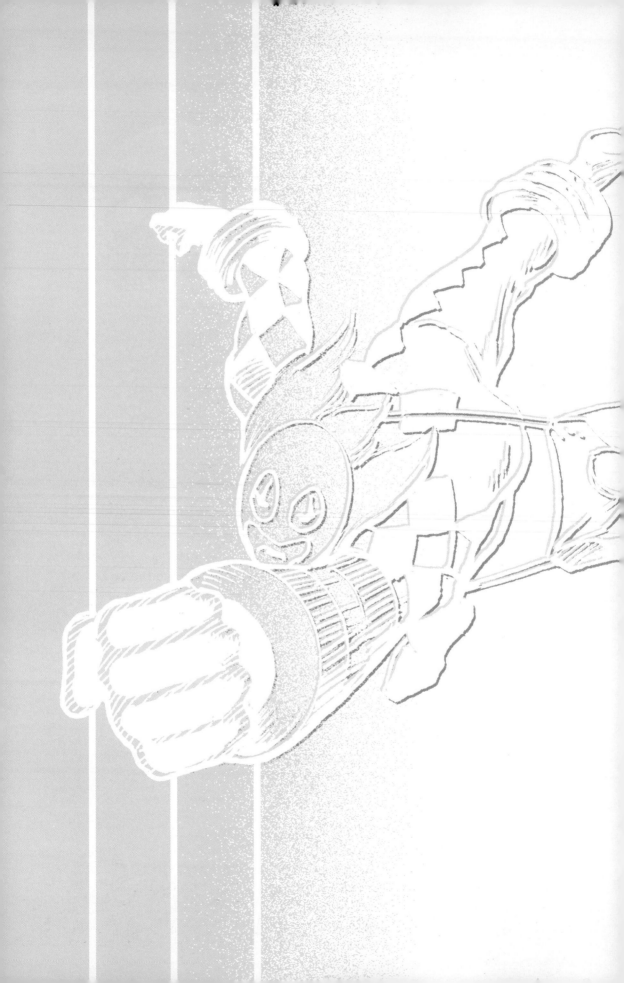

Once upon a time...

...there was a **little old man** who lived in an undistinguished rooming house on the **north side** of Astro City.

Nordling's
Department Store
Affordable Quality
1921

If you asked him, the little old man would say that he worked **forty-five** years as a draftsman in a basement room without windows, and he intended to spend his retirement out-of-doors as much as **possible**, breathing the air, looking at the **sun** and **sky** until he finally managed to flush the **fluorescent light** from his system.

But the little old man was a **liar.**

There was no **basement room.** There was no **fluorescent light.**

And he did not walk outside to look at the sun.

Reconnaissance

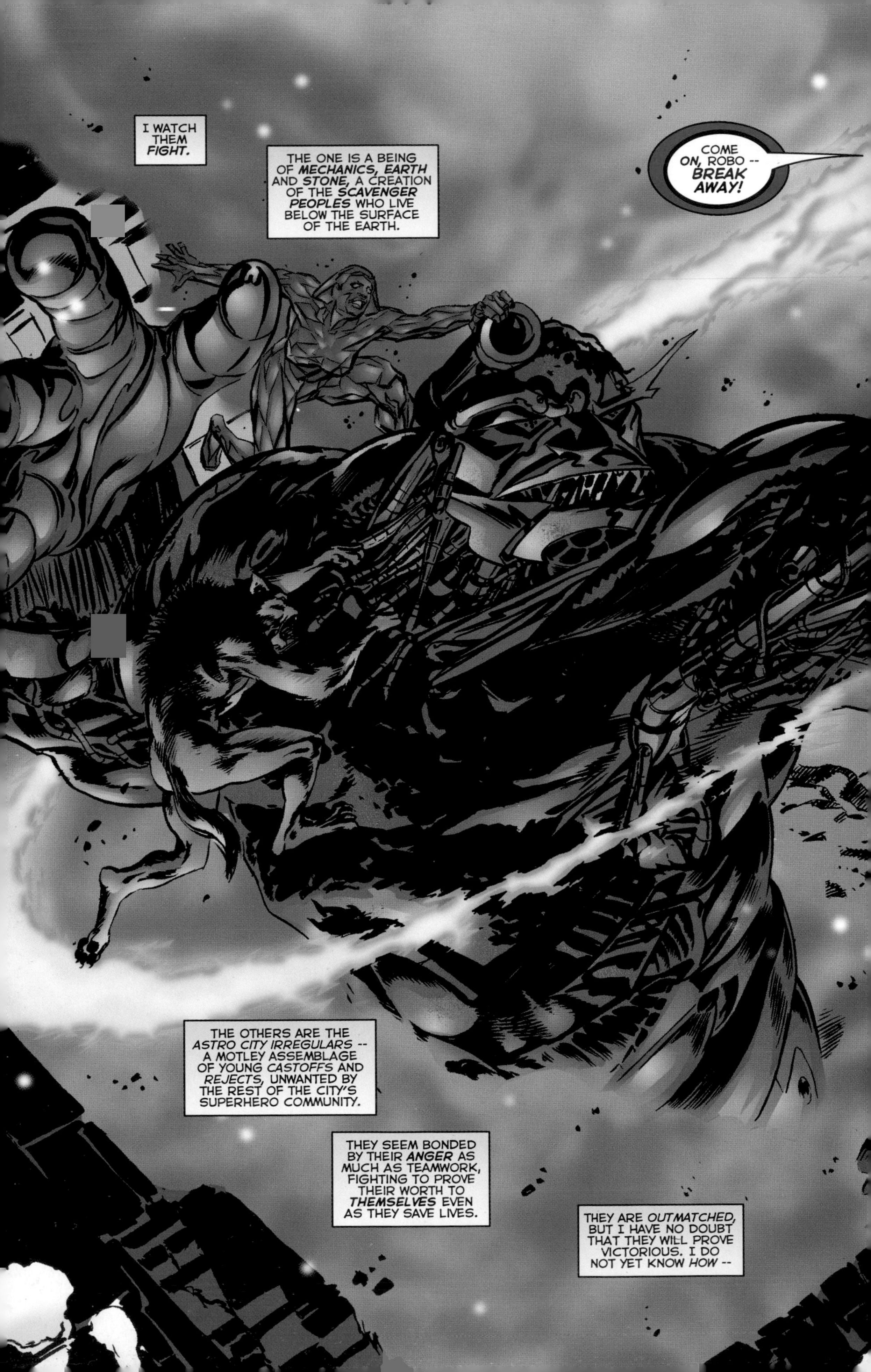
I WATCH THEM *FIGHT.*
THE ONE IS A BEING OF ***MECHANICS, EARTH*** AND ***STONE,*** A CREATION OF THE ***SCAVENGER PEOPLES*** WHO LIVE BELOW THE SURFACE OF THE EARTH.
COME *ON,* ROBO -- ***BREAK AWAY!***
THE OTHERS ARE THE *ASTRO CITY IRREGULARS* -- A MOTLEY ASSEMBLAGE OF YOUNG *CASTOFFS* AND *REJECTS,* UNWANTED BY THE REST OF THE CITY'S SUPERHERO COMMUNITY.
THEY SEEM BONDED BY THEIR ***ANGER*** AS MUCH AS TEAMWORK, FIGHTING TO PROVE THEIR WORTH TO ***THEMSELVES*** EVEN AS THEY SAVE LIVES.
THEY ARE *OUTMATCHED,* BUT I HAVE NO DOUBT THAT THEY WILL PROVE VICTORIOUS. I DO NOT YET KNOW *HOW* --

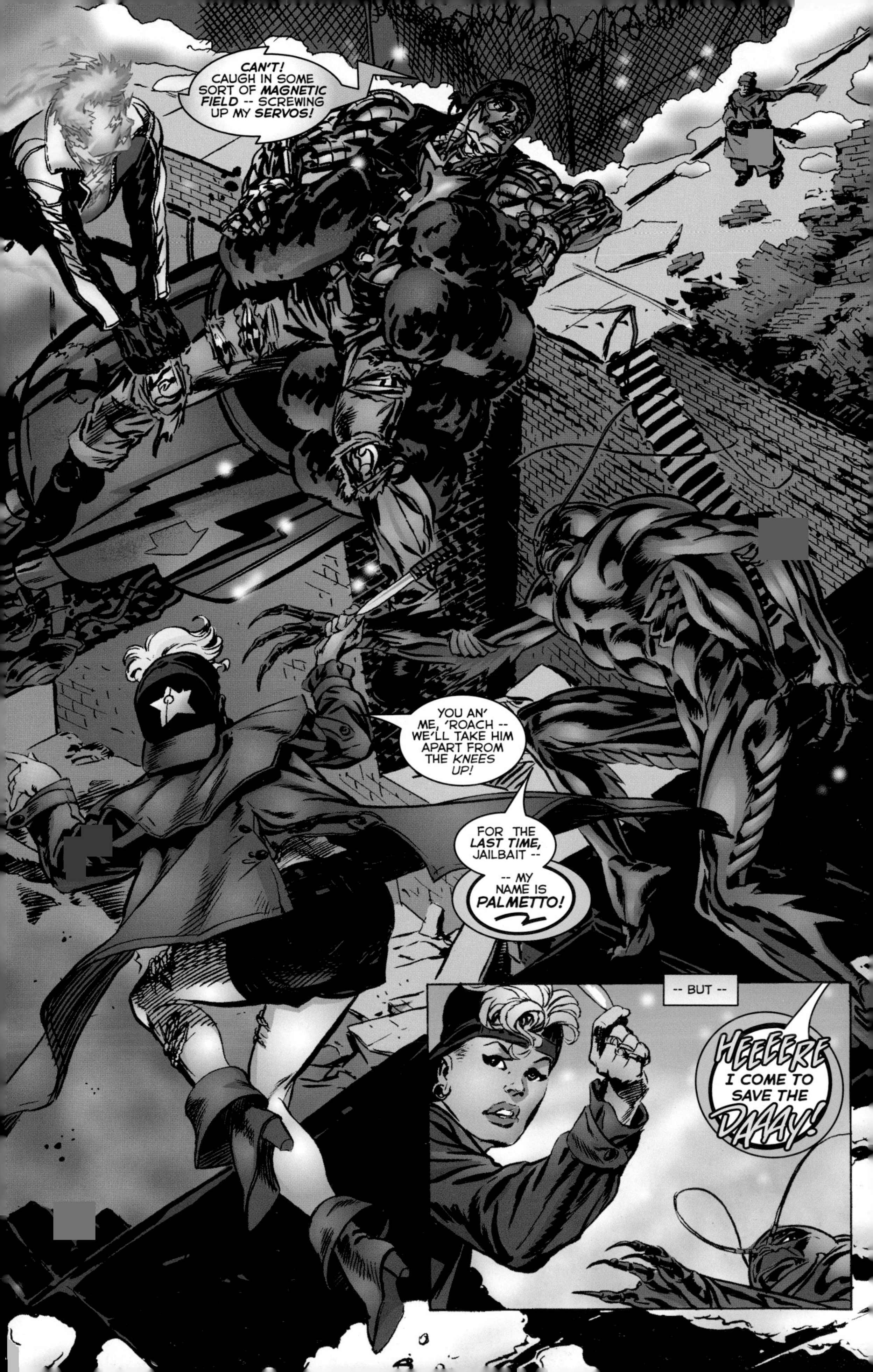
CAN'T! CAUGH IN SOME SORT OF MAGNETIC FIELD -- SCREWING UP MY SERVOS!
YOU AN' ME, 'ROACH -- WE'LL TAKE HIM APART FROM THE KNEES UP!
FOR THE LAST TIME, JAILBAIT --
-- MY NAME IS PALMETTO!
-- BUT --
HEEEERE I COME TO SAVE THE DAAAY!

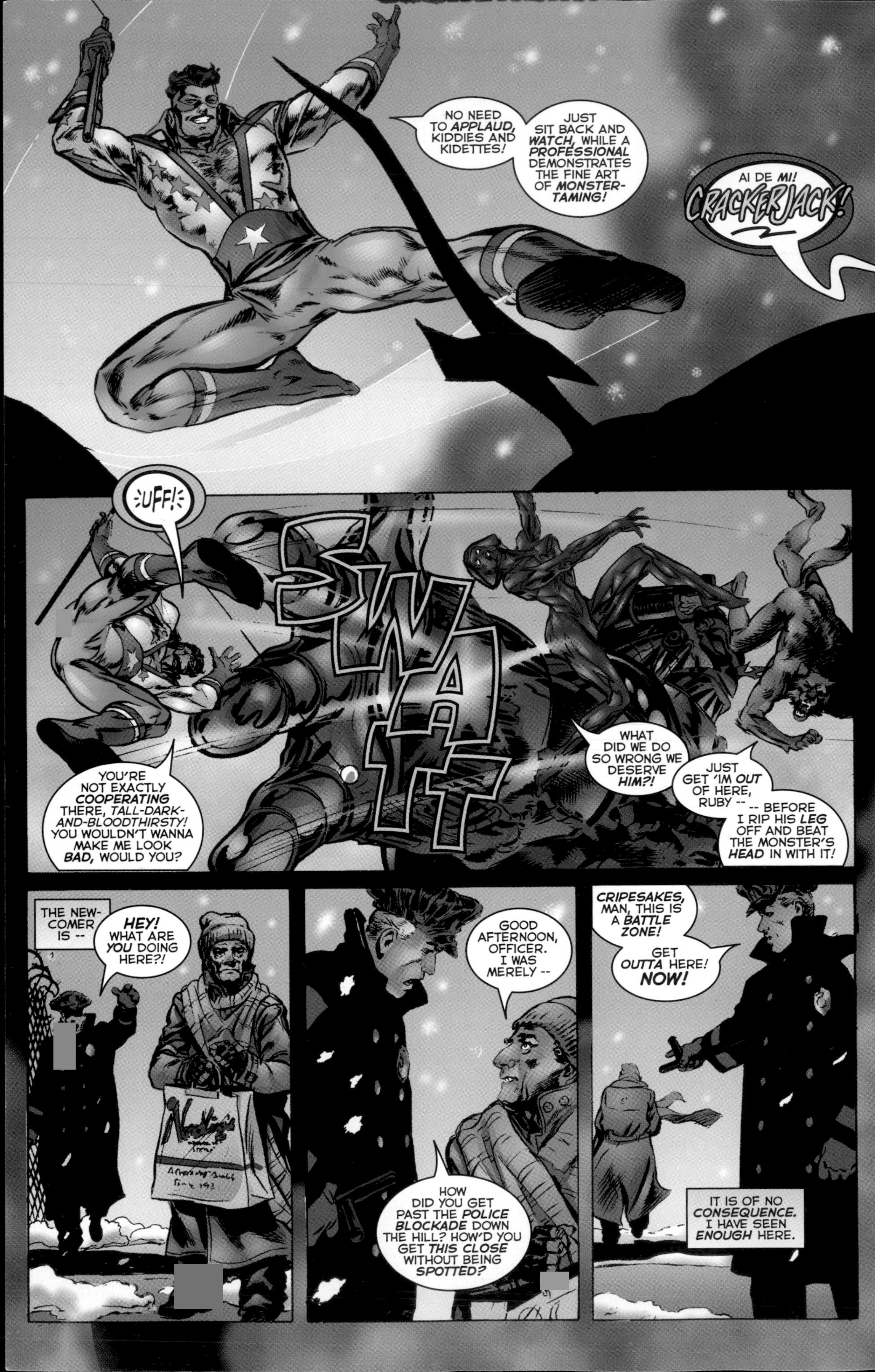
NO NEED TO *APPLAUD*, KIDDIES AND KIDETTES!
JUST SIT BACK AND *WATCH*, WHILE A *PROFESSIONAL* DEMONSTRATES THE FINE ART OF *MONSTER-TAMING!*
AI DE *MI!* CRACKERJACK!
UFF!
SMAT
YOU'RE NOT EXACTLY *COOPERATING* THERE, *TALL-DARK-AND-BLOODTHIRSTY!* YOU WOULDN'T WANNA MAKE ME LOOK *BAD*, WOULD YOU?
WHAT DID WE DO SO WRONG WE DESERVE *HIM?!*
JUST GET 'IM *OUT* OF HERE, RUBY --
-- BEFORE I RIP HIS *LEG* OFF AND BEAT THE MONSTER'S *HEAD* IN WITH IT!
THE NEW-COMER IS --
HEY! WHAT ARE *YOU* DOING HERE?!
GOOD AFTERNOON, OFFICER. I WAS MERELY --
HOW DID YOU GET PAST THE *POLICE BLOCKADE* DOWN THE HILL? HOW'D YOU GET *THIS CLOSE* WITHOUT BEING *SPOTTED?*
CRIPESAKES, MAN, THIS IS A *BATTLE ZONE!*
GET *OUTTA* HERE! *NOW!*
IT IS OF NO *CONSEQUENCE*. I HAVE SEEN *ENOUGH* HERE.

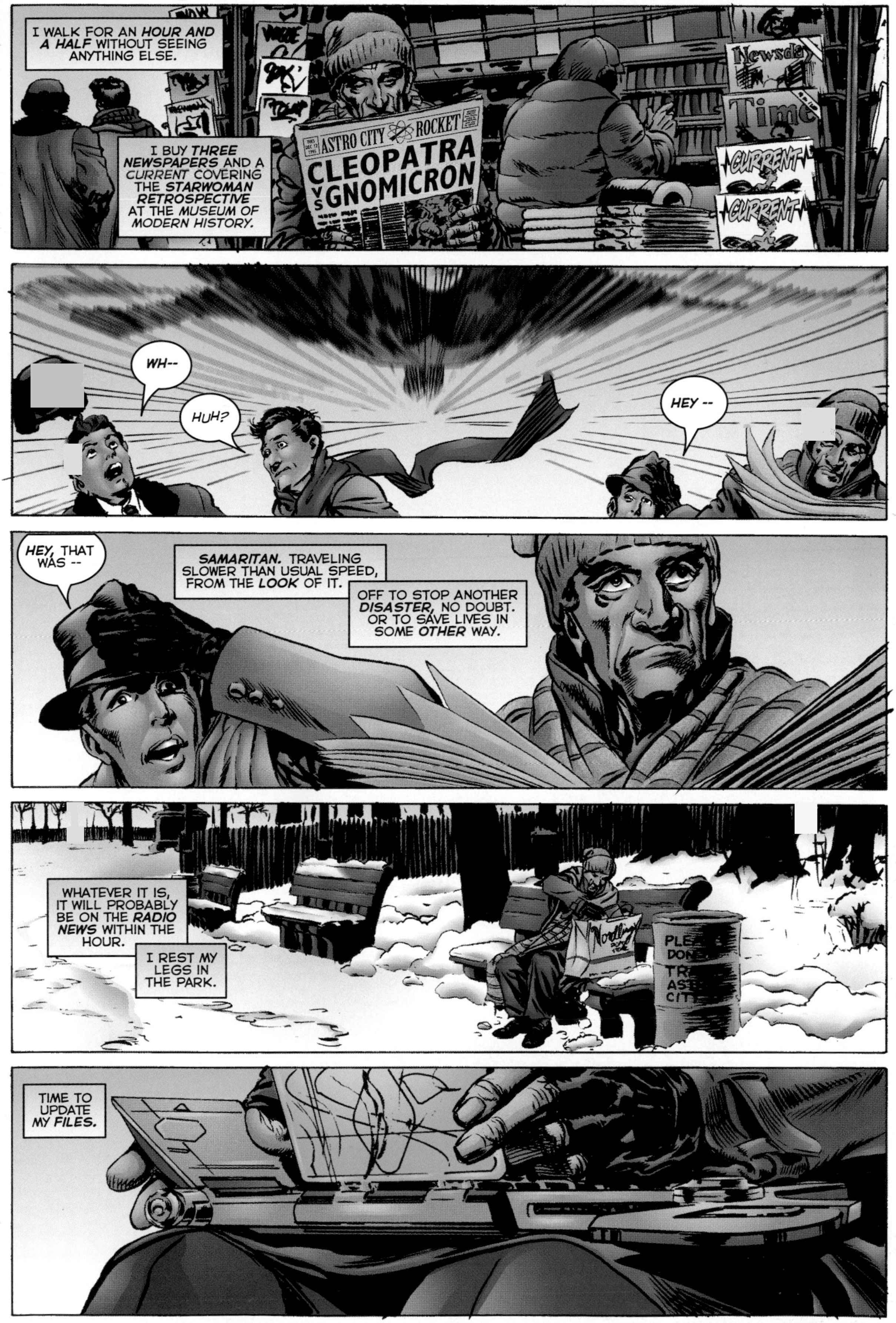
I WALK FOR AN HOUR AND A HALF WITHOUT SEEING ANYTHING ELSE.
I BUY THREE NEWSPAPERS AND A CURRENT COVERING THE STARWOMAN RETROSPECTIVE AT THE MUSEUM OF MODERN HISTORY.
ASTRO CITY ROCKET
CLEOPATRA VS GNOMICRON
Newsday
Time
CURRENT
CURRENT
WH--
HUH?
HEY --
HEY, THAT WAS --
SAMARITAN. TRAVELING SLOWER THAN USUAL SPEED, FROM THE LOOK OF IT.
OFF TO STOP ANOTHER DISASTER, NO DOUBT. OR TO SAVE LIVES IN SOME OTHER WAY.
WHATEVER IT IS, IT WILL PROBABLY BE ON THE RADIO NEWS WITHIN THE HOUR.
I REST MY LEGS IN THE PARK.
TIME TO UPDATE MY FILES.

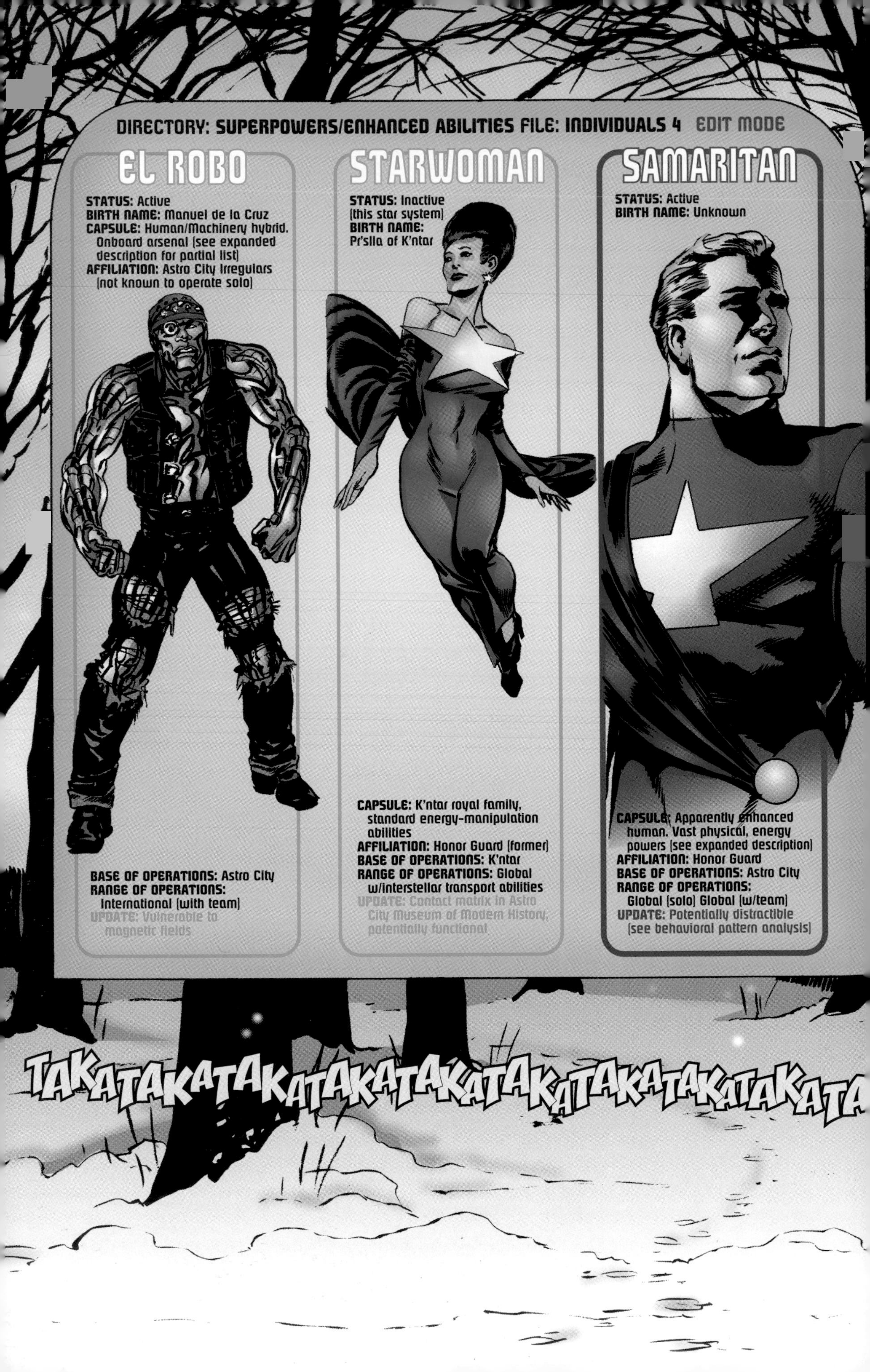

DIRECTORY: SUPERPOWERS/ENHANCED ABILITIES FILE: INDIVIDUALS 4 EDIT MODE
EL ROBO
STATUS: Active
BIRTH NAME: Manuel de la Cruz
CAPSULE: Human/Machinery hybrid. Onboard arsenal (see expanded description for partial list)
AFFILIATION: Astro City Irregulars (not known to operate solo)
BASE OF OPERATIONS: Astro City
RANGE OF OPERATIONS: International (with team)
UPDATE: Vulnerable to magnetic fields
STARWOMAN
STATUS: Inactive (this star system)
BIRTH NAME: Pr'slla of K'ntar
CAPSULE: K'ntar royal family, standard energy-manipulation abilities
AFFILIATION: Honor Guard (former)
BASE OF OPERATIONS: K'ntar
RANGE OF OPERATIONS: Global w/interstellar transport abilities
UPDATE: Contact matrix in Astro City Museum of Modern History, potentially functional
SAMARITAN
STATUS: Active
BIRTH NAME: Unknown
CAPSULE: Apparently enhanced human. Vast physical, energy powers (see expanded description)
AFFILIATION: Honor Guard
BASE OF OPERATIONS: Astro City
RANGE OF OPERATIONS: Global (solo) Global (w/team)
UPDATE: Potentially distractible (see behavioral pattern analysis)
TAKATAKATAKATAKATAKATAKATAKATAKATAKATA

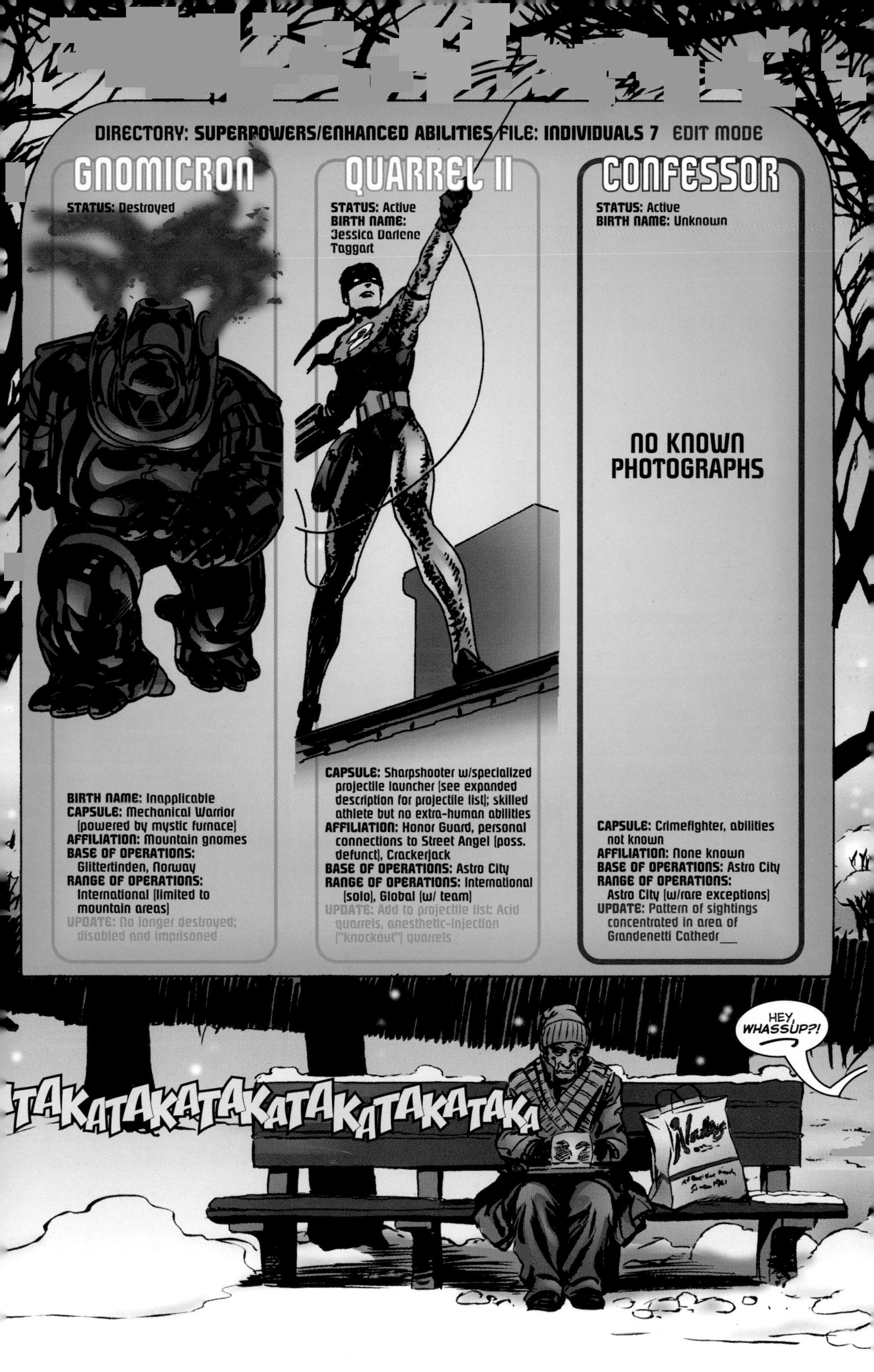
DIRECTORY: SUPERPOWERS/ENHANCED ABILITIES FILE: INDIVIDUALS 7 EDIT MODE
GNOMICRON
STATUS: Destroyed
BIRTH NAME: Inapplicable
CAPSULE: Mechanical Warrior (powered by mystic furnace)
AFFILIATION: Mountain gnomes
BASE OF OPERATIONS: Glittertinden, Norway
RANGE OF OPERATIONS: International (limited to mountain areas)
UPDATE: No longer destroyed; disabled and imprisoned
QUARREL II
STATUS: Active
BIRTH NAME: Jessica Darlene Taggart
CAPSULE: Sharpshooter w/specialized projectile launcher (see expanded description for projectile list); skilled athlete but no extra-human abilities
AFFILIATION: Honor Guard, personal connections to Street Angel (poss. defunct), Crackerjack
BASE OF OPERATIONS: Astro City
RANGE OF OPERATIONS: International (solo), Global (w/ team)
UPDATE: Add to projectile list: Acid quarrels, anesthetic-injection ("knockout") quarrels
CONFESSOR
STATUS: Active
BIRTH NAME: Unknown
NO KNOWN PHOTOGRAPHS
CAPSULE: Crimefighter, abilities not known
AFFILIATION: None known
BASE OF OPERATIONS: Astro City
RANGE OF OPERATIONS: Astro City (w/rare exceptions)
UPDATE: Pattern of sightings concentrated in area of Grandenetti Cathedr___
HEY, WHASSUP?!
TAKATAKATAKATAKATAKATAKATAKA

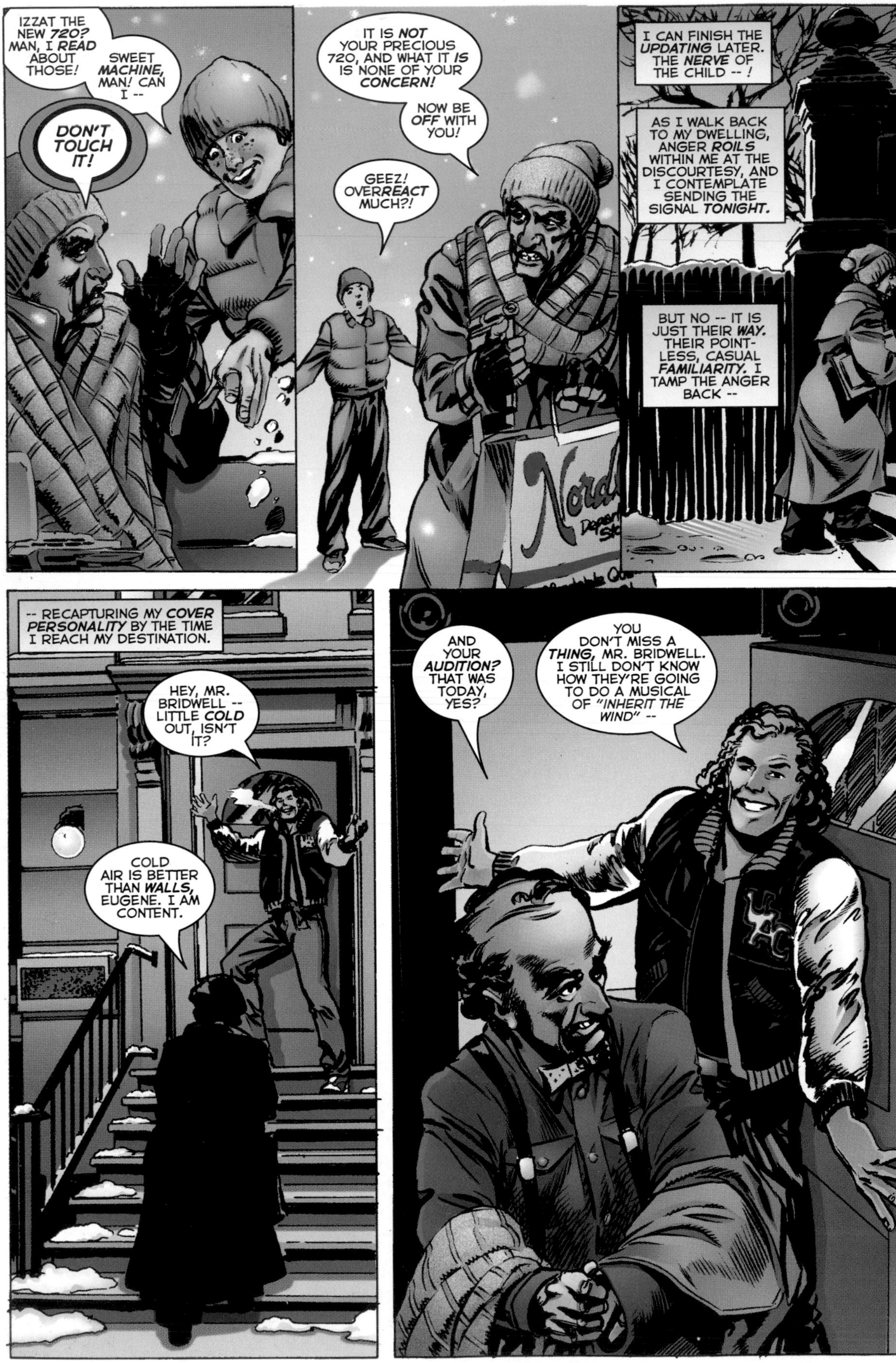
IZZAT THE NEW 720? MAN, I READ ABOUT THOSE!
SWEET MACHINE, MAN! CAN I --
DON'T TOUCH IT!
IT IS NOT YOUR PRECIOUS 720, AND WHAT IT IS IS NONE OF YOUR CONCERN!
NOW BE OFF WITH YOU!
GEEZ! OVERREACT MUCH?!
I CAN FINISH THE UPDATING LATER. THE NERVE OF THE CHILD -- !
AS I WALK BACK TO MY DWELLING, ANGER ROILS WITHIN ME AT THE DISCOURTESY, AND I CONTEMPLATE SENDING THE SIGNAL TONIGHT.
BUT NO -- IT IS JUST THEIR WAY. THEIR POINTLESS, CASUAL FAMILIARITY. I TAMP THE ANGER BACK --
-- RECAPTURING MY COVER PERSONALITY BY THE TIME I REACH MY DESTINATION.
HEY, MR. BRIDWELL -- LITTLE COLD OUT, ISN'T IT?
COLD AIR IS BETTER THAN WALLS, EUGENE. I AM CONTENT.
AND YOUR AUDITION? THAT WAS TODAY, YES?
YOU DON'T MISS A THING, MR. BRIDWELL. I STILL DON'T KNOW HOW THEY'RE GOING TO DO A MUSICAL OF "INHERIT THE WIND" --

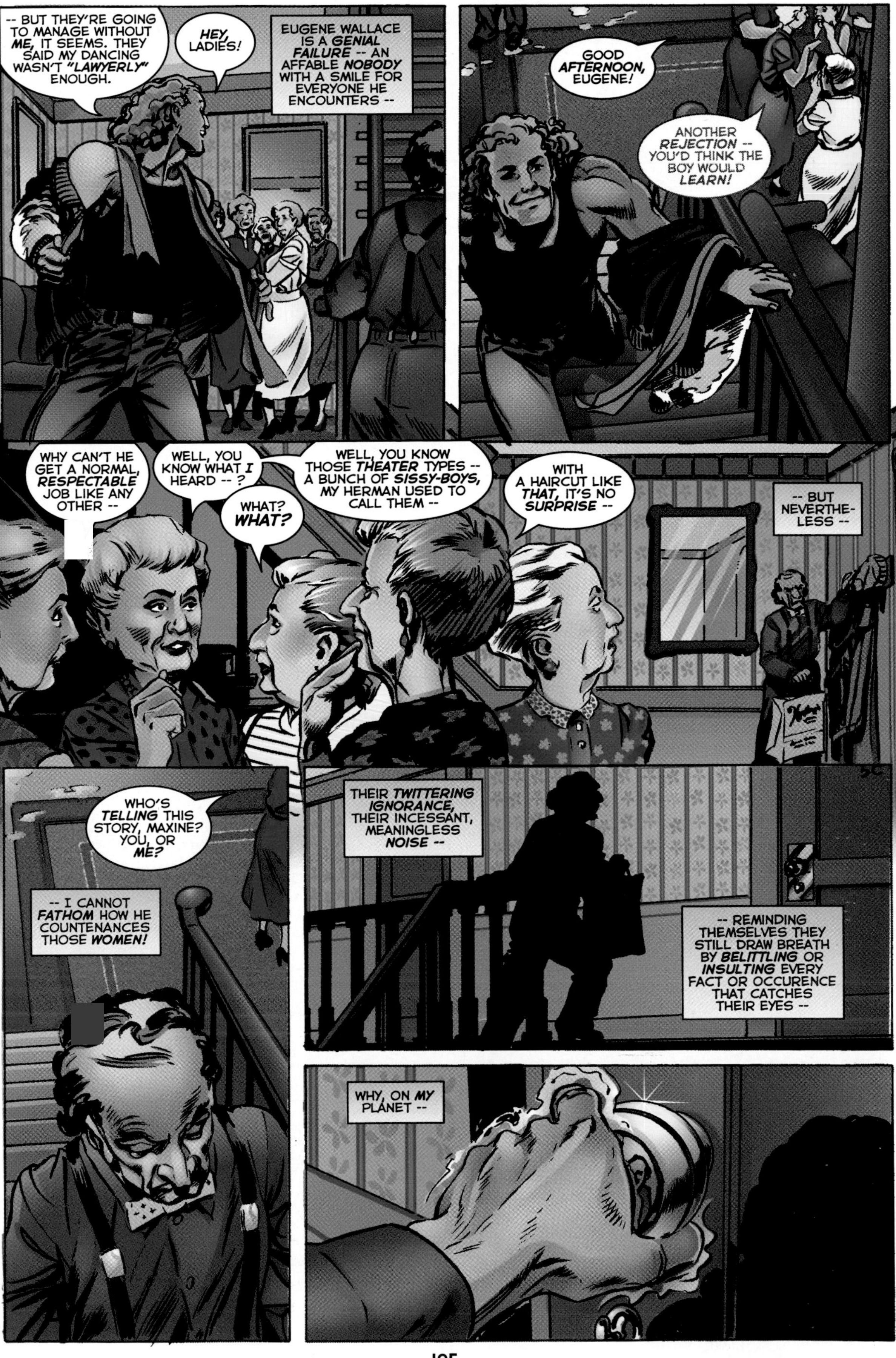
-- BUT THEY'RE GOING TO MANAGE WITHOUT ME, IT SEEMS. THEY SAID MY DANCING WASN'T "LAWYERLY" ENOUGH.
HEY, LADIES!
EUGENE WALLACE IS A GENIAL FAILURE -- AN AFFABLE NOBODY WITH A SMILE FOR EVERYONE HE ENCOUNTERS --
GOOD AFTERNOON, EUGENE!
ANOTHER REJECTION -- YOU'D THINK THE BOY WOULD LEARN!
WHY CAN'T HE GET A NORMAL, RESPECTABLE JOB LIKE ANY OTHER --
WELL, YOU KNOW WHAT I HEARD -- ?
WHAT? WHAT?
WELL, YOU KNOW THOSE THEATER TYPES -- A BUNCH OF SISSY-BOYS, MY HERMAN USED TO CALL THEM --
WITH A HAIRCUT LIKE THAT, IT'S NO SURPRISE --
-- BUT NEVERTHELESS --
WHO'S TELLING THIS STORY, MAXINE? YOU, OR ME?
-- I CANNOT FATHOM HOW HE COUNTENANCES THOSE WOMEN!
THEIR TWITTERING IGNORANCE, THEIR INCESSANT, MEANINGLESS NOISE --
-- REMINDING THEMSELVES THEY STILL DRAW BREATH BY BELITTLING OR INSULTING EVERY FACT OR OCCURENCE THAT CATCHES THEIR EYES --
WHY, ON MY PLANET --

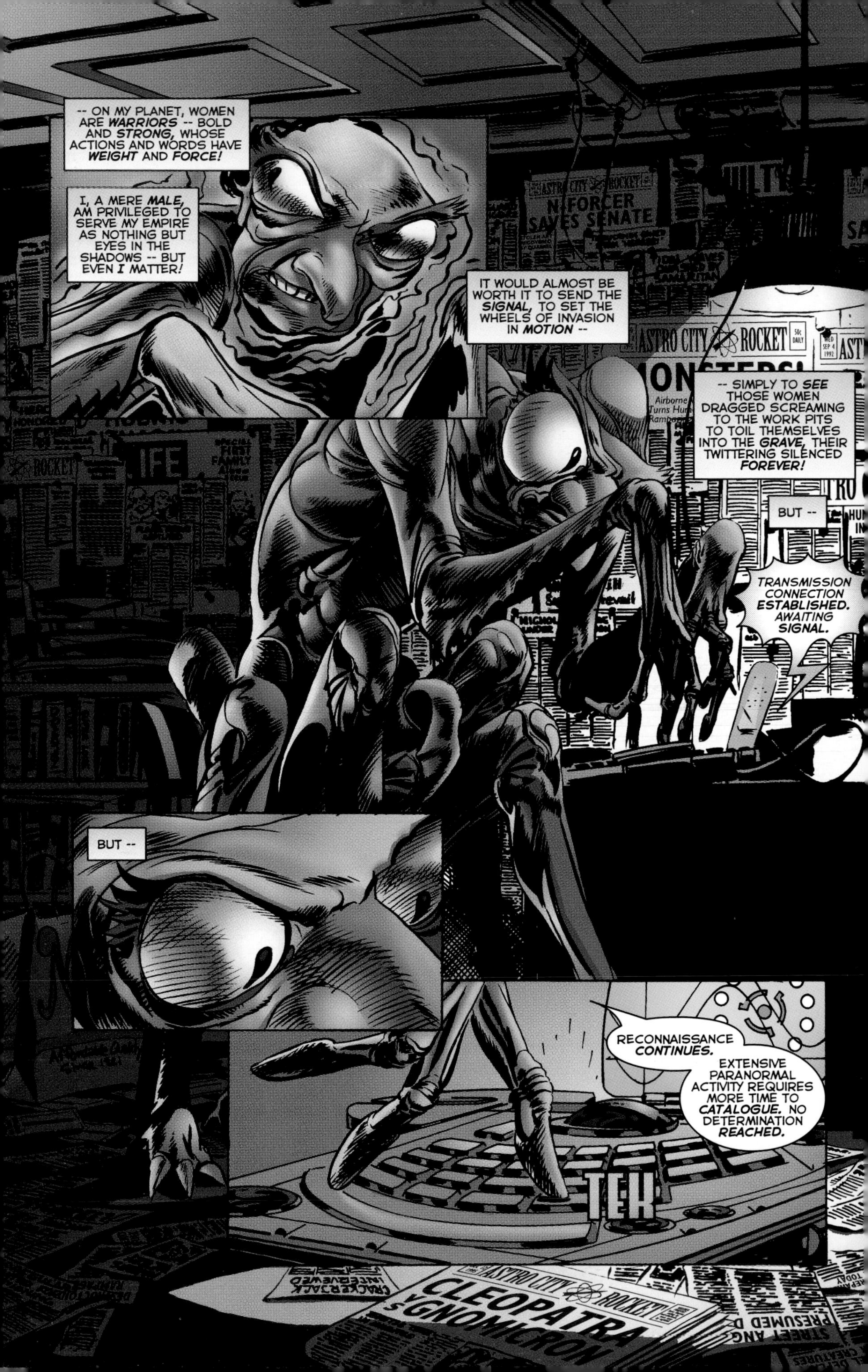
-- ON MY PLANET, WOMEN ARE WARRIORS -- BOLD AND STRONG, WHOSE ACTIONS AND WORDS HAVE WEIGHT AND FORCE!
I, A MERE MALE, AM PRIVILEGED TO SERVE MY EMPIRE AS NOTHING BUT EYES IN THE SHADOWS -- BUT EVEN I MATTER!
IT WOULD ALMOST BE WORTH IT TO SEND THE SIGNAL, TO SET THE WHEELS OF INVASION IN MOTION --
-- SIMPLY TO SEE THOSE WOMEN DRAGGED SCREAMING TO THE WORK PITS TO TOIL THEMSELVES INTO THE GRAVE, THEIR TWITTERING SILENCED FOREVER!
BUT --
TRANSMISSION CONNECTION ESTABLISHED. AWAITING SIGNAL.
BUT --
RECONNAISSANCE CONTINUES.
EXTENSIVE PARANORMAL ACTIVITY REQUIRES MORE TIME TO CATALOGUE. NO DETERMINATION REACHED.
TEK
ASTRO CITY ROCKET
N-FORCER SAVES SENATE
MONSTERS!
CLEOPATRA'S GNOMICRON

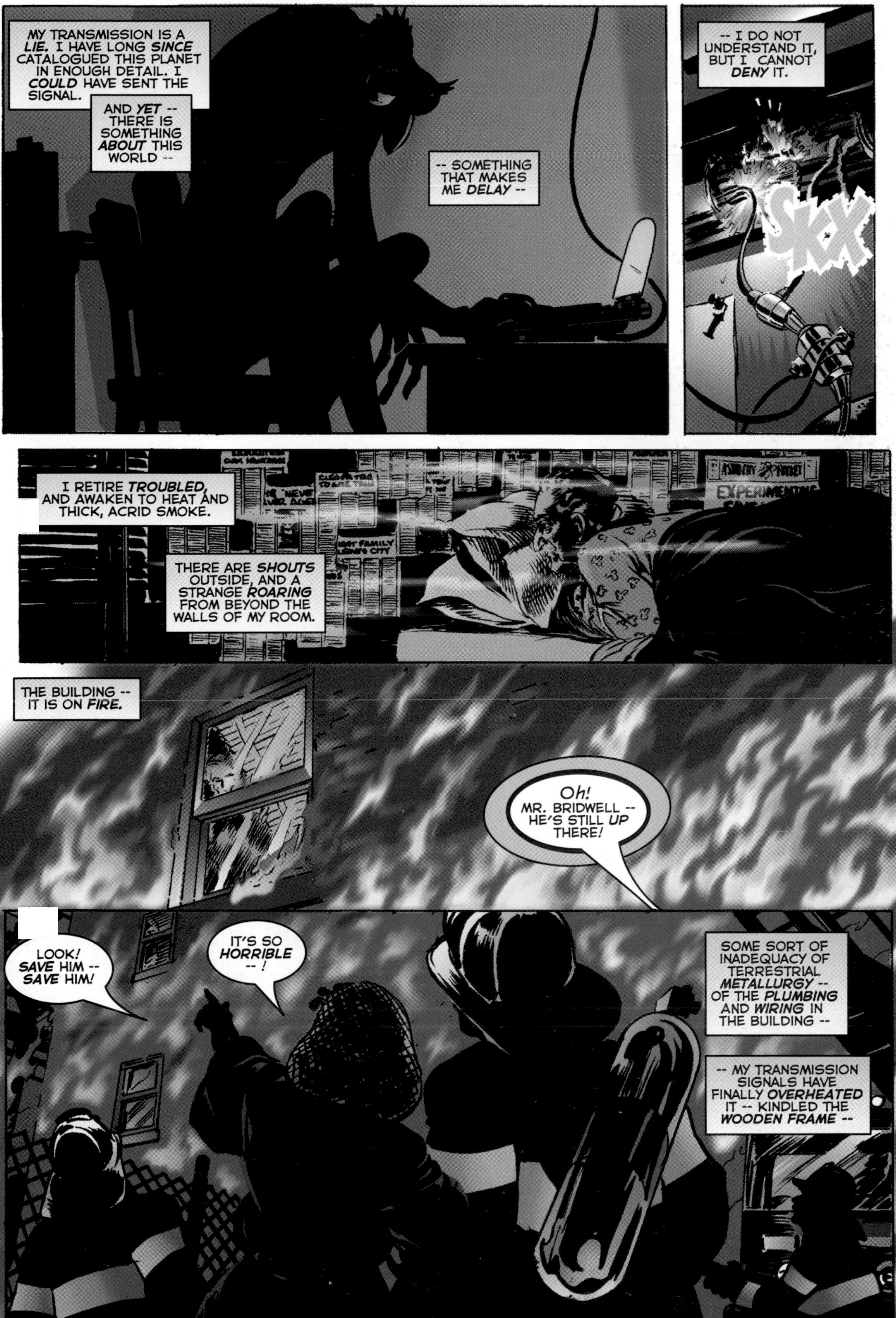
MY TRANSMISSION IS A LIE. I HAVE LONG SINCE CATALOGUED THIS PLANET IN ENOUGH DETAIL. I COULD HAVE SENT THE SIGNAL.
AND YET -- THERE IS SOMETHING ABOUT THIS WORLD --
-- SOMETHING THAT MAKES ME DELAY --
-- I DO NOT UNDERSTAND IT, BUT I CANNOT DENY IT.
SKX
I RETIRE TROUBLED, AND AWAKEN TO HEAT AND THICK, ACRID SMOKE.
THERE ARE SHOUTS OUTSIDE, AND A STRANGE ROARING FROM BEYOND THE WALLS OF MY ROOM.
THE BUILDING -- IT IS ON FIRE.
Oh! MR. BRIDWELL -- HE'S STILL UP THERE!
LOOK! SAVE HIM -- SAVE HIM!
IT'S SO HORRIBLE -- !
SOME SORT OF INADEQUACY OF TERRESTRIAL METALLURGY -- OF THE PLUMBING AND WIRING IN THE BUILDING --
-- MY TRANSMISSION SIGNALS HAVE FINALLY OVERHEATED IT -- KINDLED THE WOODEN FRAME --

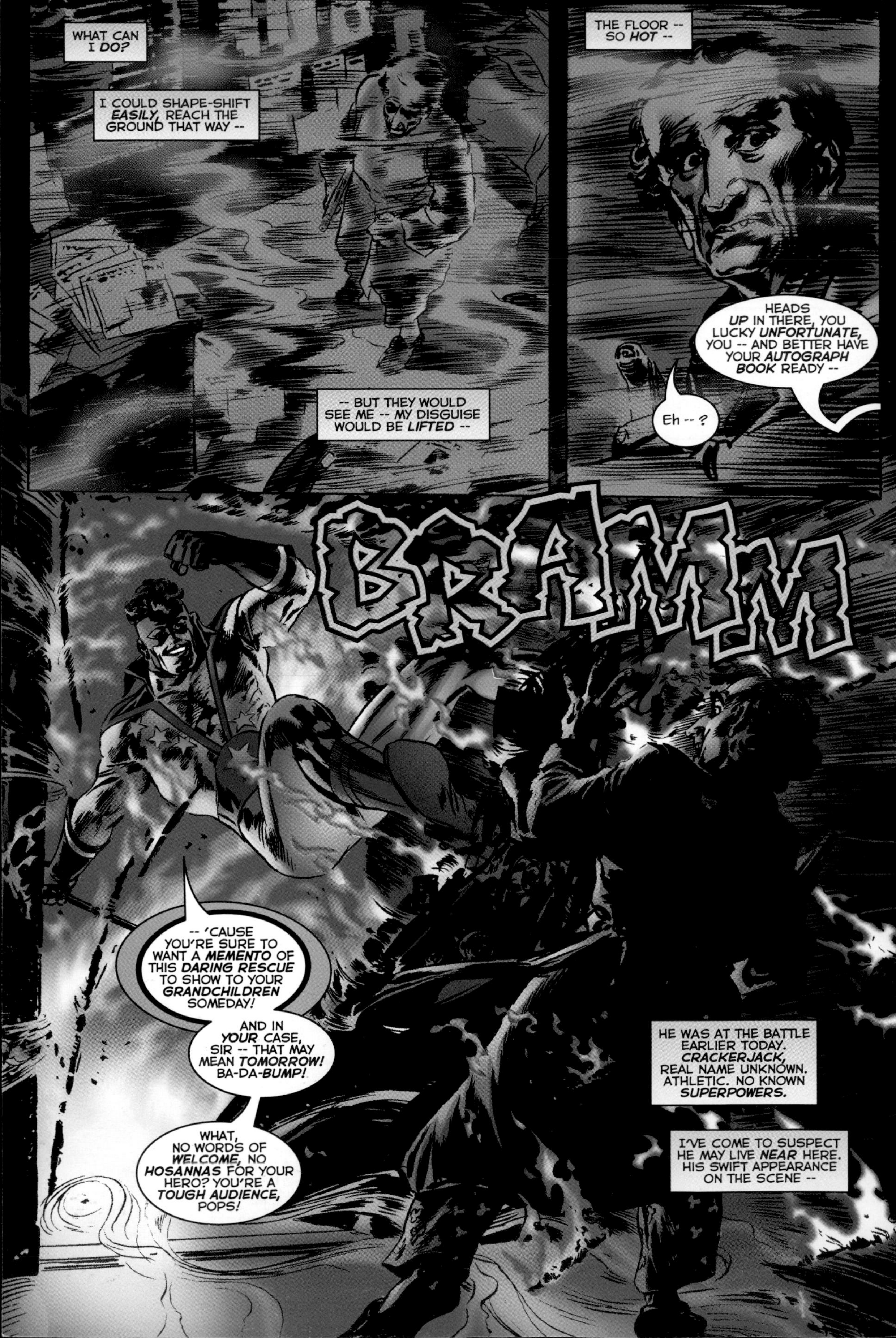
WHAT CAN I DO?
I COULD SHAPE-SHIFT EASILY, REACH THE GROUND THAT WAY --
-- BUT THEY WOULD SEE ME -- MY DISGUISE WOULD BE LIFTED --
THE FLOOR -- SO HOT --
HEADS UP IN THERE, YOU LUCKY UNFORTUNATE, YOU -- AND BETTER HAVE YOUR AUTOGRAPH BOOK READY --
Eh -- ?
BRAMM
-- 'CAUSE YOU'RE SURE TO WANT A MEMENTO OF THIS DARING RESCUE TO SHOW TO YOUR GRANDCHILDREN SOMEDAY!
AND IN YOUR CASE, SIR -- THAT MAY MEAN TOMORROW! BA-DA-BUMP!
WHAT, NO WORDS OF WELCOME, NO HOSANNAS FOR YOUR HERO? YOU'RE A TOUGH AUDIENCE, POPS!
HE WAS AT THE BATTLE EARLIER TODAY. CRACKERJACK, REAL NAME UNKNOWN. ATHLETIC. NO KNOWN SUPERPOWERS.
I'VE COME TO SUSPECT HE MAY LIVE NEAR HERE. HIS SWIFT APPEARANCE ON THE SCENE --

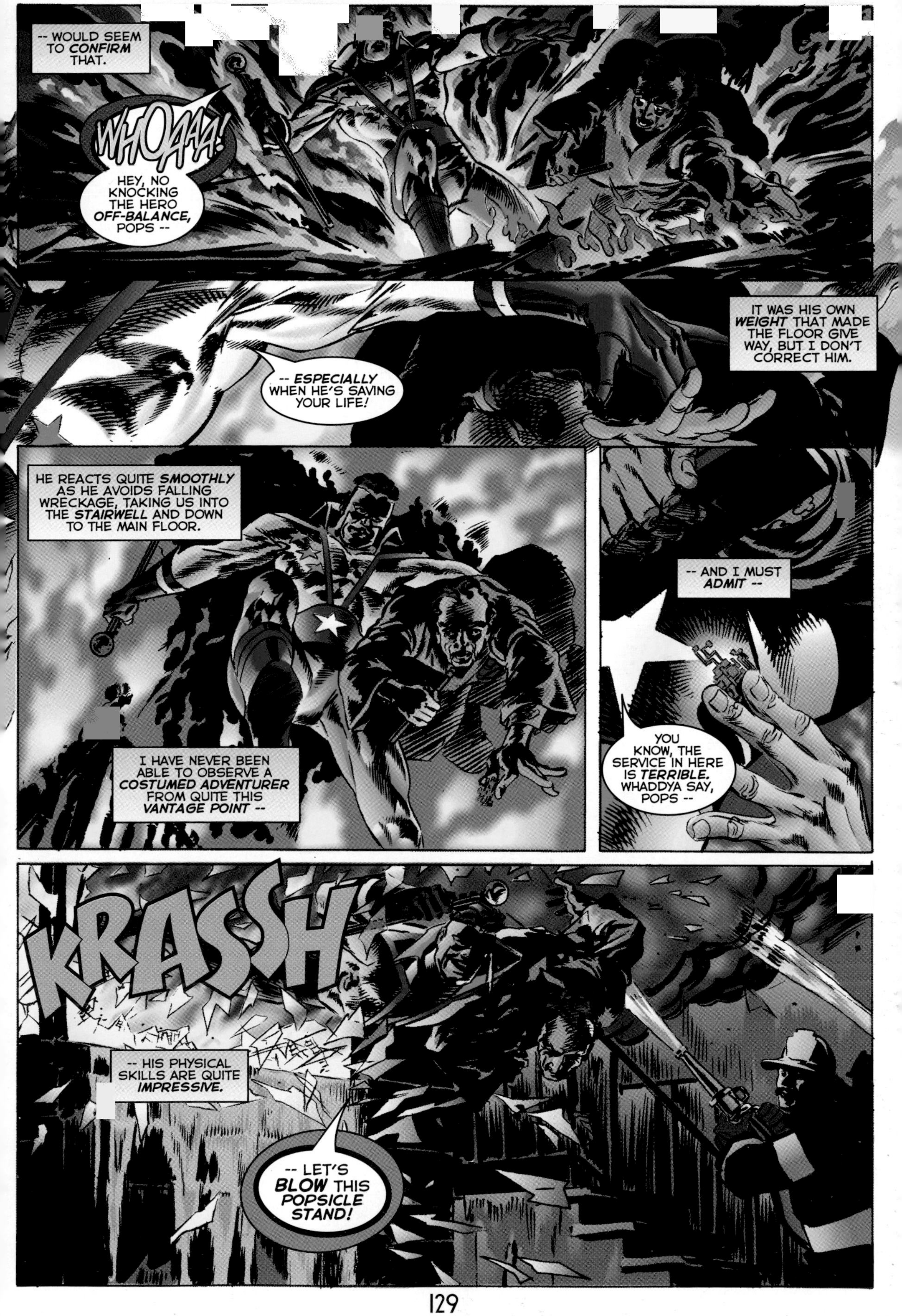
-- WOULD SEEM TO CONFIRM THAT.
WHOAAA!
HEY, NO KNOCKING THE HERO OFF-BALANCE, POPS --
IT WAS HIS OWN WEIGHT THAT MADE THE FLOOR GIVE WAY, BUT I DON'T CORRECT HIM.
-- ESPECIALLY WHEN HE'S SAVING YOUR LIFE!
HE REACTS QUITE SMOOTHLY AS HE AVOIDS FALLING WRECKAGE, TAKING US INTO THE STAIRWELL AND DOWN TO THE MAIN FLOOR.
I HAVE NEVER BEEN ABLE TO OBSERVE A COSTUMED ADVENTURER FROM QUITE THIS VANTAGE POINT --
-- AND I MUST ADMIT --
YOU KNOW, THE SERVICE IN HERE IS TERRIBLE. WHADDYA SAY, POPS --
KRASSH
-- HIS PHYSICAL SKILLS ARE QUITE IMPRESSIVE.
-- LET'S BLOW THIS POPSICLE STAND!

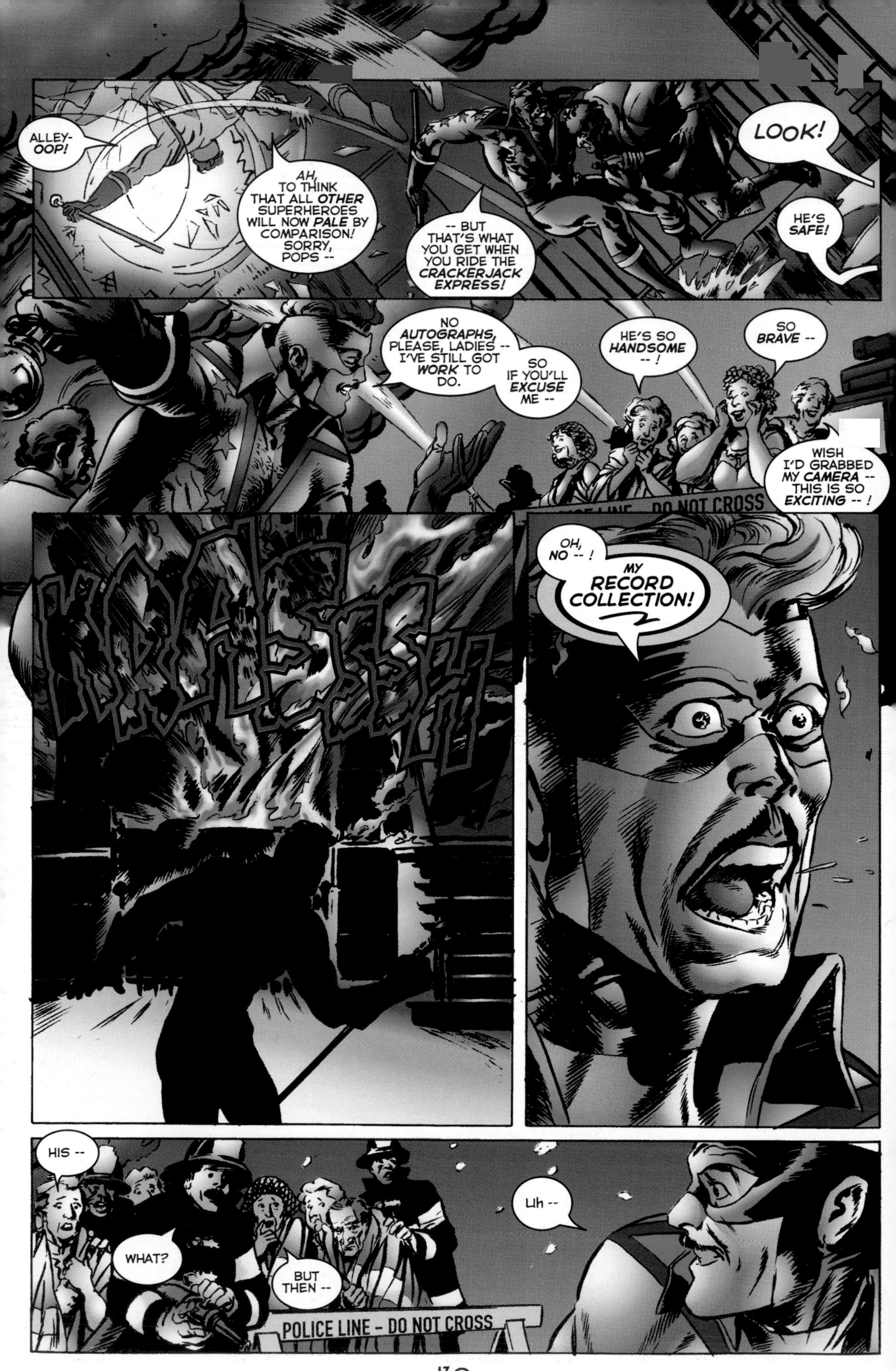
ALLEY-OOP!
AH, TO THINK THAT ALL OTHER SUPERHEROES WILL NOW PALE BY COMPARISON! SORRY, POPS --
-- BUT THAT'S WHAT YOU GET WHEN YOU RIDE THE CRACKERJACK EXPRESS!
LOOK!
HE'S SAFE!
NO AUTOGRAPHS, PLEASE, LADIES -- I'VE STILL GOT WORK TO DO.
SO IF YOU'LL EXCUSE ME --
HE'S SO HANDSOME -- !
SO BRAVE --
WISH I'D GRABBED MY CAMERA -- THIS IS SO EXCITING -- !
OH, NO -- !
MY RECORD COLLECTION!
HIS --
WHAT?
BUT THEN --
Uh --
POLICE LINE - DO NOT CROSS

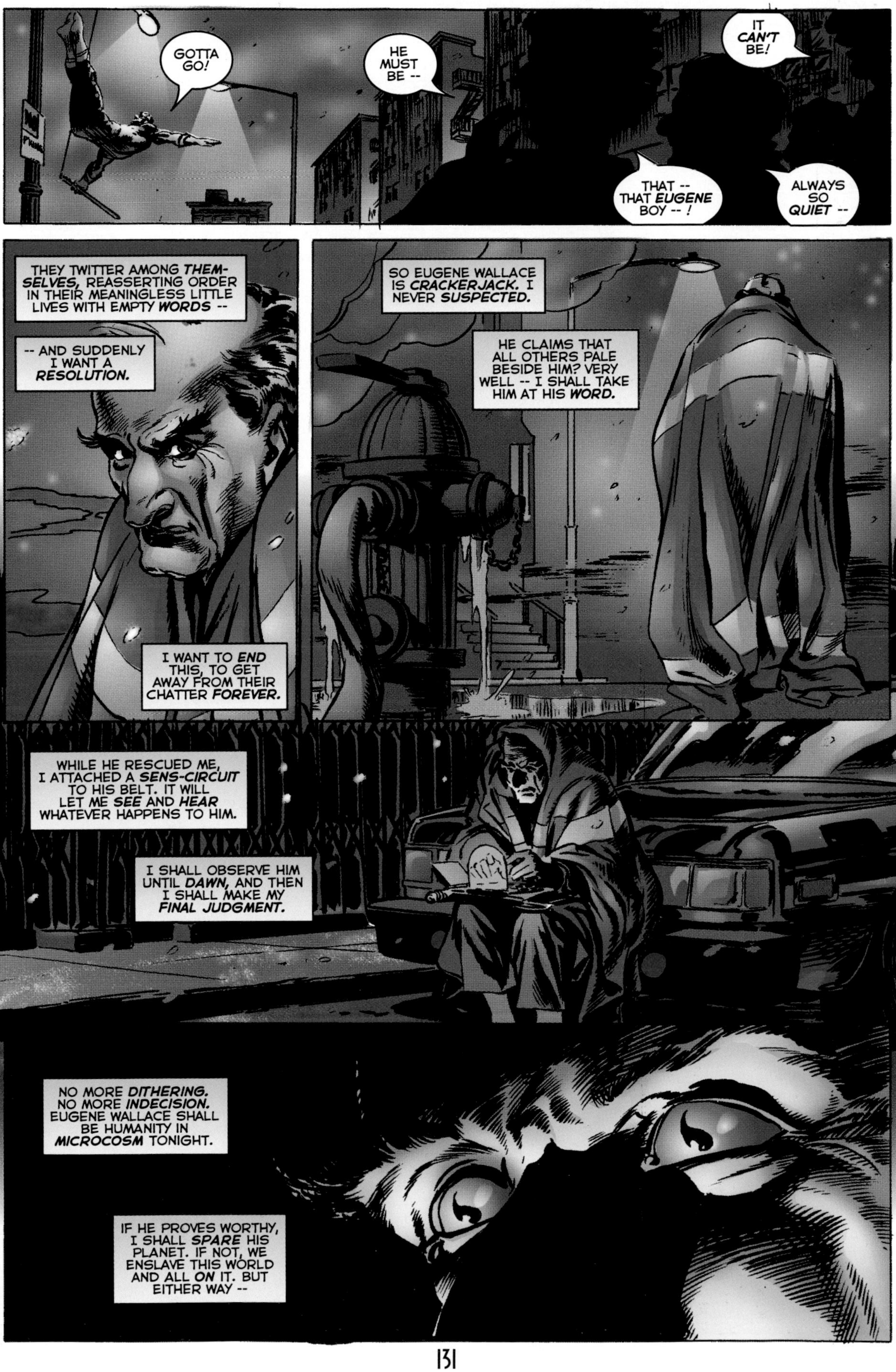

GOTTA GO!
HE MUST BE --
IT CAN'T BE!
THAT -- THAT EUGENE BOY -- !
ALWAYS SO QUIET --
THEY TWITTER AMONG THEMSELVES, REASSERTING ORDER IN THEIR MEANINGLESS LITTLE LIVES WITH EMPTY WORDS --
-- AND SUDDENLY I WANT A RESOLUTION.
I WANT TO END THIS, TO GET AWAY FROM THEIR CHATTER FOREVER.
SO EUGENE WALLACE IS CRACKERJACK. I NEVER SUSPECTED.
HE CLAIMS THAT ALL OTHERS PALE BESIDE HIM? VERY WELL -- I SHALL TAKE HIM AT HIS WORD.
WHILE HE RESCUED ME, I ATTACHED A SENS-CIRCUIT TO HIS BELT. IT WILL LET ME SEE AND HEAR WHATEVER HAPPENS TO HIM.
I SHALL OBSERVE HIM UNTIL DAWN, AND THEN I SHALL MAKE MY FINAL JUDGMENT.
NO MORE DITHERING. NO MORE INDECISION. EUGENE WALLACE SHALL BE HUMANITY IN MICROCOSM TONIGHT.
IF HE PROVES WORTHY, I SHALL SPARE HIS PLANET. IF NOT, WE ENSLAVE THIS WORLD AND ALL ON IT. BUT EITHER WAY --

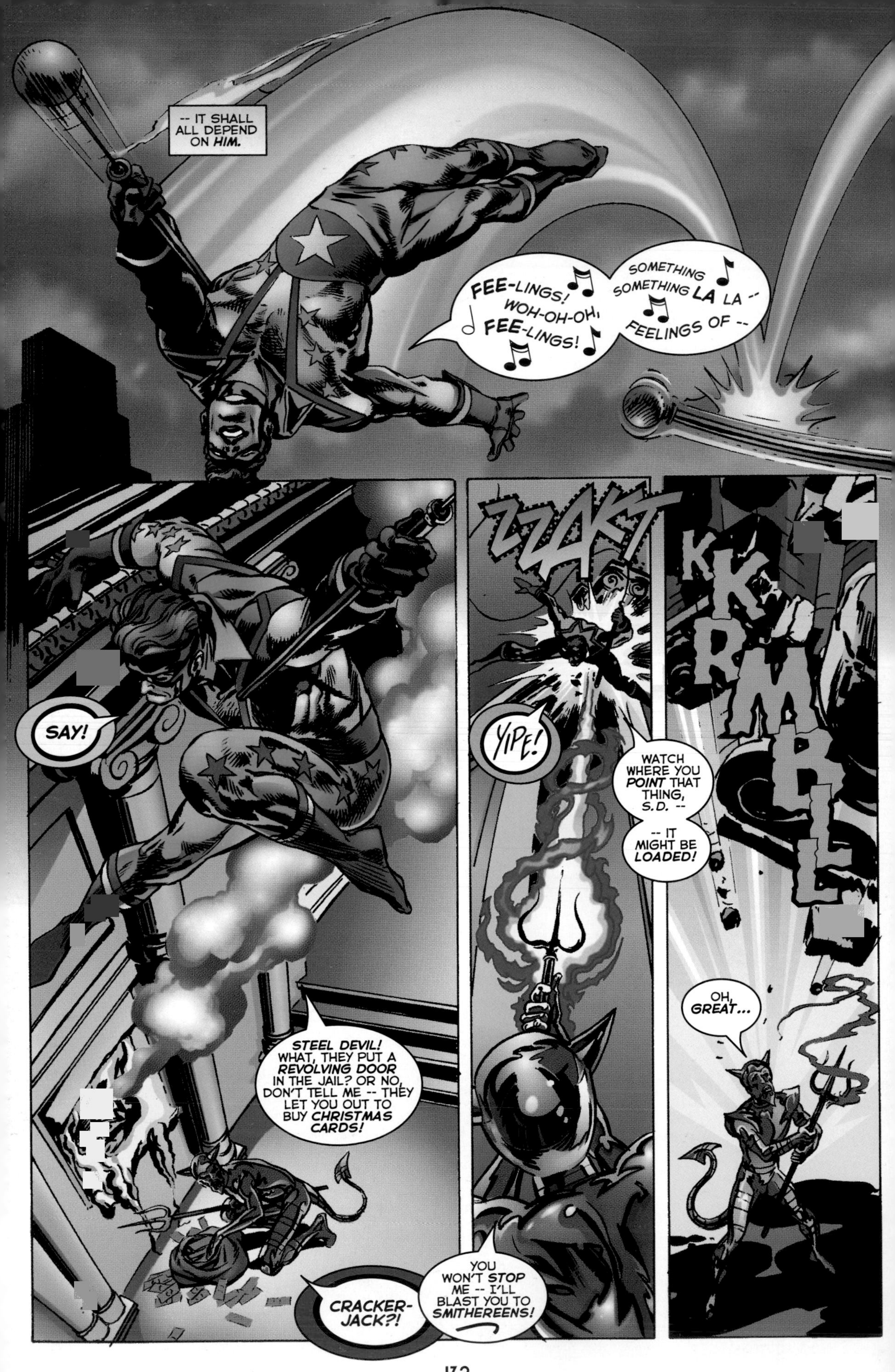
-- IT SHALL ALL DEPEND ON HIM.
FEE-LINGS! WOH-OH-OH, FEE-LINGS!
SOMETHING SOMETHING LA LA -- FEELINGS OF --
SAY!
STEEL DEVIL! WHAT, THEY PUT A REVOLVING DOOR IN THE JAIL? OR NO, DON'T TELL ME -- THEY LET YOU OUT TO BUY CHRISTMAS CARDS!
CRACKER-JACK?!
YOU WON'T STOP ME -- I'LL BLAST YOU TO SMITHEREENS!
ZZAKT
YIPE!
WATCH WHERE YOU POINT THAT THING, S.D. --
-- IT MIGHT BE LOADED!
KKRMBL
OH, GREAT...

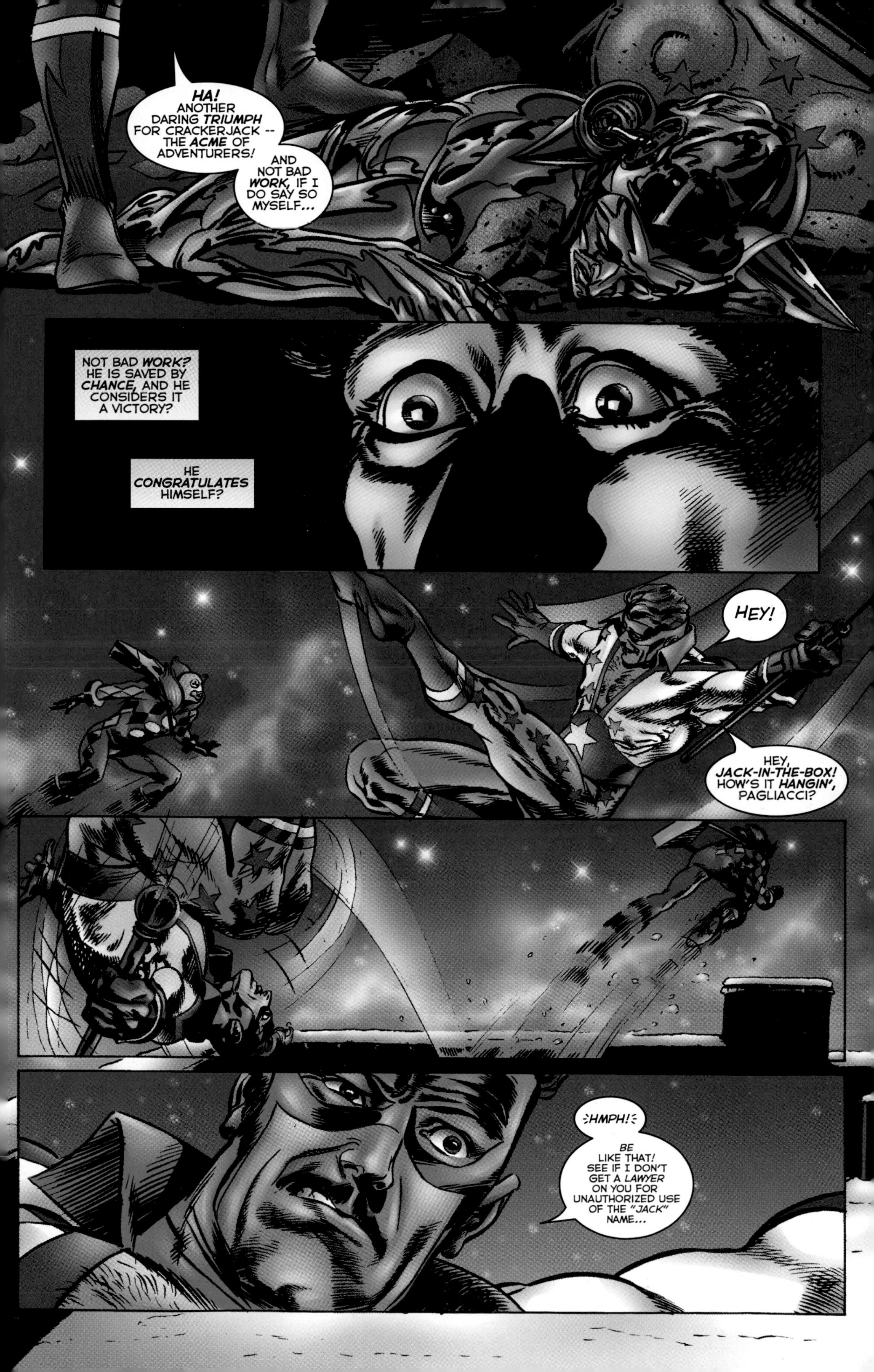

HA! ANOTHER DARING TRIUMPH FOR CRACKERJACK -- THE ACME OF ADVENTURERS!
AND NOT BAD WORK, IF I DO SAY SO MYSELF...
NOT BAD WORK? HE IS SAVED BY CHANCE, AND HE CONSIDERS IT A VICTORY?
HE CONGRATULATES HIMSELF?
HEY!
HEY, JACK-IN-THE-BOX! HOW'S IT HANGIN', PAGLIACCI?
HMPH!
BE LIKE THAT! SEE IF I DON'T GET A LAWYER ON YOU FOR UNAUTHORIZED USE OF THE "JACK" NAME...

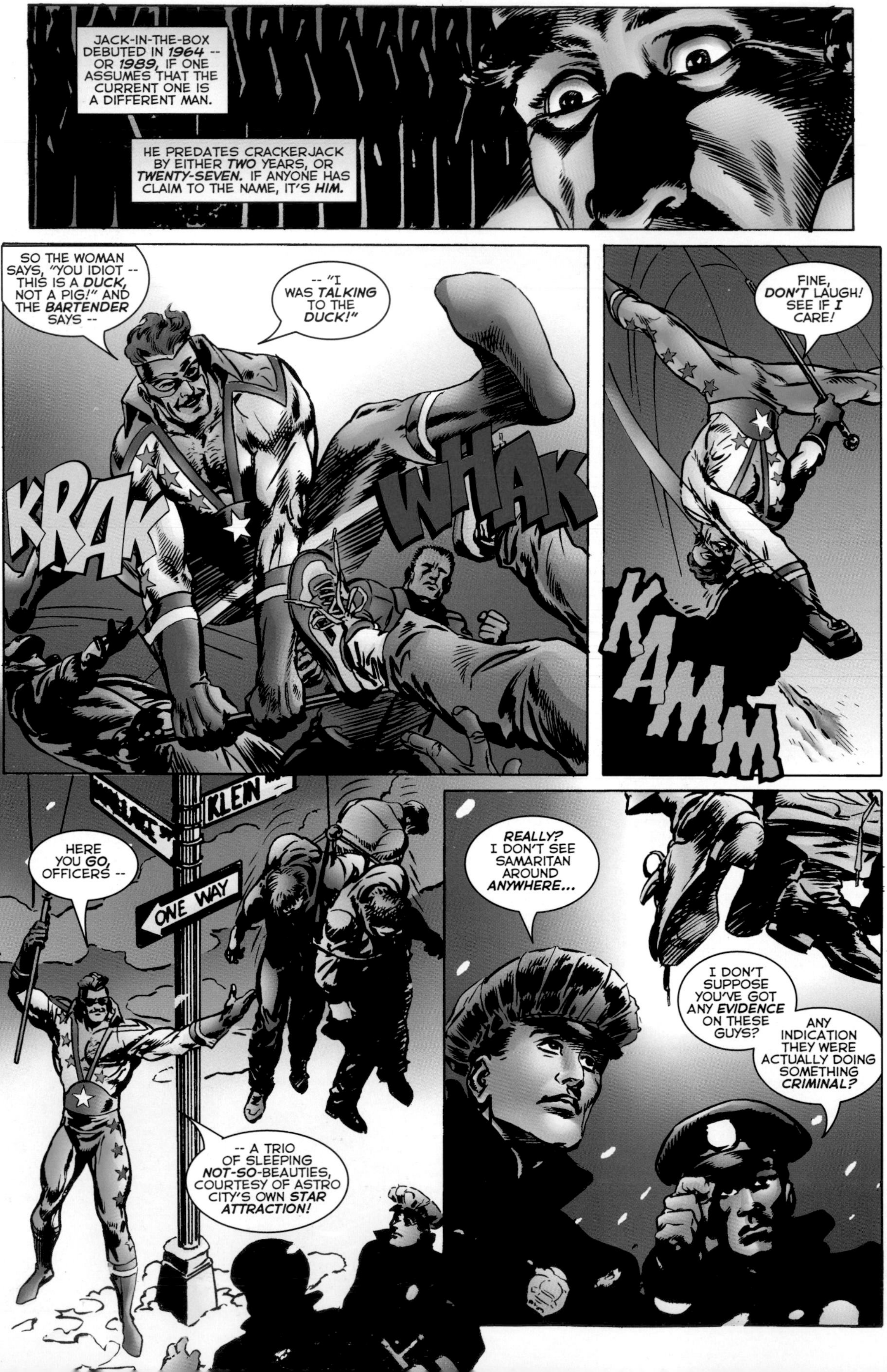
JACK-IN-THE-BOX DEBUTED IN 1964 -- OR 1989, IF ONE ASSUMES THAT THE CURRENT ONE IS A DIFFERENT MAN.
HE PREDATES CRACKERJACK BY EITHER TWO YEARS, OR TWENTY-SEVEN. IF ANYONE HAS CLAIM TO THE NAME, IT'S HIM.
SO THE WOMAN SAYS, "YOU IDIOT -- THIS IS A DUCK, NOT A PIG!" AND THE BARTENDER SAYS --
-- "I WAS TALKING TO THE DUCK!"
KRAK
WHAK
FINE, DON'T LAUGH! SEE IF I CARE!
KAMM
KLEIN
ONE WAY
HERE YOU GO, OFFICERS --
-- A TRIO OF SLEEPING NOT-SO-BEAUTIES, COURTESY OF ASTRO CITY'S OWN STAR ATTRACTION!
REALLY? I DON'T SEE SAMARITAN AROUND ANYWHERE...
I DON'T SUPPOSE YOU'VE GOT ANY EVIDENCE ON THESE GUYS?
ANY INDICATION THEY WERE ACTUALLY DOING SOMETHING CRIMINAL?

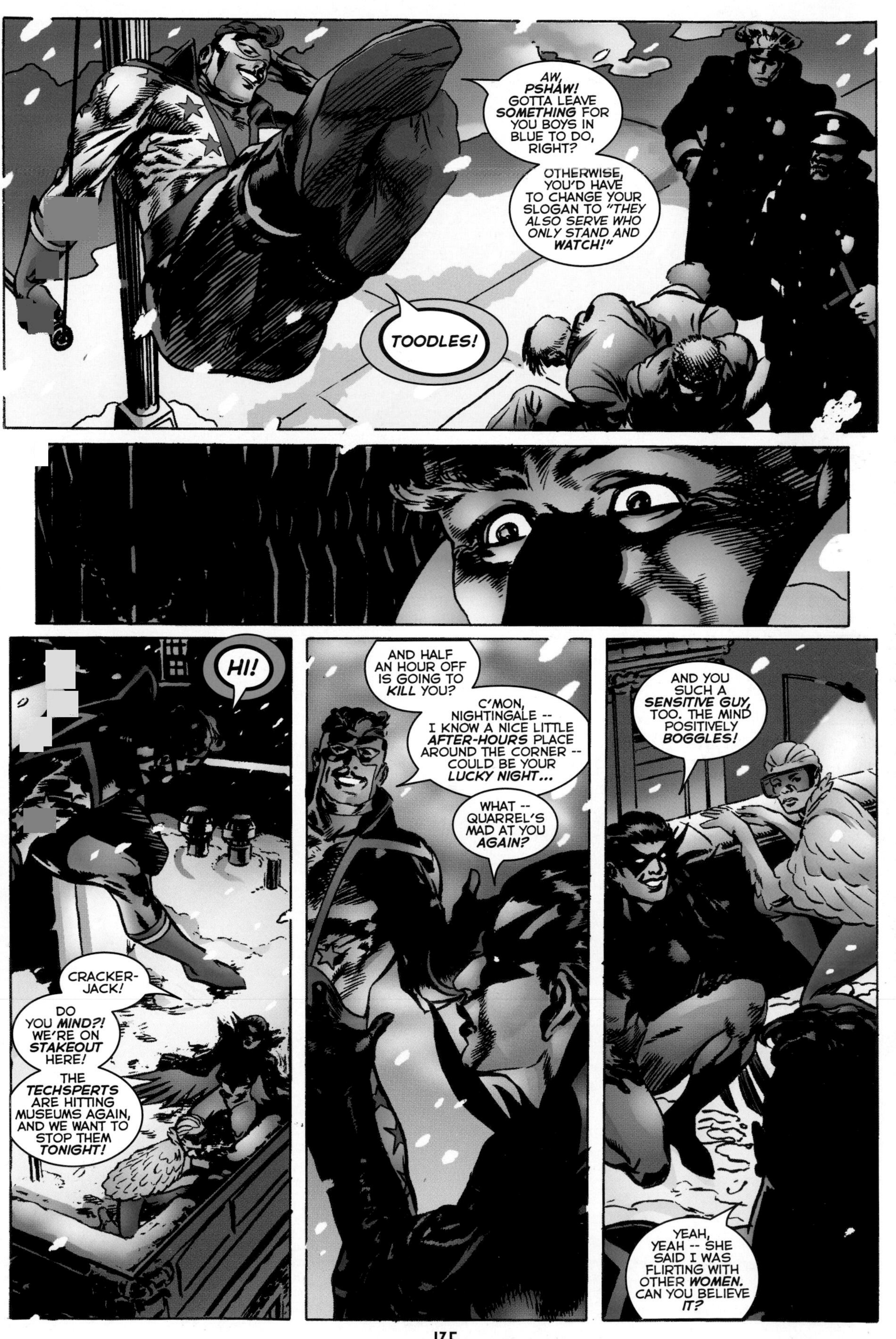

AW, PSHAW! GOTTA LEAVE SOMETHING FOR YOU BOYS IN BLUE TO DO, RIGHT?
OTHERWISE, YOU'D HAVE TO CHANGE YOUR SLOGAN TO "THEY ALSO SERVE WHO ONLY STAND AND WATCH!"
TOODLES!
HI!
CRACKER-JACK!
DO YOU MIND?! WE'RE ON STAKEOUT HERE!
THE TECHSPERTS ARE HITTING MUSEUMS AGAIN, AND WE WANT TO STOP THEM TONIGHT!
AND HALF AN HOUR OFF IS GOING TO KILL YOU?
C'MON, NIGHTINGALE -- I KNOW A NICE LITTLE AFTER-HOURS PLACE AROUND THE CORNER -- COULD BE YOUR LUCKY NIGHT...
WHAT -- QUARREL'S MAD AT YOU AGAIN?
AND YOU SUCH A SENSITIVE GUY, TOO. THE MIND POSITIVELY BOGGLES!
YEAH, YEAH -- SHE SAID I WAS FLIRTING WITH OTHER WOMEN. CAN YOU BELIEVE IT?

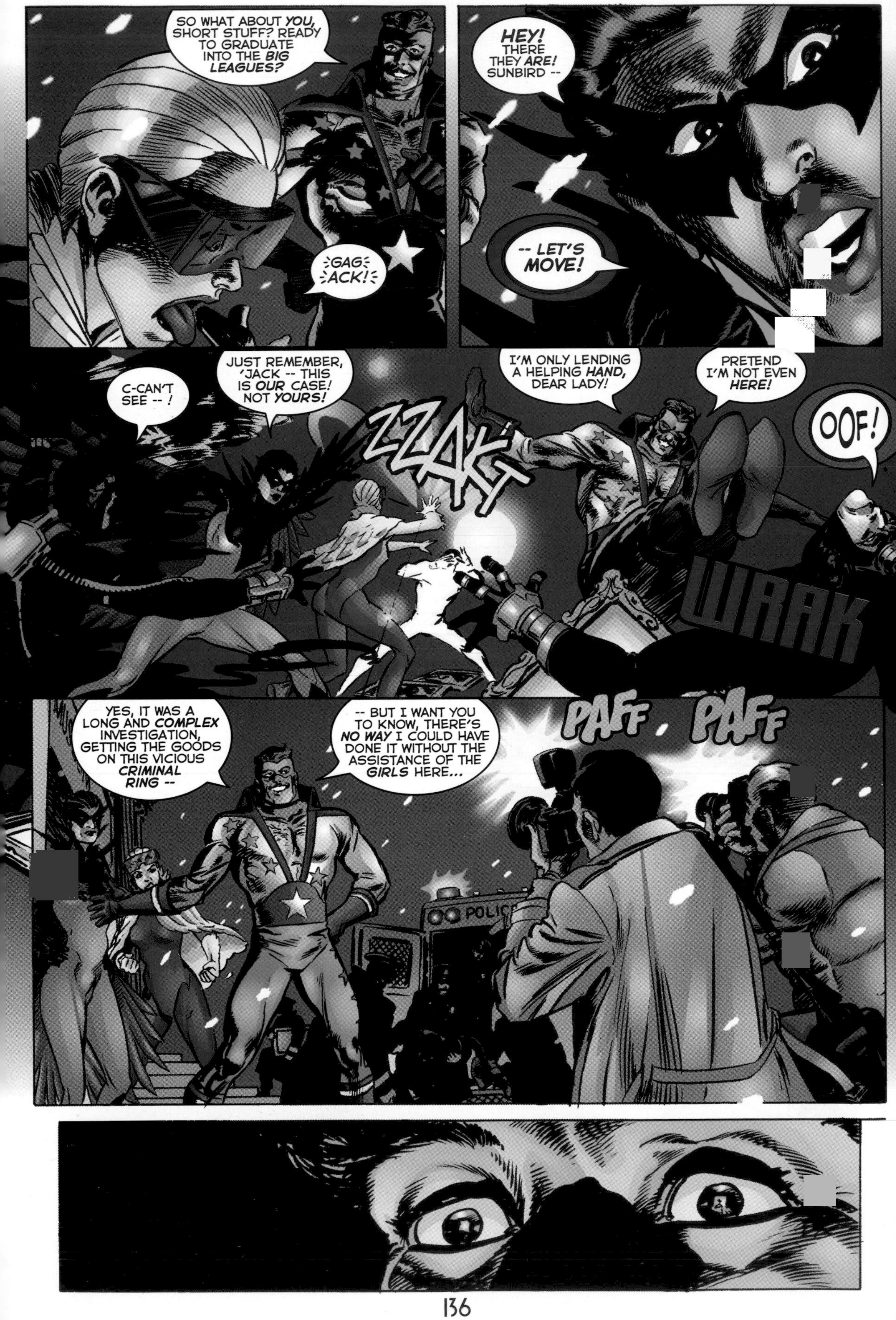
SO WHAT ABOUT YOU, SHORT STUFF? READY TO GRADUATE INTO THE BIG LEAGUES?
GAG ACK!
HEY! THERE THEY ARE! SUNBIRD --
-- LET'S MOVE!
C-CAN'T SEE -- !
JUST REMEMBER, 'JACK -- THIS IS OUR CASE! NOT YOURS!
ZZAKT
I'M ONLY LENDING A HELPING HAND, DEAR LADY!
PRETEND I'M NOT EVEN HERE!
OOF!
WRAK
YES, IT WAS A LONG AND COMPLEX INVESTIGATION, GETTING THE GOODS ON THIS VICIOUS CRIMINAL RING --
-- BUT I WANT YOU TO KNOW, THERE'S NO WAY I COULD HAVE DONE IT WITHOUT THE ASSISTANCE OF THE GIRLS HERE...
PAFF PAFF
POLICE

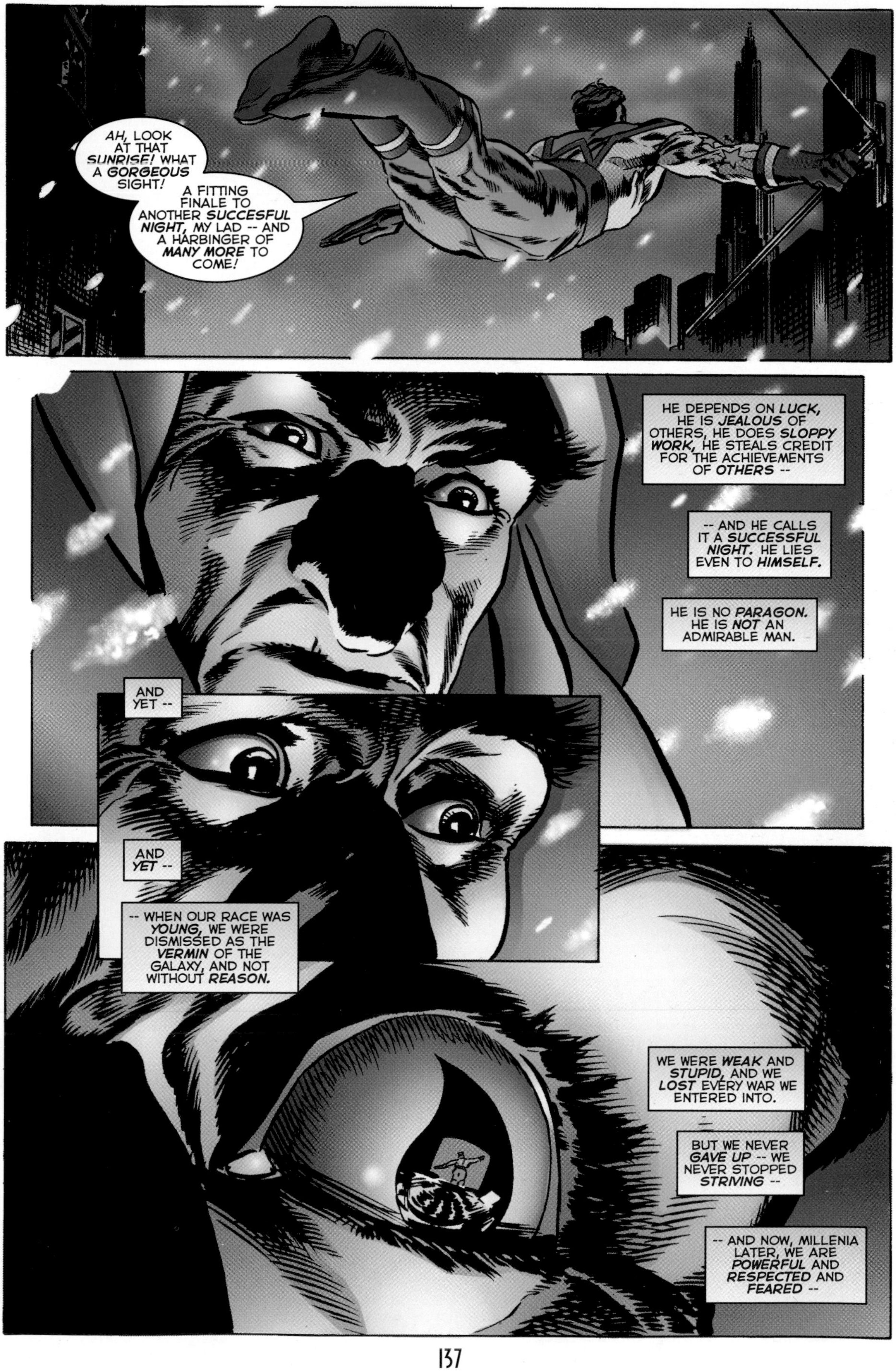
AH, LOOK AT THAT SUNRISE! WHAT A GORGEOUS SIGHT!
A FITTING FINALE TO ANOTHER SUCCESFUL NIGHT, MY LAD -- AND A HARBINGER OF MANY MORE TO COME!
HE DEPENDS ON LUCK, HE IS JEALOUS OF OTHERS, HE DOES SLOPPY WORK, HE STEALS CREDIT FOR THE ACHIEVEMENTS OF OTHERS --
-- AND HE CALLS IT A SUCCESSFUL NIGHT. HE LIES EVEN TO HIMSELF.
HE IS NO PARAGON. HE IS NOT AN ADMIRABLE MAN.
AND YET --
AND YET --
-- WHEN OUR RACE WAS YOUNG, WE WERE DISMISSED AS THE VERMIN OF THE GALAXY, AND NOT WITHOUT REASON.
WE WERE WEAK AND STUPID, AND WE LOST EVERY WAR WE ENTERED INTO.
BUT WE NEVER GAVE UP -- WE NEVER STOPPED STRIVING --
-- AND NOW, MILLENIA LATER, WE ARE POWERFUL AND RESPECTED AND FEARED --

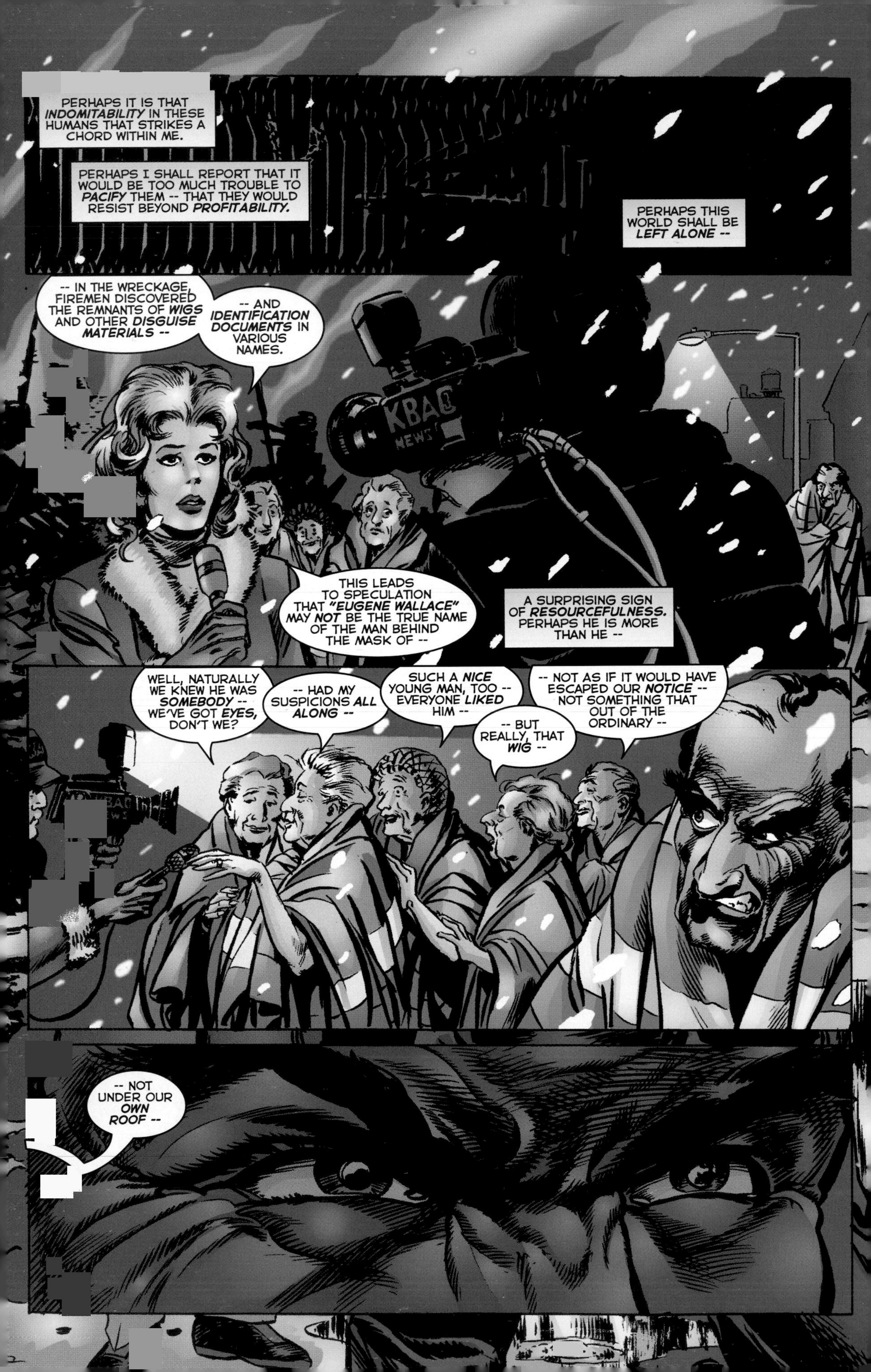
PERHAPS IT IS THAT INDOMITABILITY IN THESE HUMANS THAT STRIKES A CHORD WITHIN ME.
PERHAPS I SHALL REPORT THAT IT WOULD BE TOO MUCH TROUBLE TO PACIFY THEM -- THAT THEY WOULD RESIST BEYOND PROFITABILITY.
PERHAPS THIS WORLD SHALL BE LEFT ALONE --
-- IN THE WRECKAGE, FIREMEN DISCOVERED THE REMNANTS OF WIGS AND OTHER DISGUISE MATERIALS --
-- AND IDENTIFICATION DOCUMENTS IN VARIOUS NAMES.
KBAC NEWS
THIS LEADS TO SPECULATION THAT "EUGENE WALLACE" MAY NOT BE THE TRUE NAME OF THE MAN BEHIND THE MASK OF --
A SURPRISING SIGN OF RESOURCEFULNESS. PERHAPS HE IS MORE THAN HE --
WELL, NATURALLY WE KNEW HE WAS SOMEBODY -- WE'VE GOT EYES, DON'T WE?
-- HAD MY SUSPICIONS ALL ALONG --
SUCH A NICE YOUNG MAN, TOO -- EVERYONE LIKED HIM --
-- BUT REALLY, THAT WIG --
-- NOT AS IF IT WOULD HAVE ESCAPED OUR NOTICE -- NOT SOMETHING THAT OUT OF THE ORDINARY --
-- NOT UNDER OUR OWN ROOF --

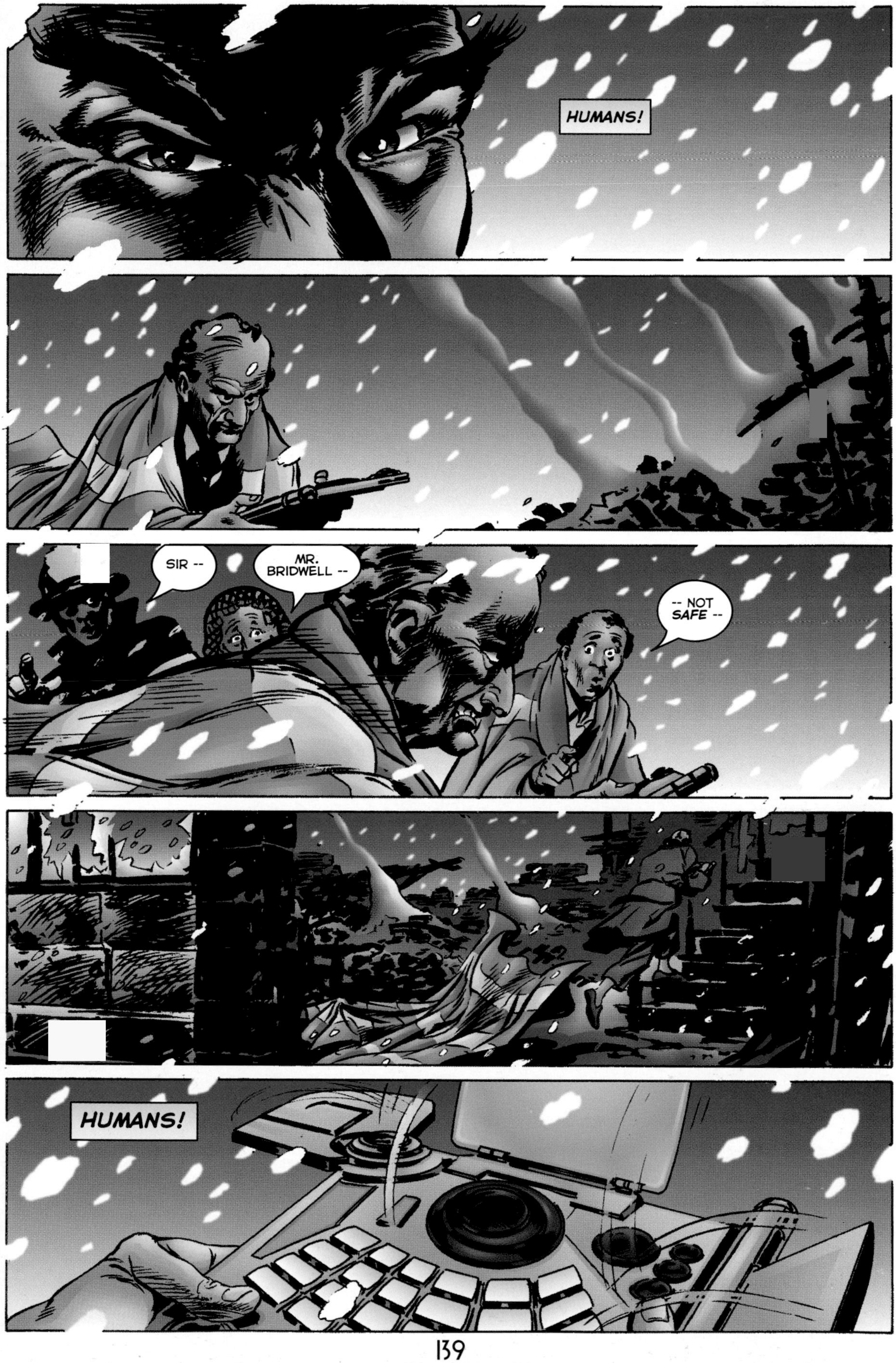

HUMANS!
SIR --
MR. BRIDWELL --
-- NOT SAFE --
HUMANS!

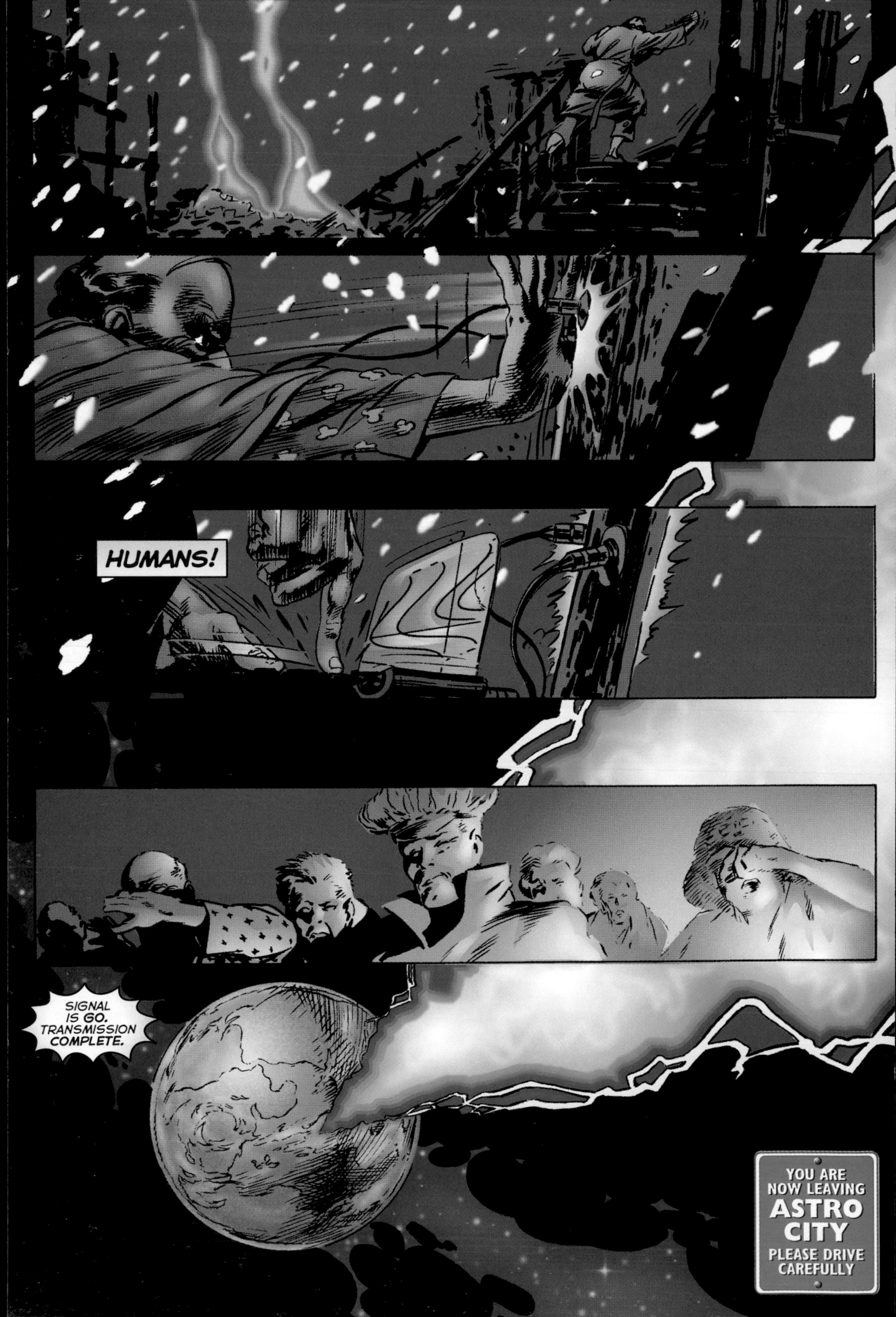
HUMANS!
SIGNAL IS GO. TRANSMISSION COMPLETE.
YOU ARE NOW LEAVING ASTRO CITY PLEASE DRIVE CAREFULLY

CHAPTER 6

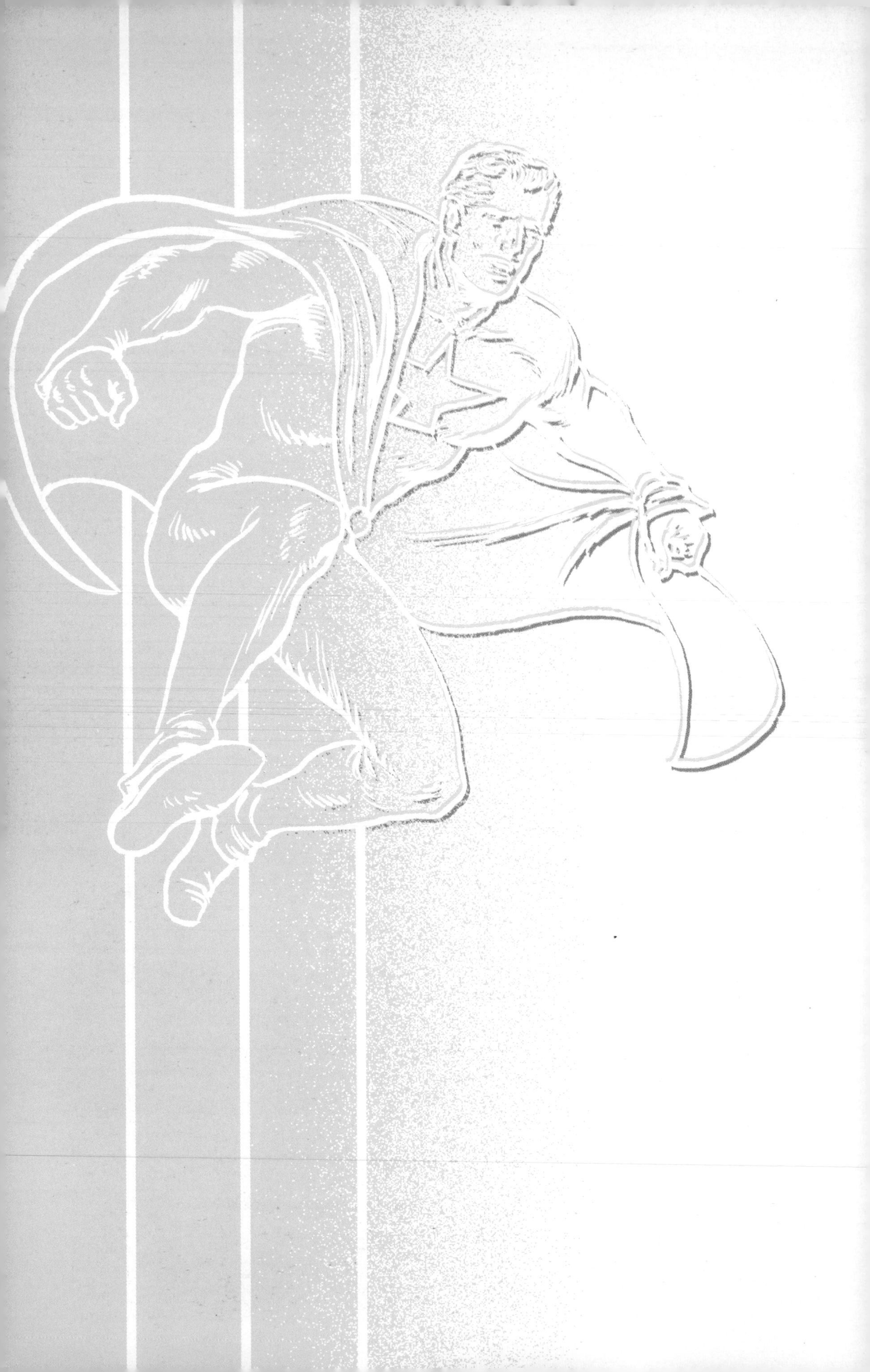

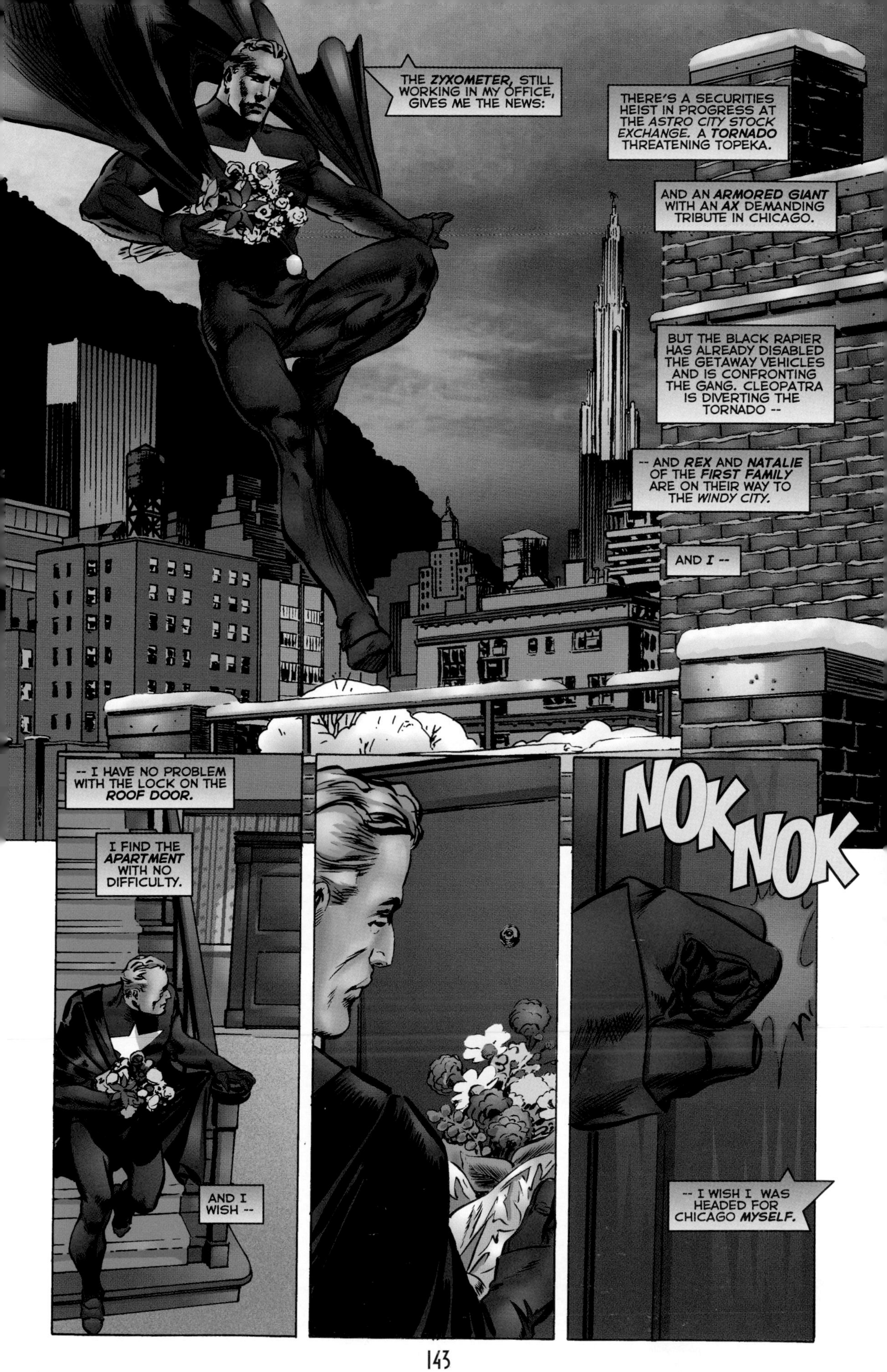
THE ZYXOMETER, STILL WORKING IN MY OFFICE, GIVES ME THE NEWS:
THERE'S A SECURITIES HEIST IN PROGRESS AT THE ASTRO CITY STOCK EXCHANGE. A TORNADO THREATENING TOPEKA.
AND AN ARMORED GIANT WITH AN AX DEMANDING TRIBUTE IN CHICAGO.
BUT THE BLACK RAPIER HAS ALREADY DISABLED THE GETAWAY VEHICLES AND IS CONFRONTING THE GANG. CLEOPATRA IS DIVERTING THE TORNADO --
-- AND REX AND NATALIE OF THE FIRST FAMILY ARE ON THEIR WAY TO THE WINDY CITY.
AND I --
-- I HAVE NO PROBLEM WITH THE LOCK ON THE ROOF DOOR.
I FIND THE APARTMENT WITH NO DIFFICULTY.
AND I WISH --
NOK NOK
-- I WISH I WAS HEADED FOR CHICAGO MYSELF.

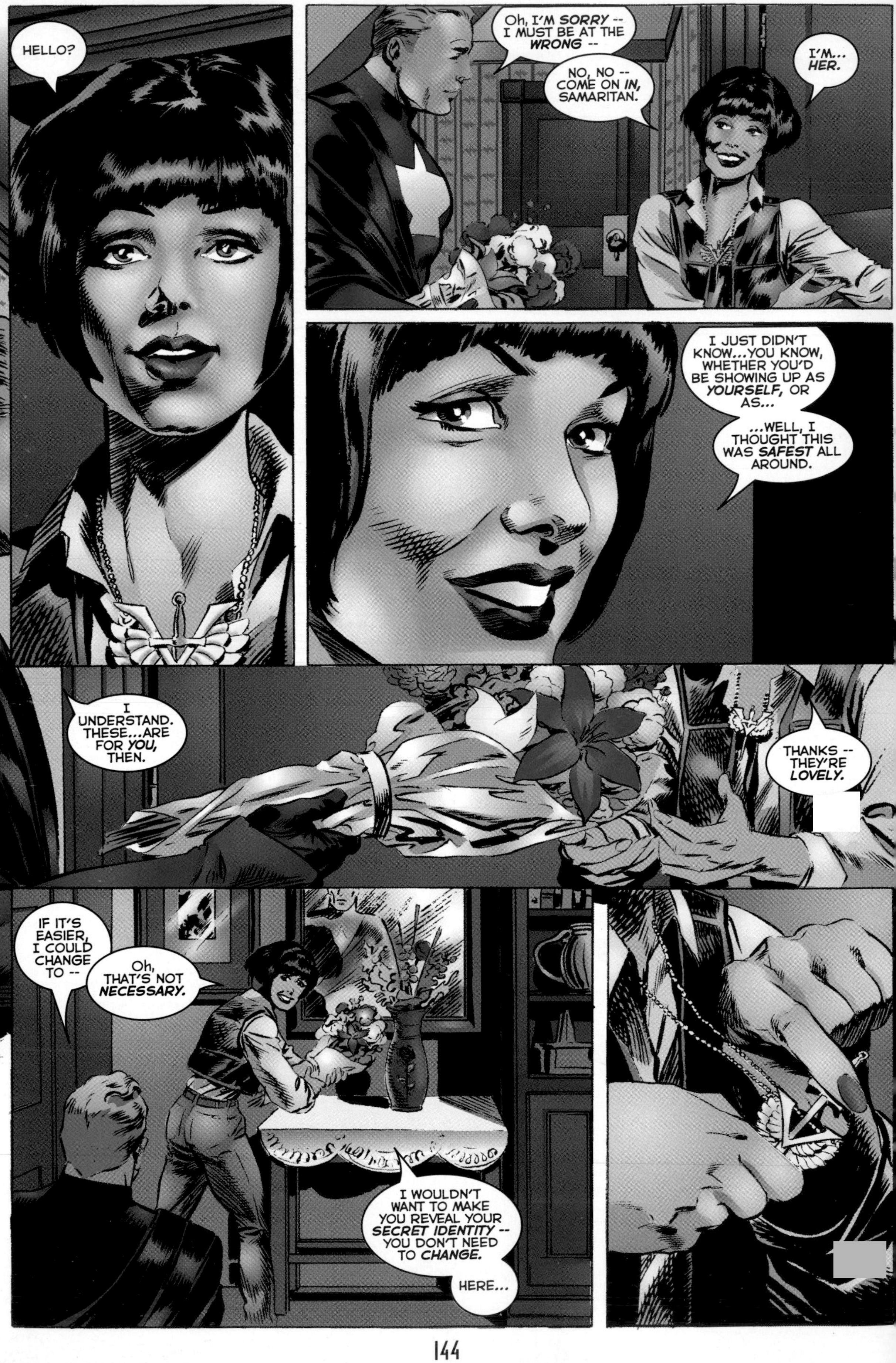
HELLO?
Oh, I'M SORRY -- I MUST BE AT THE WRONG --
NO, NO -- COME ON IN, SAMARITAN.
I'M... HER.
I JUST DIDN'T KNOW...YOU KNOW, WHETHER YOU'D BE SHOWING UP AS YOURSELF, OR AS...
...WELL, I THOUGHT THIS WAS SAFEST ALL AROUND.
I UNDERSTAND. THESE...ARE FOR YOU, THEN.
THANKS -- THEY'RE LOVELY.
IF IT'S EASIER, I COULD CHANGE TO --
Oh, THAT'S NOT NECESSARY.
I WOULDN'T WANT TO MAKE YOU REVEAL YOUR SECRET IDENTITY -- YOU DON'T NEED TO CHANGE.
HERE...

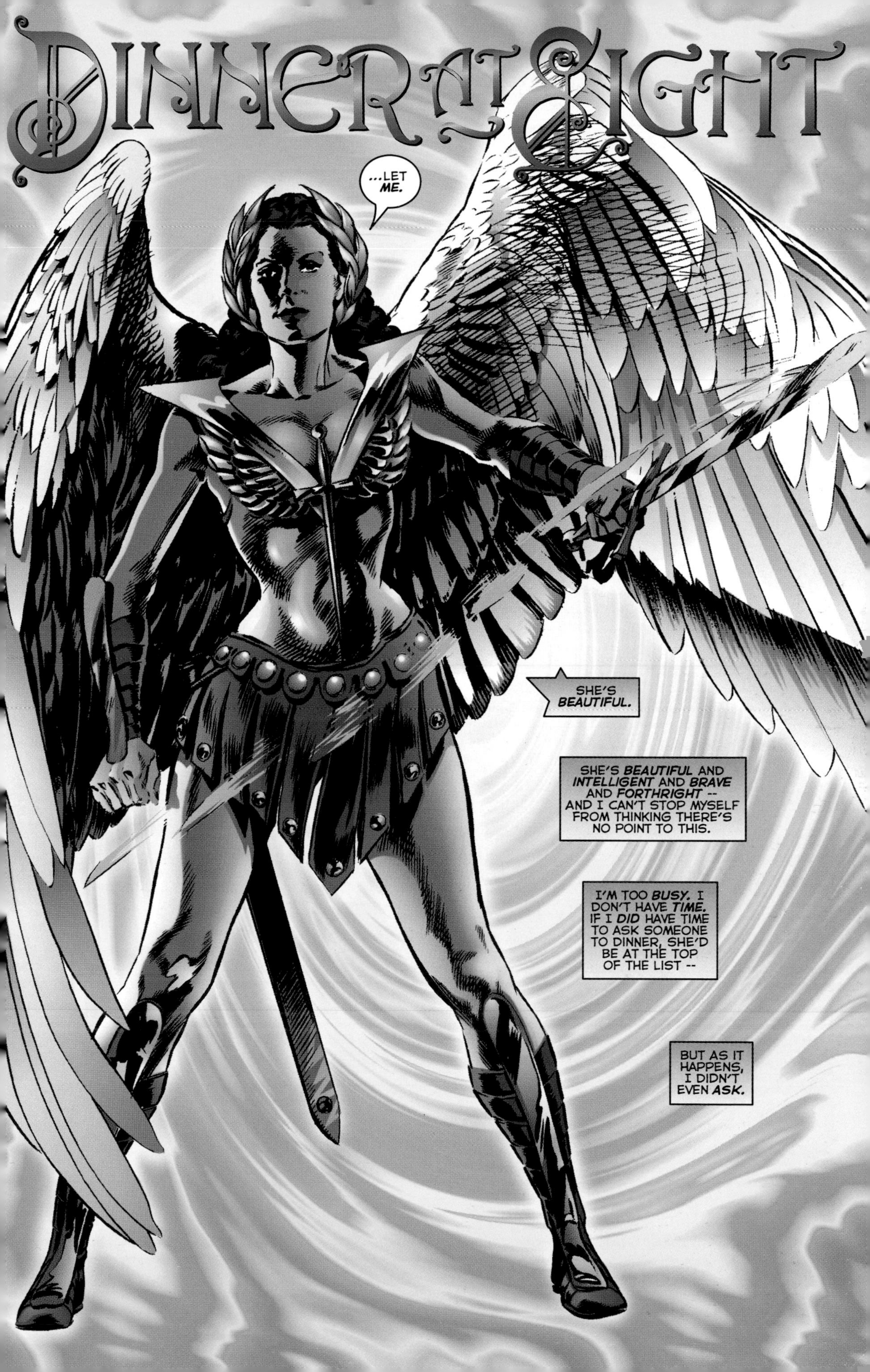

DINNER AT EIGHT
...LET ME.
SHE'S BEAUTIFUL.
SHE'S BEAUTIFUL AND INTELLIGENT AND BRAVE AND FORTHRIGHT -- AND I CAN'T STOP MYSELF FROM THINKING THERE'S NO POINT TO THIS.
I'M TOO BUSY. I DON'T HAVE TIME. IF I DID HAVE TIME TO ASK SOMEONE TO DINNER, SHE'D BE AT THE TOP OF THE LIST --
BUT AS IT HAPPENS, I DIDN'T EVEN ASK.

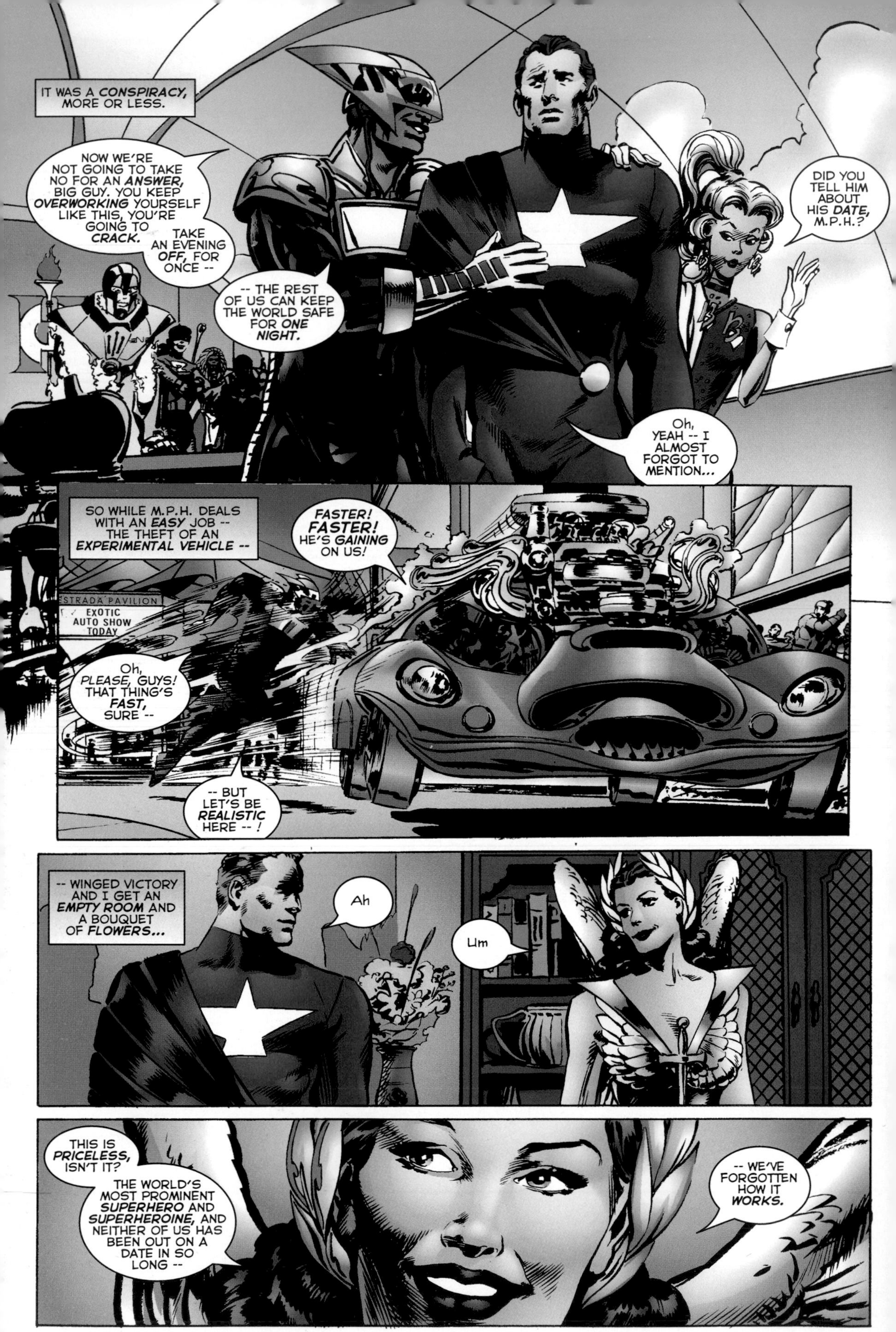
IT WAS A *CONSPIRACY,* MORE OR LESS.
NOW WE'RE NOT GOING TO TAKE NO FOR AN ***ANSWER,*** BIG GUY. YOU KEEP ***OVERWORKING*** YOURSELF LIKE THIS, YOU'RE GOING TO ***CRACK.***
TAKE AN EVENING ***OFF,*** FOR ONCE --
-- THE REST OF US CAN KEEP THE WORLD SAFE FOR ***ONE NIGHT.***
DID YOU TELL HIM ABOUT HIS ***DATE,*** M.P.H.?
Oh, YEAH -- I ALMOST FORGOT TO MENTION...
SO WHILE M.P.H. DEALS WITH AN *EASY* JOB -- THE THEFT OF AN ***EXPERIMENTAL VEHICLE*** --
FASTER! FASTER! HE'S ***GAINING*** ON US!
ESTRADA PAVILION
EXOTIC AUTO SHOW TODAY
Oh, *PLEASE,* GUYS! THAT THING'S ***FAST,*** SURE --
-- BUT LET'S BE ***REALISTIC*** HERE -- !
-- WINGED VICTORY AND I GET AN ***EMPTY ROOM*** AND A BOUQUET OF ***FLOWERS...***
Ah
Um
THIS IS ***PRICELESS,*** ISN'T IT?
THE WORLD'S MOST PROMINENT ***SUPERHERO*** AND ***SUPERHEROINE,*** AND NEITHER OF US HAS BEEN OUT ON A DATE IN SO LONG --
-- WE'VE FORGOTTEN HOW IT ***WORKS.***

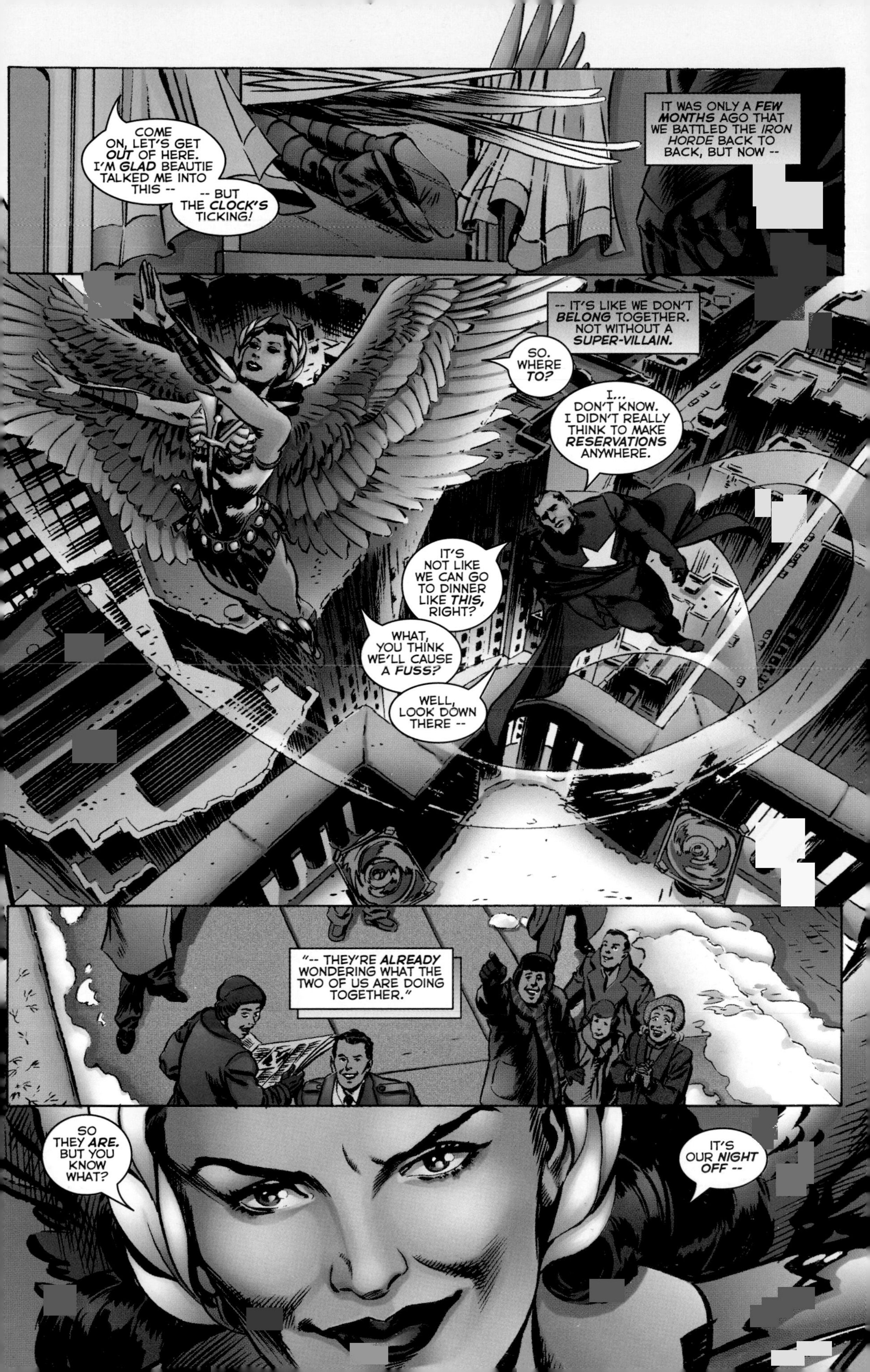
COME ON, LET'S GET OUT OF HERE. I'M GLAD BEAUTIE TALKED ME INTO THIS --
-- BUT THE CLOCK'S TICKING!
IT WAS ONLY A FEW MONTHS AGO THAT WE BATTLED THE IRON HORDE BACK TO BACK, BUT NOW --
-- IT'S LIKE WE DON'T BELONG TOGETHER. NOT WITHOUT A SUPER-VILLAIN.
SO. WHERE TO?
I... DON'T KNOW. I DIDN'T REALLY THINK TO MAKE RESERVATIONS ANYWHERE.
IT'S NOT LIKE WE CAN GO TO DINNER LIKE THIS, RIGHT?
WHAT, YOU THINK WE'LL CAUSE A FUSS?
WELL, LOOK DOWN THERE --
"-- THEY'RE ALREADY WONDERING WHAT THE TWO OF US ARE DOING TOGETHER."
SO THEY ARE. BUT YOU KNOW WHAT?
IT'S OUR NIGHT OFF --

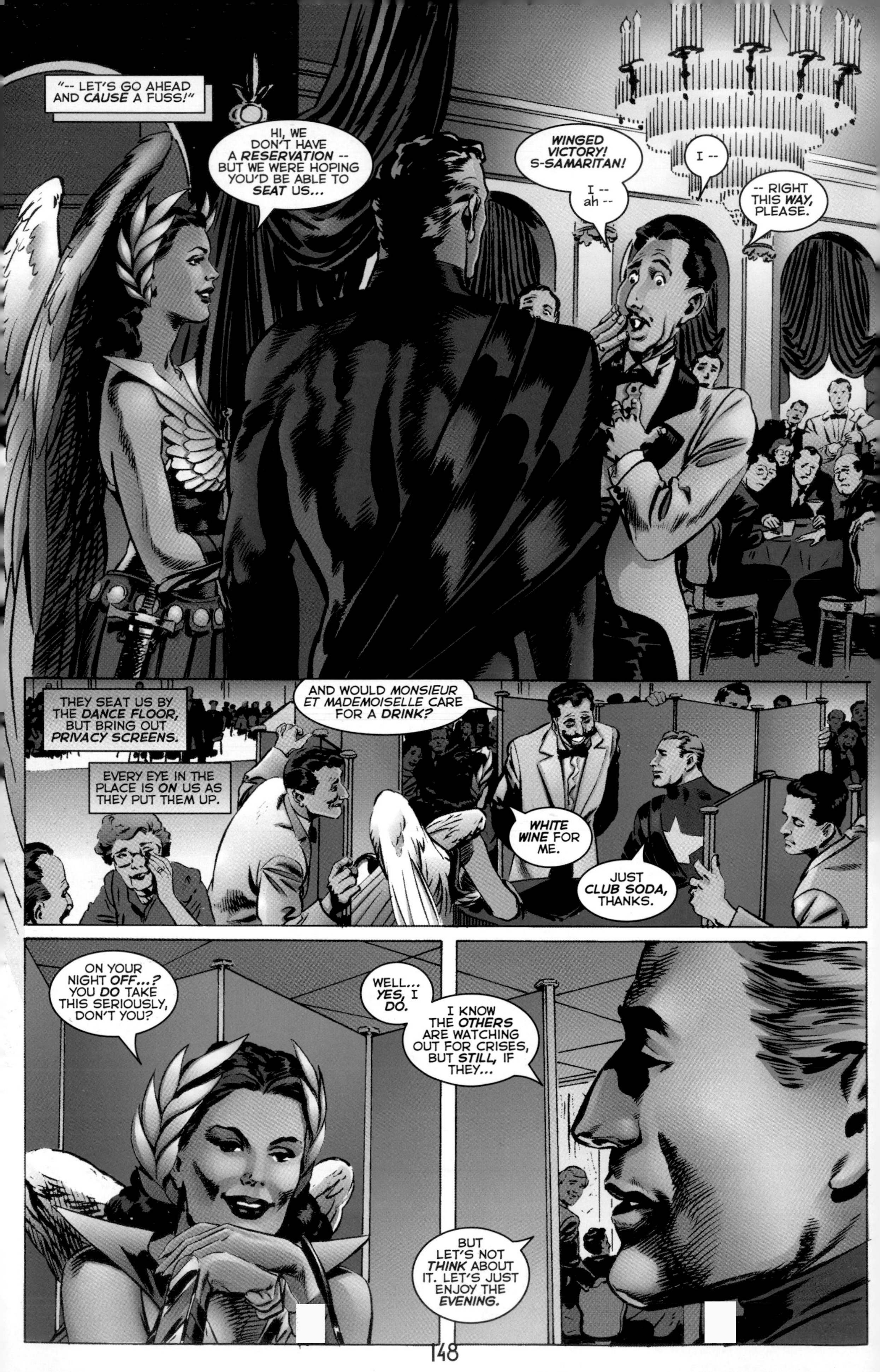

"-- LET'S GO AHEAD AND CAUSE A FUSS!"
HI, WE DON'T HAVE A RESERVATION -- BUT WE WERE HOPING YOU'D BE ABLE TO SEAT US...
WINGED VICTORY! S-SAMARITAN!
I -- ah --
I --
-- RIGHT THIS WAY, PLEASE.
THEY SEAT US BY THE DANCE FLOOR, BUT BRING OUT PRIVACY SCREENS.
EVERY EYE IN THE PLACE IS ON US AS THEY PUT THEM UP.
AND WOULD MONSIEUR ET MADEMOISELLE CARE FOR A DRINK?
WHITE WINE FOR ME.
JUST CLUB SODA, THANKS.
ON YOUR NIGHT OFF...? YOU DO TAKE THIS SERIOUSLY, DON'T YOU?
WELL... YES, I DO.
I KNOW THE OTHERS ARE WATCHING OUT FOR CRISES, BUT STILL, IF THEY...
BUT LET'S NOT THINK ABOUT IT. LET'S JUST ENJOY THE EVENING.

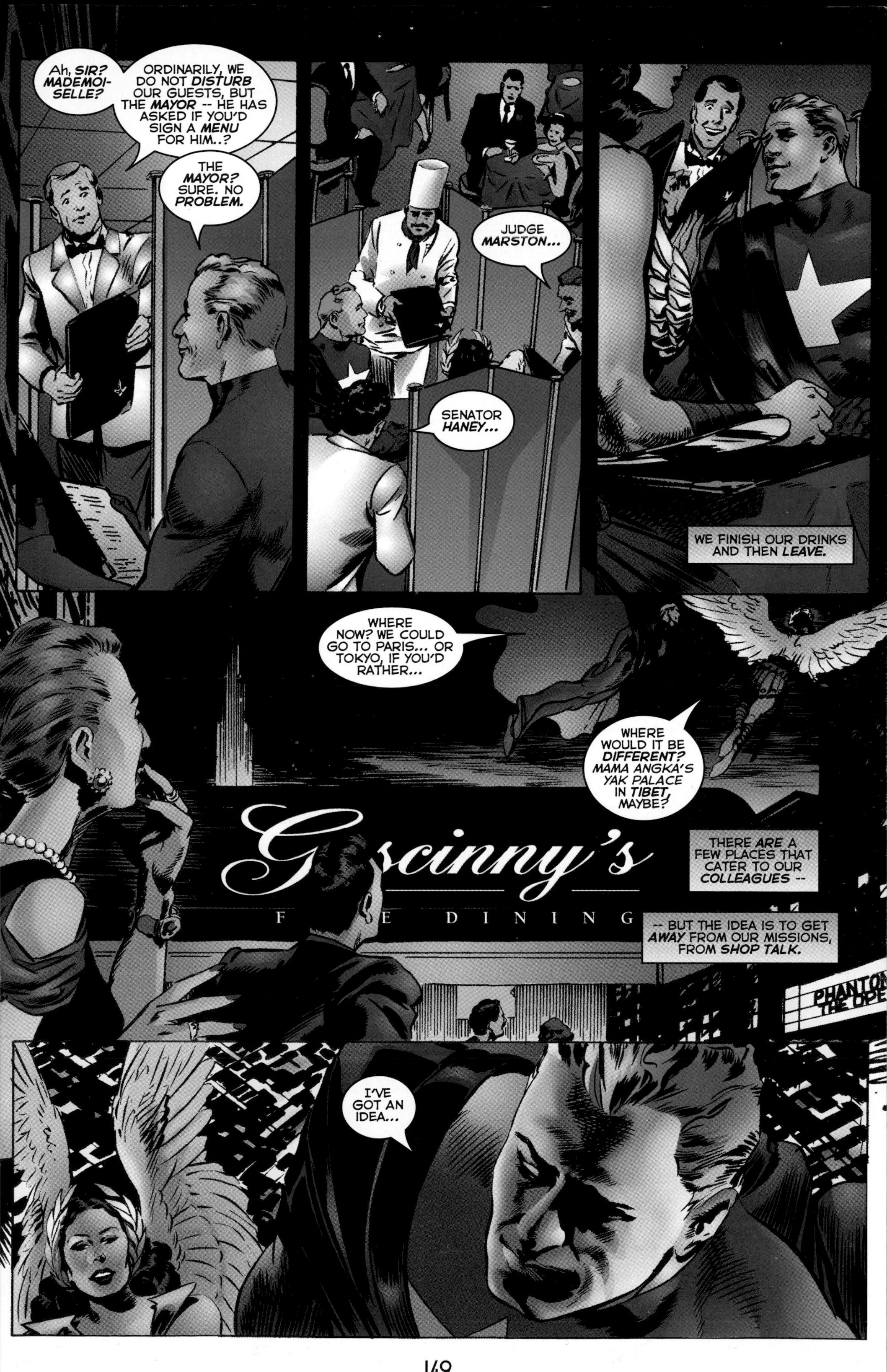
Ah, SIR? MADEMOISELLE?
ORDINARILY, WE DO NOT DISTURB OUR GUESTS, BUT THE MAYOR -- HE HAS ASKED IF YOU'D SIGN A MENU FOR HIM..?
THE MAYOR? SURE. NO PROBLEM.
JUDGE MARSTON...
SENATOR HANEY...
WE FINISH OUR DRINKS AND THEN LEAVE.
WHERE NOW? WE COULD GO TO PARIS... OR TOKYO, IF YOU'D RATHER...
WHERE WOULD IT BE DIFFERENT? MAMA ANGKA'S YAK PALACE IN TIBET, MAYBE?
THERE ARE A FEW PLACES THAT CATER TO OUR COLLEAGUES --
-- BUT THE IDEA IS TO GET AWAY FROM OUR MISSIONS, FROM SHOP TALK.
I'VE GOT AN IDEA...

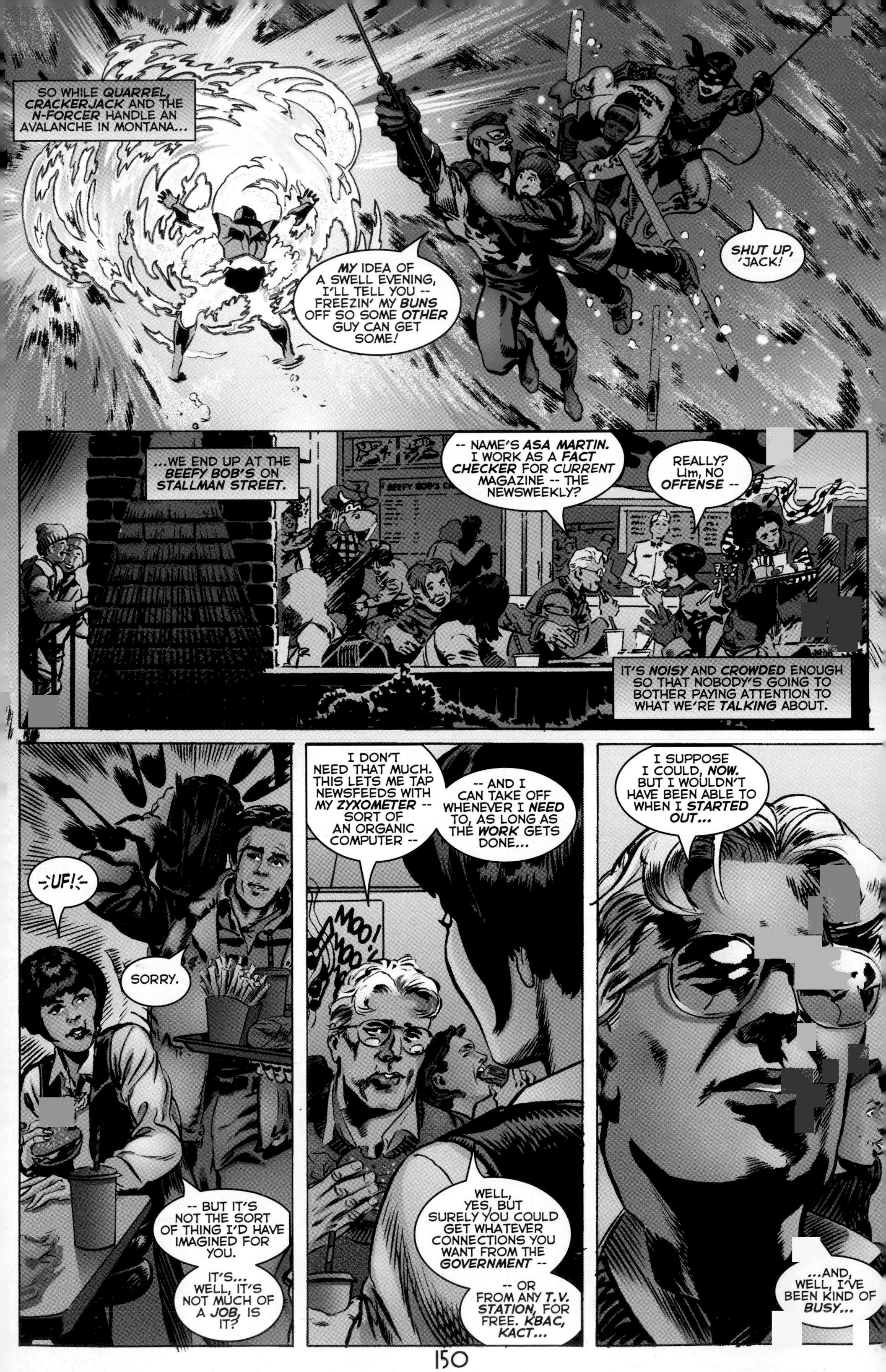
SO WHILE QUARREL, CRACKERJACK AND THE N-FORCER HANDLE AN AVALANCHE IN MONTANA...
MY IDEA OF A SWELL EVENING, I'LL TELL YOU -- FREEZIN' MY BUNS OFF SO SOME OTHER GUY CAN GET SOME!
SHUT UP, 'JACK!
...WE END UP AT THE BEEFY BOB'S ON STALLMAN STREET.
-- NAME'S ASA MARTIN. I WORK AS A FACT CHECKER FOR CURRENT MAGAZINE -- THE NEWSWEEKLY?
REALLY? Um, NO OFFENSE --
IT'S NOISY AND CROWDED ENOUGH SO THAT NOBODY'S GOING TO BOTHER PAYING ATTENTION TO WHAT WE'RE TALKING ABOUT.
-UF!-
SORRY.
-- BUT IT'S NOT THE SORT OF THING I'D HAVE IMAGINED FOR YOU.
IT'S... WELL, IT'S NOT MUCH OF A JOB, IS IT?
I DON'T NEED THAT MUCH. THIS LETS ME TAP NEWSFEEDS WITH MY ZYXOMETER -- SORT OF AN ORGANIC COMPUTER --
-- AND I CAN TAKE OFF WHENEVER I NEED TO, AS LONG AS THE WORK GETS DONE...
MOO!
WELL, YES, BUT SURELY YOU COULD GET WHATEVER CONNECTIONS YOU WANT FROM THE GOVERNMENT --
-- OR FROM ANY T.V. STATION, FOR FREE. KBAC, KACT...
I SUPPOSE I COULD, NOW. BUT I WOULDN'T HAVE BEEN ABLE TO WHEN I STARTED OUT...
...AND, WELL, I'VE BEEN KIND OF BUSY...

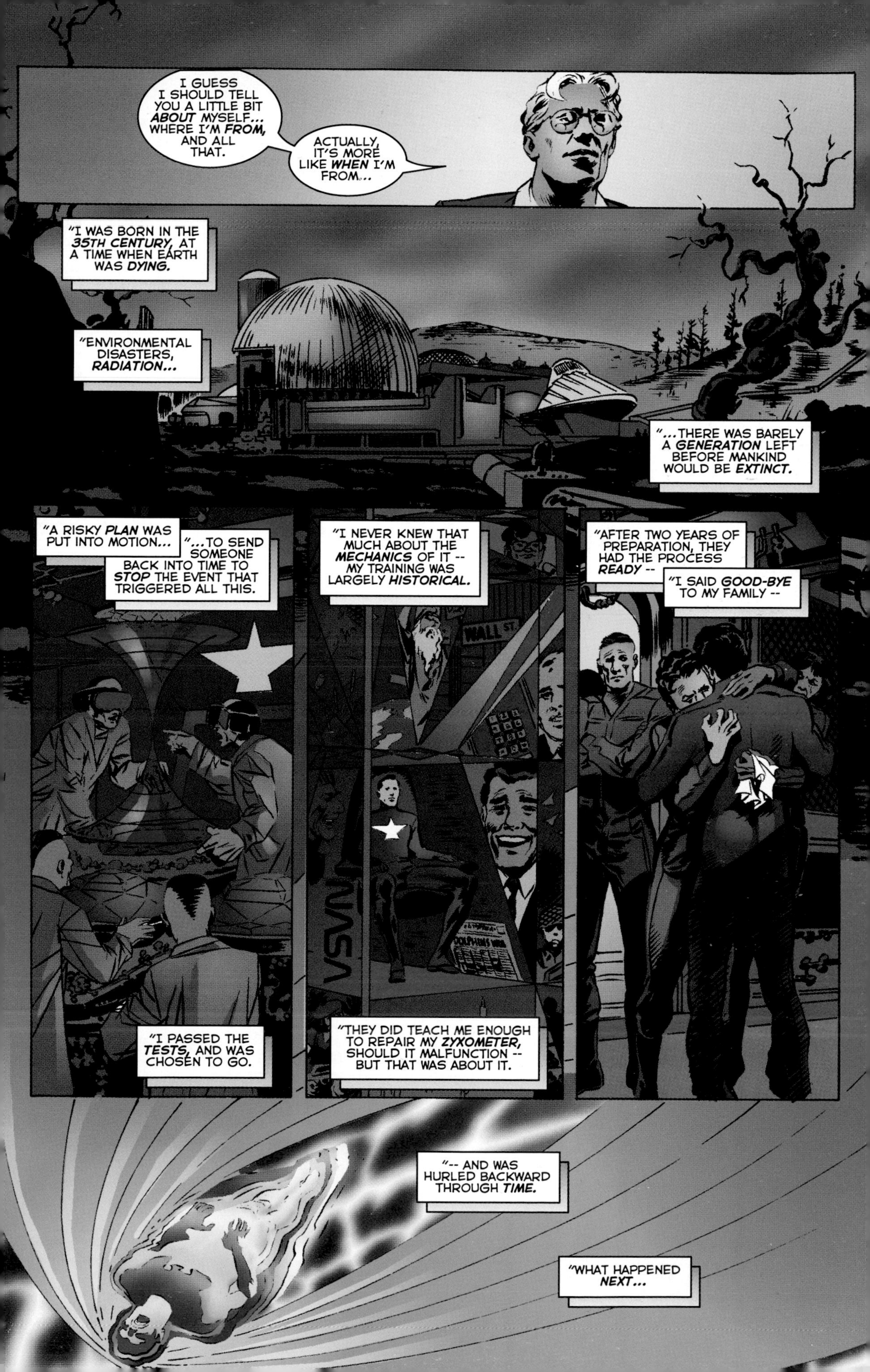
I GUESS I SHOULD TELL YOU A LITTLE BIT ABOUT MYSELF... WHERE I'M FROM, AND ALL THAT.
ACTUALLY, IT'S MORE LIKE WHEN I'M FROM...
"I WAS BORN IN THE 35TH CENTURY, AT A TIME WHEN EARTH WAS DYING.
"ENVIRONMENTAL DISASTERS, RADIATION...
"...THERE WAS BARELY A GENERATION LEFT BEFORE MANKIND WOULD BE EXTINCT.
"A RISKY PLAN WAS PUT INTO MOTION...
"...TO SEND SOMEONE BACK INTO TIME TO STOP THE EVENT THAT TRIGGERED ALL THIS.
"I PASSED THE TESTS, AND WAS CHOSEN TO GO.
"I NEVER KNEW THAT MUCH ABOUT THE MECHANICS OF IT -- MY TRAINING WAS LARGELY HISTORICAL.
WALL ST.
NASA
"THEY DID TEACH ME ENOUGH TO REPAIR MY ZYXOMETER, SHOULD IT MALFUNCTION -- BUT THAT WAS ABOUT IT.
"AFTER TWO YEARS OF PREPARATION, THEY HAD THE PROCESS READY --
"I SAID GOOD-BYE TO MY FAMILY --
"-- AND WAS HURLED BACKWARD THROUGH TIME.
"WHAT HAPPENED NEXT...

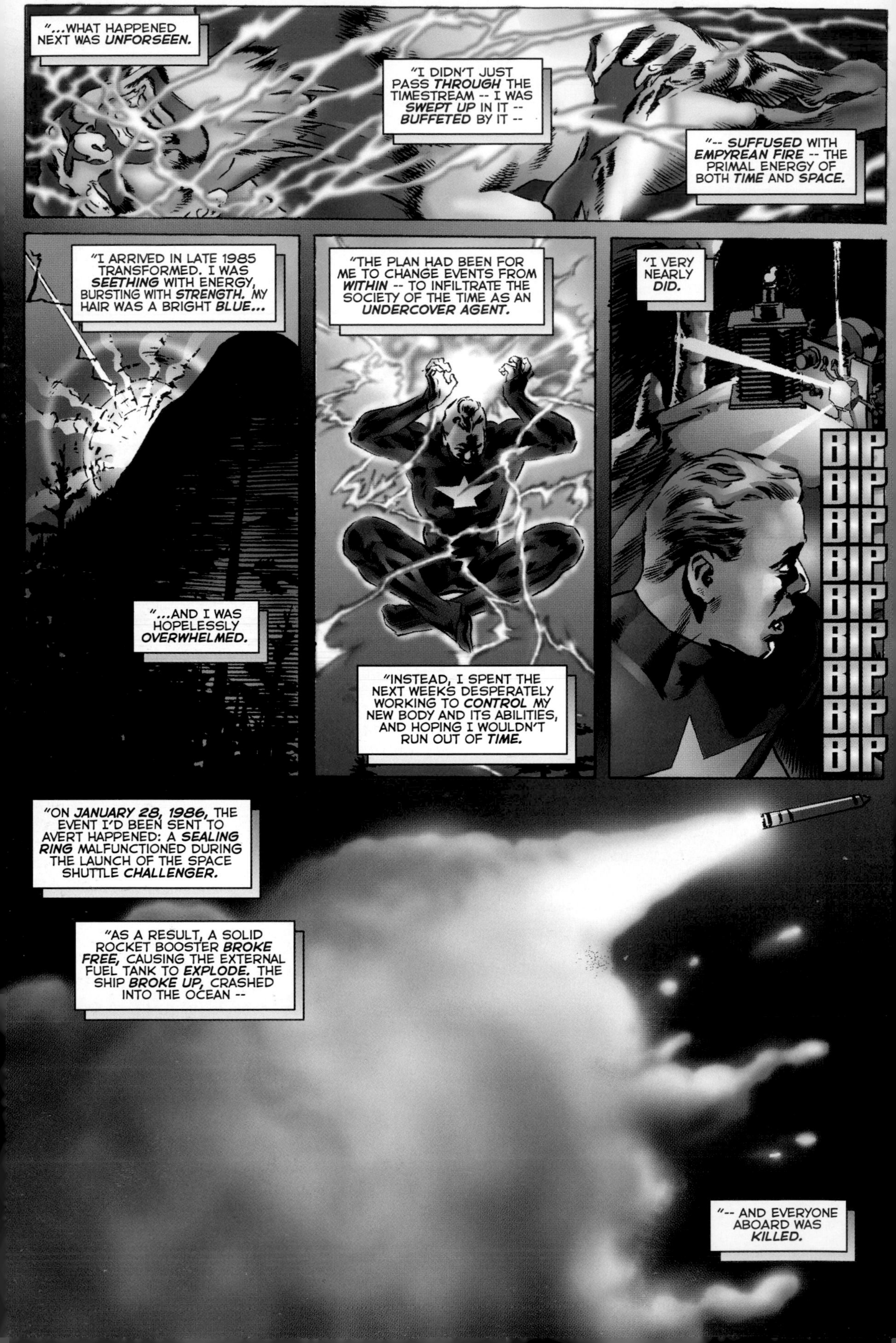
"...WHAT HAPPENED NEXT WAS UNFORSEEN.
"I DIDN'T JUST PASS THROUGH THE TIMESTREAM -- I WAS SWEPT UP IN IT -- BUFFETED BY IT --
"-- SUFFUSED WITH EMPYREAN FIRE -- THE PRIMAL ENERGY OF BOTH TIME AND SPACE.
"I ARRIVED IN LATE 1985 TRANSFORMED. I WAS SEETHING WITH ENERGY, BURSTING WITH STRENGTH. MY HAIR WAS A BRIGHT BLUE...
"...AND I WAS HOPELESSLY OVERWHELMED.
"THE PLAN HAD BEEN FOR ME TO CHANGE EVENTS FROM WITHIN -- TO INFILTRATE THE SOCIETY OF THE TIME AS AN UNDERCOVER AGENT.
"INSTEAD, I SPENT THE NEXT WEEKS DESPERATELY WORKING TO CONTROL MY NEW BODY AND ITS ABILITIES, AND HOPING I WOULDN'T RUN OUT OF TIME.
"I VERY NEARLY DID.
BIP BIP BIP BIP BIP BIP BIP BIP BIP
"ON JANUARY 28, 1986, THE EVENT I'D BEEN SENT TO AVERT HAPPENED: A SEALING RING MALFUNCTIONED DURING THE LAUNCH OF THE SPACE SHUTTLE CHALLENGER.
"AS A RESULT, A SOLID ROCKET BOOSTER BROKE FREE, CAUSING THE EXTERNAL FUEL TANK TO EXPLODE. THE SHIP BROKE UP, CRASHED INTO THE OCEAN --
"-- AND EVERYONE ABOARD WAS KILLED.

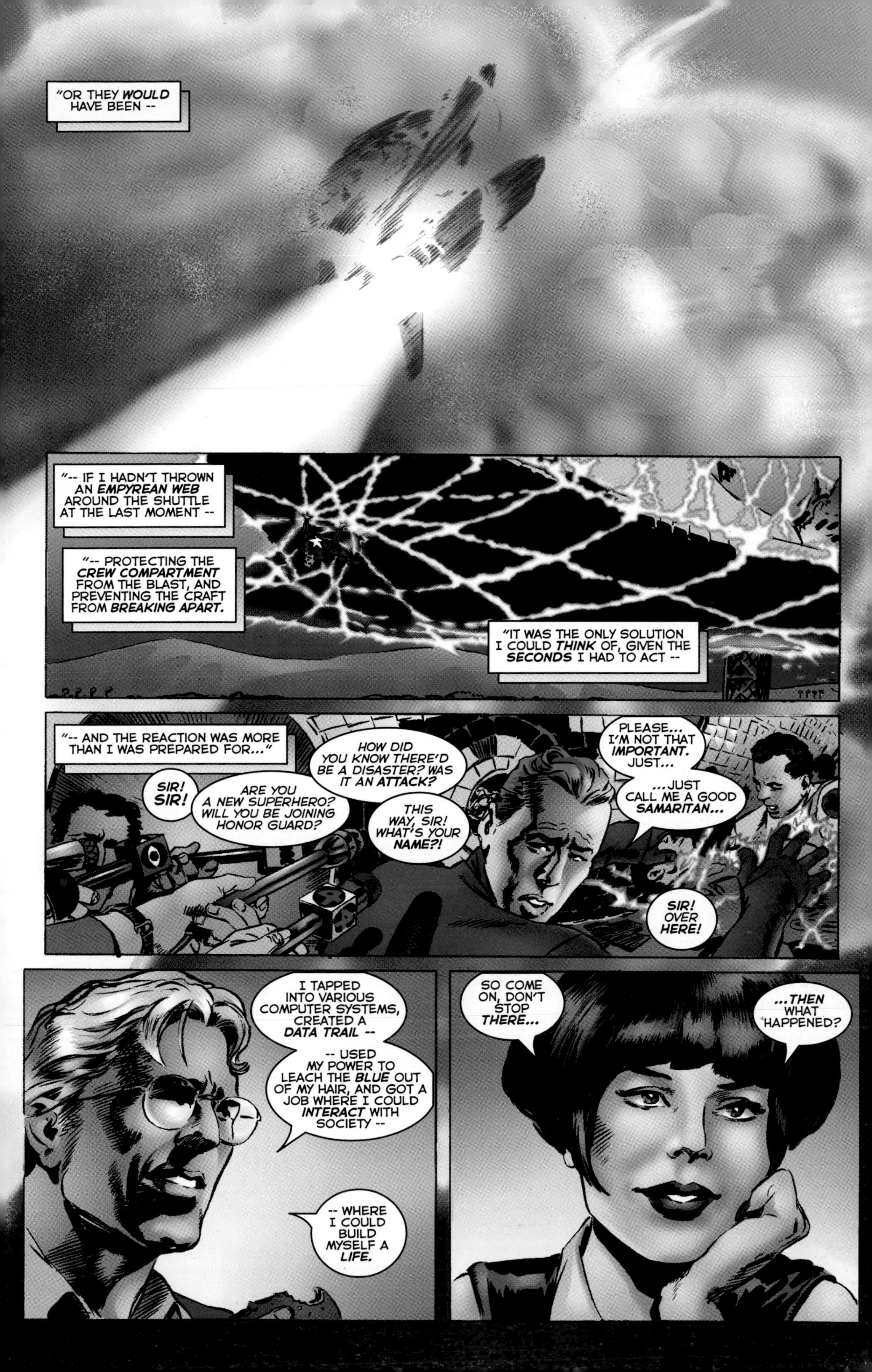
"OR THEY WOULD HAVE BEEN --
"-- IF I HADN'T THROWN AN EMPYREAN WEB AROUND THE SHUTTLE AT THE LAST MOMENT --
"-- PROTECTING THE CREW COMPARTMENT FROM THE BLAST, AND PREVENTING THE CRAFT FROM BREAKING APART.
"IT WAS THE ONLY SOLUTION I COULD THINK OF, GIVEN THE SECONDS I HAD TO ACT --
"-- AND THE REACTION WAS MORE THAN I WAS PREPARED FOR..."
SIR! SIR!
ARE YOU A NEW SUPERHERO? WILL YOU BE JOINING HONOR GUARD?
HOW DID YOU KNOW THERE'D BE A DISASTER? WAS IT AN ATTACK?
THIS WAY, SIR! WHAT'S YOUR NAME?!
PLEASE... I'M NOT THAT IMPORTANT. JUST...
...JUST CALL ME A GOOD SAMARITAN...
SIR! OVER HERE!
I TAPPED INTO VARIOUS COMPUTER SYSTEMS, CREATED A DATA TRAIL --
-- USED MY POWER TO LEACH THE BLUE OUT OF MY HAIR, AND GOT A JOB WHERE I COULD INTERACT WITH SOCIETY --
-- WHERE I COULD BUILD MYSELF A LIFE.
SO COME ON, DON'T STOP THERE...
...THEN WHAT HAPPENED?

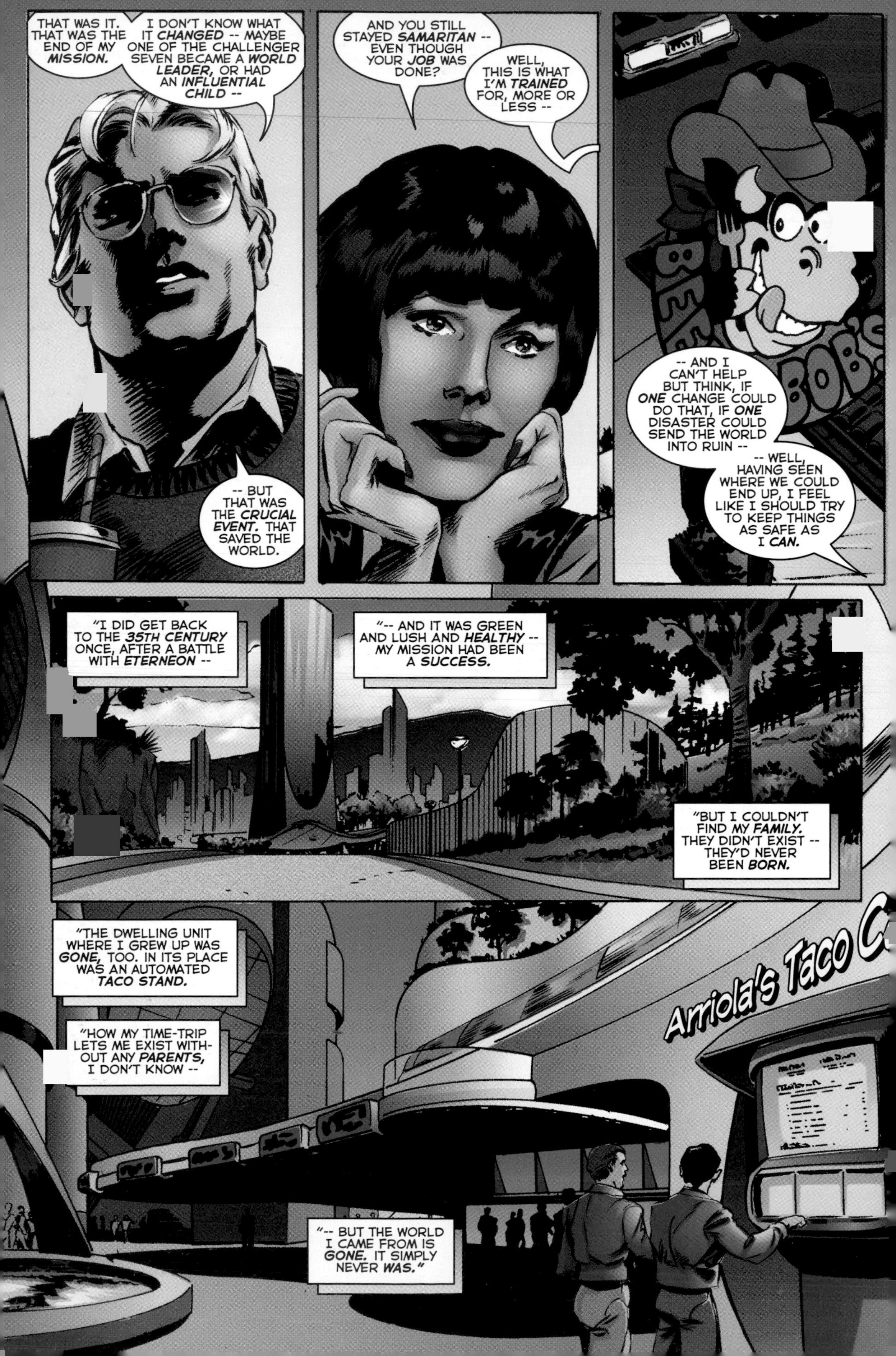
THAT WAS IT. THAT WAS THE END OF MY MISSION.
I DON'T KNOW WHAT IT CHANGED -- MAYBE ONE OF THE CHALLENGER SEVEN BECAME A WORLD LEADER, OR HAD AN INFLUENTIAL CHILD --
-- BUT THAT WAS THE CRUCIAL EVENT. THAT SAVED THE WORLD.
AND YOU STILL STAYED SAMARITAN -- EVEN THOUGH YOUR JOB WAS DONE?
WELL, THIS IS WHAT I'M TRAINED FOR, MORE OR LESS --
-- AND I CAN'T HELP BUT THINK, IF ONE CHANGE COULD DO THAT, IF ONE DISASTER COULD SEND THE WORLD INTO RUIN --
-- WELL, HAVING SEEN WHERE WE COULD END UP, I FEEL LIKE I SHOULD TRY TO KEEP THINGS AS SAFE AS I CAN.
"I DID GET BACK TO THE 35TH CENTURY ONCE, AFTER A BATTLE WITH ETERNEON --
"-- AND IT WAS GREEN AND LUSH AND HEALTHY -- MY MISSION HAD BEEN A SUCCESS.
"BUT I COULDN'T FIND MY FAMILY. THEY DIDN'T EXIST -- THEY'D NEVER BEEN BORN.
"THE DWELLING UNIT WHERE I GREW UP WAS GONE, TOO. IN ITS PLACE WAS AN AUTOMATED TACO STAND.
"HOW MY TIME-TRIP LETS ME EXIST WITHOUT ANY PARENTS, I DON'T KNOW --
Arriola's Taco C
"-- BUT THE WORLD I CAME FROM IS GONE. IT SIMPLY NEVER WAS."

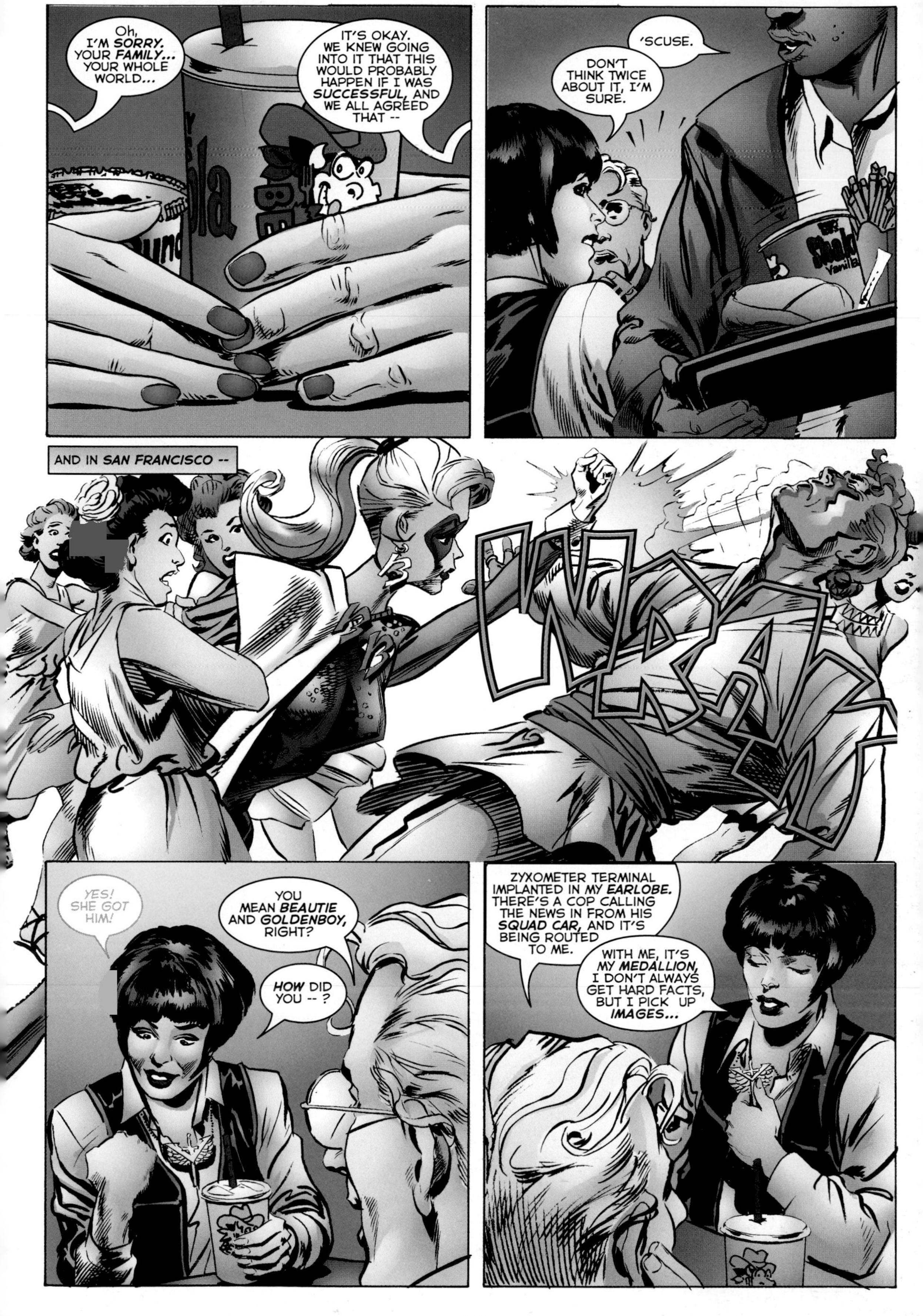

Oh, I'M SORRY. YOUR FAMILY... YOUR WHOLE WORLD...
IT'S OKAY. WE KNEW GOING INTO IT THAT THIS WOULD PROBABLY HAPPEN IF I WAS SUCCESSFUL, AND WE ALL AGREED THAT --
'SCUSE.
DON'T THINK TWICE ABOUT IT, I'M SURE.
AND IN SAN FRANCISCO --
WRAK
YES! SHE GOT HIM!
YOU MEAN BEAUTIE AND GOLDENBOY, RIGHT?
HOW DID YOU -- ?
ZYXOMETER TERMINAL IMPLANTED IN MY EARLOBE. THERE'S A COP CALLING THE NEWS IN FROM HIS SQUAD CAR, AND IT'S BEING ROUTED TO ME.
WITH ME, IT'S MY MEDALLION. I DON'T ALWAYS GET HARD FACTS, BUT I PICK UP IMAGES...

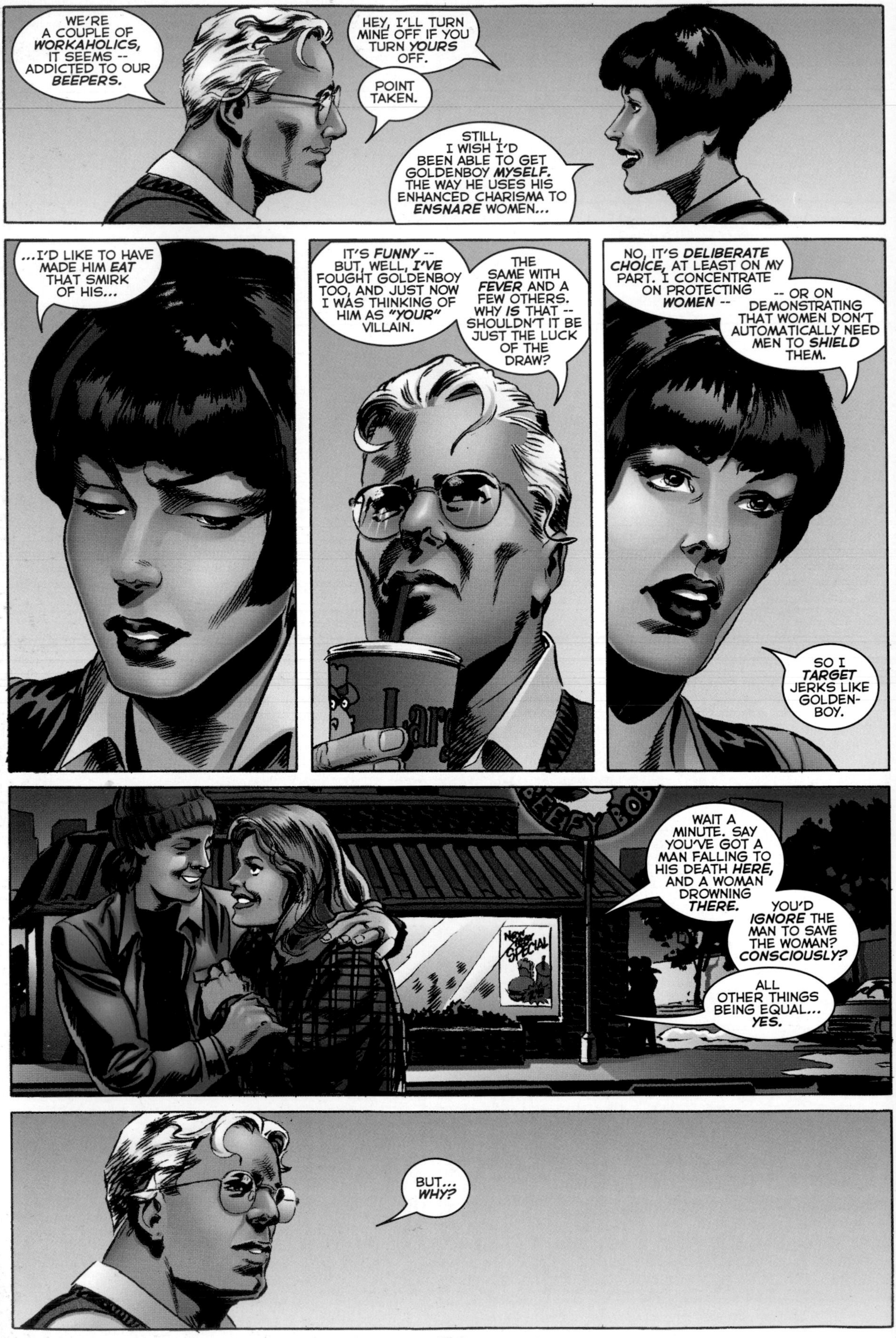
WE'RE A COUPLE OF WORKAHOLICS, IT SEEMS -- ADDICTED TO OUR BEEPERS.
HEY, I'LL TURN MINE OFF IF YOU TURN YOURS OFF.
POINT TAKEN.
STILL, I WISH I'D BEEN ABLE TO GET GOLDENBOY MYSELF. THE WAY HE USES HIS ENHANCED CHARISMA TO ENSNARE WOMEN...
...I'D LIKE TO HAVE MADE HIM EAT THAT SMIRK OF HIS...
IT'S FUNNY -- BUT, WELL, I'VE FOUGHT GOLDENBOY TOO, AND JUST NOW I WAS THINKING OF HIM AS "YOUR" VILLAIN.
THE SAME WITH FEVER AND A FEW OTHERS. WHY IS THAT -- SHOULDN'T IT BE JUST THE LUCK OF THE DRAW?
NO, IT'S DELIBERATE CHOICE, AT LEAST ON MY PART. I CONCENTRATE ON PROTECTING WOMEN --
-- OR ON DEMONSTRATING THAT WOMEN DON'T AUTOMATICALLY NEED MEN TO SHIELD THEM.
SO I TARGET JERKS LIKE GOLDEN-BOY.
BEEFY BOB
WAIT A MINUTE. SAY YOU'VE GOT A MAN FALLING TO HIS DEATH HERE, AND A WOMAN DROWNING THERE.
YOU'D IGNORE THE MAN TO SAVE THE WOMAN? CONSCIOUSLY?
ALL OTHER THINGS BEING EQUAL... YES.
BUT... WHY?

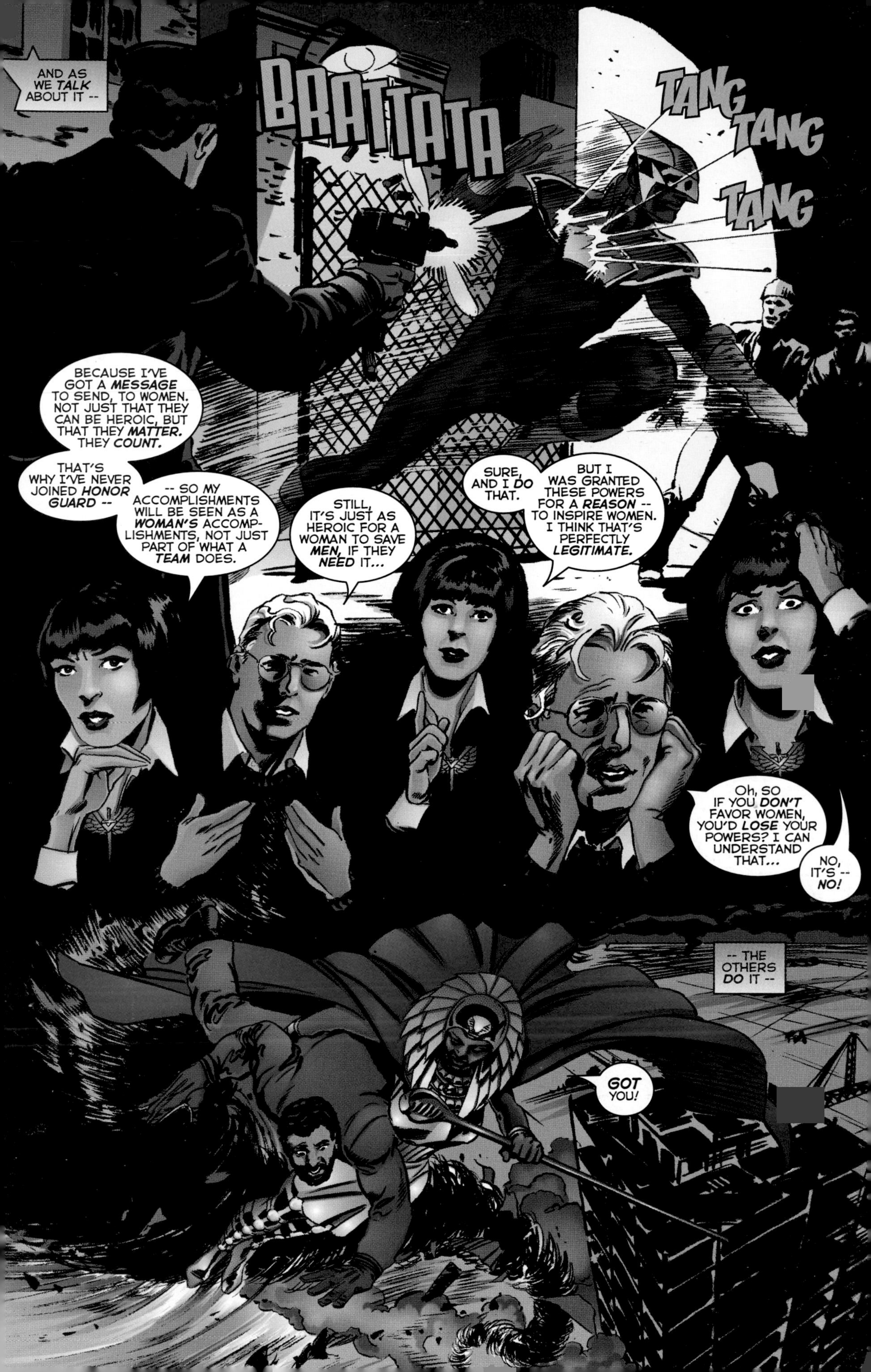

AND AS WE TALK ABOUT IT --
BRATTATA
TANG TANG TANG
BECAUSE I'VE GOT A MESSAGE TO SEND, TO WOMEN. NOT JUST THAT THEY CAN BE HEROIC, BUT THAT THEY MATTER. THEY COUNT.
THAT'S WHY I'VE NEVER JOINED HONOR GUARD --
-- SO MY ACCOMPLISHMENTS WILL BE SEEN AS A WOMAN'S ACCOMPLISHMENTS, NOT JUST PART OF WHAT A TEAM DOES.
STILL, IT'S JUST AS HEROIC FOR A WOMAN TO SAVE MEN, IF THEY NEED IT...
SURE, AND I DO THAT.
BUT I WAS GRANTED THESE POWERS FOR A REASON -- TO INSPIRE WOMEN. I THINK THAT'S PERFECTLY LEGITIMATE.
Oh, SO IF YOU DON'T FAVOR WOMEN, YOU'D LOSE YOUR POWERS? I CAN UNDERSTAND THAT...
NO, IT'S -- NO!
-- THE OTHERS DO IT --
GOT YOU!

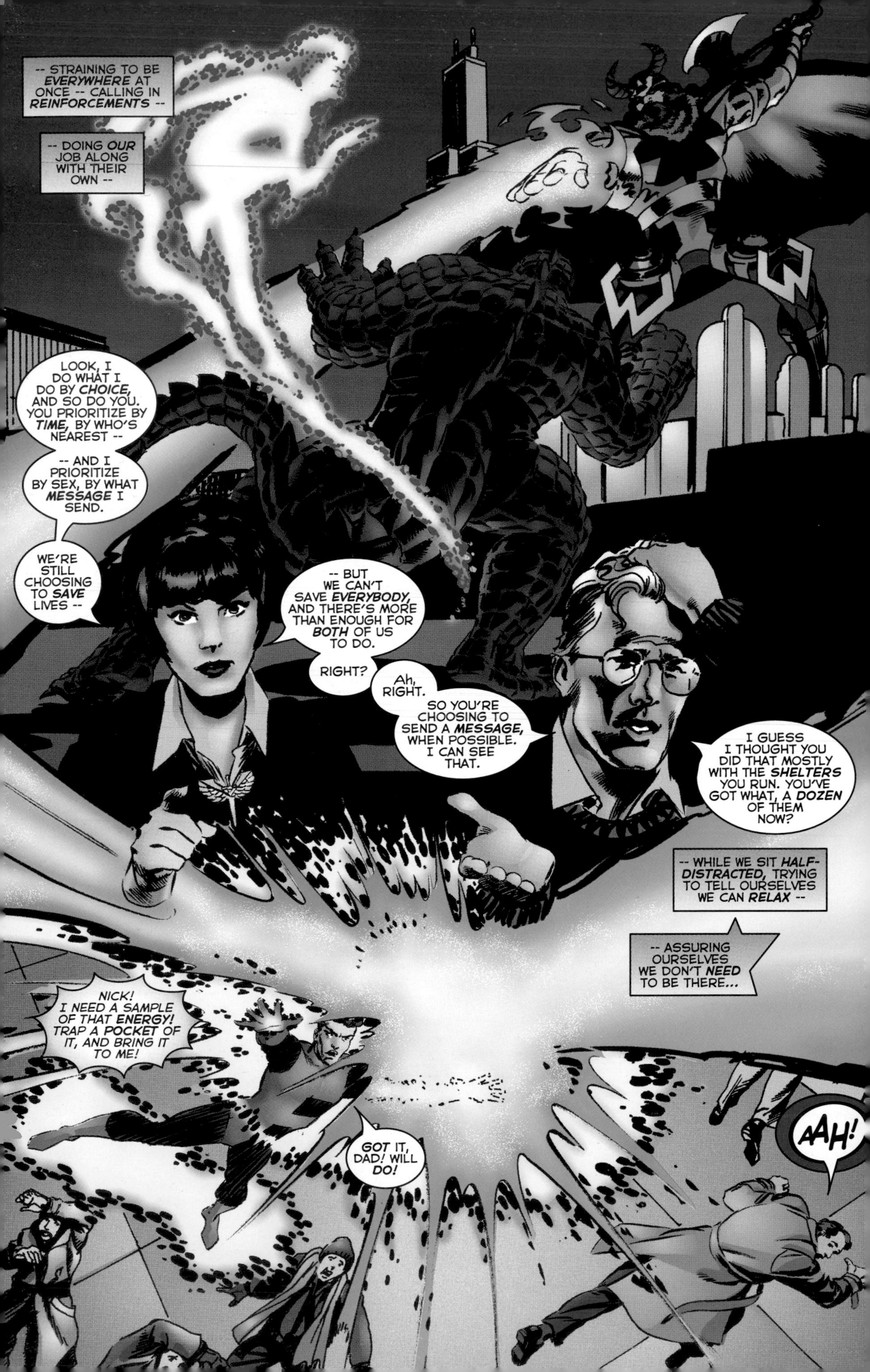
-- STRAINING TO BE EVERYWHERE AT ONCE -- CALLING IN REINFORCEMENTS --
-- DOING OUR JOB ALONG WITH THEIR OWN --
LOOK, I DO WHAT I DO BY CHOICE, AND SO DO YOU. YOU PRIORITIZE BY TIME, BY WHO'S NEAREST --
-- AND I PRIORITIZE BY SEX, BY WHAT MESSAGE I SEND.
WE'RE STILL CHOOSING TO SAVE LIVES --
-- BUT WE CAN'T SAVE EVERYBODY, AND THERE'S MORE THAN ENOUGH FOR BOTH OF US TO DO.
RIGHT?
Ah, RIGHT.
SO YOU'RE CHOOSING TO SEND A MESSAGE, WHEN POSSIBLE. I CAN SEE THAT.
I GUESS I THOUGHT YOU DID THAT MOSTLY WITH THE SHELTERS YOU RUN. YOU'VE GOT WHAT, A DOZEN OF THEM NOW?
-- WHILE WE SIT HALF-DISTRACTED, TRYING TO TELL OURSELVES WE CAN RELAX --
-- ASSURING OURSELVES WE DON'T NEED TO BE THERE...
NICK! I NEED A SAMPLE OF THAT ENERGY! TRAP A POCKET OF IT, AND BRING IT TO ME!
GOT IT, DAD! WILL DO!
AAH!

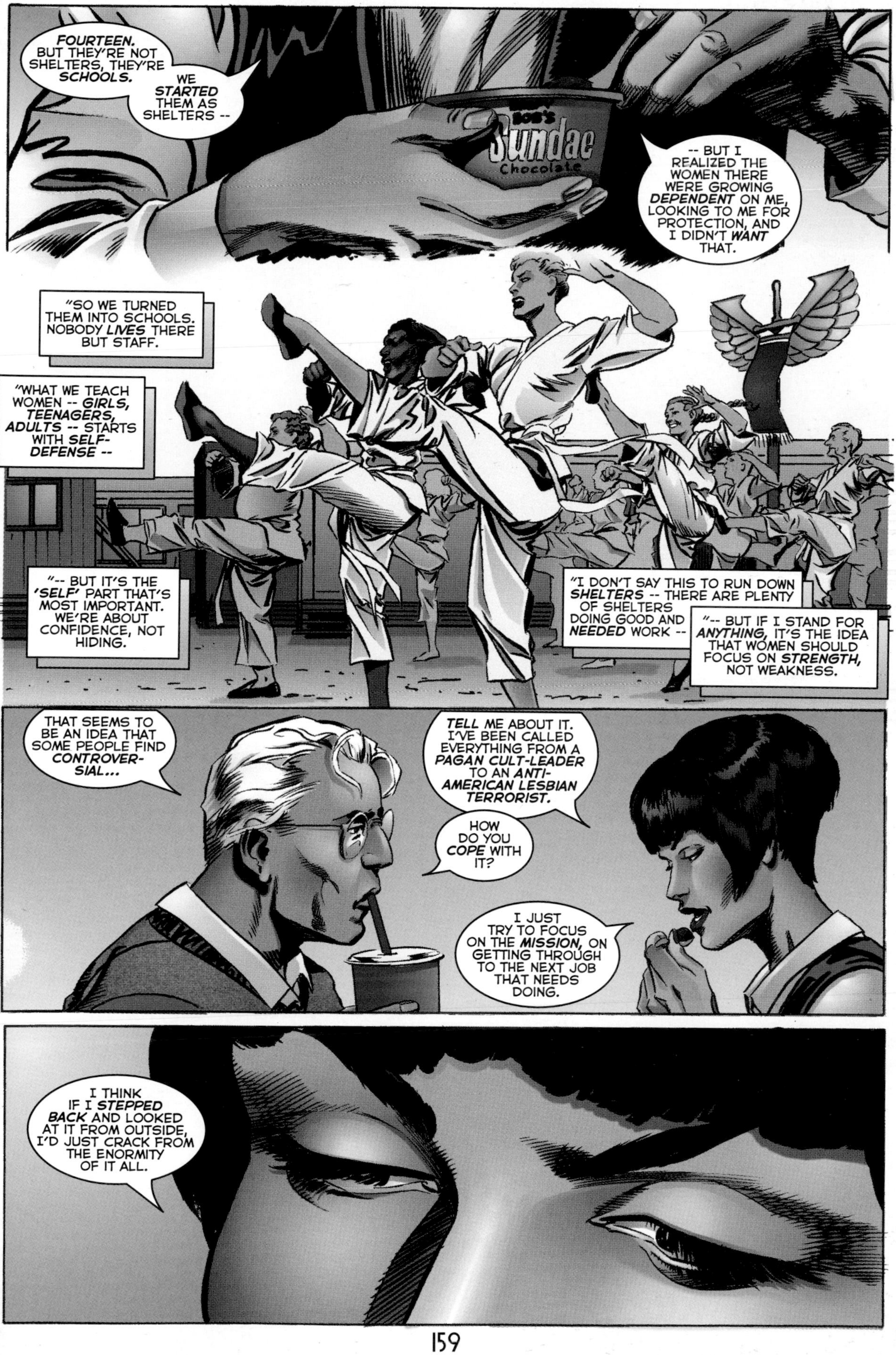

FOURTEEN. BUT THEY'RE NOT SHELTERS, THEY'RE SCHOOLS.
WE STARTED THEM AS SHELTERS --
BOB'S Sundae Chocolate
-- BUT I REALIZED THE WOMEN THERE WERE GROWING DEPENDENT ON ME, LOOKING TO ME FOR PROTECTION, AND I DIDN'T WANT THAT.
"SO WE TURNED THEM INTO SCHOOLS. NOBODY LIVES THERE BUT STAFF.
"WHAT WE TEACH WOMEN -- GIRLS, TEENAGERS, ADULTS -- STARTS WITH SELF-DEFENSE --
"-- BUT IT'S THE 'SELF' PART THAT'S MOST IMPORTANT. WE'RE ABOUT CONFIDENCE, NOT HIDING.
"I DON'T SAY THIS TO RUN DOWN SHELTERS -- THERE ARE PLENTY OF SHELTERS DOING GOOD AND NEEDED WORK --
"-- BUT IF I STAND FOR ANYTHING, IT'S THE IDEA THAT WOMEN SHOULD FOCUS ON STRENGTH, NOT WEAKNESS.
THAT SEEMS TO BE AN IDEA THAT SOME PEOPLE FIND CONTROVERSIAL...
TELL ME ABOUT IT. I'VE BEEN CALLED EVERYTHING FROM A PAGAN CULT-LEADER TO AN ANTI-AMERICAN LESBIAN TERRORIST.
HOW DO YOU COPE WITH IT?
I JUST TRY TO FOCUS ON THE MISSION, ON GETTING THROUGH TO THE NEXT JOB THAT NEEDS DOING.
I THINK IF I STEPPED BACK AND LOOKED AT IT FROM OUTSIDE, I'D JUST CRACK FROM THE ENORMITY OF IT ALL.

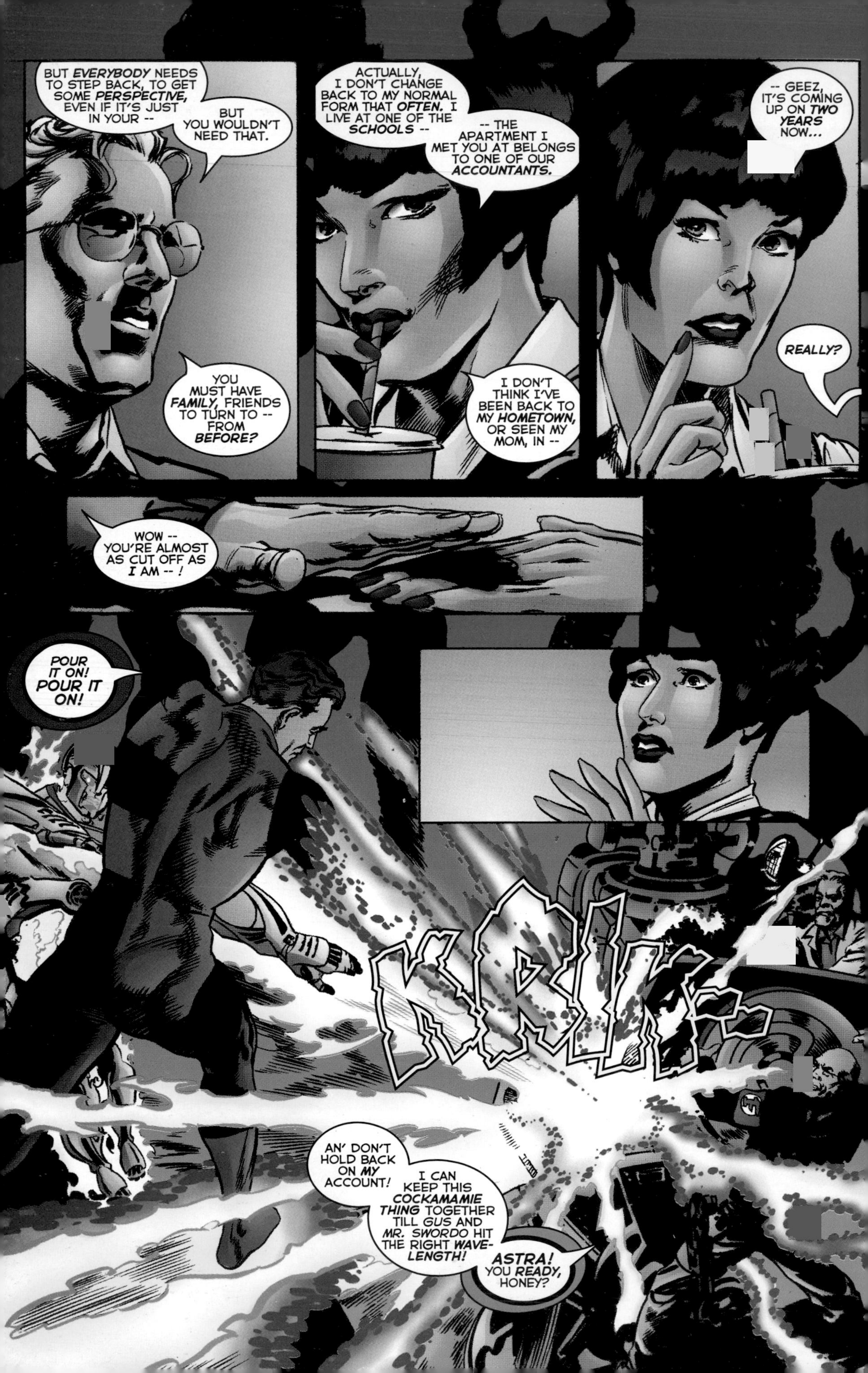
BUT EVERYBODY NEEDS TO STEP BACK, TO GET SOME PERSPECTIVE, EVEN IF IT'S JUST IN YOUR --
BUT YOU WOULDN'T NEED THAT.
YOU MUST HAVE FAMILY, FRIENDS TO TURN TO -- FROM BEFORE?
ACTUALLY, I DON'T CHANGE BACK TO MY NORMAL FORM THAT OFTEN. I LIVE AT ONE OF THE SCHOOLS --
-- THE APARTMENT I MET YOU AT BELONGS TO ONE OF OUR ACCOUNTANTS.
I DON'T THINK I'VE BEEN BACK TO MY HOMETOWN, OR SEEN MY MOM, IN --
-- GEEZ, IT'S COMING UP ON TWO YEARS NOW...
REALLY?
WOW -- YOU'RE ALMOST AS CUT OFF AS I AM -- !
POUR IT ON! POUR IT ON!
KRAK
AN' DON'T HOLD BACK ON MY ACCOUNT!
I CAN KEEP THIS COCKAMAMIE THING TOGETHER TILL GUS AND MR. SWORDO HIT THE RIGHT WAVE-LENGTH!
ASTRA! YOU READY, HONEY?

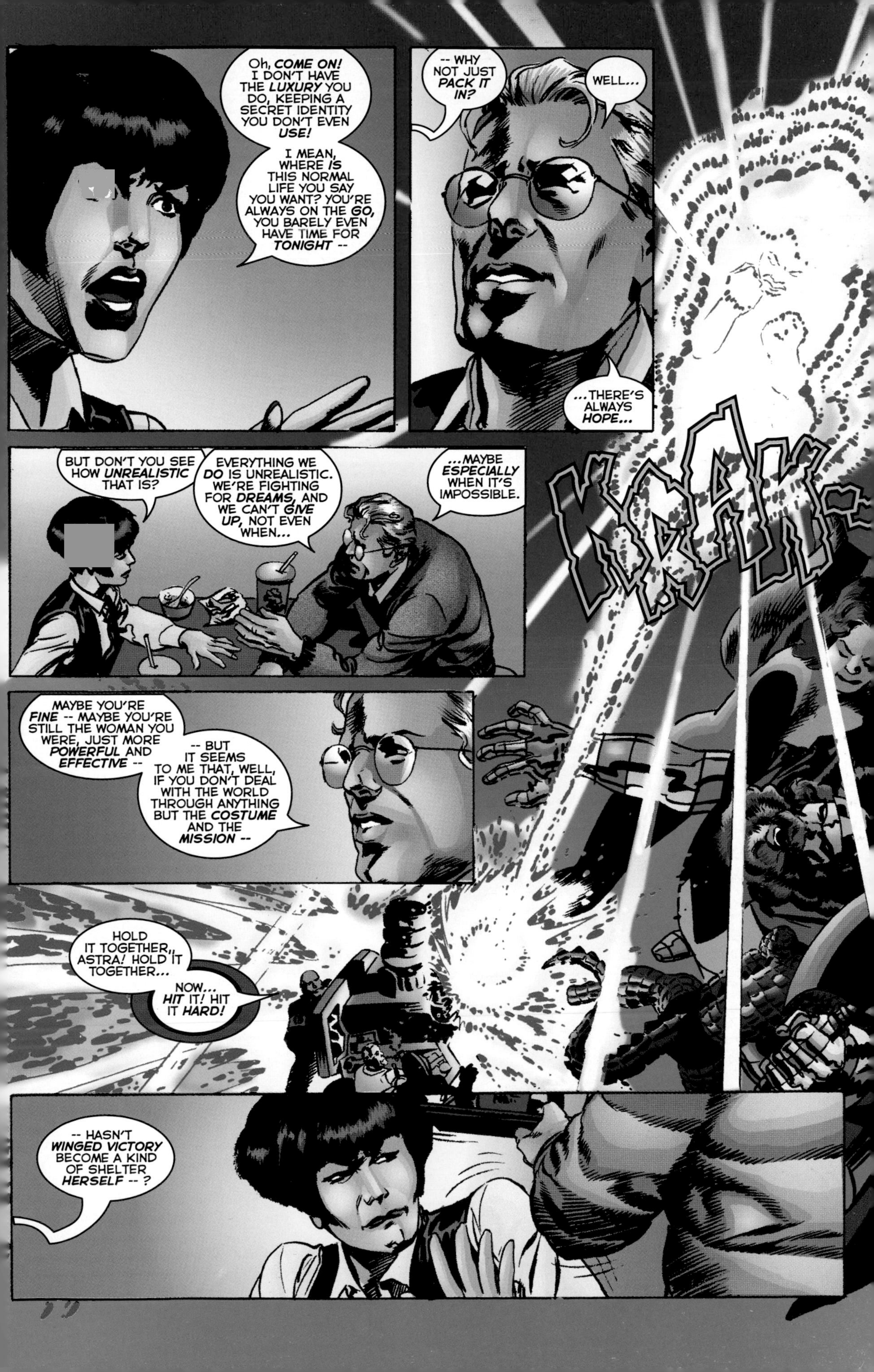
Oh, COME ON! I DON'T HAVE THE LUXURY YOU DO, KEEPING A SECRET IDENTITY YOU DON'T EVEN USE!
I MEAN, WHERE IS THIS NORMAL LIFE YOU SAY YOU WANT? YOU'RE ALWAYS ON THE GO, YOU BARELY EVEN HAVE TIME FOR TONIGHT --
-- WHY NOT JUST PACK IT IN?
WELL...
...THERE'S ALWAYS HOPE...
BUT DON'T YOU SEE HOW UNREALISTIC THAT IS?
EVERYTHING WE DO IS UNREALISTIC. WE'RE FIGHTING FOR DREAMS, AND WE CAN'T GIVE UP, NOT EVEN WHEN...
...MAYBE ESPECIALLY WHEN IT'S IMPOSSIBLE.
KRAAK
MAYBE YOU'RE FINE -- MAYBE YOU'RE STILL THE WOMAN YOU WERE, JUST MORE POWERFUL AND EFFECTIVE --
-- BUT IT SEEMS TO ME THAT, WELL, IF YOU DON'T DEAL WITH THE WORLD THROUGH ANYTHING BUT THE COSTUME AND THE MISSION --
HOLD IT TOGETHER, ASTRA! HOLD IT TOGETHER...
NOW... HIT IT! HIT IT HARD!
-- HASN'T WINGED VICTORY BECOME A KIND OF SHELTER HERSELF -- ?

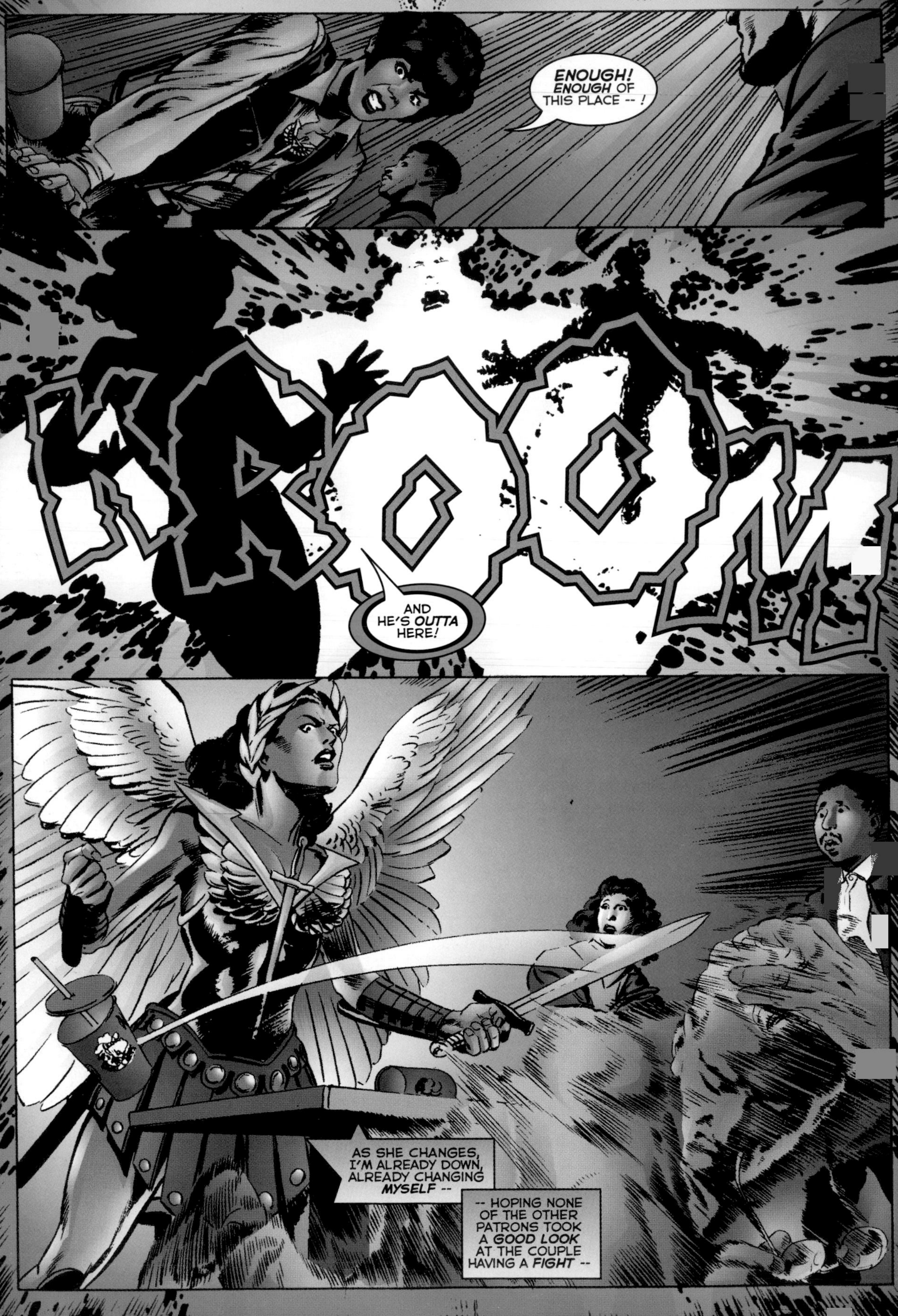
ENOUGH! ENOUGH OF THIS PLACE -- !
KRAOOM
AND HE'S OUTTA HERE!
AS SHE CHANGES, I'M ALREADY DOWN, ALREADY CHANGING MYSELF --
-- HOPING NONE OF THE OTHER PATRONS TOOK A GOOD LOOK AT THE COUPLE HAVING A FIGHT --

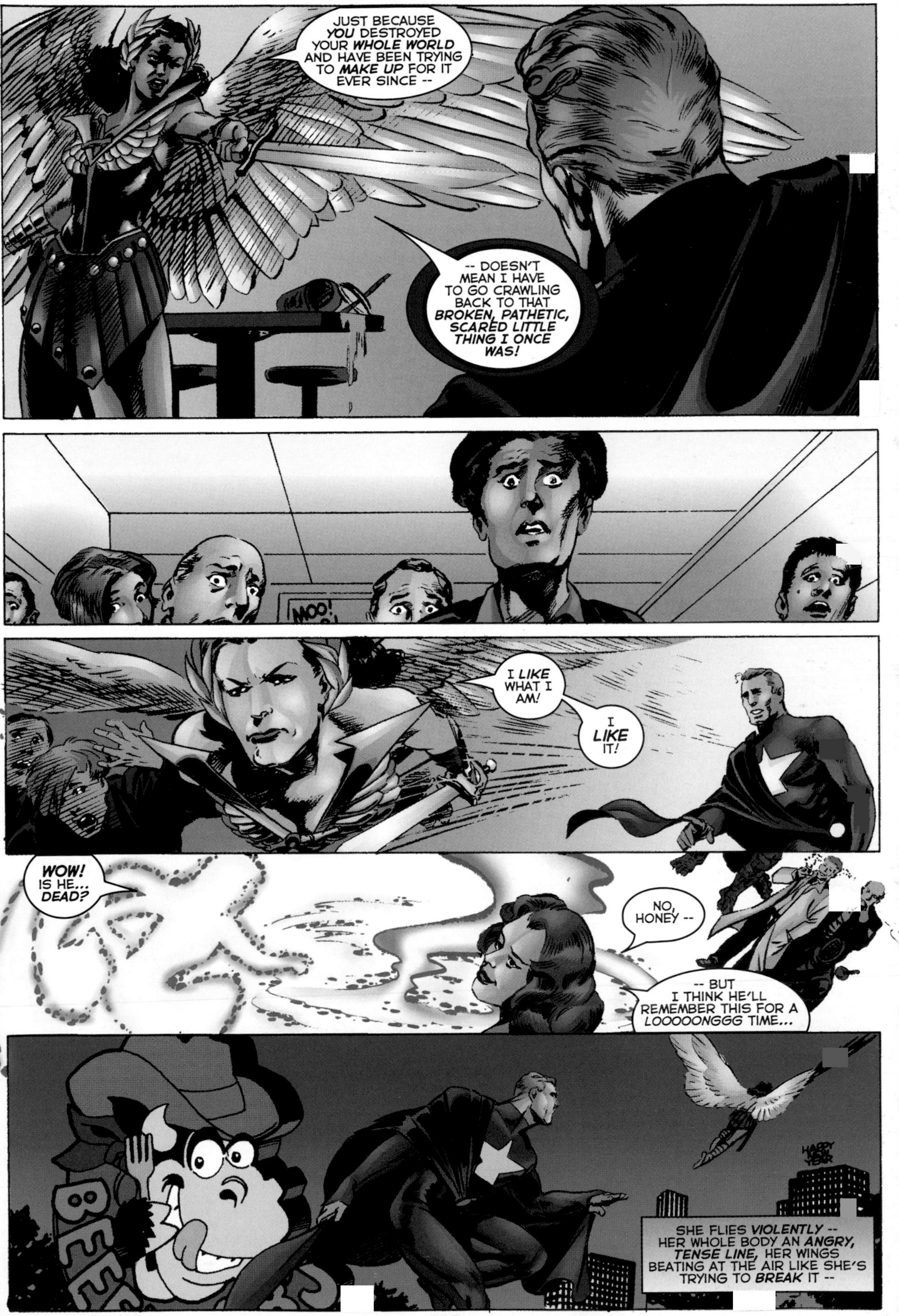
JUST BECAUSE YOU DESTROYED YOUR WHOLE WORLD AND HAVE BEEN TRYING TO MAKE UP FOR IT EVER SINCE --
-- DOESN'T MEAN I HAVE TO GO CRAWLING BACK TO THAT BROKEN, PATHETIC, SCARED LITTLE THING I ONCE WAS!
MOO!
I LIKE WHAT I AM!
I LIKE IT!
WOW! IS HE... DEAD?
NO, HONEY --
-- BUT I THINK HE'LL REMEMBER THIS FOR A LOOOOONGGG TIME...
HAPPY NEW YEAR
SHE FLIES VIOLENTLY -- HER WHOLE BODY AN ANGRY, TENSE LINE, HER WINGS BEATING AT THE AIR LIKE SHE'S TRYING TO BREAK IT --

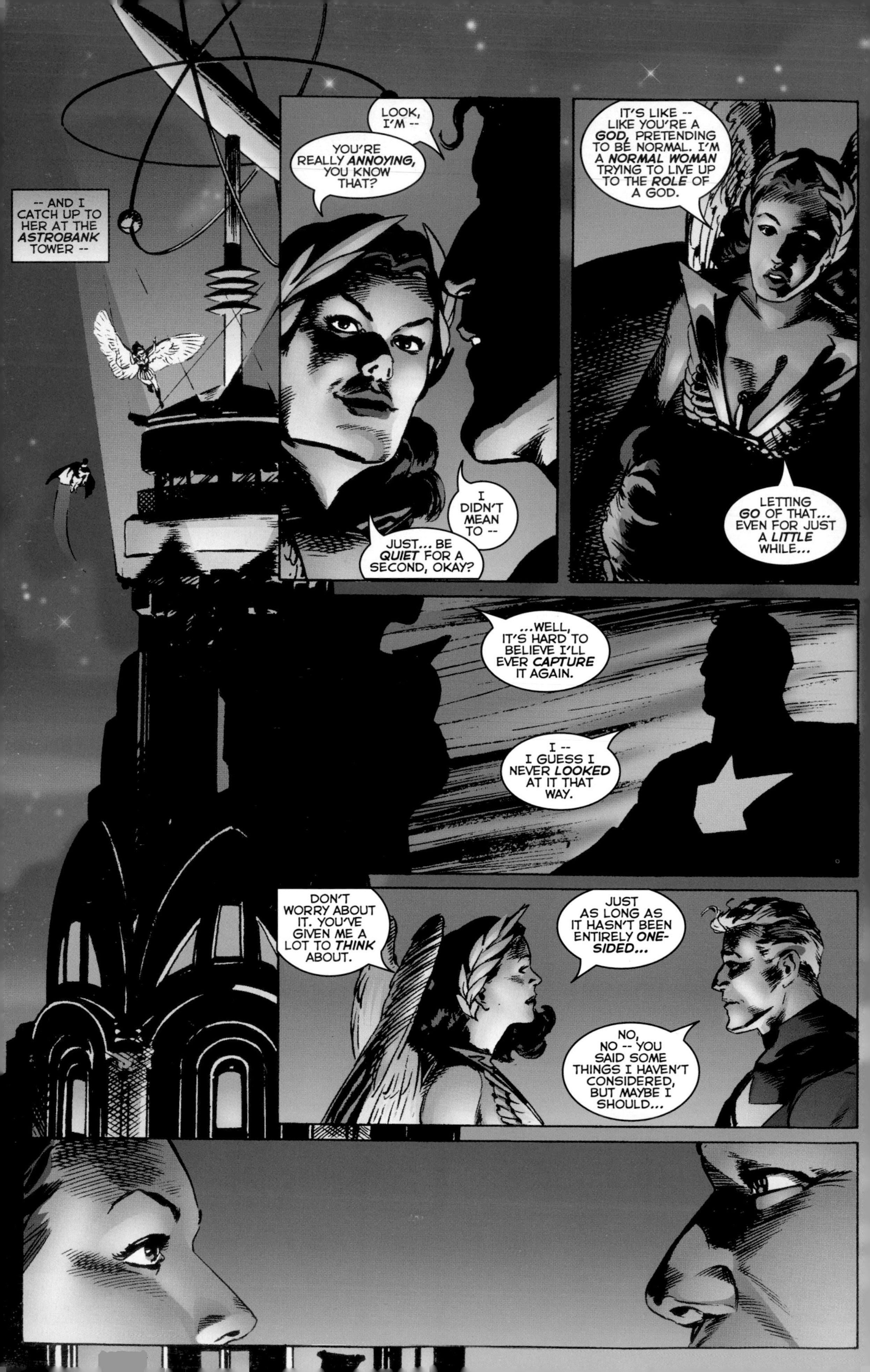
-- AND I CATCH UP TO HER AT THE ASTROBANK TOWER --
LOOK, I'M --
YOU'RE REALLY ANNOYING, YOU KNOW THAT?
I DIDN'T MEAN TO --
JUST... BE QUIET FOR A SECOND, OKAY?
IT'S LIKE -- LIKE YOU'RE A GOD, PRETENDING TO BE NORMAL. I'M A NORMAL WOMAN TRYING TO LIVE UP TO THE ROLE OF A GOD.
LETTING GO OF THAT... EVEN FOR JUST A LITTLE WHILE...
...WELL, IT'S HARD TO BELIEVE I'LL EVER CAPTURE IT AGAIN.
I -- I GUESS I NEVER LOOKED AT IT THAT WAY.
DON'T WORRY ABOUT IT. YOU'VE GIVEN ME A LOT TO THINK ABOUT.
JUST AS LONG AS IT HASN'T BEEN ENTIRELY ONE-SIDED...
NO, NO -- YOU SAID SOME THINGS I HAVEN'T CONSIDERED, BUT MAYBE I SHOULD...

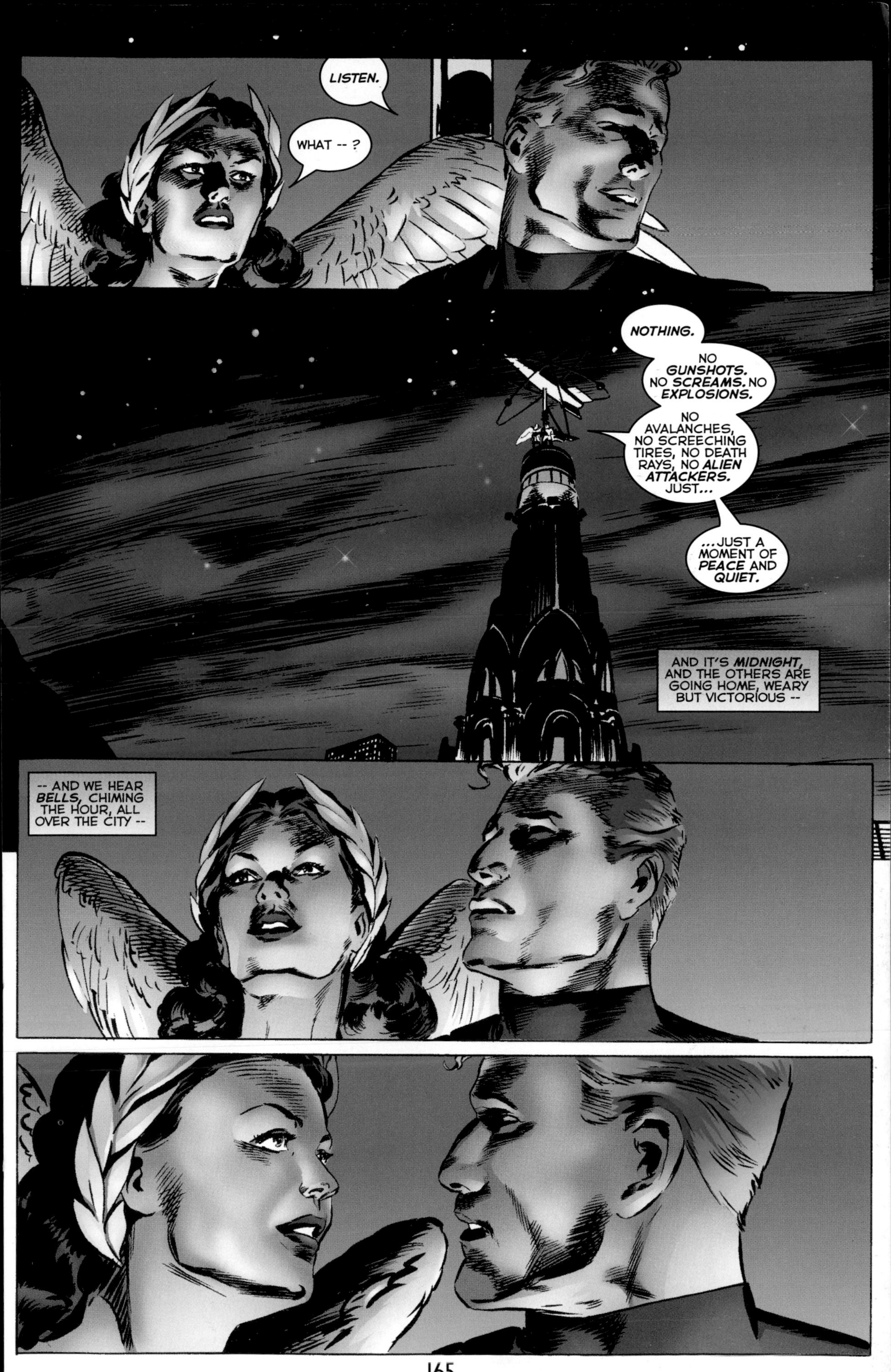

LISTEN.
WHAT -- ?
NOTHING.
NO GUNSHOTS. NO SCREAMS. NO EXPLOSIONS.
NO AVALANCHES, NO SCREECHING TIRES, NO DEATH RAYS, NO ALIEN ATTACKERS. JUST...
...JUST A MOMENT OF PEACE AND QUIET.
AND IT'S MIDNIGHT, AND THE OTHERS ARE GOING HOME, WEARY BUT VICTORIOUS --
-- AND WE HEAR BELLS, CHIMING THE HOUR, ALL OVER THE CITY --

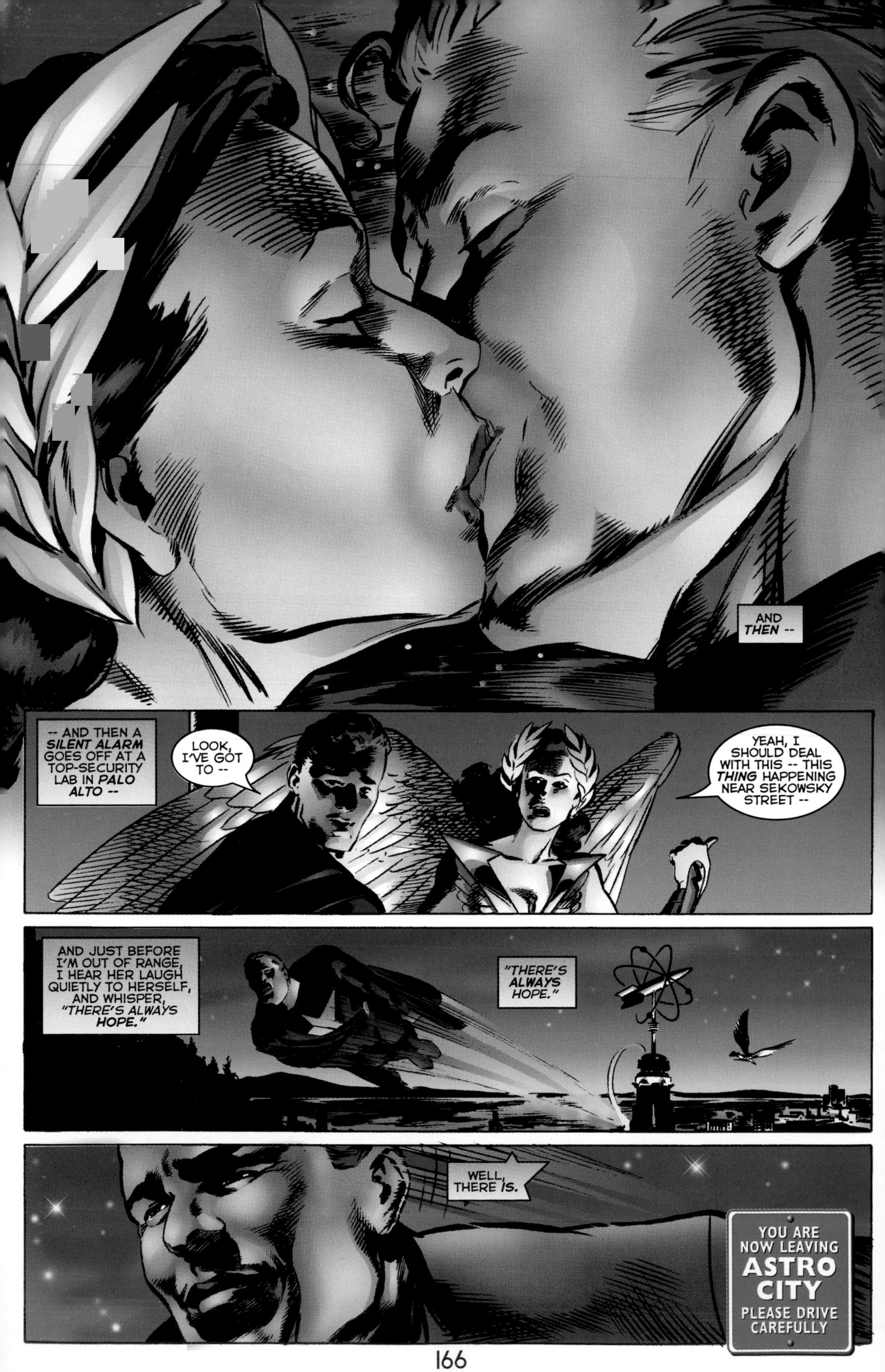
AND THEN --
-- AND THEN A SILENT ALARM GOES OFF AT A TOP-SECURITY LAB IN PALO ALTO --
LOOK, I'VE GOT TO --
YEAH, I SHOULD DEAL WITH THIS -- THIS THING HAPPENING NEAR SEKOWSKY STREET --
AND JUST BEFORE I'M OUT OF RANGE, I HEAR HER LAUGH QUIETLY TO HERSELF, AND WHISPER, "THERE'S ALWAYS HOPE."
"THERE'S ALWAYS HOPE."
WELL, THERE IS.
YOU ARE NOW LEAVING ASTRO CITY PLEASE DRIVE CAREFULLY

INFRASTRUCTURE

City Planning

Creating an entire city from the ground up, one with over 75 years of superhero history, isn't the easiest of challenges. When you've got one writer and two artists (three, if you count Art Nichols's lettercolumn cityscape), you can't just make things up as you go along. Everything's got to be worked out in advance — and while at times, I feel like Alex, Brent and I are burying each other under continual round-robin faxes, with revisions of this and designs for that, it's been a major thrill to see this world come to life, neighborhood by neighborhood and sketch by sketch.

— Kurt Busiek

Below ▼ Brent's notes on how to draw the "rocket" beacon atop the AstroBank tower — based on a two-dimensional design by Alex, which was in turn inspired by faxes I sent him of the old, discontinued library-system genre-sticker for "science fiction."

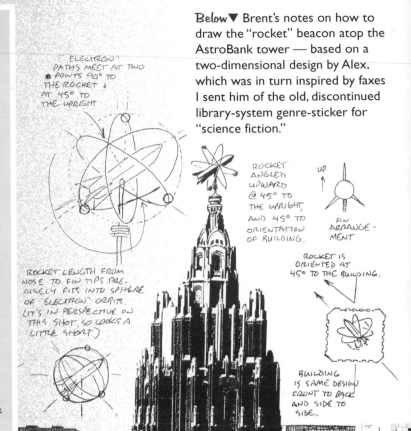

"ELECTRON" PATHS MEET AT TWO POINTS 90° TO THE ROCKET & AT 45° TO THE UPRIGHT

ROCKET ANGLED UPWARD @ 45° TO THE UPRIGHT, AND 45° TO ORIENTATION OF BUILDING.

ROCKET IS ORIENTED AT 45° TO THE BUILDING.

FIN ARRANGE-MENT

UP

ROCKET LENGTH FROM NOSE TO FIN TIPS PRE-CISELY FITS INTO SPHERE OF "ELECTRON" ORBITS. (IT'S IN PERSPECTIVE ON THIS SHOT, SO LOOKS A LITTLE SHORT)

BUILDING IS SAME DESIGN FRONT TO BACK AND SIDE TO SIDE.

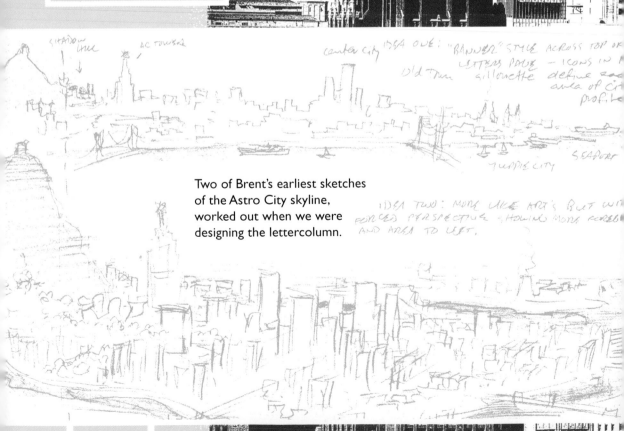

SHADOW LINE

AC TOWERS

center city IDEA ONE: "BANNER" STYLE ACROSS TOP OF LETTERS PAGE — ICONS IN SILHOUETTE DEFINE EACH AREA OF CITY

Old Town

profile

SEAPORT

YUPPIE CITY

Two of Brent's earliest sketches of the Astro City skyline, worked out when we were designing the lettercolumn.

IDEA TWO: MORE LIKE ART'S BUT WITH FORCED PERSPECTIVE SHOWING MORE FOREGROUND AND AREA TO LEFT.

City Planning

In the inset is my very first rough map (and rough it is indeed!) of Astro City and its environs, and below, Brent's reworking of it into something that looks more like an actual city. This is very early — we hadn't named the rivers or most of the neighborhoods yet, the prison island got a new name by the time #1 got lettered, and we added some stuff here and there — but it's got all the basics.

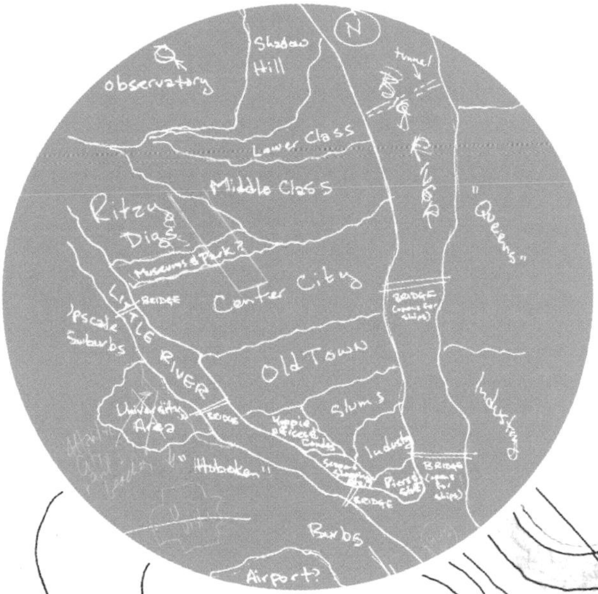

N
Shadow Hill
observatory
tunnel
Lower Class
Middle Class
Ritzy Digs
Museums & Park?
RIVER
"Queens"
Center City
BRIDGE
Upscale Suburbs
LITTLE RIVER
Old Town
Slums
University Area
Yuppie Places
Industry
"Hoboken"
Burbs
Airport?

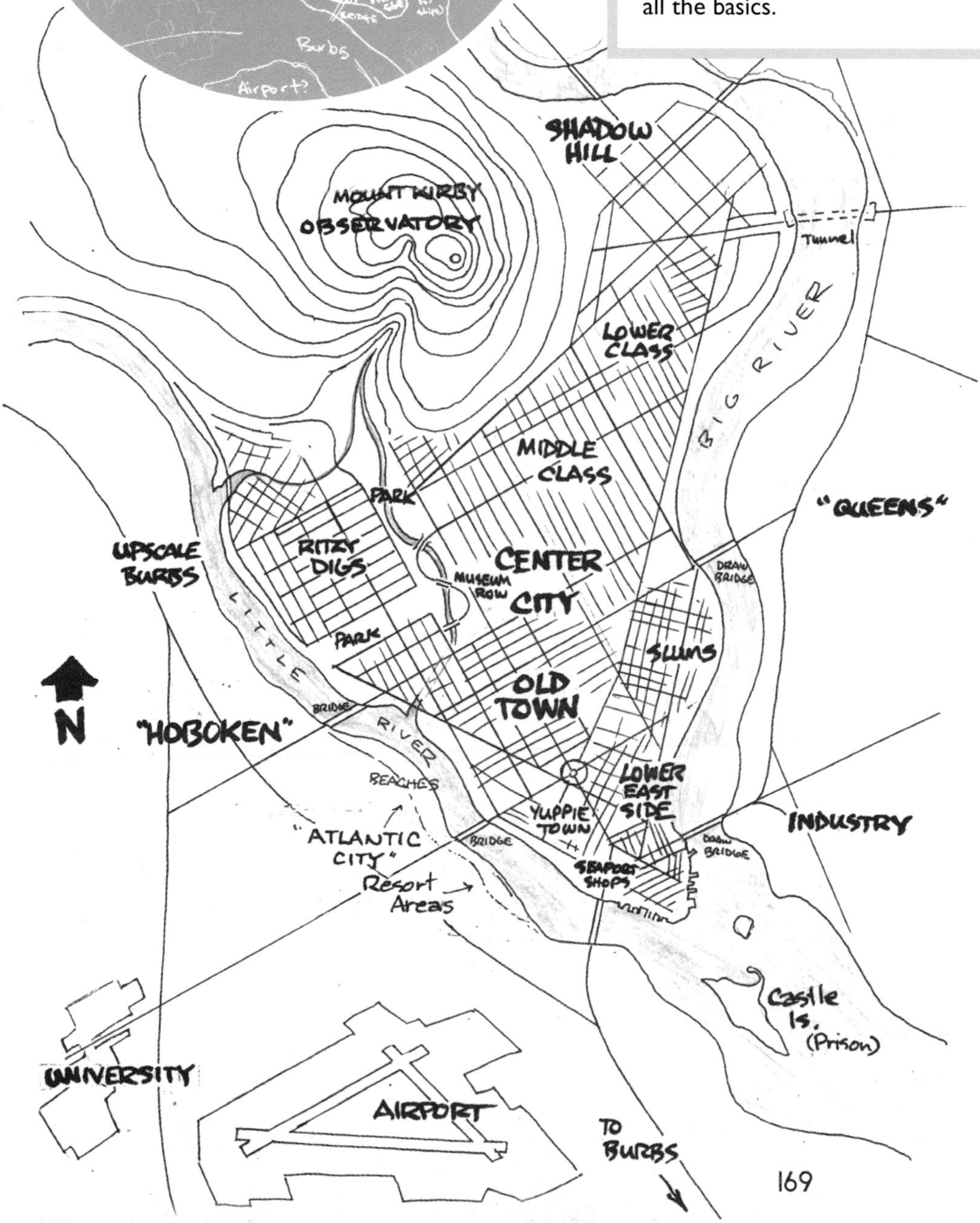

SHADOW HILL
MOUNT KIRBY OBSERVATORY
Tunnel
LOWER CLASS
BIG RIVER
MIDDLE CLASS
PARK
"QUEENS"
UPSCALE BURBS
RITZY DIGS
CENTER CITY
MUSEUM ROW
DRAW BRIDGE
LITTLE
PARK
SLUMS
OLD TOWN
N
"HOBOKEN"
BRIDGE
RIVER
BEACHES
LOWER EAST SIDE
YUPPIE TOWN
INDUSTRY
"ATLANTIC CITY"
BRIDGE
DRAW BRIDGE
SEAPORT SHOPS
Resort Areas
Castle Is. (Prison)
UNIVERSITY
AIRPORT
TO BURBS

Samaritan

Some of Alex's dozens (hundreds?) of sketches working out a design for Samaritan, showing the development of his chest-symbol and some attempts to figure out a distinctive cape. The cape design we finally went with is an extreme stylization of a Greek toga.

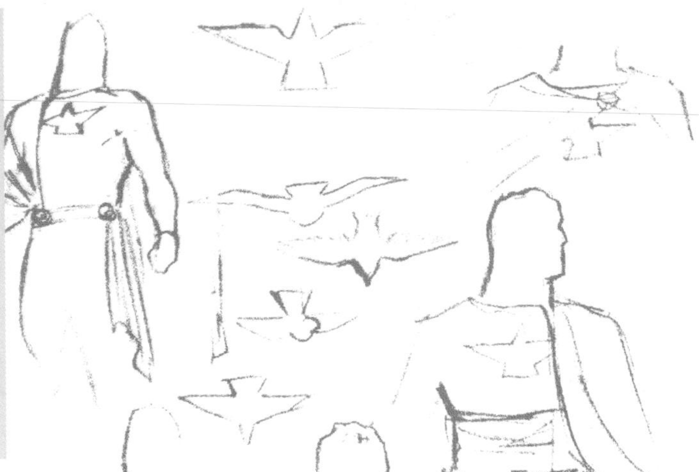

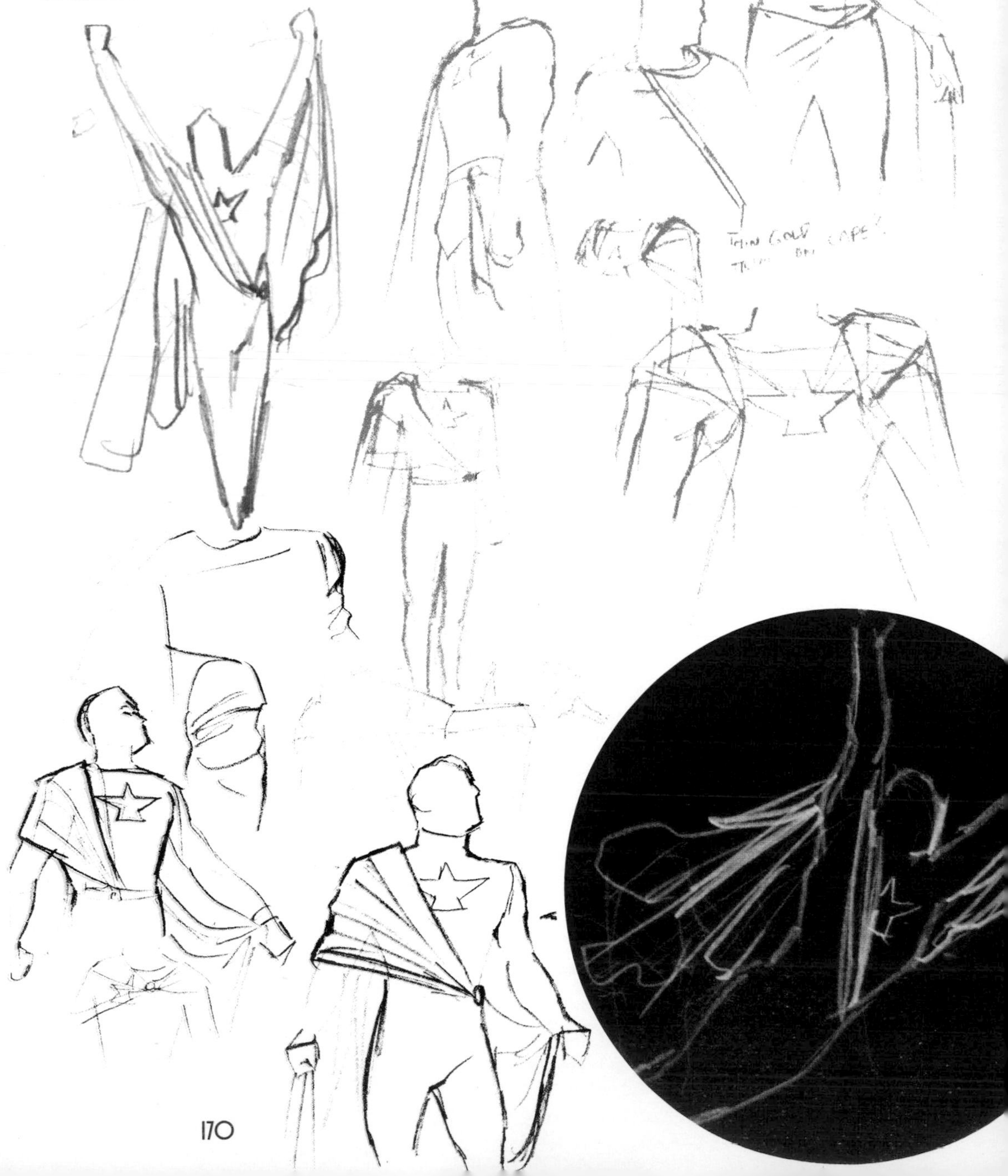

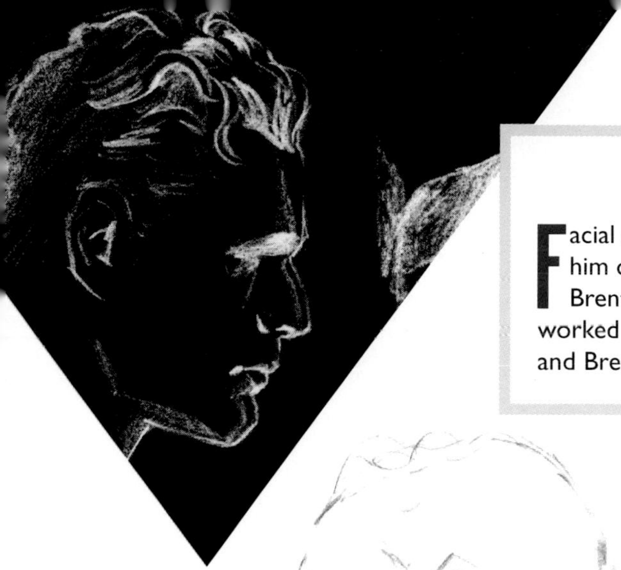

Samaritan

Facial studies of Samaritan. Even if Alex was painting him on the cover to #1 with his face obscured, Brent had to draw him all through the issue, so Alex worked out his face from many angles to make sure he and Brent would be drawing exactly the same man.

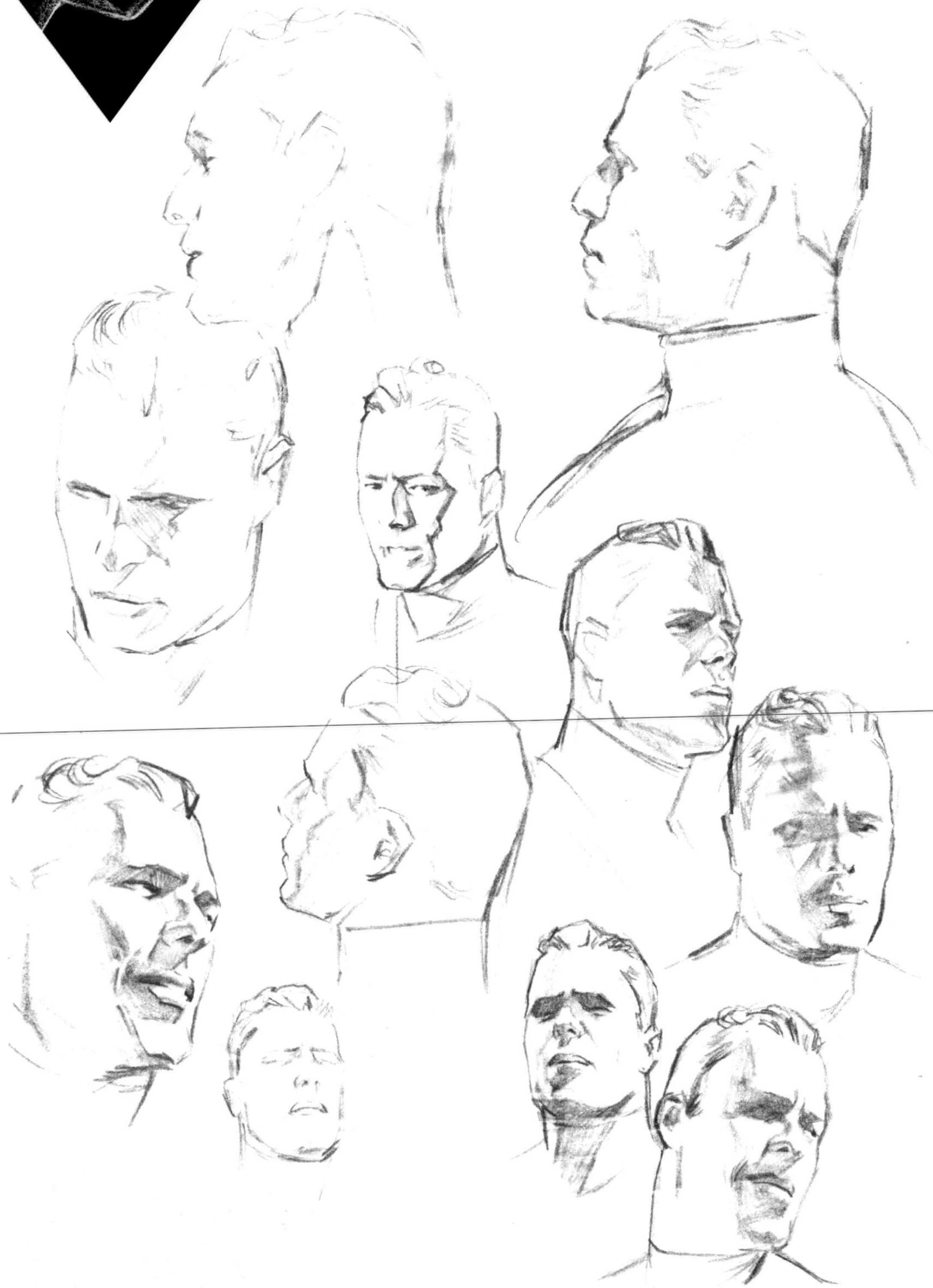

Honor Guard

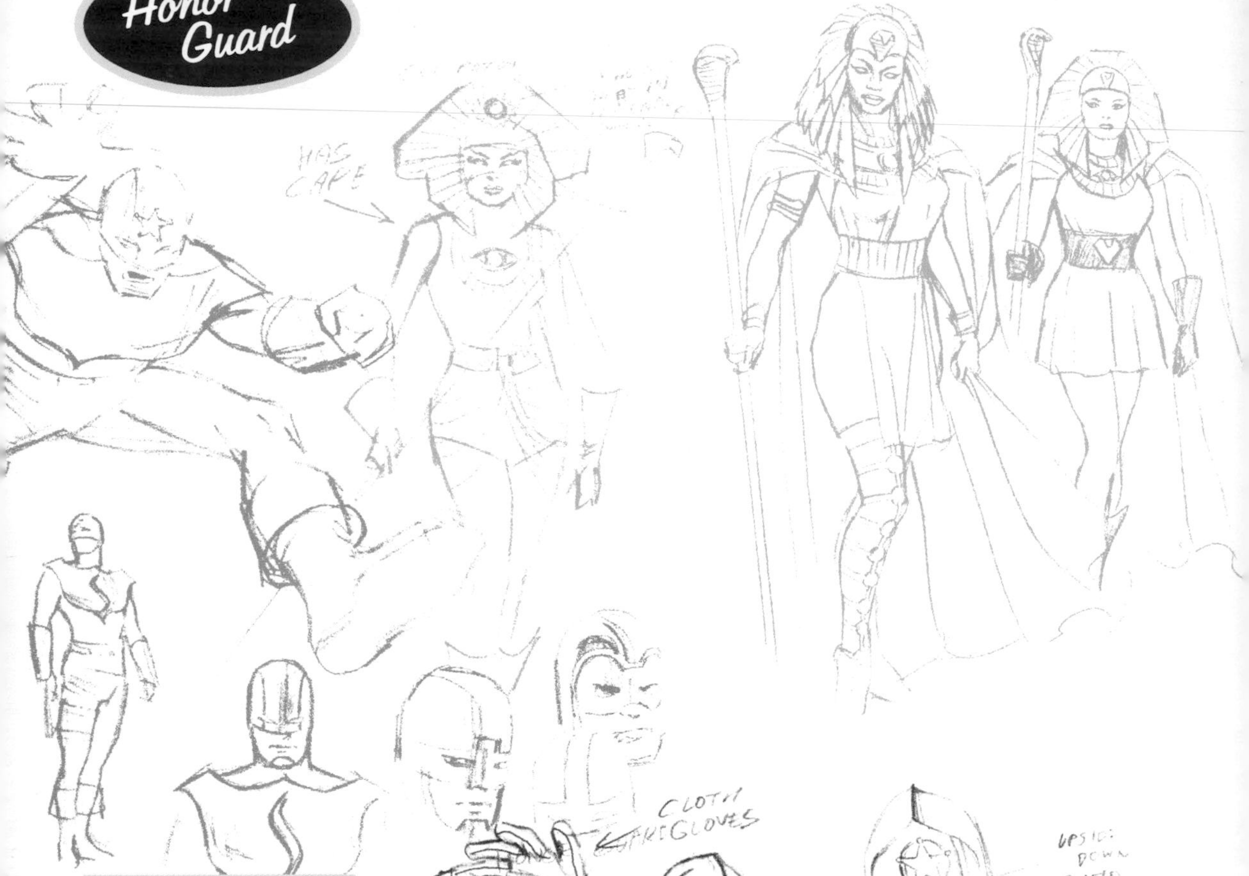

HAS CAPE

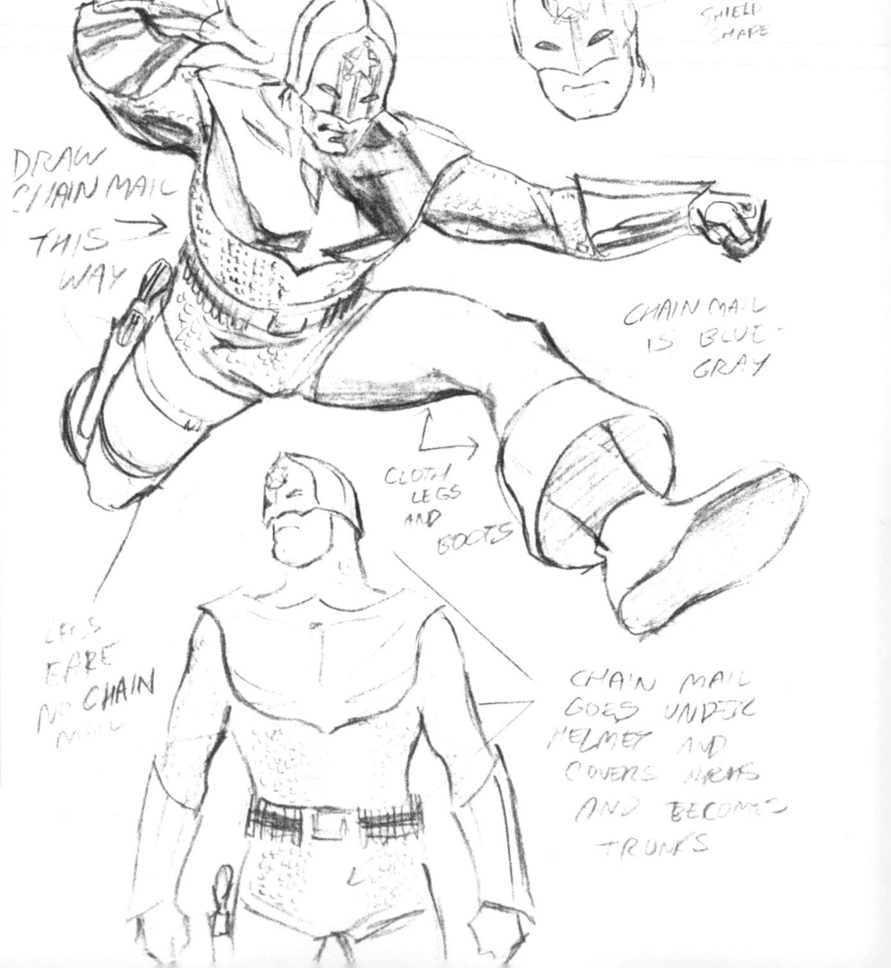

CLOTH GLOVES
UPSIDE DOWN SHIELD SHAPE
DRAW CHAIN MAIL THIS WAY
CHAIN MAIL IS BLUE-GRAY
CLOTH LEGS AND BOOTS
LEGS BARE NO CHAIN MAIL
CHAIN MAIL GOES UNDER HELMET AND COVERS ARMS AND BECOMES TRUNKS

Upper right ◀
Three designs for Cleopatra. The one furthest left is striking and memorable, but it didn't quite say "hero" to me. The two others became the modern Cleopatra and the 1959 Cleopatra respectively.

Above, ▲ *and lower right* ▶
Early sketches for the Silver Agent, including variant helmet and chest-shield ideas

Honor Guard

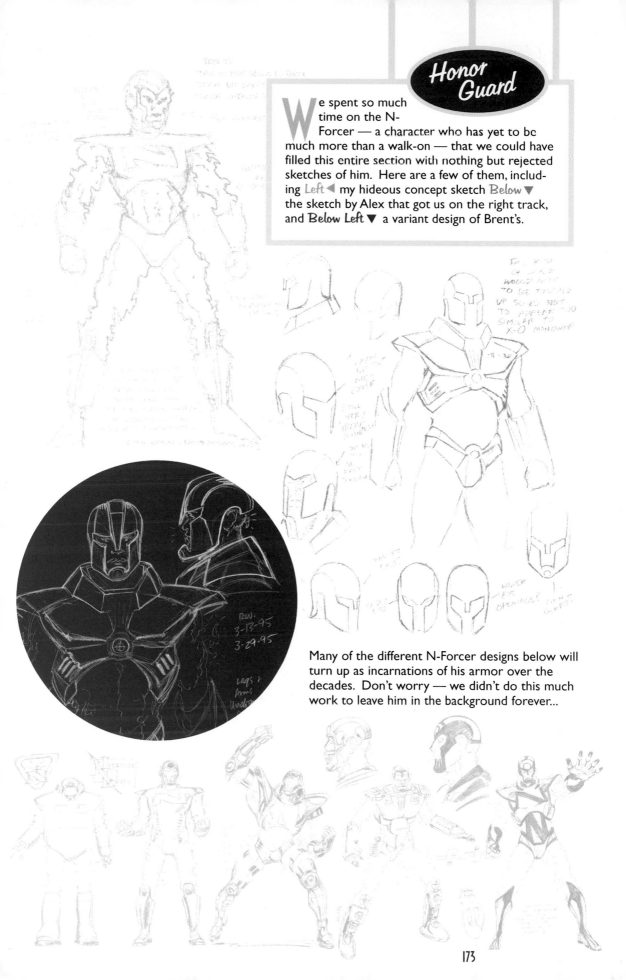

We spent so much time on the N-Forcer — a character who has yet to be much more than a walk-on — that we could have filled this entire section with nothing but rejected sketches of him. Here are a few of them, including *Left* ◀ my hideous concept sketch *Below* ▼ the sketch by Alex that got us on the right track, and *Below Left* ▼ a variant design of Brent's.

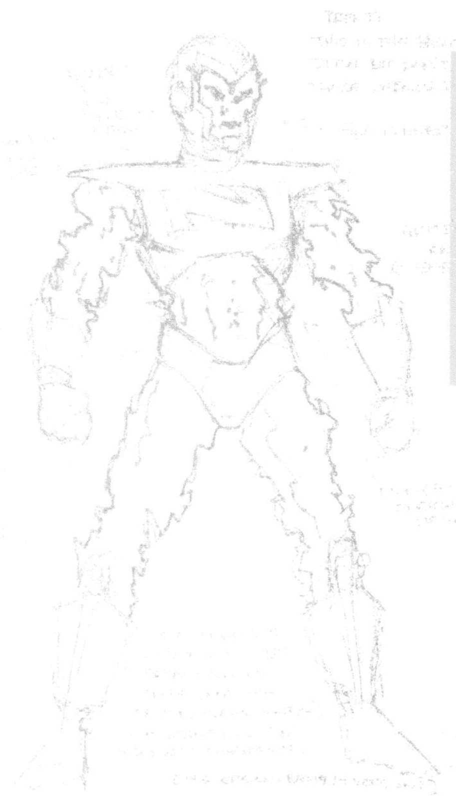

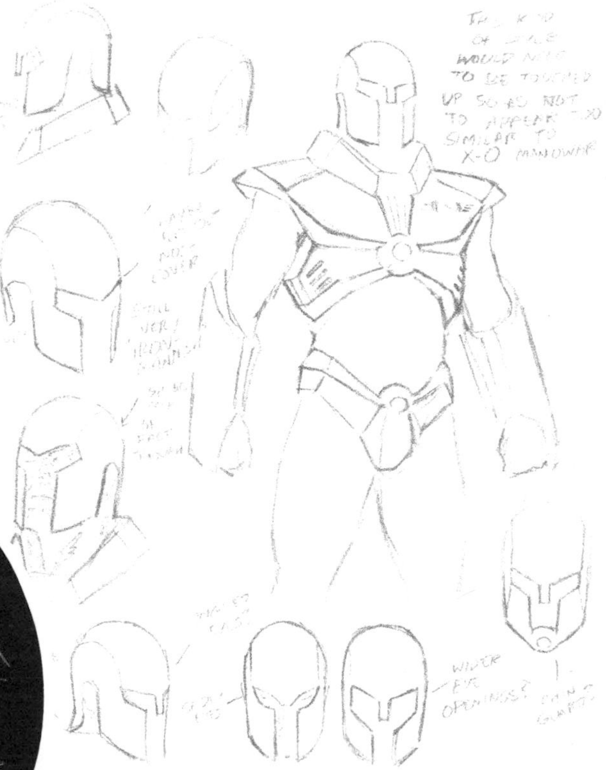
WOULD NEED TO BE TOUCHED UP SO AS NOT TO APPEAR TOO SIMILAR TO X-O MANOWAR

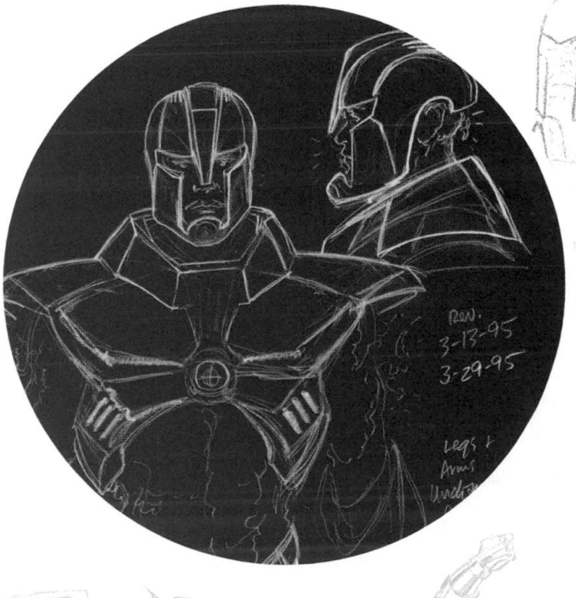
REV. 3-13-95
3-29-95

Many of the different N-Forcer designs below will turn up as incarnations of his armor over the decades. Don't worry — we didn't do this much work to leave him in the background forever...

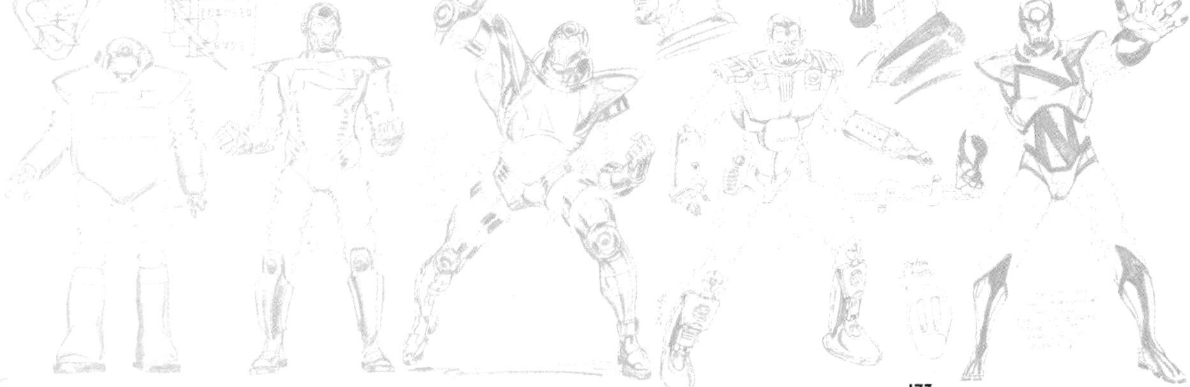

Honor Guard

More Honor Guard designs: To the right ▶ Brent's original sketch of Quarrel, and a suggestion for revised leggings from Alex. **Below, counterclockwise from bottom left** ▼ My original sketch for Starwoman (you can see now why I work with professionals…), Brent's design sketches for Beautie, with Alex's mask suggestions, . Opposite page, top ▶ Brent's initial sketch for M.P.H. and the final design.

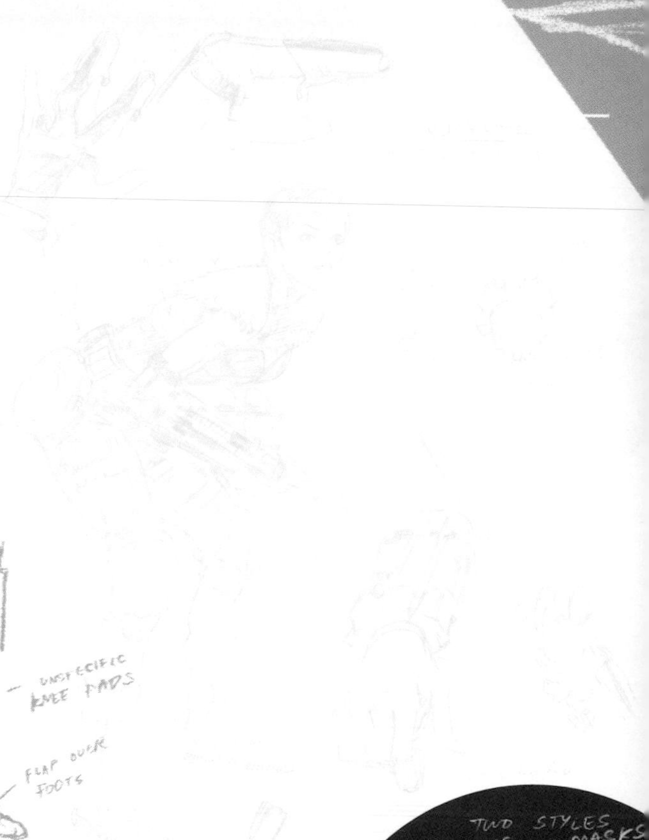

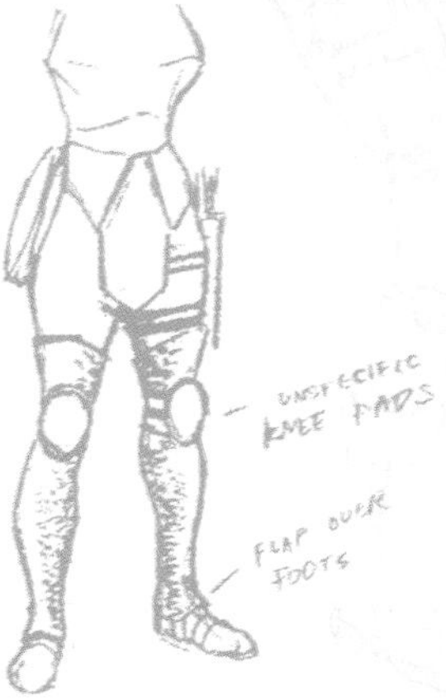

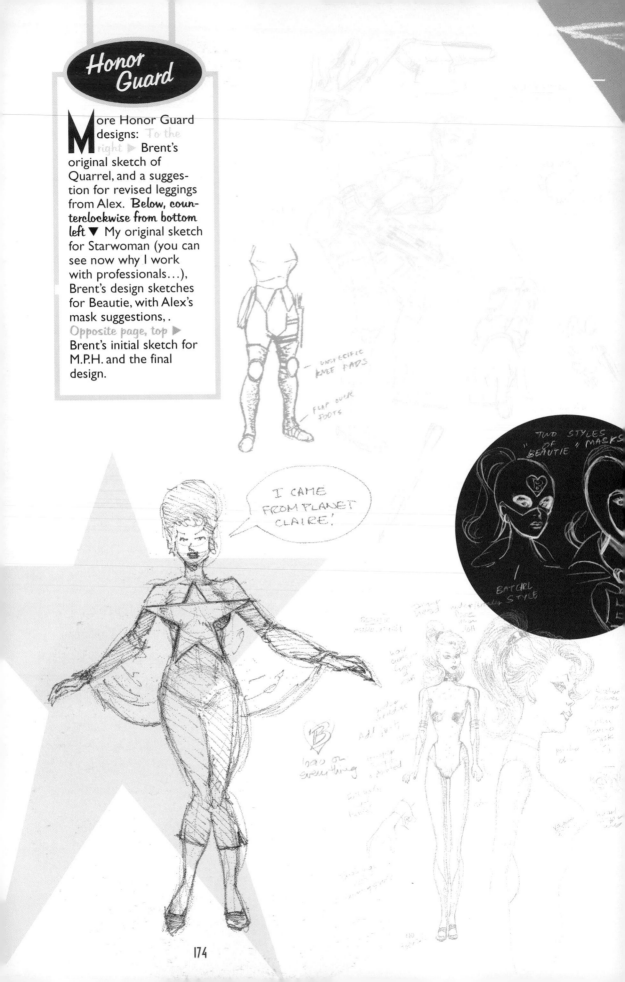

UNSPECIFIC KNEE PADS
FLAP OVER FOOTS

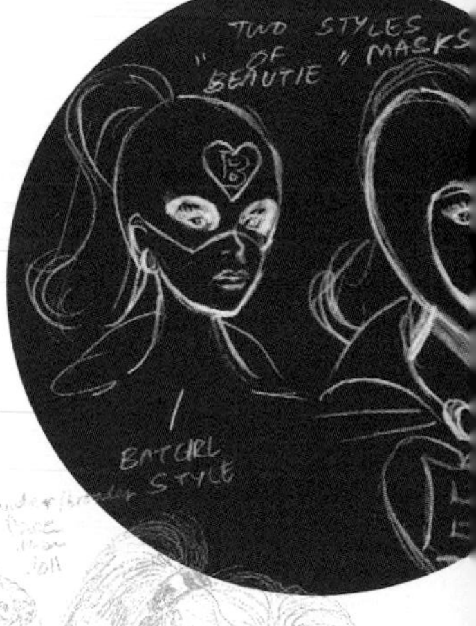

TWO STYLES OF "BEAUTIE" MASKS
BATGIRL STYLE

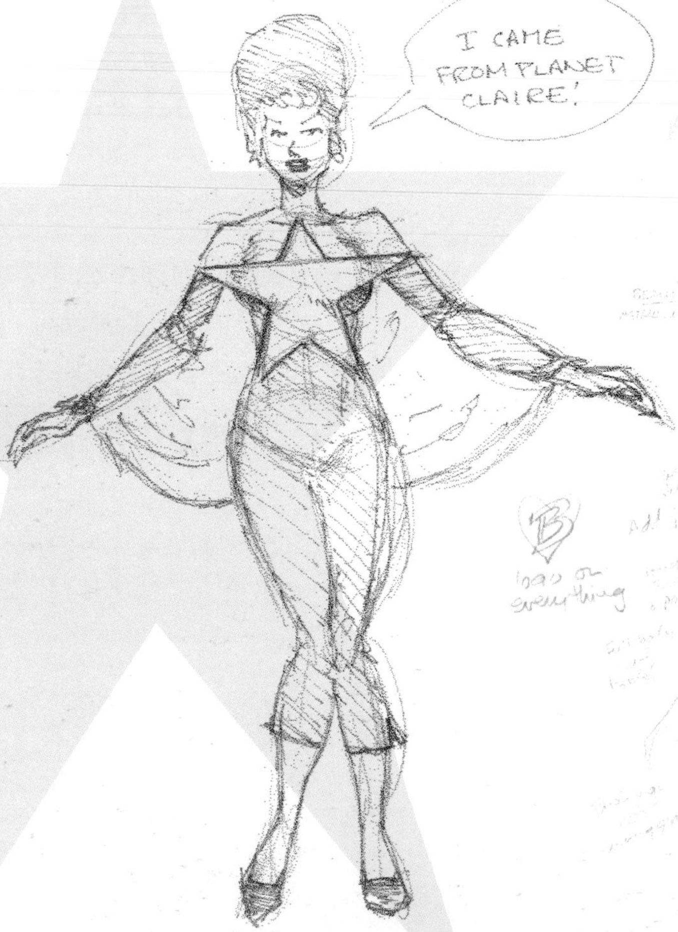

I CAME FROM PLANET CLAIRE!

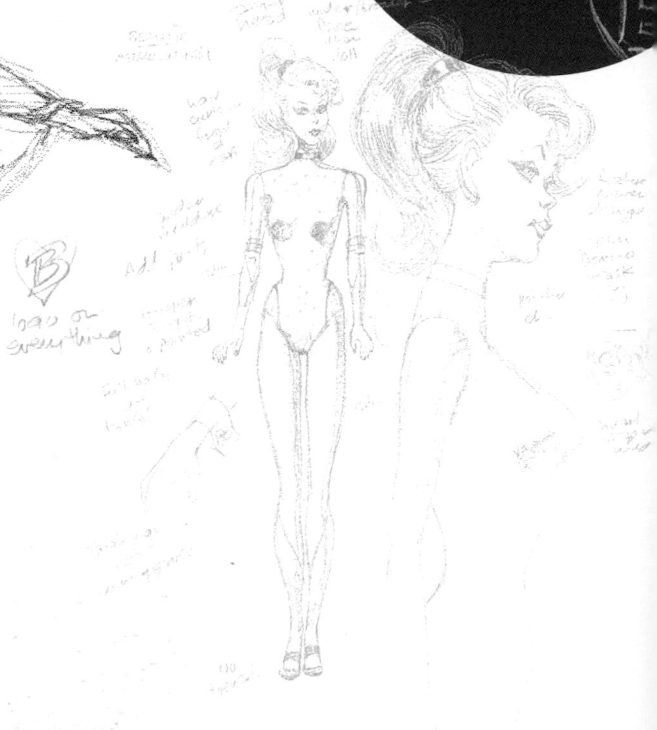

logo on everything

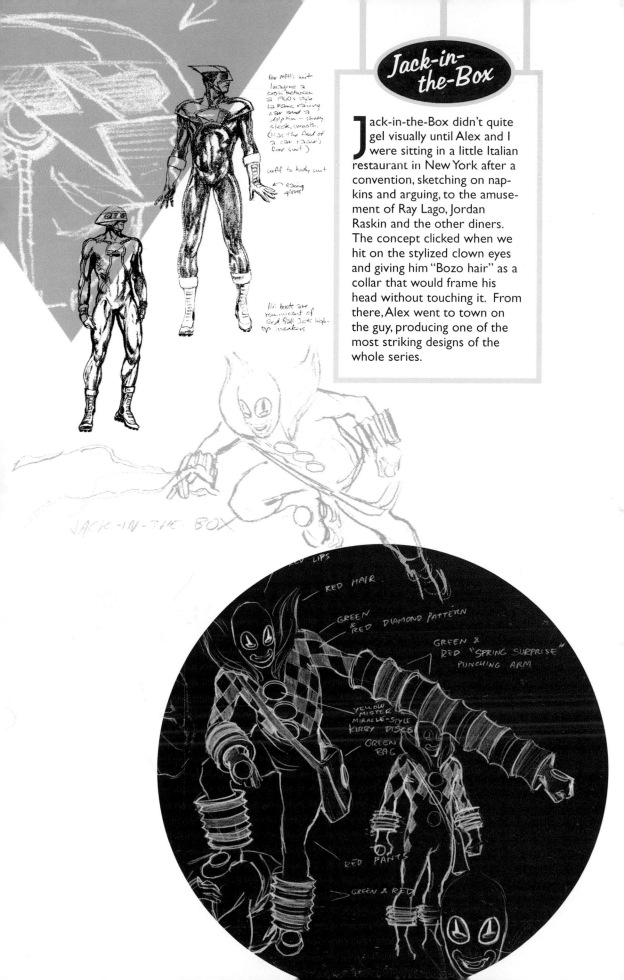

Jack-in-the-Box

Jack-in-the-Box didn't quite gel visually until Alex and I were sitting in a little Italian restaurant in New York after a convention, sketching on napkins and arguing, to the amusement of Ray Lago, Jordan Raskin and the other diners. The concept clicked when we hit on the stylized clown eyes and giving him "Bozo hair" as a collar that would frame his head without touching it. From there, Alex went to town on the guy, producing one of the most striking designs of the whole series.

For MPH's suit imagine a cross between a 1940's style LeMans racing car and a dolphin — shinny, sleek, smooth. (Has the feel of a car racer's fire suit)

cuff to body suit

Racing gloves

His boots are reminiscent of Red Ball Jets high-top sneakers

JACK-IN-THE-BOX

RED LIPS

RED HAIR

GREEN & RED DIAMOND PATTERN

GREEN & RED "SPRING SURPRISE" PUNCHING ARM

YELLOW MISTER MIRACLE-STYLE KIRBY DISCS

GREEN BAG

RED PANTS

GREEN & RED

Shark Men

Even "cannon fodder" has to be designed — this is Brent's design drawing of one of Shirak's "devourers," drawn to help Alex paint the cover to #2.

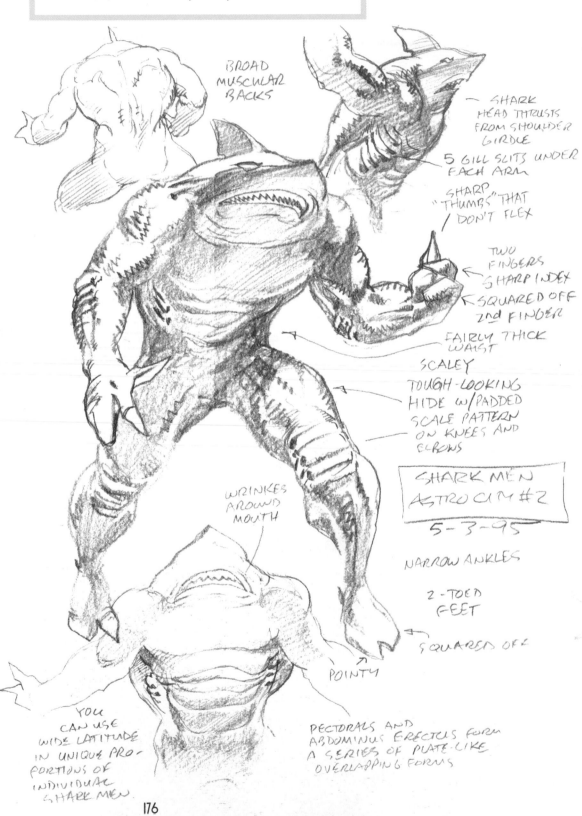

BROAD MUSCULAR BACKS

SHARK HEAD THRUSTS FROM SHOULDER GIRDLE

5 GILL SLITS UNDER EACH ARM

SHARP "THUMBS" THAT DON'T FLEX

TWO FINGERS SHARP INDEX SQUARED OFF 2nd FINGER

FAIRLY THICK WAIST

SCALEY TOUGH-LOOKING HIDE w/PADDED SCALE PATTERN ON KNEES AND ELBOWS

SHARK MEN ASTRO CITY #2 5-3-95

NARROW ANKLES

2-TOED FEET

SQUARED OFF

WRINKLES AROUND MOUTH

POINTY

YOU CAN USE WIDE LATITUDE IN UNIQUE PROPORTIONS OF INDIVIDUAL SHARK MEN.

PECTORALS AND ABDOMINUS ERECTUS FORM A SERIES OF PLATE-LIKE OVERLAPPING FORMS

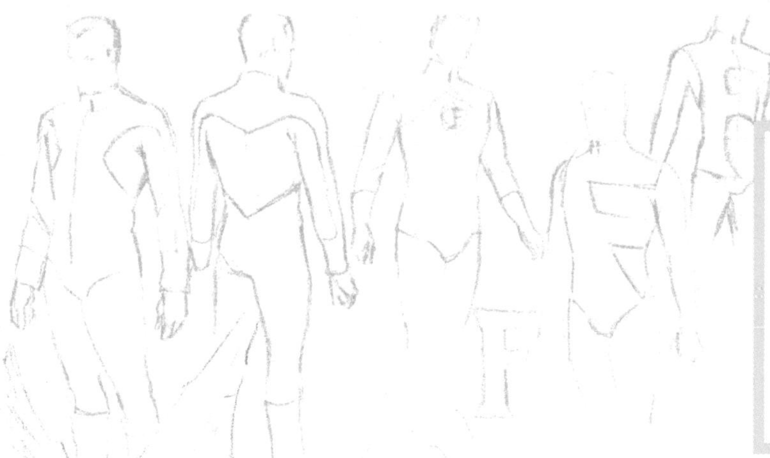

First Family

Across the top ◀ Initial design ideas for the First Family's uniforms, starting with something too "Star Trek: The Next Generation" and getting closer to what we finally used.

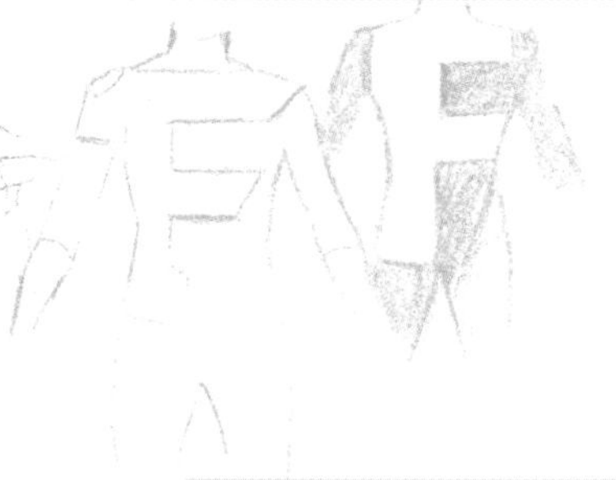

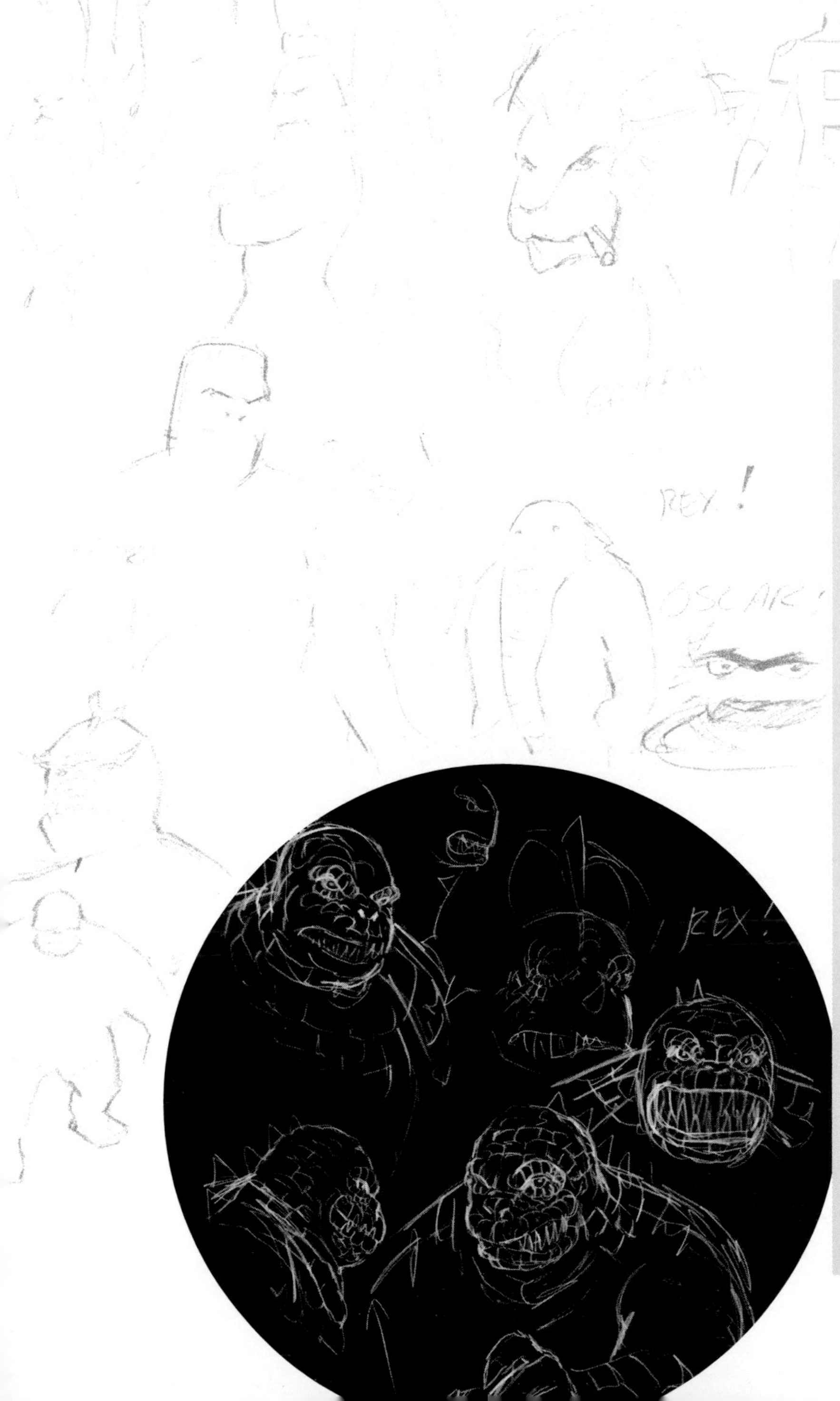
REX!
OSCAR
REX!

All we knew about Rex of the First Family, when we started out, was that he'd be married to Dr. Furst's adoptive daughter Natalie, he'd be a monster, and he'd be the son of one of the team's arch-enemies. We tried lots of different concepts, from a lion-man to a gryphon to a rock-creature, but nothing clicked ...

...until we realized that the name "Rex," originally invented during the "lion-man" stage, could apply as easily to a tyrannosaur. After that, it was easy.

All sketches on this page are by Alex.

Ordinary People

Some of the "little people," sketched by Alex to co-ordinate his cover paintings with what Brent drew in the interior art, plus reference photos shot by Alex for the covers.

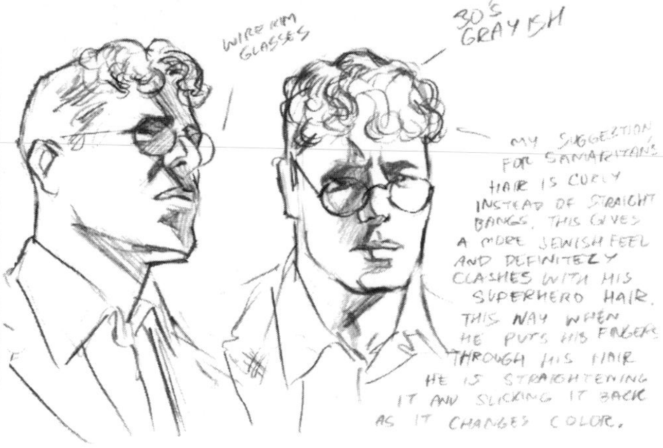
WIRE RIM GLASSES
30'S GRAYISH
MY SUGGESTION FOR SAMARITAN'S HAIR IS CURLY INSTEAD OF STRAIGHT BANGS. THIS GIVES A MORE JEWISH FEEL AND DEFINITELY CLASHES WITH HIS SUPERHERO HAIR. THIS WAY WHEN HE PUTS HIS FINGERS THROUGH HIS HAIR HE IS STRAIGHTENING IT AND SLICKING IT BACK AS IT CHANGES COLOR.

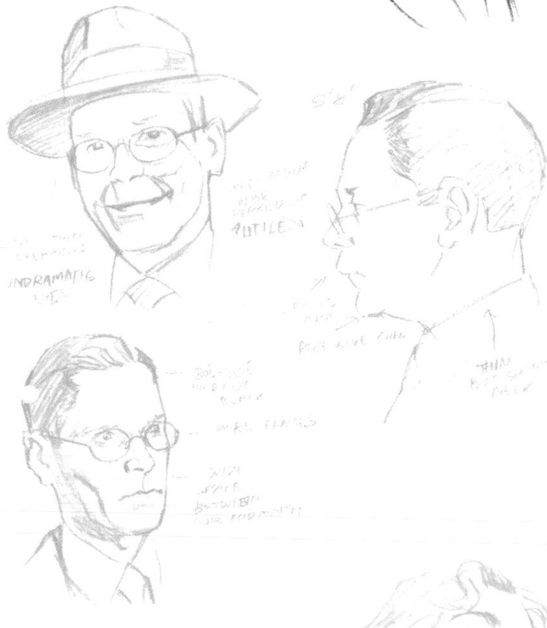

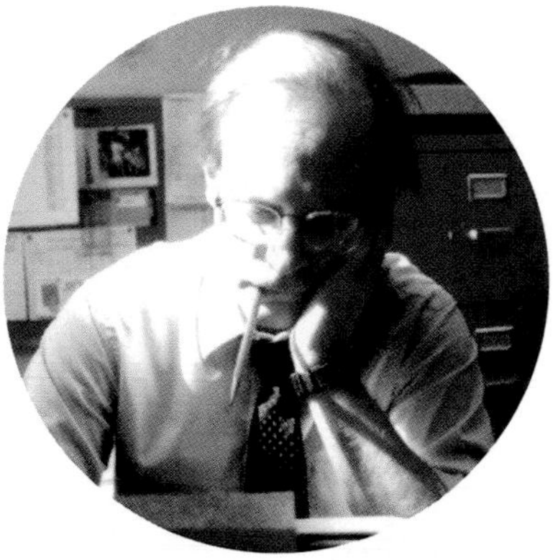

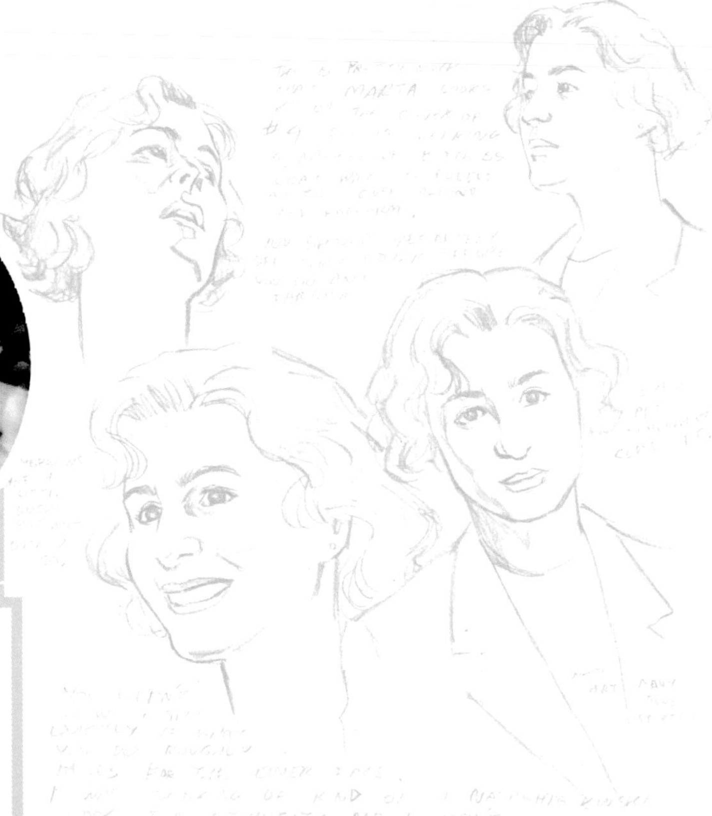

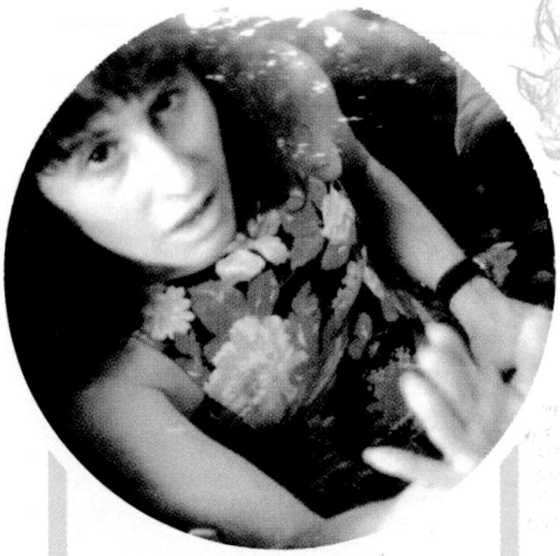

From the top down ▲ Asa "Samaritan" Martin from #1 and #6 (we changed his hair, but kept the face the same), Eliot Mills from #2, and Marta from #4.

COVER GALLERY

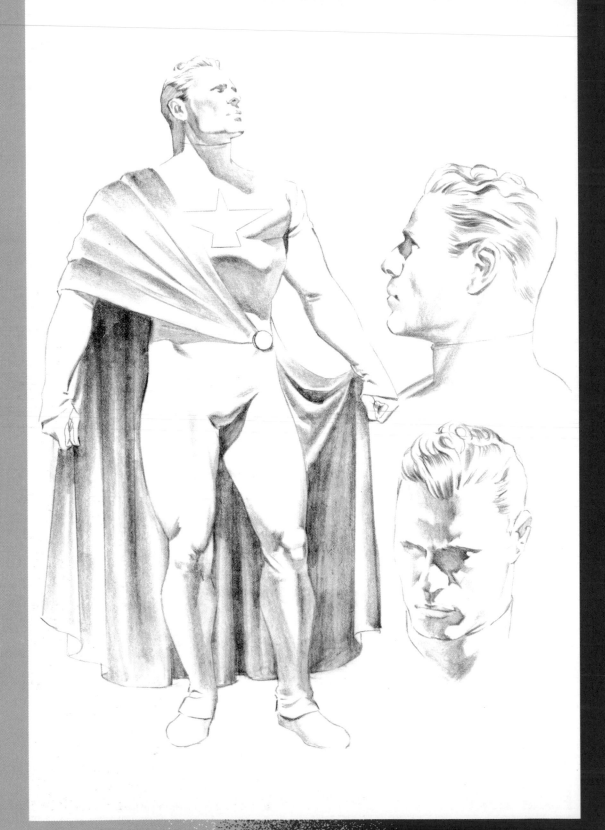

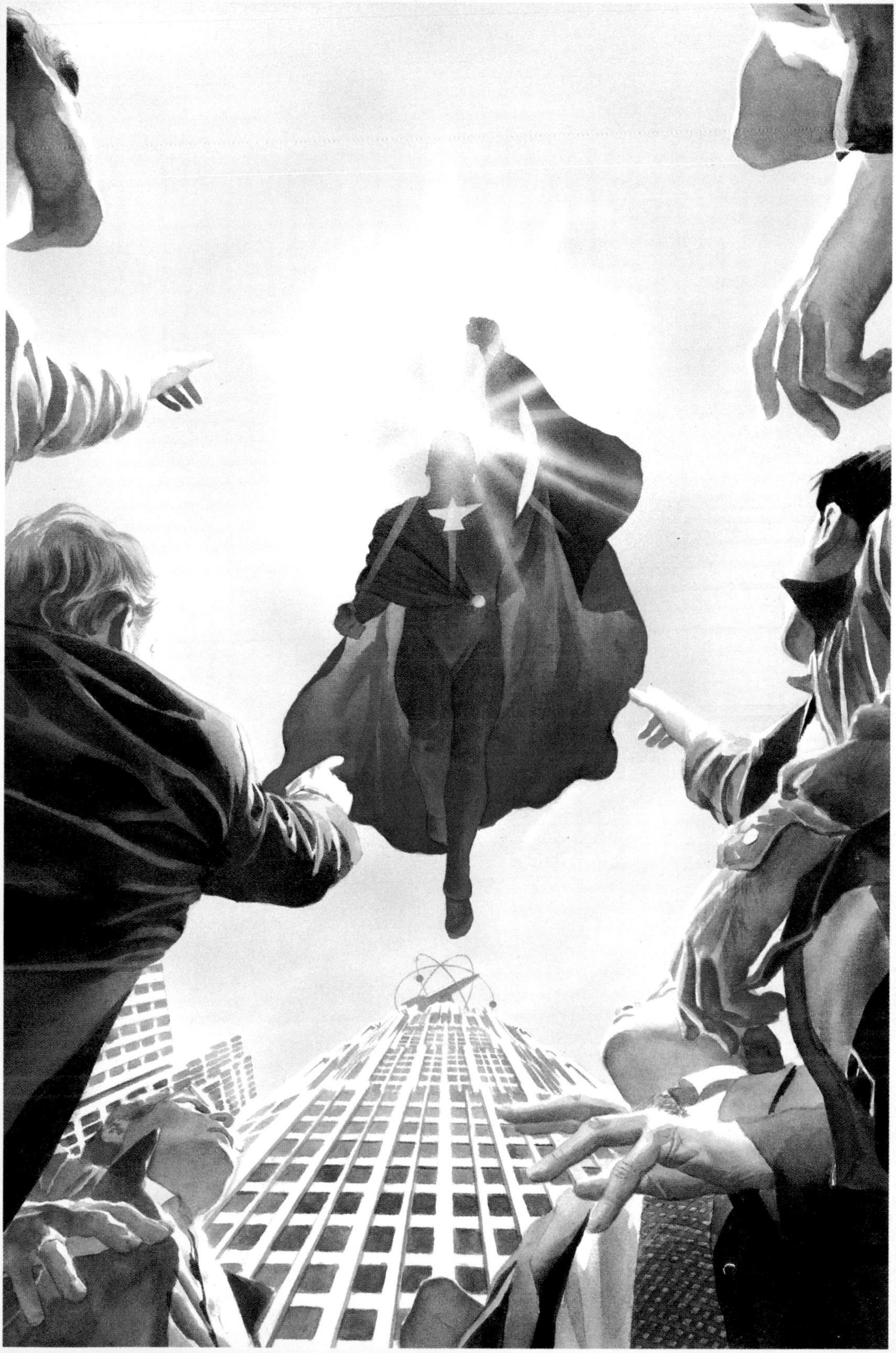

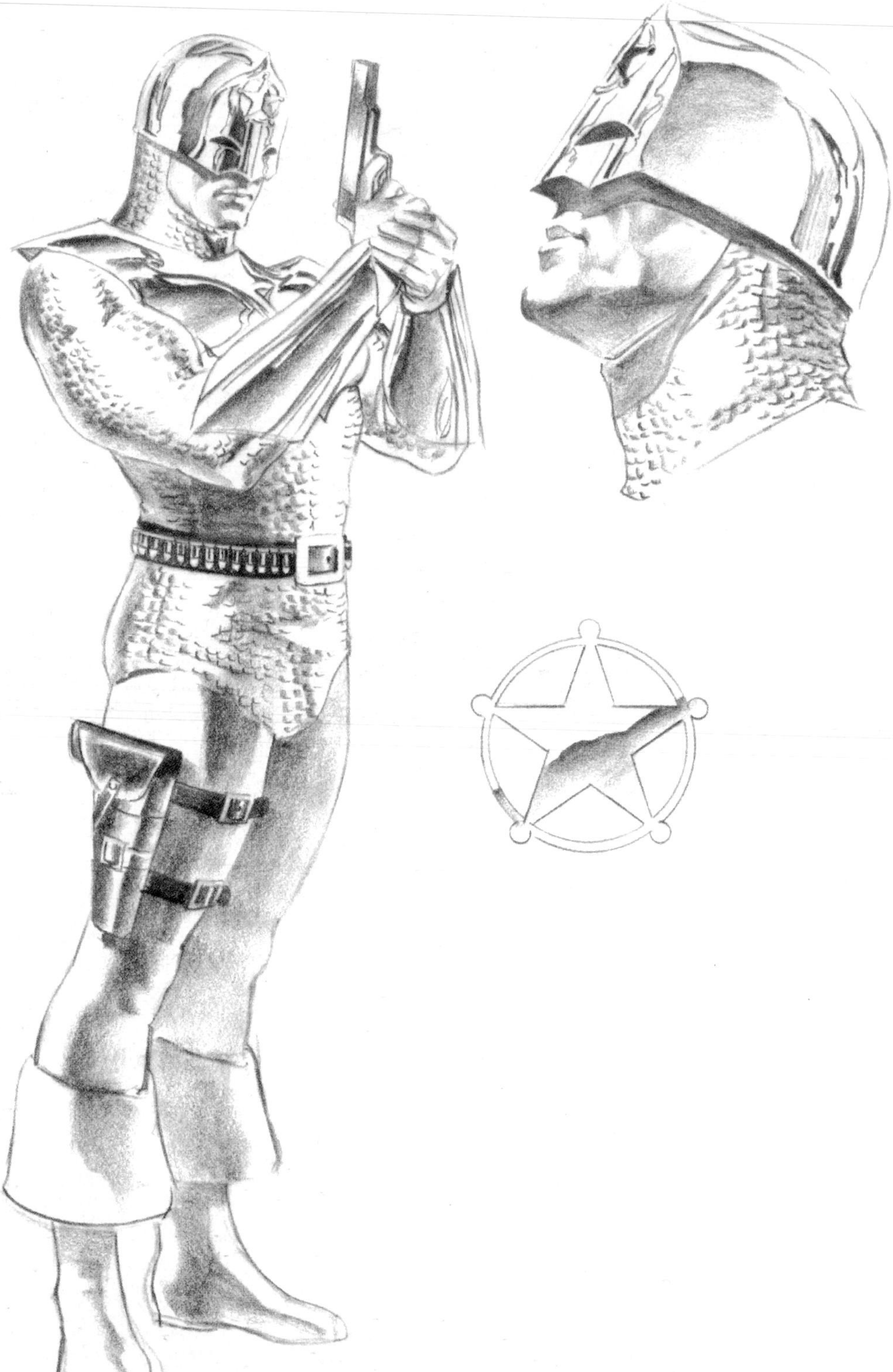

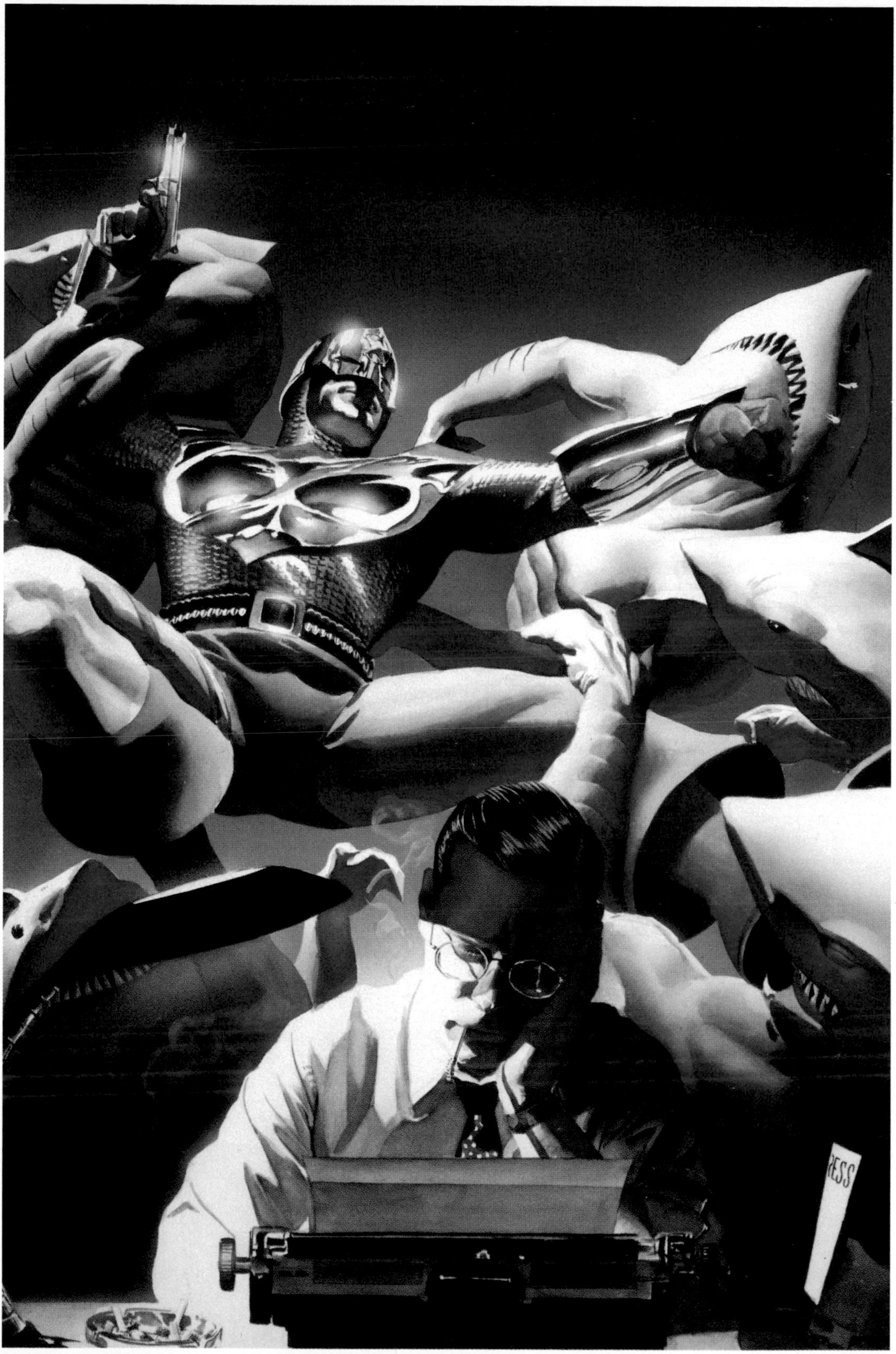

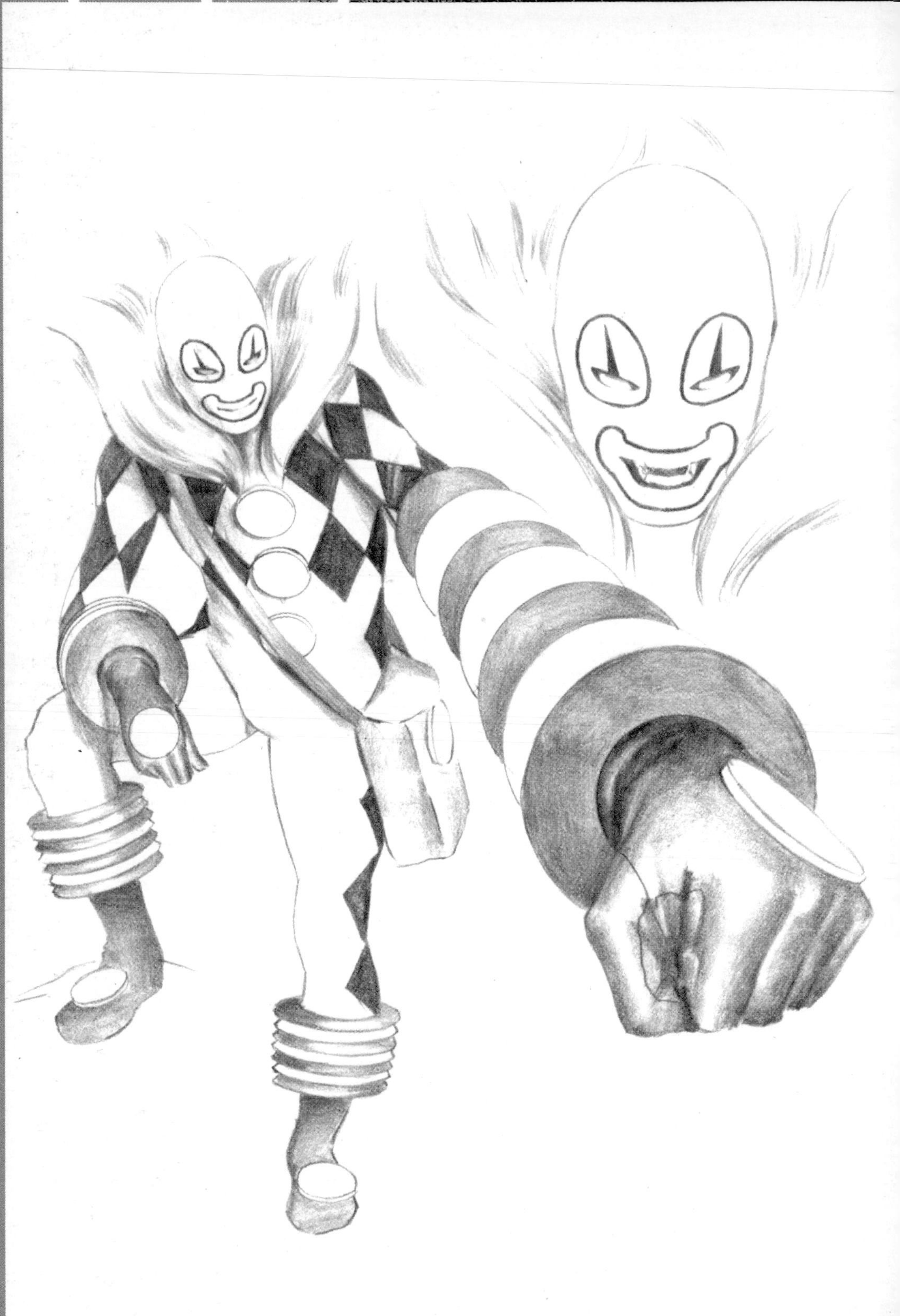

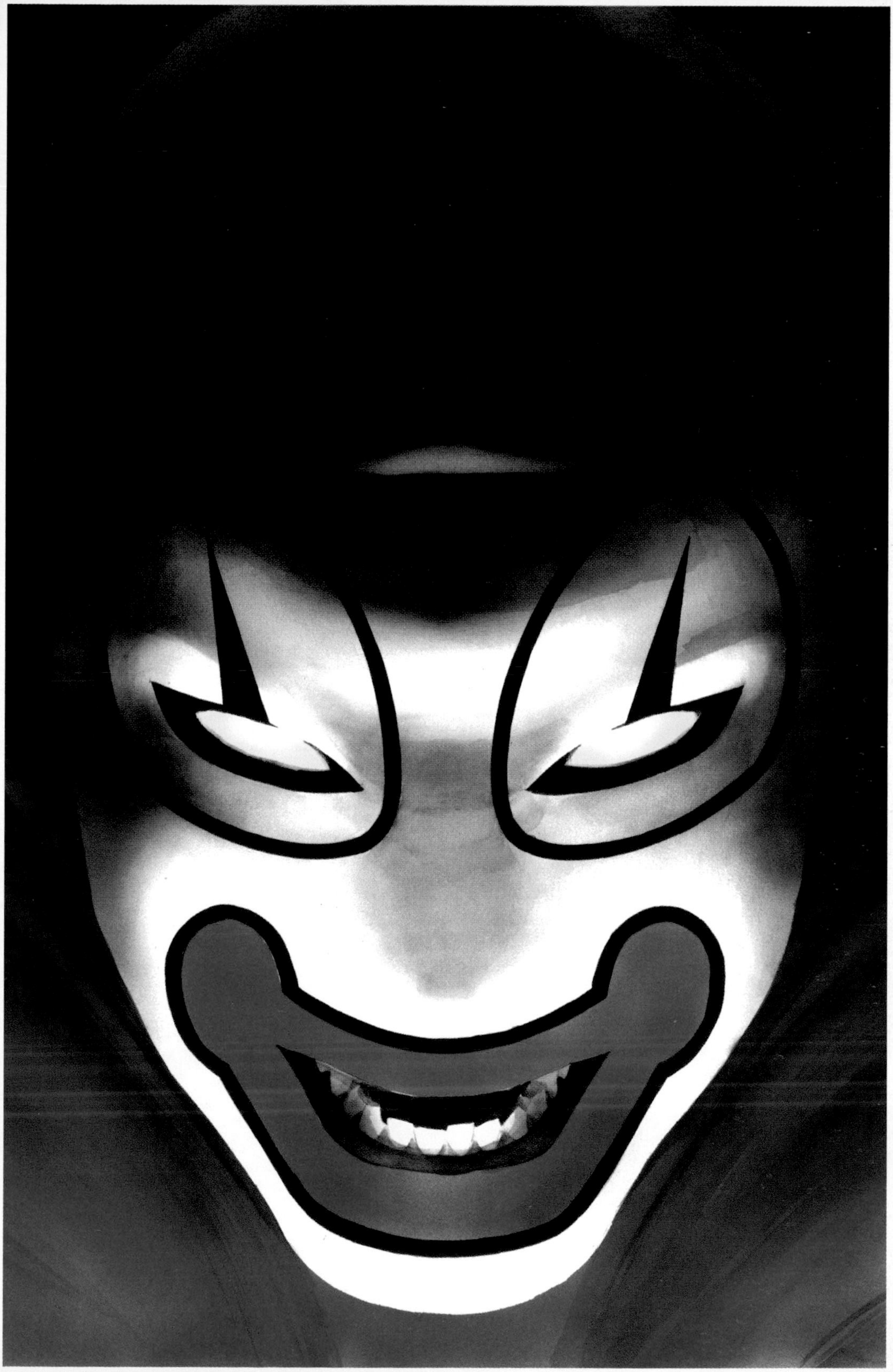

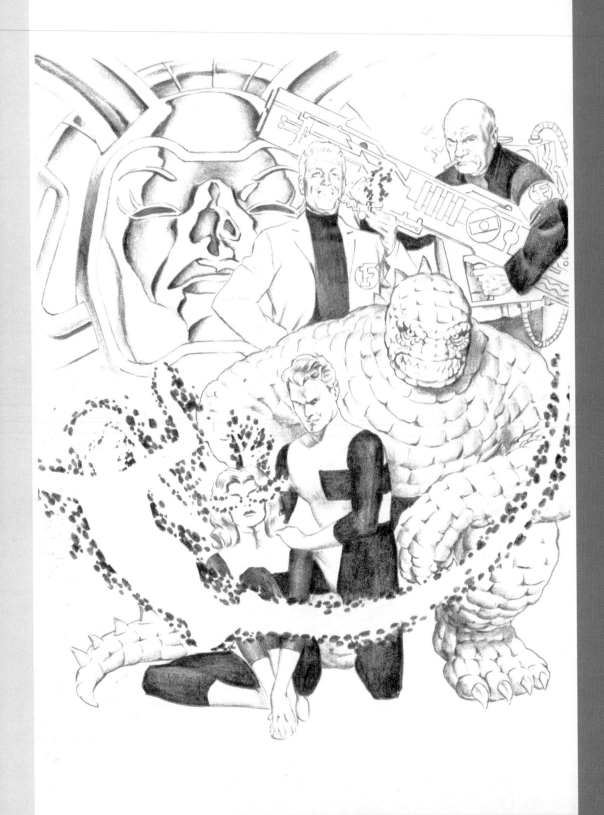

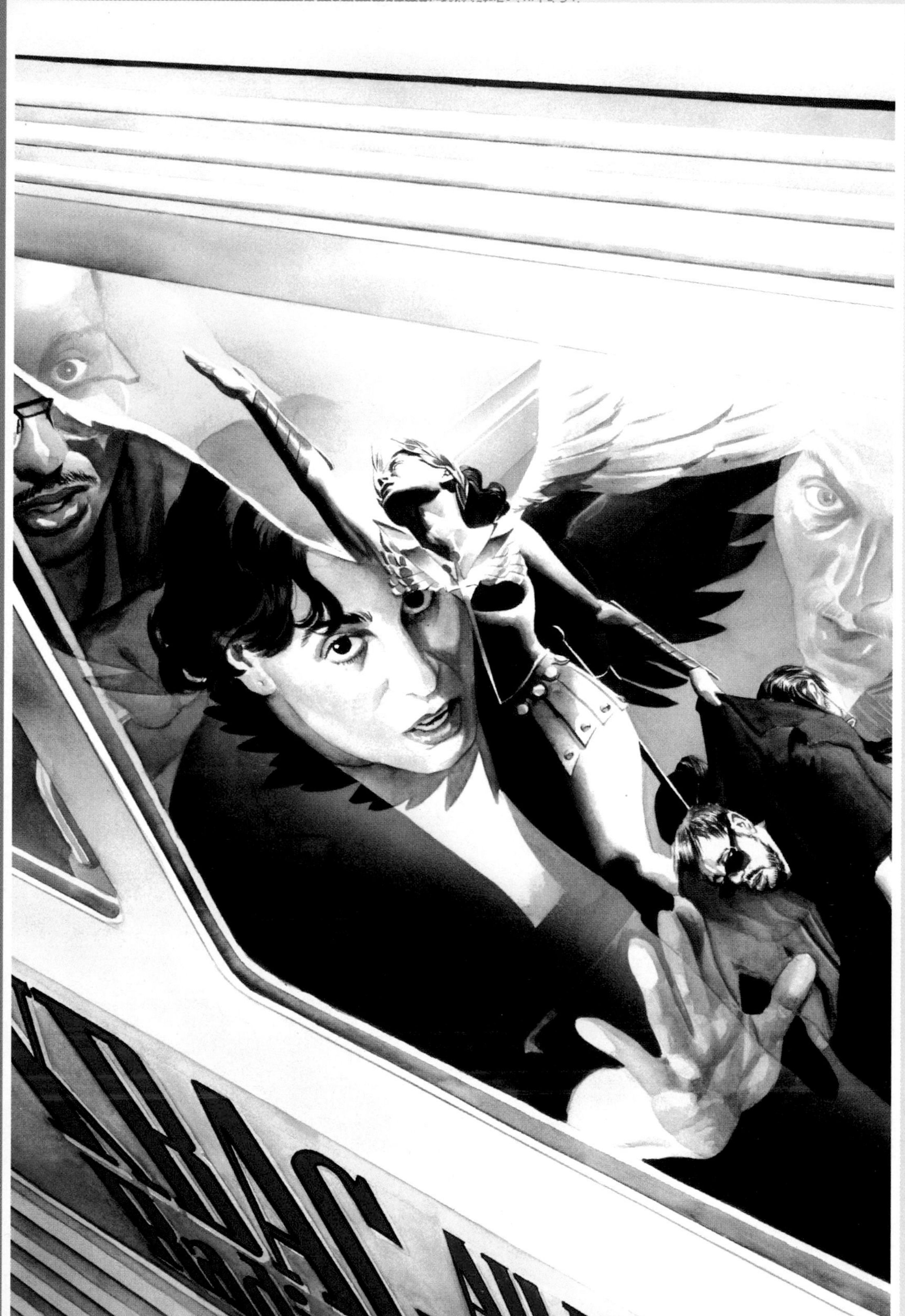

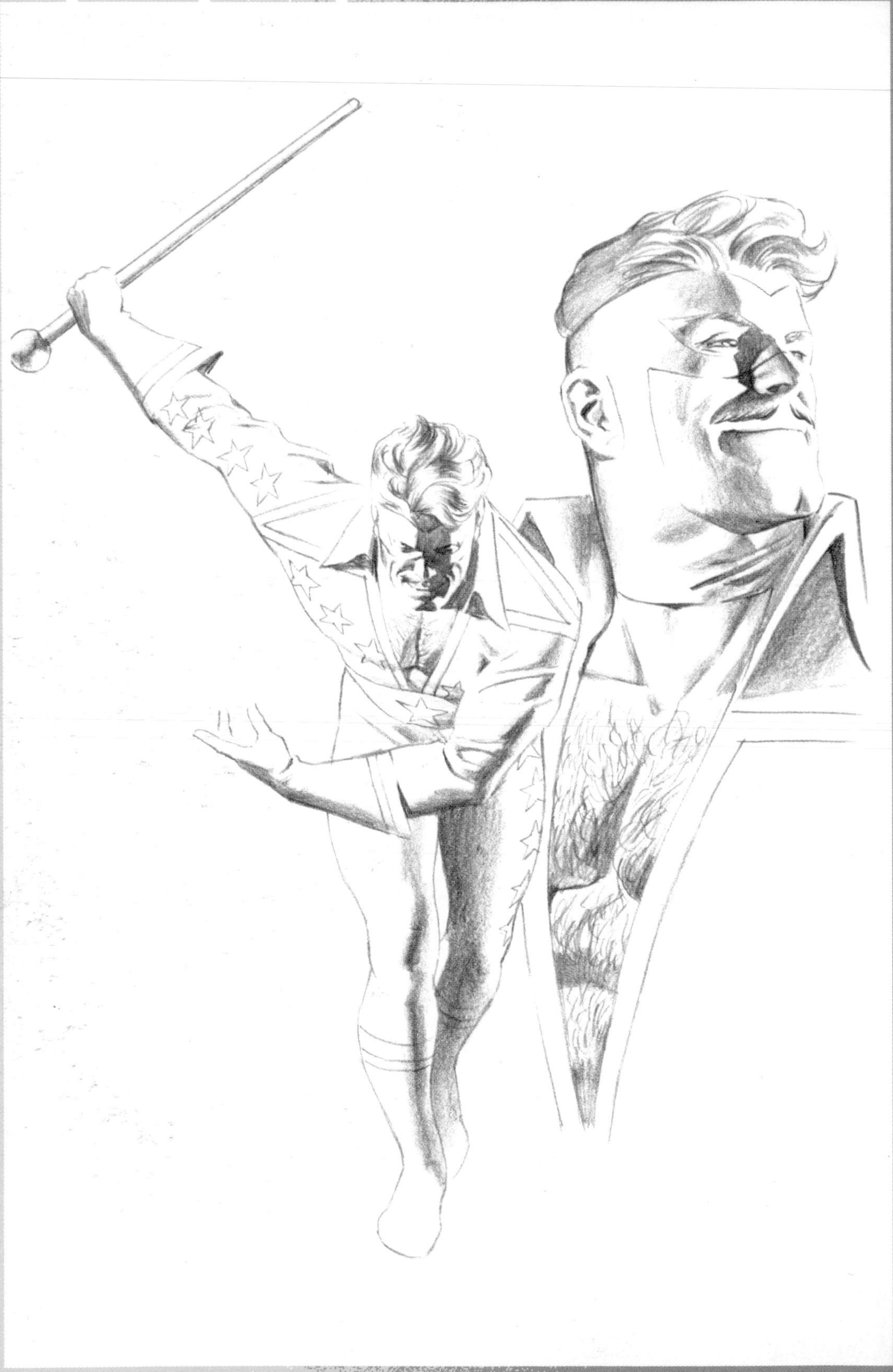

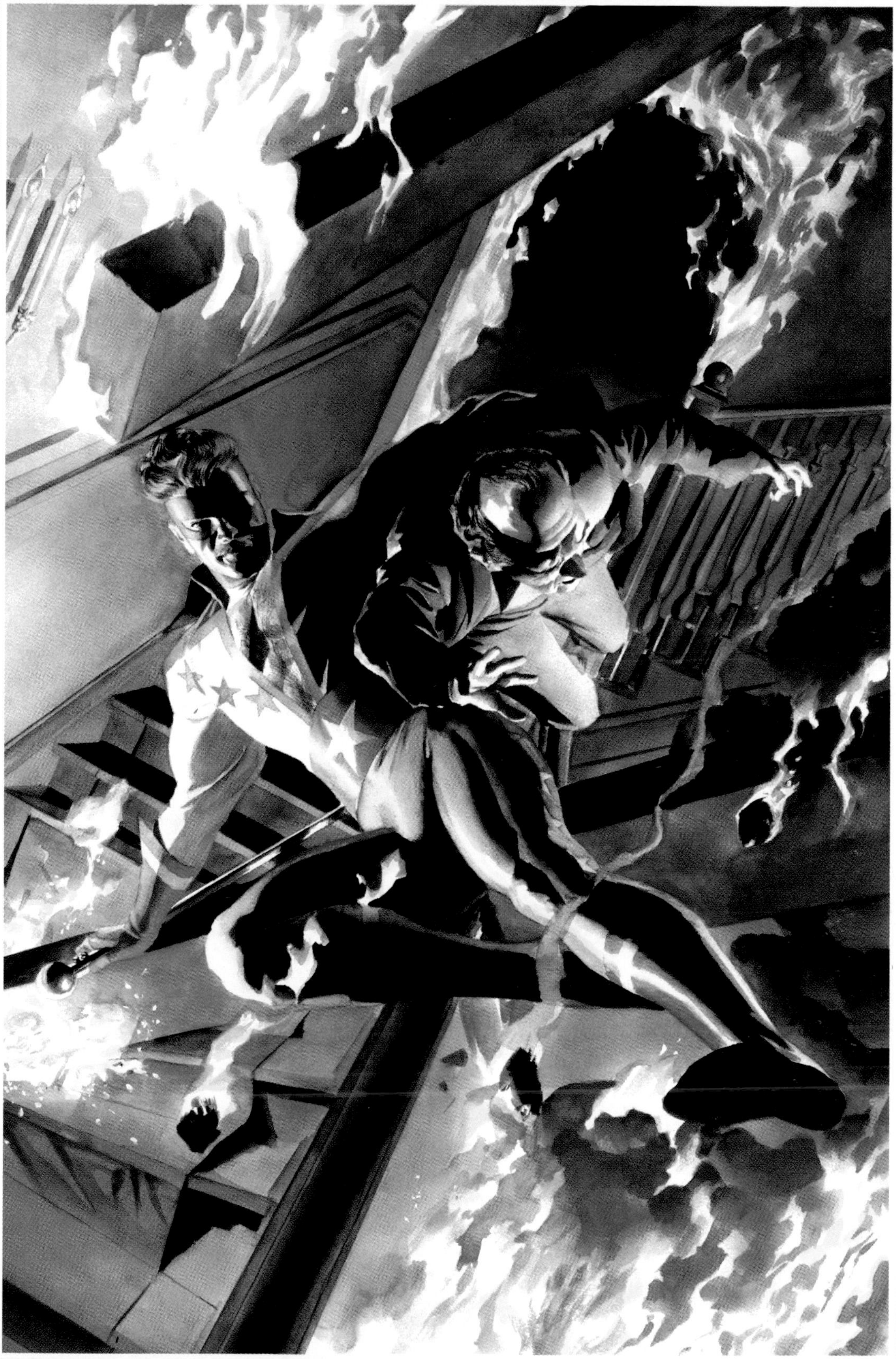

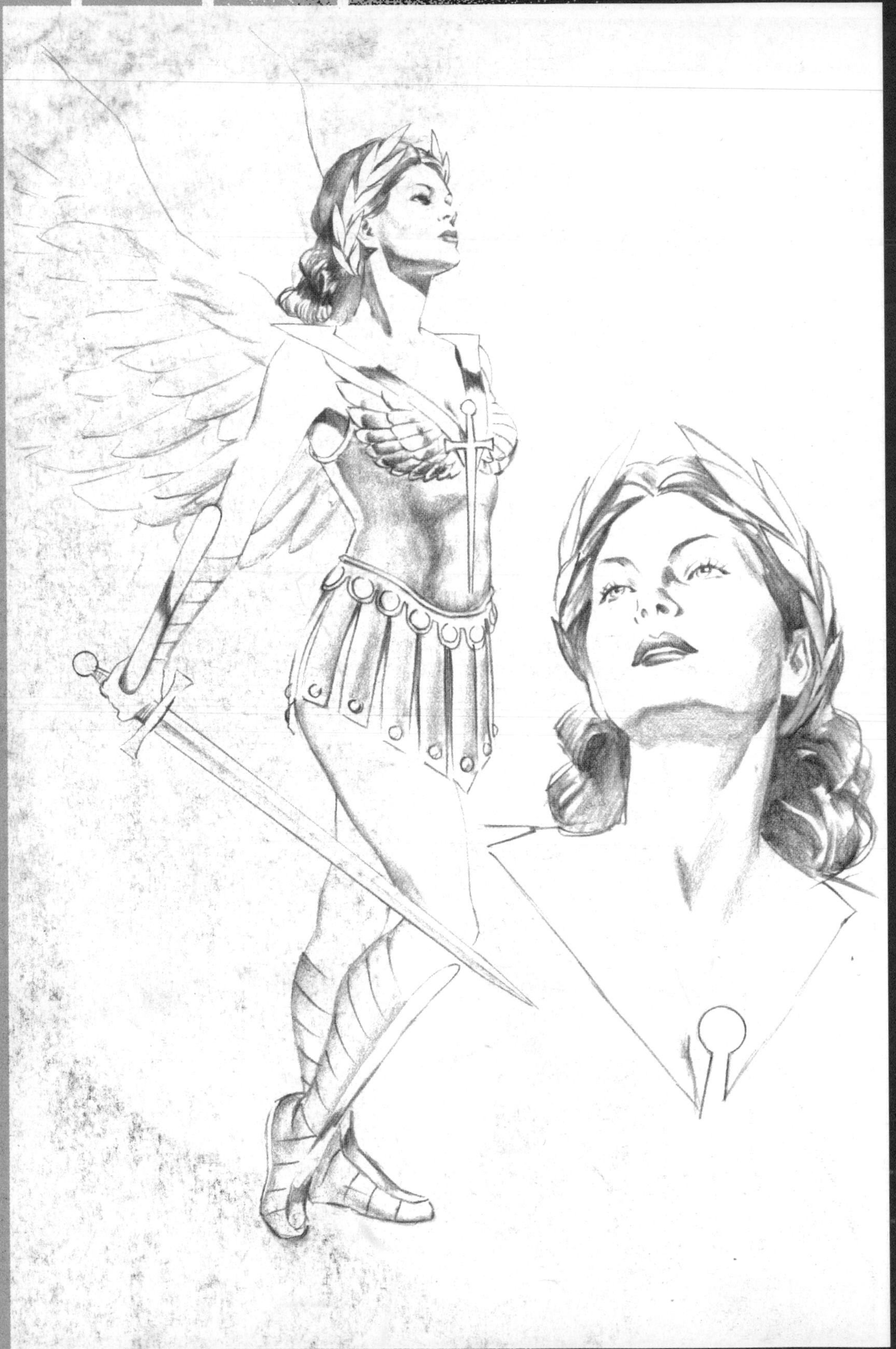

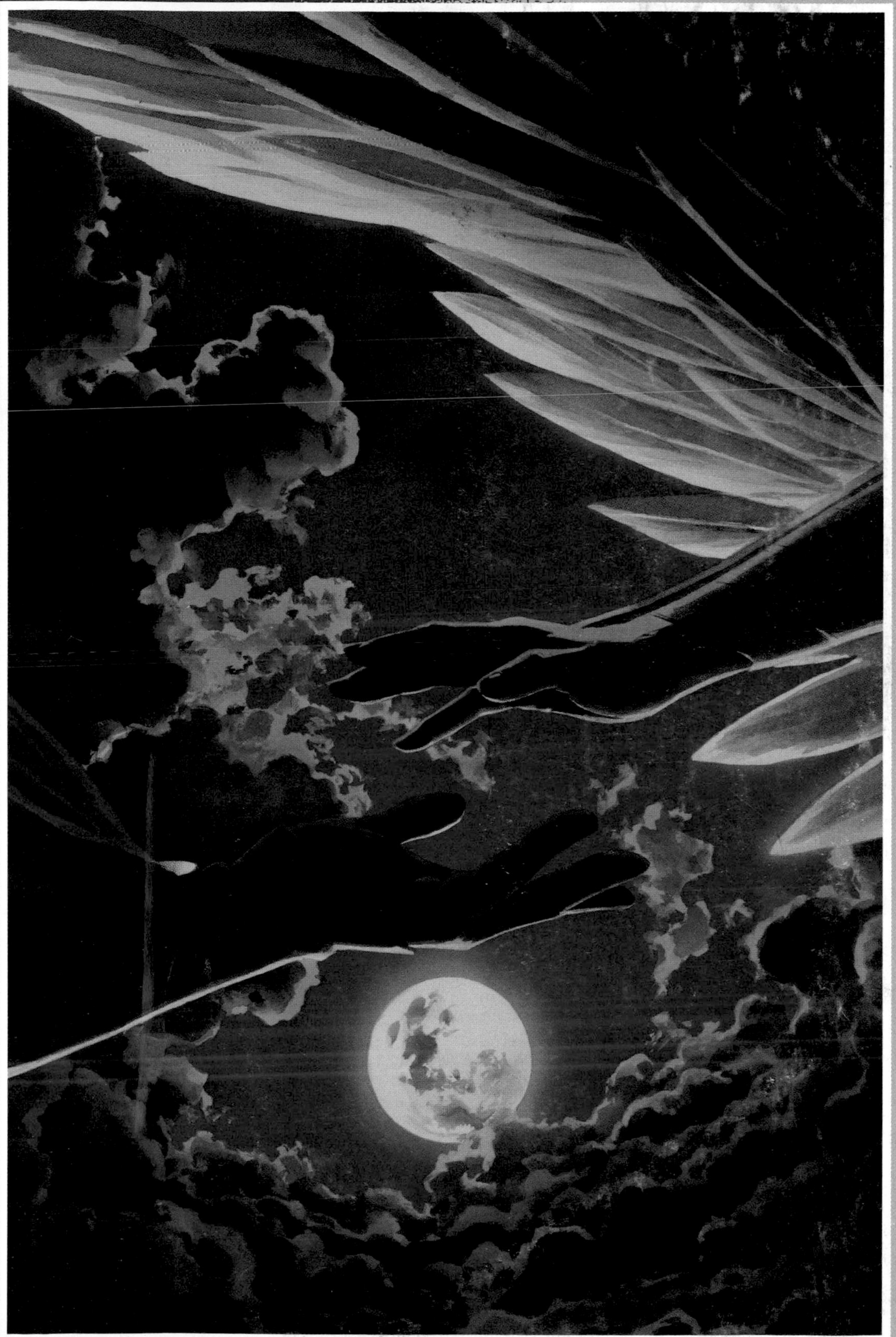

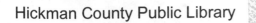

ACKNOWLEDGEMENTS

I'd like to thank Scott and Ivy McCloud, Richard Howell, James Fry, Karl and Barbara Kesel, Mark Waid, Ron Randall, Steve Mattsson, Lawrence Watt-Evans, Shirley Anderston, Roger Stern and Carmela Merlo for listening and giving me feedback when I needed it; Lou Bank, Bob Schreck, Jim Valentino and Jeff Smith for encouraging me to go ahead and do this; Maura Healy for legal assistance; Brian Hibbs and Rory Root for retail advice; Dave Sim, Colleen Doran, Martin Wagner and Paul Pope for promotional advice and assistance; Larry Marder and the Image partners for giving us a home; Jim Lee and the Homage guys for giving us another; the late Carol Kalish for lessons, encouragement and support that will last for the rest of my life; and above all my mother, Sydney Kirk Thompson Kennedy, both for telling me that I could do whatever I wanted if I worked for it, and for sending me a newspaper clipping that I carried around for sixteen years before it became issue #2.

— *Kurt Busiek*

I want to thank my mother, Carol, who encouraged me to fly on my own; the many fathers both young and old who inspired me; my HO!B.O.B. brothers Frank, Ken, Gary, Ron, Chuck and Stan; Todd, who knows why; my brother Aaron, my sister Cinda, and my nephew Cody Ray; Kurt and Ann Busiek for making these acknowledgments necessary; Sharon Cho, Mike Friedrich and Lyn Dunagan of Star*Reach Productions for their services; the Spellbinders, Pras Stillman, Dave Smeds, Steve Mills, Brian, Danaan, and Rhiannon Crist, Margaret Raymond, Walter Sauers, Bob Fleming, Cherie Kushner, Marion Gibbons, Olivia Raymond and cat yronwode for their creative support and, finally, my wife Shirley who is my Winged Victory in every way.

— *Brent Eric Anderson*

My thanks go to my models Frank Kasy, Mark Braun, Meg Guttman and Lisa Beaderstadt for their continued involvement in my work and their infinite patience.

— *Alex Ross*

YOU ARE
NOW LEAVING
**ASTRO
CITY**
PLEASE DRIVE
CAREFULLY